Lecture Notes in Computer Science

Vol. 1: GI-Gesellschaft für Informatik e.V. 3. Jahrestagung, Hamburg, 8.–10. Oktober 1973. Herausgegeben im Auftrag der Gesellschaft für Informatik von W. Brauer. XI, 508 Seiten. 1973. DM 32,–

Vol. 2: GI-Gesellschaft für Informatik e.V. 1. Fachtagung über Automatentheorie und Formale Sprachen, Bonn, 9.–12. Juli 1973. Herausgegeben im Auftrag der Gesellschaft für Informatik von K.-H. Böhling und K. Indermark. VII, 322 Seiten. 1973. DM 26,–

Vol. 3: 5th Conference on Optimization Techniques, Part I. (Series: I.F.I.P. TC7 Optimization Conferences.) Edited by R. Conti and A. Ruberti. XIII, 565 pages. 1973. DM 38.–

Vol. 4: 5th Conference on Optimization Techniques, Part II. (Series: I.F.I.P. TC7 Optimization Conferences.) Edited by R. Conti and A. Ruberti. XIII, 389 pages. 1973. DM 28,–

Vol. 5: International Symposium on Theoretical Programming. Edited by A. Ershov and V. A. Nepomniaschy. VI, 407 pages. 1974. DM 30,–

Vol. 6: B. T. Smith, J. M. Boyle, B. S. Garbow, Y. Ikebe, V. C. Klema, and C. B. Moler, Matrix Eigensystem Routines – EISPACK Guide. X, 387 pages. 1974. DM 28,–

Vol. 7: 3. Fachtagung über Programmiersprachen, Kiel, 5.–7. März 1974. Herausgegeben von B. Schlender und W. Frielinghaus. VI, 225 Seiten. 1974. DM 20,–

Vol. 8: GI-NTG Fachtagung über Struktur und Betrieb von Rechensystemen, Braunschweig, 20.–22. März 1974. Herausgegeben im Auftrag der GI und der NTG von H.-O. Leilich. VI, 340 Seiten. 1974. DM 26,–

Vol. 9: GI-BIFOA Internationale Fachtagung: Informationszentren in Wirtschaft und Verwaltung. Köln, 17./18. Sept. 1973. Herausgegeben im Auftrag der GI und dem BIFOA von P. Schmitz. VI, 259 Seiten. 1974. DM 22,–

Vol. 10: Computing Methods in Applied Sciences and Engineering, Part 1. International Symposium, Versailles, December 17–21, 1973. Edited by R. Glowinski and J. L. Lions. X, 497 pages. 1974. DM 34,–

Vol. 11: Computing Methods in Applied Sciences and Engineering, Part 2. International Symposium, Versailles, December 17–21, 1973. Edited by R. Glowinski and J. L. Lions. X, 434 pages. 1974. DM 30,–

Vol. 12: GFK-GI-GMR Fachtagung Prozessrechner 1974. Karlsruhe, 10.–11. Juni 1974. Herausgegeben von G. Krüger und R. Friehmelt. XI, 620 Seiten. 1974. DM 42,–

Vol. 13: Rechnerstrukturen und Betriebsprogrammierung, Erlangen, 1970. (GI-Gesellschaft für Informatik e.V.) Herausgegeben von W. Händler und P. P. Spies. VII, 333 Seiten. 1974. DM 30,–

Vol. 14: Automata, Languages and Programming – 2nd Colloquium, University of Saarbrücken, July 29–August 2, 1974. Edited by J. Loeckx. VIII, 611 pages. 1974. DM 48,–

Vol. 15: L Systems. Edited by A. Salomaa and G. Rozenberg. VI, 338 pages. 1974. DM 30,–

Vol. 16: Operating Systems, International Symposium, Rocquencourt 1974. Edited by E. Gelenbe and C. Kaiser. VIII, 310 pages. 1974. DM 30,–

Vol. 17: Rechner-Gestützter Unterricht RGU '74, Fachtagung, Hamburg, 12.–14. August 1974, ACU-Arbeitskreis Computer-Unterstützter Unterricht. Herausgegeben im Auftrag der GI von K. Brunnstein, K. Haefner und W. Händler. X, 417 Seiten. 1974. DM 35,–

Vol. 18: K. Jensen and N. Wirth, PASCAL – User Manual and Report. VI, 167 pages. 2nd Edition 1975. DM 20,–

Vol. 19: Programming Symposium. Proceeding, Colloque sur la Programmation, Paris, April 9–11, 1974. V, 425 pages. 1974. DM 35,–

Vol. 20: J. Engelfriet, Simple Program Schemes and Formal Languages. VII, 254 pages. 1974. DM 25,–

Vol. 21: Compiler Construction, An Advanced Course. Edited by F. L. Bauer and J. Eickel. XIV. 621 pages. 1974. DM 42,–

Vol. 22: Formal Aspects of Cognitive Processes. Proceedings Interdisciplinary Conference, Ann Arbor, March 1972. Edited by T. Storer and D. Winter. V, 214 pages. 1975. DM 23,–

Vol. 23: Programming Methodology. 4th Informatik Symposium IBM Germany Wildbad, September 25–27, 1974. Edited by C. E Hackl. VI, 501 pages. 1975. DM 39,–

Vol. 24: Parallel Processing. Proceedings of the Sagamore Com puter Conference, August 20–23, 1974. Edited by T. Feng. VI 433 pages. 1975. DM 35,–

Vol. 25: Category Theory Applied to Computation and Control Proceedings of the First International Symposium, San Francisco February 25–26, 1974. Edited by E. G. Manes. X, 245 pages 1975. DM 25,–

Vol. 26: GI-4. Jahrestagung, Berlin, 9.–12. Oktober 1974. Her ausgegeben im Auftrag der GI von D. Siefkes. IX, 748 Seiten 1975. DM 49,–

Vol. 27: Optimization Techniques. IFIP Technical Conference Novosibirsk, July 1–7, 1974. (Series: I.F.I.P. TC7 Optimizatio Conferences.) Edited by G. I. Marchuk. VIII, 507 pages. 1975 DM 39,–

Vol. 28: Mathematical Foundations of Computer Science. 3r Symposium at Jadwisin near Warsaw, June 17–22, 1974. Edite by A Blikle. VIII, 484 pages. 1975. DM 37,–

Vol. 29: Interval Mathematics. Proceedings of the Internation Symposium, Karlsruhe, West Germany, May 20–24, 1975. Edite by K. Nickel. VI, 331 pages. 1975. DM 30,–

Vol. 30: Software Engineering. An Advanced Course. Edited b F. L. Bauer. (Formerly published 1973 as Lecture Notes in Ec nomics and Mathematical Systems, Vol. 81) XII, 545 pages. 197 DM 42,–

Vol. 31: S. H. Fuller, Analysis of Drum and Disk Storage Units. I 283 pages. 1975. DM 28,–

Vol. 32: Mathematical Foundations of Computer Science 197 Proceedings 1975. Edited by J. Bečvář. X, 476 pages. 1975. DM 39

Vol. 33: Automata Theory and Formal Languages, Kaiserslaute May 20–23, 1975. Herausgegeben im Auftrag der GI von H. Bra hage. II, 292 Seiten. 1975. DM 28,–

Lecture Notes in Computer Science

Edited by G. Goos and J. Hartmanis
Series: GI, Gesellschaft für Informatik e.V.

33

Automata Theory and Formal Languages 2nd GI Conference

Kaiserslautern, May 20–23, 1975

Edited by H. Brakhage on behalf of GI

Springer-Verlag
Berlin · Heidelberg · New York 1975

Program Committee
Prof. Dr. Karl-Heinz Böhling
Institut für Angewandte Mathematik und Informatik
der Universität Bonn
Prof. Dr. Wilfried Brauer
Institut für Informatik der Universität Hamburg
Prof. Dr. Günter Hotz
Institut für Angewandte Mathematik
der Universität des Saarlandes
Prof. Dr. Claus-Peter Schnorr
Fachbereich Mathematik an der Universität Frankfurt

Editor and Local Chairman
Prof. Dr. H. Brakhage
Universität Kaiserslautern
Fachbereich Mathematik
Pfaffenbergstr.
675 Kaiserslautern/BRD

Library of Congress Cataloging in Publication Data
Main entry under title:

Automata theory and formal languages.

(Lecture notes in computer science ; 33)
English or German.
Bibliography: p.
Includes index.
1. Machine theory--Congresses. 2. Automata--Congresses. 3. Formal languages--Congresses. I. Brakhage, H., 1926- II. Gesellschaft für Informatik. III. Title. IV. Series.
QA267.A924 629.8'91 75-28494

AMS Subject Classifications (1970): 02-XX, 68-XX, 94-XX
CR Subject Classifications (1974): 1.3, 4.12, 5.21, 5.22, 5.23, 5.24, 5.25, 5.26, 5.27, 5.31, 5.32, 5.7, 6.1

ISBN 3-540-07407-4 Springer-Verlag Berlin · Heidelberg · New York
ISBN 0-387-07407-4 Springer-Verlag New York · Heidelberg · Berlin

Offsetdruck: Julius Beltz, Hemsbach/Bergstr.

V O R W O R T

Die GI-Fachtagungen Automatentheorie und Formale Sprachen haben das Ziel, in regelmäßigen Abständen über den aktuellen Stand der Forschung zu unterrichten und die Zusammenarbeit der auf diesem Gebiet tätigen Wissenschaftler zu fördern. Die erste Fachtagung fand vom 9. - 12. Juli 1973 an der Universität Bonn statt. Der vorliegende Tagungsband enthält die Vorträge, die auf der zweiten Fachtagung vom 2o. - 23. Mai 1975 an der Universität Kaiserslautern gehalten wurden. Das Programmkomitee hat an der Form der Tagung ohne Parallelsitzungen festgehalten und war daher gezwungen, aus der erfreulich großen Anzahl von Vortragsanmeldungen eine Auswahl zu treffen, die ihm in vielen Fällen schwergefallen ist. Bei der Auswahl der Hauptvorträge sollte einer der Vorträge die Kooperation über das engere Fachgebiet hinaus fördern, während bei den übrigen drei Hauptvorträgen bewußt ein Schwerpunkt im Bereich der Komplexitätsfragen gesetzt wurde. Dankenswerterweise hat Herr Professor Collins eine im Umfang über seinen Hauptvortrag wesentlich hinausgehende erste ausführliche Darstellung seiner Resultate für den Tagungsband zur Verfügung gestellt.

Allen Vortragenden, Teilnehmern und Helfern und allen, die darüber hinaus zum Gelingen der Tagung beigetragen haben, sei an dieser Stelle herzlich gedankt. Das Bundesministerium für Forschung und Technologie hat durch seine finanzielle Förderung die Durchführung der Tagung ermöglicht. Für großzügige Unterstützung ist insbesondere der Universitätsleitung und dem Freundeskreis der Universität Kaiserslautern sowie Spendern aus der Industrie zu danken. An den organisatorischen Arbeiten haben sich die Kollegen des Organisationskomitees, die Herren Professor Dr. Loos, Leitender Regierungsdirektor Dr. Maaß und Professor Dr. Wippermann tatkräftig beteiligt. Dem Springer-Verlag und den Herausgebern der Reihe Lecture Notes in Computer Science ist für die Aufnahme des Tagungsbandes in diese Reihe zu danken.

Kaiserslautern, im Mai 1975 — Der Herausgeber

I N H A L T S V E R Z E I C H N I S

Dienstagvormittag

Dienstagnachmittag

Mittwochvormittag

FORMAL LANGUAGE THEORY AND THEORETICAL COMPUTER SCIENCE[†]

Ronald V. Book

Department of Computer Science
Yale University
10 Hillhouse Avenue
New Haven, Conn. 06520, U.S.A.

In the last fifteen years the area of formal language theory and abstract automata has enjoyed a great deal of attention from the research community in theoretical computer science. However, in the last few years the main interest in theoretical computer science has been directed elsewhere. In these notes I shall consider the role of formal language theory in theoretical computer science by discussing some areas in which formal language theory may find applications.

Behind the activities in theoretical computer science lie the major problems of understanding the nature of computation and its relationship to computing methodology. While this area is mathematical and abstract in spirit, it is not pure mathematics: indeed, theoretical computer science derives much of its motivation from the abstraction of the practical problems of computation.

Abstraction for the sake of abstraction and beauty is one of the goals of modern pure mathematics [1]. However, as part of theoretical computer science, formal language theory must speak to problems concerning the nature of computation. In Part I of these notes I point to results of language theory which stem from or lend insight to the more general study of computability and computational complexity. In Part II I discuss several problem areas where formal language theory may find interesting and fruitful application. In this context I urge the reader to consult the paper "Programming languages, natural languages, and mathematics" by Peter Naur [2].

[†] The preparation of this paper was supported in part by the National Science Foundaion under Grant GJ-30409 and by the Department of Computer Science, Yale University.

Part I

Formal language theory is concerned with the specification and manipulation of se of strings of symbols, i.e., languages. It is my thesis here that as an area of interest within theoretical computer science formal language theory should be closely tied to the study of computability theory and computational complexity. Computability theo is concerned with the representation of algorithms and languages, and computational complexity considers the inherent difficulty of evaluating functions and deciding predicates. Within the scope of these studies are the questions of determinism versus nc determinism, trade-offs between measures and representations, differences in computational power stemming from different choices of atomic operations, and the existence hierarchies.

We shall explore two topics in order to illustrate how the common features and th differences between formal language theory and computability theory can interact fruitfully. In both cases it is shown that the questions and results of formal language theory take on new significance when reconsidered in terms of computability theory an computational complexity.

A. *Universal Sets*

One of the most basic notions in computability theory is the notion of a "univer machine." This notion allows a representation of the concept of "self-reference" in terms of a class of algorithms. It is particularly useful when one wishes to establi that some question is undecidable by working from first principals.

In formal language theory there are concepts that are related to the notion of universal machine. Consider the specification of a class of languages by means of an algebraic definition: the smallest class containing some specific language (the generator) and closed under specified operations. One example of this is the concept of principal AFL [3]: the smallest class of languages containing the generator and clo under union, concatenation, Kleene *, intersection with regular sets, homomorphic mappings, and inverse homomorphism. Many classes of languages studied in traditional formal language theory are principal AFLs; e.g., the context-free languages, the regu sets, the context-sensitive languages. These structures have representation theorems which are generalizations of the Chomsky-Schutzenberger Theorem for context-free languages: A language L is context-free if and only if there exists a regular set R, a nonerasing homomorphism h_1, and a homomorphism h_2 such that $L = h_1(h_2^{-1}(D_2) \cap R)$, where D_2 is the Dyck set on two letters. Besides providing certain information regarding the algebraic structure of these classes, the existence of this type of generator can be identified with a characteristic of an appropriate class of abstract automata that accept the languages involved: finitely encodable abstract families of acceptors [3].

From the standpoint of computability and computational complexity, the notion o generator with respect to some algebraic structure can be useful [31] but the more general notion of a language being "complete" for a class with respect to some type of "reducibility " is more important when considering the inherent computational complexity of the membership problem for languages in the class. However Greibach [4] has shown that in certain classes of languages the algebraic structure yields information about questions such as the complexity of the membership problem.

There exists a "hardest" context-free language [4]: a language with the property that the inherent time complexity of the membership problem for this language yields the order of the achievable least upper bound for the time necessary for the general context-free membership problem. Formally, there is a context-free language L_0 with the property that for any context-free language L there exists a homomorphism h such that for all strings w, $w \in L$ if and only if $h(w) \in L_0$.[†] Thus if one has an algorithm Θ for deciding membership in L_0, then for any context-free language L one can obtain an algorithm Θ_L for deciding membership in L and the order of the running time of Θ_L is the order of the running time of Θ. In this sense L_0 is a "hardest" context-free language. Similar considerations hold for space bounds.

Greibach's result says something further regarding the algebraic structure of the class <u>CF</u> of context-free languages, in particular that <u>CF</u> $= \{h^{-1}(L_0) \mid h$ a homomorphism$\}$. Following [5], let us call a class C a <u>principal cylinder</u> if there is some $L_0 \in C$ such that $C = \{h^{-1}(L_0) \mid h$ a homomorphism$\}$. Thus if C is a principal cylinder with generator L_0, then for every $L \in C$ there exists a function f such that for all w, $w \in L$ if and only if $f(w) \in L_0$, and f is very simple to compute (being a homomorphism). In this way a class of languages is a principal cylinder if and only if it has a language which is complete with respect to homomorphic mappings (viewed as a type of many-one reducibility) and closed under inverse homomorphism.

There are a number of classes of languages which are principal cylinders, and viewing them as such is useful when one considers these classes as complexity classes [6]. For example, each of the following classes is a principal cylinder:

(i) For any $\varepsilon > 0$, the class of languages accepted in space n^{ε} by deterministic (nondeterministic) Turing machines;

(ii) For any $k \geq 1$, the class of languages accepted in time n^k by nondeterministic Turing machines;

(iii) The class of languages accepted in exponential time by deterministic (nondeterministic) Turing machines.

If we consider the notion of a principal cylinder, then we have an example of the algebraic structure of a class of languages yielding insight into the computational complexity of the class. However we can discuss the notion of a class having a hardest language without reference to the algebraic structure.

Let C be a class of languages and let $B \in C$. Then B is a <u>hardest</u> language

† For the purpose of this discussion, the empty word is ignored.

for C (B is C -hardest) if the following condition is satisfied: if there exists an algorithm Θ for deciding membership in L_0 and Θ has running time $t(n)$, then for every $L \in C$ there exists a modification Θ_L of Θ and constants c_1, c_2 such that Θ_L is an algorithm for deciding membership in L and Θ_L has running time $c_1 t(c_2 n)$.

In this way the complexity of recognition of a C -hardest language is at least as great as the least upper bound of the complexity of recognition of all languages in C and thus the inherent time complexity of the recognition problem for this language yields the order of the achievable least upper bound for the inherent time complexity of the general recognition problem for the class C.

If C is a principal cylinder with generator L_0, then L_0 is a C -hardest language -- this is in the spirit of Greibach's result on the context-free languages [4 However there are classes which are not principal cylinders but do have hardest languages [7]: the deterministic context-free languages, the languages accepted in real time by deterministic multitape Turing machines, the intersection closure of the class of context-free languages. Thus the notion of a class having a hardest language is distinct from the notion of a class being a principal cylinder.

While the definition of hardest language is fairly broad, one can use elementary techniques to show that certain well-studied classes do not have hardest languages. For example, the class P of languages accepted in polynomial time by deterministic Turing machines (or random-access machines or string algorithms) does not have a hardest language. The proof of this fact depends on a simple property of algebraic structures. The class P can be decomposed into an infinite hierarchy of classes of languages: for each $k \geq 1$, $\mathrm{DTIME}(n^k)$ denotes the class of languages accepted in time n^k by deterministic Turing machines, then for every $j \geq 1$ $\mathrm{DTIME}(n^j) \subsetneq \mathrm{DTIME}(n^{j+1})$ and $P = \bigcup_j \mathrm{DTIME}(n^j)$. If P has a hardest language L_0, then there is some least k such that $L_0 \in \mathrm{DTIME}(n^k)$. From the properties of the class $\mathrm{DTIME}(n^k)$ and the definition of hardest language, this implies that $P \subseteq \mathrm{DTIME}(n^k)$ so that the hierarchy $\mathrm{DTIME}(n) \subsetneq \mathrm{DTIME}(n^2) \subsetneq \ldots$ is only finite ending with $\mathrm{DTIME}(n^k)$, a contradiction.

One should note the difference between the fact that P does not have a hardest language and the results in [8] showing that there are certain languages which are complete for P with respect to the class of reducibilities computed in log space (that is, there are languages $L_0 \in P$ with the property that for every $L \in P$ there is a function f which can be computed by a deterministic Turing machine using only log space such that for all w, $w \in L$ if and only if $f(w) \in L_0$). A function computed in log space can be computed in polynomial time. However the result presented above shows that not all of the reducibilities used in [8] can be computed in linear time The argument used above shows even more: the reducibilities used in [8] cannot all computed in time n^k for any fixed k.

The concept of a universal element is central to computability theory. Studies of generators and complete sets play important roles in formal language theory and i computational complexity. These closely related notions each represent some aspects of the self-referential properties of a class. The results described here suggest that attention be given to the comparative power of the basis operations needed for these representations, as part of the development of a conceptual framework to provide a unified view of results of this type.

B. *Nondeterminism*

The mathematical construct of nondeterminism has surfaced periodically in the forefront of activity in formal language theory. It arises when acceptance of languages by automata and their generation by grammars, and closure properties of classes of languages are considered. While nondeterminism is essential for presentation of certain classes of languages, e.g., the context-free languages, it is not clear what role this construct plays in computability theory and computational complexity - indeed, the underlying notion of nondeterminism is not well understood.

Abstract automata are said to operate nondeterministically if the transition function (which specifies what to do at each step) is multi-valued -- there is not a unique move to be performed at each step but rather a finite set of possible next moves. The automaton arbitrarily chooses (guesses) which move to perform and any choice is valid. In this way computations of a nondeterministic automaton on a given input may be represented as a tree in which each node has branches corresponding to the possible next steps. Such a device is said to accept an input if there exists some path through the tree ending in a node that indicates an accepting configuration of the automaton.

A nondeterministic automaton may be considered as a representation of a nondeterministic algorithm [32], an algorithm in which the notion of choice is allowed. However in this case all the branches of the tree must be explored and all choices followed, so that the entire tree must be searched. All configurations resulting from the data underlying the algorithm must be generated until either a solution is encountered or all possibilities are exhausted. The implementation of such algorithms is usually carried out by means of backtracking, and these nondeterministic algorithms are a useful design tool for parsing [33] and for programs to solve combinatorial search problems, and nondeterministic algorithms provide an efficient specification for algorithms which deterministically simulate nondeterministic processes.

It was once thought that nondeterminism was a mathematical construct that arose in the study of automata theory and formal languages but had nothing to do with other aspects of computer science. This view has changed since the observation by Cook [34] of the importance of the class NP of languages accepted in polynomial time by nondeterministic Turing machines (or random-access machines or programs written in some general purpose language). It has been shown by Cook, Karp [35], and others (see [36]) that a wide variety of important computational problems in combinatorial mathematics, mathematical programming, and logic can be naturally represented so as to be in NP. It is not known whether these problems are in the class P of languages accepted in polynomial time by deterministic algorithms. While every language in NP can be accepted by some deterministic algorithm, the known results force the deterministic algorithm to operat in exponential instead of polynomial time. In computational complexity, it is widely accepted that a computational problem is tractable if and only if there is an algorith for its solution whose running time is bounded by a polynomial in the size of the inpu Thus it is not known if some of the problems in NP are tractable. Any proof of their tractability is likely to yield some fundamental insights into the nature of computing since it would show that the results of backtracking and of combinatorial searching can be obtained efficiently. See [37, 38] for results in this area and for some inter pretations of the role of the question "does P equal NP?" plays in theoretical compute science.

Let us consider the known results regarding nondeterminism in resource bounded o restricted access automata. For the two extreme cases of finite-state acceptors and arbitrary Turing machines, nondeterminism adds nothing to the power of acceptance; bo deterministic and nondeterministic finite-state acceptors characterize the class of a regular sets, and both deterministic and nondeterministic Turing acceptors characteri the class of all recursively enumerable sets. Between these extremes there is just o case for which it is known that the deterministic and nondeterministic modes of opera tion are equivalent: auxiliary pushdown acceptors. An auxiliary pushdown acceptor [39] has a two-way read-only input tape, and auxiliary storage tape which is bounded size (as a function of the length of the input), and an auxiliary storage tape which a pushdown store and is unbounded. If f is a well-behaved space bound, then a language is accepted by a deterministic auxiliary pushdown acceptor which uses at most $f(n)$ space on its auxiliary storage tape if and only if that language is accepted by a nondeterministic auxiliary pushdown acceptor which operates in time $2^{cf(n)}$ for sc $c > 0$.

There are a few cases where it is known that a language can be accepted by a non deterministic device with certain characteristics but cannot be accepted by any deter ministic device with those characteristics. Some examples of this include the follow ing:

(i) pushdown store acceptors (nondeterministic pushdown store acceptors accept all and only context-free languages while deterministic pushdown store acceptors ac cept only deterministic context-free languages, the languages generated by $LR(k)$ grammars);

(ii) on-line one counter acceptors (the language $\{w\,c\,y \mid w,y \in \{a,b\}^*, w \neq y\}$ is accepted in real time by a nondeterministic on-line one counter acceptor but is not accepted by any deterministic on-line one counter acceptor);

(iii) multitape Turing acceptors which operate in real time (the class of languages accepted in real time by nondeterministic multitape Turing acceptors are the quasi-realtime languages of [40] while the class of languages accepted in real time by deterministic multitape Turing acceptors are the real-time definable la guages [41, 42]; the former is closed under linear erasing and can be decompos into only a finite hierarchy based on the number of storage tapes while the latter is not closed under linear erasing and can be decomposed into an infinite hierarchy based on the number of tapes);

(iv) multitape Turing acceptors which operate in real time and are reversal-bounded (the class of languages accepted in real time by deterministic multitape Turing acceptors which are reversal-bounded have the property that if a language L is accepted by such a device and for every $x,y \in L$, either x is a prefix of y or y is a prefix of x, then L is regular; the class of languages accepted by the nondeterministic devices operating in this way do not have this property [43]);

(v) on-line multitape Turing acceptors which are reversal-bounded (the class of languages accepted by deterministic reversal-bounded Turing acceptors is a subclass of the recursive sets while every recursively enumerable set is accepted by a nondeterministic reversal-bounded acceptor [44]).

In each of the cases (i) - (v), each language L_1 accepted by a nondeterministic device of the class in question can be represented as the homomorphic image of a language L_2 accepted by a deterministic device of that class. When the nondeterministic device is forced to operate in real time, then the corresponding homomorphic mappings are nonerasing (i.e., $h(w) = e$ if and only if $w = e$), and the class of languages accepted by the nondeterministic devices is closed under nonerasing homomorphism while the class corresponding to the deterministic devices is not.

Generally, a class of languages accepted by nondeterministic devices which are on-line and have finite-state control are closed under nonerasing homomorphism. In such a setting the operation of nonerasing homomorphism corresponds to the notion of bounded existential quantification. Thus in the cases above, the homomorphism (or existential quantifier) chooses (a representation of) an accepting computation of the device on the input given. The deterministic device is able to check if indeed the choice is a representation of an accepting computation. In this way an accepting computation of an on-line nondeterministic device can be viewed as having two distinct phases, one which allows a choice or "guess" and one which checks to see if the choice has the appropriate qualities. This view of nondeterministic operation is brought forth strongly in the proofs in [40, 45] where a machine first "guesses" what the input will be and performs a computation on this guess before checking whether the guess is correct.

Representing languages accepted by on-line nondeterministic devices in terms of homomorphisms or existential quantifiers and languages accepted by deterministic devices is consistent with Karp's presentation of NP-complete problems (languages) [35]. Further, the strategy of "guessing" and then "checking" is fundamental to the structure of the specific "hardest context-free language" presented by Greibach in [4].

When one considers devices which have two-way input tapes, then the above representation does not seem applicable. For example, we see no way of representing the languages accepted by nondeterministic linear bounded automata in terms of the languages accepted by deterministic linear bounded automata. While the question of deter minism vs. nondeterminism can be treated in terms of complete sets and reducibilities in this case as well as in the case of on-line devices [46], the role of nondeterminis is even less understood in the case of two-way devices.

One area where nondeterminism appears to be a useful tool but where it has previously played little role is in the representation and analysis of logical predicates Recently the class of rudimentary relations of Smullyan -- the smallest class of strin relations containing the concatenation relations and closed under the Boolean operations, explicit transformation, and a form of bounded (existential and universal) qua tification -- has been studied as a class RUD of formal languages [47]. This class contains all context-free languages, all languages accepted in real time by nondeterministic multitape Turing machines, and all languages accepted in log(n) space by non deterministic Turing machines. On the other hand, every language in RUD is accepted in linear space by a deterministic Turing machine.

This class is of interest for various reasons. It is closed under most of the operations associated with classes specified by nondeterministic devices -- union, co catenation, Kleene *, nonerasing homomorphism, inverse homomorphism, linear erasing, reversal -- as well as under complementation, a property usually associated with a class specified by deterministic devices. Wrathall [47] has shown that RUD can be re resented in terms of nondeterministic devices: RUD is the smallest class of language containing the empty set and closed under the operation of relative acceptance by non deterministic linear time-bounded oracle machines. This class can be decomposed into a hierarchy based on the number of applications of the oracle machine. It is not kno whether this hierarchy is infinite and this question is closely tied to the questions of determinism vs. nondeterminism in automata based on computational complexity. The results presented in [47] show that the study of closure operations usually associate with classes of formal language theory can yield insight into the questions arising in computational complexity.

The study of nondeterminism takes on an extremely important role in theoretical computer science when it is removed from the context of formal language theory and cc sidered in terms of computability and computational complexity. The techniques, results, and insights provided by the previous (and ongoing) work in language theory ar extremely valuable when considering this problem. It is hoped that a healthy intera tion between formal language theory and computational complexity will lead to a complete understanding of this important construct.

C. Reprise

In this section I have discussed two examples of notions that can be studied in formal language theory and in computability and computational complexity. I have attempted to show that studying these notions in terms of the interplay between these areas will lead to a better understanding of the problems they reflect than studying them from either area exclusively. It is in this spirit that the role of formal language theory in theoretical computer science may find renewal.†

† In this light the reader should find [48] of interest.

Part II

In this portion of the paper, several problem areas are discussed. These areas are not part of the "classical" theory of formal languages and abstract automata. How-ever each may prove to be an area where formal language theory may find interesting and fruitful application.

A. *L Systems*

In the last few years a new area of activity has excited many researchers in auto-mata and formal language theory. This is the study of L (for Lindenmayer) systems. Originally L systems were put forth as an attempt to model certain phenomena in devel-opmental biology, and this motivation continues to provide a robust quality to the work in this field. However current activity has drawn researchers from cellular auto-mata and tessellation structures, self-reproducing automata and systems, graph genera-ting and graph recognition systems, as well as from classical automata and formal lan-guage theory.

From the biological point of view, L systems provide mathematical tools for buil ing models of actual individuals or species in order to investigate and predict their behavior. Further, it is possible to use the machinery of L systems to express gener statements about non-specific organisms and to precisely express hypotheses concernin the mechanisms behind certain phenomena. To what extent this area will affect the st of cellular behavior in development depends largely on how fully the analogy between systems and the developing organisms they model can be exploited [10].

From the mathematical point of view, L systems have provided an entirely new per-spective on languages, grammars, and automata. While the definition of application rewriting rules varies from the Chomsky-type model discussed in the classical theory, many of the questions pursued are the standard ones: characterization of weak and strong generative capacity, decidability of properties of systems and languages, clos properties, etc. However a number of questions which are not particularly meaningful in the classical theory play a prominent role in the study of this new model. For ex-ample, while the notion of derivational complexity is of interest when studying conte sensitive and general phrase-structure grammars, it is of little interest when study context-free grammars; however, the study of growth functions (closely related to the "time functions" of [12]) plays an important role in the study of L systems.

Some of the questions arising in the study of L systems are closely related to questions regarding extensions of context-free grammars. It appears that there are possibilities for these two activities to affect one another, both in terms of tech-niques (such as the study of recursion, fixed-point theorems, and tree-manipulating systems) and actual results. Further the techniques used in the study of L systems provide interesting tools for studying problems such as synchronization in general a gorithmic systems and discrete pattern recognition.

Just as much of the work in classical automata and formal language theory has strayed from the central questions (of computer science) regarding models for computation and should be regarded as a part of applied mathematics, much of the research in L systems should be viewed as an exciting new aspect of modern applied mathematics.

The literature in the area of L systems appears to grow without bound (or at least at the same rate that cells interact and grow). The interested reader can find a brief introduction in [9] and there is an excellent book [13] by G.T. Herman and G. Rozenberg which will introduce the mathematically sophisticated reader to most problem areas currently studied. There are three recent conference proceedings [11, 14, 15] which will help the reader to learn about relatively current research.

B. Program Schemes

Many results and techniques from automata and formal language theory have found application in the study of the mathematical theory of computation. This has been particularly true in the study of the comparative power of different types and features of programming languages when explicit functions are banished and abstract uninterpreted programs are considered. This is the realm of program schemes.

Program schemes can be viewed as abstract models of programs where assignment statements use unspecified functions and the test statements that control the direction of flow through a program during a computation make use of unspecified predicates. Thus, a single program scheme is an abstract model of a family of different programs, each program arising from the program scheme through a specific interpretation of the function and predicate symbols used to define the scheme. In this way the scheme represents the control structure of the program and the interpretation represents the meaning of its instructions.

Many of the results concerning flowchart schemes and recursion schemes depend on the type of "syntactic" arguments used in the study of acceptance of formal languages by abstract automata. Also, many results in language theory can be applied to problems after some rephrasing. This is particularly true when considering problems regarding the decidability of questions such as weak and strong equivalence, inclusion, and translation.

Here we point out only a few of the results that directly connect the study of schemes to formal language theory. Friedman [23] has shown that the inclusion problem for simple deterministic languages is undecidable and has applied this result to show that the inclusion problem for monadic recursion schemes is undecidable. Further, Friedman [24] has reduced the question of equivalence of deterministic pushdown store acceptors to the question of strong equivalence of monadic recursion schemes, a result that is quite surprising in that it shows the two questions to be reciprocally reducible.

Nivat [21] and his students and colleagues in Paris have made some interesting connections among questions of semantics, polyadic recursion schemes, and general rewriting systems. Downey [19] has also used general rewriting systems to study recursion in language definition. Rosen [18] has used techniques involving context-free grammars to study the structure of computations by recursion schemes. Engelfriet [20] has made an explicit attempt to exploit the connections between language theory and schemes.

Finally, it should be noted that the fundamental paper [17] of Luckham, Park, an Paterson on flowchart schemes makes frequent use of concepts from automata and langua theory as do others [16, 20].

C. Pattern Rocognition

Many constructs from formal language theory have been used in the study of automatic recognition and generation of patterns, particularly in the case of picture pro cessing techniques. This application of language theoretic notions is particularly fruitful when the approach to pattern recognition is syntactic or structural as oppos to decision-theoretic. Some of this work is surveyed in [25].

Recently it has been shown that techniques from formal language theory are extremely useful in certain problems of automatic speech recognition. Lipton and Snyde [26] have treated the parsing of speech as a problem of parsing probabilistic input a have presented an efficient optimal algorithm for this problem. The algorithm they u is a generalization of a well known parsing algorithm for context-free grammars. Lev son [27] has taken a similar approach and his work indicates that the area of automat speech recognition may be an extremely fruitful area for the application of notions c automata and formal language theory.

D. Parallel Computation

One area in which notions from automata and formal language theory may find app cation is that of parallel computation. A wide variety of models of parallel comput tion have been presented in the literature. Most models have been motivated by prob arising in the study of operating systems and these models have properties that refl the characteristics of certain systems. Some of these models have been explored by researchers in theoretical computer science because of their ability to express gene problems of sequencing, synchronization, and communication and interaction between p cesses. In particular, Petri nets and vector addition systems have received a great deal of attention.

Some of the questions modeled in these systems (e.g., deadlock, liveness) have been represented in terms of abstract automata in order to determine whether or not they are decidable and, if so, to determine the inherent complexity of the decision problem. In this area language theory may be useful since many of the properties st died can be represented by means of language-theoretic notions. Examples of this ma be found in [28, 29, 30].

References

[1] G.H. Hardy. *A Mathematician's Apology.* Cambridge Univ. Press, 1940, reprinted 1967.

[2] P. Naur. Programming languages, natural languages, and mathematics. Conference Record, *2nd ACM Symp. Principles of Programming Languages.* Palo Alto, Calif., 1975, 137-148.

[3] S. Ginsburg and S.A. Greibach. Principal AFL. *J. Computer System Sci.* 4 (1970), 308-338.

[4] S.A. Greibach. The hardest context-free language. *SIAM J. Computing* 2 (1973), 304-310.

[5] L. Boasson and M. Nivat. Le cylindre des langages lineaires n'est pas principal. *Proc. 2nd GI - Profession Conf. Automata Theory and Formal Languages.* Springer Verlag, to appear.

[6] R. Book. Comparing complexity classes. *J. Computer System Sci.* 9 (1974), 213-229.

[7] R. Book. On hardest sets. In preparation.

[8] N. Jones and W. Laaser. Complete problems for deterministic polynomial time recognizable languages. *Proc. 6th ACM Symp. Theory of Computing.* Seattle, Wash., 1974, 40-46.

[9] A. Salomaa. *Formal Languages.* Academic Press. New York, 1973.

[10] P.G. Doucet. On the applicability of L-systems in developmental biology. In [11].

[11] A. Lindenmayer and G. Rozenberg (eds.). Abstract of papers presented at a Conference on Formal Languages, Automata, and Development. Univ. Utrecht, Utrecht, The Netherlands, 1975.

[12] R. Book. Time-bounded grammars and their languages. *J. Computer System Sci.* 4 (1971), 397-429.

[13] G.T. Herman and G. Rozenberg. *Developmental Systems and Languages.* North-Holland Publ. Co. Amsterdam, 1974.

[14] G. Rozenberg and A. Salomaa (eds.). *L Systems.* Lecture Notes in Computer Science, Vol. 15. Springer-Verlag, 1974.

[15] *Proceedings of the 1974 Conference on Biologically Motivated Automata Theory.* McLean, Va. Published by the IEEE Computer Society.

[16] S. Garland and D. Luckham. Program schemes, recursion schemes, and formal languages. *J. Computer System Sci.* 7 (1973), 119-160.

[17] D. Luckham, D. Park, and M. Paterson. On formalized computer programs. *J. Computer System Sci.* 4 (1970), 220-249.

[18] B.K. Rosen. Program equivalence and context-free grammars. *Proc. 13th IEEE Symposium on Switching and Automata Theory.* College Park, Md., 1972, 7-18.

[19] P.J. Downey. Formal languages and recursion schemes. *Proc. 8th Princeton Conference on Information Science and Systems.* Princeton, N.J., 1974.

[20] J. Engelfriet. *Simple Program Schemes and Formal Languages.* Lecture Notes in Computer Science, Vol. 20. Springer-Verlag, 1974.

[21] M Nivat. On the interpretation of recursive program schemes. IRIA Technical Report, 1974.

[22] E. Ashcroft, Z. Manna, and A. Pnueli. Decidable properties of monadic functiona schemes. *J. Assoc. Comput. Mach.* 20 (1973), 489-499.

[23] E.P. Friedman. The inclusion problem for simple languages. *Theoretical Compute Science* 1 (1975). To appear.

[24] E.P. Friedman. Relationships between monadic recursion schemes and deterministi context-free languages. *Proc. 15th IEEE Symposium on Switching and Automata Theory*. New Orleans, La., 1974, 43-51.

[25] K. Fu. *Syntactic Methods in Pattern Recognition*. Academic Press. New York, 1974.

[26] R. Lipton and L. Snyder. On the parsing of speech. Technical Report Number 37, Department of Computer Science, Yale University, 1975.

[27] S. Levinson. An Artificial Intelligence Approach to Automatic Speech Recognition. Doctoral Dissertation, U. Rhode Island, 1974.

[28] J.L. Peterson. Computation sequence sets. Unpublished manuscript.

[29] W.H. Byrn. Sequential Processes, Deadlocks, and Semaphore Primitives. Doctoral Dissertation, Harvard University, 1974.

[30] W.E. Riddle. Modeling and Analysis of Supervisory Systems. Doctoral Dissertation, Stanford University, 1972.

[31] R. Book. On languages accepted in polynomial time. *SIAM J. Computing* 1 (1972) 281-287.

[32] R. Floyd. Nondeterministic algorithms. *J. Assoc. Comput. Mach.* 14 (1967), 636-644.

[33] A. Aho and J. Ullman. *The Theory of Parsing, Translating, and Compiling, Vol.* Prentice-Hall Publ. Co., 1972.

[34] S. Cook. The complexity of theorem-proving procedures. *Proc. 3rd ACM Symp. Theory of Computing*. Shaker Hts., Ohio, 1973, 343-353.

[35] R. Karp. Reducibilities among combinatorial problems. In *Complexity of Comput Computation* (R. Miller and J. Thatcher, eds.). Plenum, N.Y., 1972, 85-104.

[36] A. Aho, J. Hopcroft, and J. Ullman. *The Design and Analysis of Computer Algorithms*. Addison-Wesley, 1974.

[37] R. Karp (ed.). *Complexity of Computation*. SIAM-AMS Proc. VII, Amer. Math. Soc Providence, R.I., 1974.

[38] J. Hartmanis and J. Simon. Feasible computations. *Proc. GI-Jahrestagung 74*. Springer-Verlag, to appear.

[39] S. Cook. Characterizations of pushdown machines in terms of time-bounded computers. *J. Assoc. Comput. Mach.* 18 (1971), 4-18.

[40] R. Book and S.A. Greibach. Quasi-realtime languages. *Math. Systems Theory* 4 (1970), 97-111.

[41] A. Rosenberg. Real-time definable languages. *J. Assoc. Comput. Mach.* 14 (196 645-662.

[42] S. Aanderaa. On k-tape versus (k+1)-tape real time computation. In [37].

[43] R. Book and M. Nivat. On linear languages and intersections of classes of languages. In preparation.

[44] B. Baker and R. Book. Reversal-bounded multi-pushdown machines. *J. Computer System Sci.* 8 (1974), 315-332.

[45] R. Book, M. Nivat, and M. Paterson. Reversal-bounded acceptors and intersections of linear languages. *SIAM J. Computing* 3 (1974), 283-295.

[46] J. Hartmanis and H. Hunt. The LBA problem and its importance in the theory of computing. In [37].

[47] C. Wrathall. Rudimentary predicates and relative computation. In preparation.

[48] H. Hunt, D. Rosenkrantz, and T. Szymanski. On the equivalence, containment, and covering problems for the regular and context-free languages. *J. Computer System Sci.*, to appear.

LE CYLINDRE DES LANGAGES LINEAIRES N'EST PAS PRINCIPAL

L. BOASSON et M. NIVAT

La présente communication répond à une question posée par S. Greibach [1,4]: existe-t-il un langage linéaire dont tout langage linéaire soit image dans un homomorphisme inverse? La réponse est non ainsi qu'il est suggéré dans [4].

Rappelons qu'un langage linéaire est un langage algébrique (ou "context-free") engendrable par une grammaire algébrique linéaire (i.e. dont les membres droits de règles contiennent au plus une lettre non-terminale). Par définition, une famille de langages $\mathcal{L}$ constitue un <u>cylindre</u> si elle est fermée par homomorphisme inverse et intersection par les langages rationnels (ou réguliers). Notons qu'un cylindre fermé par homomorphisme est un cône rationnel [1]. Un cylindre $\mathcal{C}$ est principal s'il existe un langage L tel que le plus petit cylindre contenant L soit précisément $\mathcal{C}$. Le but de cette communication est d'établir le

<u>Théorème</u>: <u>La famille</u> Lin <u>des langages linéaires constitue un cylindre qui n'est pas principal</u>.

Notons que la famille Lin, qui constitue un cône rationnel, est principale en tant que cône et pas en tant que cylindre, alors qu'au contraire la famille des langages algébriques est principale non seulement en tant que cône rationnel, mais aussi en tant que cylindre [4]. La question reste ouverte de savoir si le cylindre des langages à compteur est principal ou non.

Nous donnons ci-dessous les principaux éléments nécessaires à l'établissement de la preuve du théorème annoncé.

<u>A - Les langages $\hat{S}_n$</u>:

Sur l'alphabet $Z_n = Y_n \cup \bar{Y}_n$ où $Y_n = \{a_i \mid i=1,\dots,n\}$ et $\bar{Y}_n = \{\bar{a}_i \mid i=1,\dots,n\}$, on définit de façon classique le langage symétrique S_n

$$S_n = \{a_{i_1}a_{i_2}\dots a_{i_p}\bar{a}_{i_p}\dots\bar{a}_{i_2}\bar{a}_{i_1} \mid p \geqslant 1 \quad a_{i_j} \in Y_n\} .$$

Désignant par R_n le langage rationnel $\{a_i\bar{a}_i \mid i=1,\dots,n\}^+$, on construit le langage S''_n à partir de S_n en substituant dans ce dernier langage à chaque occurrence de $a \in Y$ le langage rationnel aR_n et à chaque $\bar{a} \in \bar{Y}$ le langage rationnel $(\bar{a}R_n \cup \bar{a})$. Notons que, puisque S_n est un langage linéaire et que l'opération ainsi définie est une substitution rationnelle, S''_n est également linéaire. Il en va alors de même du langage $S'_n = R_n.S''_n$.

Considérant alors deux nouveaux symboles $\#$ et α, on peut définir le langage

$$\hat{S}'_n = \{\# u_1\alpha v_1\alpha w_1 \# \ldots \# u_p\alpha v_p\alpha w_p \mid p \geq 1,\ u_i, w_i \in (Z_n \cup \{\alpha\})^* \text{ et } v_1 \ldots v_p \in S'_n\}$$

Il est facile de voir que $\hat{S}'_n$ est un langage linéaire (comme S'_n) et donc que le langage $\hat{S}_n$ défini ci-dessous l'est aussi:

$$\hat{S}_n = \{g \mid g = \# \alpha a_1 \alpha \# f \in \hat{S}'_n \text{ et } \# f \in K_n\} \text{ où}$$

K_n est le langage rationnel $(\{\#\alpha,\alpha\}\ \bar{Y}(Y^2 \cup Y \cup \{1\}))^*$.

L'intérêt des langages $\hat{S}_n$ vient du

Lemme 1: Le langage L sur l'alphabet X est linéaire propre si et seulement si il existe un entier n et un homomorphisme ϕ de X^* dans Z_n^* tel que

$$L = \phi^{-1}\hat{S}_n .$$

Ce lemme est établi en étudiant d'assez près la forme normale de Greibach [2] des grammaires linéaires (la preuve est ensuite analogue à celle de [4] pour les langages algébriques). Cette étude des règles linéaires unilatères droites (i.e. de la forme $v \to v'_m$ où v' est un non-terminal) suggère un traitement simultané de règles linéaires unilatères

et permet de démontrer qu'à tout langage linéaire L on peut associer un langage linéaire pur L' (i.e. engendré par une grammaire linéaire sans règle unilatère) et une substitution rationnelle propre σ telle que $L = \sigma(L')$. Il en résulte que le langage symétrique S_2 est un générateur fidèle [1] du cône rationnel Lin et, en vertu d'un résultat de [1] la

Proposition: Si L est un générateur du cône rationnel Lin, $L \cup \{1\}$ en est un générateur fidèle.

B - Le résultat principal:

Nous commençons par une remarque d'ordre général: le langage L' sur l'alphabet $X_{L'}$ est élément du cylindre engendré par le langage L sur l'alphabet X_L si et seulement si il existe un langage rationnel K (sur l'alphabet de L') et un homomorphisme ϕ du monoïde libre $X_{L'}^*$ dans X_L^* tels que $L' = \phi^{-1}L \cap K$. Ceci provient de ce que si $L' = \phi^{-1}(L \cap R)$, on a $L' = \phi^{-1}L \cap \phi^{-1}R$ et du fait que la composition de deux homomorphismes est un homomorphisme.

Nous considérons alors sur l'alphabet $X_p = \{x_1, x_2, \ldots, x_p\}$ les langages suivants:

- les rationnels $R = x_1^+ x_2^+ \ldots x_p^+$ et $\bar{R} = X_p^* - R$.
- les langages linéaires (où Z et t sont deux nouveaux symboles)

$$A_p = \{Z^n x_1^{n_1} x_2^{n_2} \ldots x_p^{n_p}\ t\ x_p^{n_p} \ldots x_2^{n_2} x_1^{n_1} Z^n \mid n \geq 1,\ n_i \geq 1 \text{ pour } i=1,\ldots,p\}$$

$$A'_p = \{Z^n x_1^{n_1} x_2^{n_2} \ldots x_p^{n_p}\ t\ x_p^{n_p} \ldots x_2^{n_2} x_1^{n_1} Z^m \mid n,m \geq 1,\ n \neq m,\ n_i \geq 1 \text{ pour } i=1,\ldots,p\}$$

$$L_p = A_p . R$$

$$L'_p = A'_p . \bar{R}$$

$$L''_p = L_p \cup L'_p .$$

Supposant alors que le langage L''_p est élément du cylindre engendré par le langage S, et donc que $L''_p = \phi^{-1} S \cap \bar{K}$ où $\bar{K}$ est un langage rationnel, on établit d'abord qu'il existe un entier r tel que

$$\bar{K} \supseteq (Z^r)^+(x_1^r)^+ \dots (x_p^r)^+ \; t(x_p^r)^+ \dots (x_1^r)^+ \; X_p^*$$

(Cette preuve est identique à celle classique qui permet d'établir que si un langage rationnel K contient tous les mots de la forme $a^n b^m$ où $n \neq m$, il existe un entier r tel que K contienne $(a^r)^+(b^r)^+$.).

Il en résulte alors facilement que si $L''_p = \phi^{-1} S \cap \bar{K}$, il existe un homomorphisme λ tel que $L_p = \lambda^{-1} S \cap K$ où K est le langage rationnel $K = Z^+ x_1^+ x_2^+ \dots x_p^+ t x_p^+ \dots x_2^+ x_1^+ Z^+ X_p^*$.

Le lemme essentiel à la preuve de notre théorie est alors le suivant:

<u>Lemme 2</u>: <u>Pour</u> $p > n^2$, <u>il n'existe pas d'homomorphisme</u> λ <u>tel que</u> $L_p = \lambda^{-1} \hat{S}_n \cap K$ <u>où</u> K <u>est le langage rationnel donné ci-dessus</u>.

L'idée de la preuve de ce lemme est la suivante. Supposant que $L_p = \lambda^{-1} \hat{S}_n \cap K$, on s'assure que, pour tout $i=1,\dots,p$ λx_i contient au moins une occurrence de #. Puis on considère comment la contrainte d'égalité des nombres de Z à gauche de t et à droite de t peut apparaître par λ: ceci impose que dans les mots de $\hat{S}_n$ dont proviennent les mots de L_p les facteurs itérants situés à droite de la dernière occurrence de Z (i.e. les occurrences de x_i) proviennent de facteurs itérants de mots de $\hat{S}_n$, et donc d'éléments de la forme $\bar{a}_i a_j$. On trouve alors que si $p > n^2$, on pourra échanger deux tels facteurs itérants ce qui est impossible dans L_p.

La preuve du théorème est alors immédiate: supposons que Lin soit un cylindre admettant le langage H comme générateur principal. Alors, puisque $H \in$ Lin, il existe en vertu du lemme 1 un entier n et un homomorphisme ϕ tel que $H = \phi^{-1} \hat{S}_n$ et donc, il existe un entier n_o tel que $\hat{S}_{n_o}$ soit générateur principal du cylindre Lin. Mais alors L''_p est, pour tout p, élément du cylindre engendré par $\hat{S}_{n_o}$; il résulte donc de nos remarques préliminaires que pour tout p, il existe un homomorphisme λ tel que $L_p = \lambda^{-1} \hat{S}_{n_o} \cap K$, ce qui contredit le lemme 2.

Pour conclure, notons qu'un tel résultat négatif n'établit pas qu'il n'y ait aucun langage linéaire de complexité "maximale". En effet, bon nombre d'opérations ne modifiant pas la classe de complexité ne sont pas prises en compte ici (par exemple, l'intersection par des langages linéaires déterministes). En outre, la preuve du résultat suggère deux possibilités : elle fournit un système générateur du cylindre Lin, la famille des $\hat{S}_n$ et il semble donc que si l'on sait reconnaître tous ces langages "raisonnablement", il en ira de même de tout langage linéaire. En outre, il apparaît qu'à défaut d'un générateur du cylindre, la substitution du langage symétrique S_2 dans $\hat{S}_2$ fournit un langage qui doit contenir dans le cylindre qu'il engendre toute la famille Lin (sans qu'il soit lui-même linéaire). Ainsi, la complexité des langages linéaires ne serait-elle pas plus "grande" que celle de ce dernier langage.

[1] BOASSON L. et M. NIVAT: Sur Diverses Familles de Langages Fermées par Transductions Rationnelles.
Acta Informatica, 2, 180-188 (1973).

[2] GINSBURG S.: The Mathematical Theory of Context-Free Languages.
Mc Graw Hill (1966).

[3] GREIBACH S.: Jump pda's, Deterministic Context-Free Languages, Principal AFDL's and Polynomial Time Recognition.
Proc. of 5th Annual ACM Symposium on Theory of Computing, Austin, (Texas), 20-28 (1973).

[4] GREIBACH S.: The Hardest Context-Free Language.
Siam J. of Comput., 2, n°4, 304-330 (1975).

L. BOASSON
U.E.R. de Mathématiques
Université de Picardie

Ad. Postale: 5, Allée Georges Rouault
75020 - PARIS (F).

M. NIVAT
U.E.R. de Mathématiques
Université Paris 7

Ad. Postale: 8 rue Portalis
75009 - PARIS (F).

LANGAGES ALGEBRIQUES DETERMINISTES

ET GROUPES ABELIENS

J-F. PERROT

J. SAKAROVITCH

Le présent travail s'inscrit dans le cadre d'une étude d'ensemble sur les monoïdes syntactiques des langages algébriques (ou "context-free") dont on trouvera les premiers résultats en [6] et [7] . Nous présentons ici un résultat relatif au caractère déterministe ou non des langages algébriques dont le monoïde syntactique est un groupe abélien.

I . INTRODUCTION

Rappelons que le monoïde syntactique d'un langage L sur un alphabet X est par définition le quotient du monoïde libre X^* par sa congruence la plus grossière saturant L,(congruence syntactique), laquelle peut être ainsi caractérisée : deux mots u et $v \in X^*$ ont même image dans le monoïde syntactique de L ssi, pour tout couple $(f, g) \in X^* \times X^*$, on a $f\,u\,g \in L \Leftrightarrow f\,v\,g \in L$.

La théorie des monoïdes syntactiques, fondée en 1955 par M.P.Schützenberger pour rendre compte de certaines propriétés combinatoires des monoïdes libres, a été développée principalement pour les langages rationnels (ou "regular events"), qui sont caractérisés par le fait que leurs monoïdes syntactiques sont finis (Théorème de Kleene). Les succès remportés dans cette direction (langages "star-free", théorie de Krohn et Rhodes), grâce à l'interprétation naturelle du monoïde syntactique comme monoïde de transitions de l'automate réduit acceptant le langage, incitent à étendre la théorie aux autres classes de langages, notamment à celles de la hiérarchie de Chomsky (cf. par exemple Smith [8]). Cette entreprise offre de nombreuses difficultés et les résultats obtenus à ce jour sont très fragmentaires, même si on se limite à la classe des langages algébriques.

II . PRESENTATION DU RESULTAT

Un langage algébrique L étant toujours pris sur un alphabet fini, son monoïde syntactique $\underline{M}(L)$ est toujours finiment engendré. Si $\underline{M}(L)$ est un groupe abélien, il est donc, d'après la théorie classique, isomorphe au produit direct $F \times Z^k$ d'un groupe abélien fini F par un groupe abélien libre Z^k, lui-même isomorphe au produit direct de k exemplaires du groupe additif Z des entiers, pour un certain entier k positif ou nul : nous dirons que le rang du groupe considéré est k. Notre résultat principal s'énonce ainsi :

Théorème 1 : Soit L un langage algébrique dont le monoïde syntactique est un groupe abélien, et soit k le rang de ce groupe. Alors L est nécessairement déterministe si $k \leqslant 1$ et non-déterministe si $k \geqslant 2$.

Notons que, pour tout groupe abélien finiment engendré G, de rang k, il existe effectivement des langages algébriques admettant G comme monoïde syntactique : on peut notamment en construire par récurrence sur k à partir de langages rationnels (admettant F comme monoïde syntactique) et de langages algébriques dont le monoïde syntactiques est isomorphe à Z (p. ex. sur l'alphabet $X = \{x, y\}$, le langage de Dyck $\{w \in X^* \quad |w|_x = |w|_y \}$) .

Cette construction est possible en vertu du fait que, si les monoïdes syntactiques de deux langages algébriques L_1 et L_2 n'ont pas de zéro, il existe un langage algébrique L_3 dont le monoïde syntactique est isomorphe au produit $\underline{M}(L_1) \times \underline{M}(L_2)$. On sait par ailleurs que le produit direct de deux monoïdes syntactiques de langages algébriques n'est pas toujours lui-même isomorphe au monoïde syntactique d'un autre langage algébrique, de sorte que pour la construction précédente l'hypothèse que $\underline{M}(L_1)$ et $\underline{M}(L_2)$ n'ont pas de zéro n'est pas superflue [6]. Dans le même sens, on doit à E. Valkema la remarque suivante :

Proposition [9] : Soient L_1 et L_2 deux langages algébriques déterministes : il existe un langage algébrique L_3 dont le monoïde syntactique est isomorphe au produit direct $\underline{M}(L_1) \times \underline{M}(L_2)$.

Notre résultat montre, en prenant $G = Z \times Z$, que le langage L_3 peut être obligatoirement non-déterministe, d'où le

Corollaire : La classe des monoïdes syntactiques de langages algébriques déterministes n'est pas fermée par produit direct.

III . DISCUSSION DU RESULTAT

a) Bien que la famille des langages algébriques déterministes soit fermée par passage au complémentaire, il n'est pas possible de caractériser ces langages par leurs monoïdes syntactiques, même à l'intérieur de la famille des langages algébriques : on observe en effet, avec $X = \{x, y\}$, que le langage non-déterministe $\{x^n y^n ; n \geqslant 1\} \cup \{x^n y^{2n} ; n \geqslant 1\}$ et le langage déterministe $\{x^n y^n ; n = 2p, p \geqslant 1\} \cup \{x^n y^{2n} ; n=2p+1, p \geqslant 1\}$ ont tous deux le même monoïde syntactique, isomorphe au quotient de Rees du monoïde X^* par son idéal bilatère $X^*yx X^*$.

b) Il reste que certains monoïdes sont ainsi faits que, L étant un langage admettant le monoïde en question comme monoïde syntactique, l'hypothèse que L est algébrique (hypothèse de nature combinatoire dans le monoïde libre) entraîne automatiquement des restrictions supplémentaires.

Le groupe additif Z et les groupes abéliens de rang 1 ne sont pas les seuls pour lesquels L supposé algébrique doit de plus être déterministe : la même démonstration donne cette propriété au groupe diédral infini, produit libre de deux groupes d'ordre 2.

De même, d'autres monoïdes que les groupes abéliens de rang $\geqslant 2$ sont tels que le langage L algébrique est obligatoirement non-déterministe : c'est notamment le cas, d'après la remarque de E. Valkema rappelée ci-dessus, pour tout monoïde M dont le carré par produit direct $M \times M$ n'est monoïde syntactique d'aucun langage algébrique (un tel monoïde contient nécessairement un zéro ; un exemple est donné en [6]) .

c) Signalons enfin que dans notre résultat c'est effectivement le non-déterminisme qui est en cause, et non l'ambiguïté inhérente, propriété plus forte, comme on aurait pu le supposer au vu des techniques de preuve employées, qui font appel aux propriétés des "paires itérantes " . Il existe en effet des langages algébriques non-ambigus dont le complémentaire est algébrique non-ambigu, et admettant Z^2 comme monoïde syntactique.

Par exemple sur l'alphabet $X = \{x, \bar{x}, y, \bar{y}\}$ considérons le langage $L = L' \cup L''$, avec

$$L' = \{w \in X^* ; |w|_x = |w|_{\bar{x}} \text{ et } |w|_y - |w|_{\bar{y}} \text{ impair}\}$$

$$L'' = \{w \in X^* ; |w|_y = |w|_{\bar{y}} \text{ et } |w|_x - |w|_{\bar{x}} \text{ impair}\}$$

L' et L" étant disjoints, l'un et l'autre déterministes (leurs monoïdes syntactiques sont isomorphes à $Z \times Z/2Z$) le langage L est lui même non-ambigu (mais aussi non-déterministe), et son monoïde syntactique est isomorphe à Z^2 .

On vérifie que $\bar{L}$ le complémentaire de L peut s'écrire

$\bar{L} = L_1 \cup L_2 \cup R_1 \cup R_2$ avec

$R_1 = \{w \in X^*; |w|_x - |w|_{\bar{x}}$ pair et $|w|_y - |w|_{\bar{y}}$ pair $\}$

$R_2 = \{w \in X^*; |w|_x - |w|_{\bar{x}}$ impair et $|w|_y - |w|_{\bar{y}}$ impair $\}$

$L_1 = \{w \in X^*; |w|_x \neq |w|_{\bar{x}}$ et $|w|_x - |w|_{\bar{x}}$ pair et $|w|_y - |w|_{\bar{y}}$ impair $\}$

$L_2 = \{w \in X^*; |w|_y \neq |w|_{\bar{y}}$ et $|w|_y - |w|_{\bar{y}}$ pair et $|w|_x - |w|_{\bar{x}}$ impair $\}$

Ces quatres langages sont disjoints deux à deux ; R_1 et R_2 sont rationnels donc non-ambigus, L_1 et L_2 sont déterministes (monoïde syntactique $Z \times Z/2Z$) donc non-ambigus eux aussi. Leur réunion est algébrique non-ambiguë.

IV . PREUVE DU THEOREME 1

a) Méthode

Etant donné un monoïde M, tout langage L dont le monoïde syntactique est isomorphe à M est de la forme $L = \varphi^{-1}(P)$, où φ est un homomorphisme du monoïde libre engendré par l'alphabet du langage sur M et où P est une partie disjonctive de M, i.e. un sous-ensemble qui n'est saturé par aucune autre congruence de M que l'égalité, (la congruence syntactique de P dans M est l'égalité) , ce qui se traduit par : pour $m', m'' \in M$, $m' \neq m''$ entraîne l'existence de $p,q \in M$ vérifiant soit $pm'q \in P$ et $pm''q \notin P$, soit $pm'q \notin P$ et $pm''q \in P$.
Il est essentiel de constater que le caractère algébrique (resp. algébrique déterministe) du langage L ne dépend pas de l'homomorphisme φ, mais seulement de la partie P, en vertu du Lemme suivant, conséquence directe de la liberté des monoïdes en question :

Lemme [7] : Etant donné un monoïde M, une partie quelconque $P \subset M$, deux homomorphismes φ_1 et φ_2 de deux monoïdes libres X_1^* et X_2^* sur M, en notant $L_1 = \varphi_1^{-1}(P)$ et $L_2 = \varphi_2^{-1}(P)$, il existe deux homomorphismes ζ et θ, $\zeta : X_1^* \to X_2^*$ et $\theta : X_2^* \to X_1^*$ vérifiant $\zeta^{-1}(L_2) = L_1$ et $\theta^{-1}(L_1) = L_2$

Les caractères des langages qui nous intéressent sont en effet conservés par homomorphisme inverse.

Notre méthode de preuve consiste donc à choisir un alphabet X et un homomorphisme φ "adaptés à la structure" du monoïde M considéré, en l'occurrence un groupe abélien G, et à montrer que, pour une partie P (disjonctive) quelconque de G, l'image inverse $L = \varphi^{-1}(P)$ ne peut être algébrique sans être aussi déterministe (ou non-déterministe).

b) Groupes de rang $\leqslant 1$

Si le rang de G est nul, G est fini et le langage L est rationnel, donc déterministe.

Si G est de rang 1, il est de la forme $G = \mathbb{Z} \times F$ où F est fini. La première partie du théorème résulte alors de la proposition suivante, un peu plus générale :

Proposition : Soit F un groupe fini et G le produit direct $G = \mathbb{Z} \times F$; Soit φ un homomorphisme d'un monoïde libre X^* sur G et $L = \varphi^{-1}(P)$ l'image inverse d'une partie quelconque P de G. Si L est algébrique alors L est déterministe .

Conformément à a) nous choisissons $X = \{x, \bar{x}\} \cup Y$, où Y est un alphabet quelconque ne contenant ni x ni $\bar{x}$ et doté d'un homomorphisme ψ envoyant Y^* sur F, et nous définissons $\varphi : X^* \to G$ par

$\varphi(x) = (1, e_F)$

$\varphi(\bar{x}) = (-1, e_F)$ $\qquad e_F$ désignant l'élément neutre de F.

$\varphi(y) = (0, \psi(y))$ pour $y \in Y$.

Notons π la projection de X^* sur $\{x, \bar{x}\}^*$ définie par $\pi(x) = x$, $\pi(\bar{x}) = \bar{x}$ et $\pi(y)$ = le mot vide. La première composante de l'image par φ

d'un mot w de X^* est un entier n ou $-n$ suivant que l'image inverse $\varphi^{-1}(\varphi(w))$ contient un mot "réduit" dont la projection par π est x^n ou $\bar{x}^n$.

Pour $g \in F$, désignons par R_g l'ensemble $\varphi^{-1}(\mathbb{Z}, g)$ des mots de X^* dont l'image dans G a g pour 2e composante : R_g est une partie rationnelle de X^*. Considérons alors $L_g = \{ u \in \{x, \bar{x}\}^* ; \varphi(u).(0,g) \in P\}$

On a $L_g = \pi(L \cap R_g)$, L_g est donc une partie algébrique de $\{x, \bar{x}\}^*$ et l'ensemble des mots réduit $K_g = L_g \cap (x^* \cup \bar{x}^*)$ est donc union d'une partie algébrique de x^* (donc rationnelle) et d'une partie algébrique de $\bar{x}^*$ (donc également rationnelle), il est rationnel ainsi que l'ensemble $\bar{K}_g$ qui s'en déduit par échange de x et $\bar{x}$ (passage à l'image opposée).

Désignons enfin par r_g un mot quelconque de X^* dont l'image $\varphi(r_g)$ est $(0,g)$.

On vérifie immédiatement, en calculant dans G, qu'un mot $w \in X^*$ est dans L ssi, pour au moins un $g \in F$ on a $\pi(wr_g) \in L_g$, ce qui a lieu ssi un mot réduit $k \in \bar{K}_g$ vérifie $\varphi(w\, r_g k) = (0, e_F)$. Désignons , suivant [3], par L/R le langage $L/R = \{u ; \exists\, v \in R$ tel que $u\, v \in L\}$.

En posant $K = \cup \{\bar{K}_g\, r_g ; g \in F\}$, et $D = \varphi^{-1}(0,e_F)$, nous obtenons

$L = \{ w \in X^* ; \exists\, k \in K, w\, k \in D\}$, soit $L = D/K$.

D'après le corollaire 2 du Théorème 3.4 de [2] on a : K étant rationnel, L est déterministe si D est lui-même déterministe. Il suffit alors d'observer que $D = \hat{D} \cap R_e$, où $R_e = \varphi^{-1}(\mathbb{Z}, e_F)$ est rationnel et $\hat{D} = \{ w \in X^* ; |w|_x = |w|_{\bar{x}} \}$ est bien connu pour être déterministe (langage de Dyck), pour établir la proposition .

<u>Remarque</u> : Le même résultat reste vrai en remplaçant $\mathbb{Z}$ par le groupe diédral infini, engendré par deux éléments x et y avec pour seules relations de définition $x^2 = y^2 = e$, ce qui montre que c'est moins la commutativité que la "maigreur" de $\mathbb{Z}$ qui est en cause. Il suffit pour le voir de reprendre la démonstration précédente en observant que l'ensemble des "mots réduits" est alors $(xy)^* \cup (yx)^* \cup y(xy)^* \cup x(yx)^*$ qui, comme $x^* \cup \bar{x}^*$ ne peut contenir de partie algébrique qui ne soit rationnelle. Le langage $\hat{D}$ est alors un langage de Dyck généralisé [2] .

c) <u>Une propriété d'itération des langages algébriques déterministes</u>

La démonstration de la partie réciproque du théorème 1 repose sur une propriété des "paires itérantes" d'un langage algébrique déterministe, propriété dont la preuve est donnée en [7].

Etant donné un langage L sur l'alphabet X, on note $\equiv_L$ l'équivalence régulière droite la plus grossière de X^* qui sature L.

On a $p \equiv_L q \Leftrightarrow \{ \forall v \in X^* \quad p v \in L \Leftrightarrow q v \in L \}$

<u>Définition</u> Soit L un langage sur l'alphabet X.

On appelle <u>paire itérante</u> du mot f dans L un quintuplet $\pi = (\alpha, u, \beta, v, \gamma)$ de X^{*5} tel que

i) $f = \alpha u \beta v \gamma$

ii) $|uv| \geqslant 1$

iii) $\forall n \in N \quad \alpha u^n \beta v^n \gamma \in L$

On appelle <u>paire itérante déterministe</u> du mot f dans L un quintuplet $\pi = (\alpha, u, \beta, v, \gamma)$ de X^{*5} tel que

i) $f = \alpha u \beta v \gamma$

ii) $|uv| \geqslant 1$

iii) $V n \in N \quad \alpha u^n \beta v^n \gamma \equiv_L \alpha u \beta v \gamma$

On appellera n-ième itéré de π le mot $f_n = \alpha u^n \beta v^n \gamma$.

Exemple : Soient $L = \{a^p b^q \;;\; p,q \in N \quad p \neq q\}$ et le mot $f = a^3 b^4$. $\pi_1 = (a, a, ab, b, b^2)$, $\pi_2 = (a, a, ab, b^2, b)$, et $\pi_3 = (1, a^3, b, b, b^2)$ sont trois paires itérantes de f dans L. π_1 et π_2 sont des paires itérantes déterministes de f dans L, mais π_3 ne l'est pas.

L'existence d'au moins une paire itérante dans tout mot suffisamment long d'un langage algébrique est assurée par les résultats classiques de Bar-Hillel, Perles et Shamir, et d'Ogden ; Boasson [1] a entamé une étude systématique de ce phénomène, nous nous inspirons ici de ses méthodes. Nos "paires itérantes déterministes" sont essentiellement une généralisation des paires itérantes mises en évidence par Ogden [5] et Harrison et Havel [4] dans les langages déterministes.

<u>Définition</u> Soit L un langage sur l'alphabet X.

Un mot f de X^* admet un <u>couple de paires itérantes déterministes disjointes dans</u> L, $C = (\pi_1, \pi_2)$ - $\pi_2 = (\alpha_1, u_1, \beta_1, v_1, \gamma_1)$ et $\pi_2 = (\alpha_2, u_2, \beta_2, v_2, \gamma_2)$ - Si, et seulement si,

i) $f = \alpha_1 u_1 \beta_1 v_1 \gamma_1 = \alpha_2 u_2 \beta_2 v_2 \gamma_2$

ii) les occurrences des quatre facteurs u_1, v_1, u_2, v_2 sont disjointes dans f deux à deux.

iii) en désignant par $f_{n,m}$ le mot obtenu en prenant simultanément le n-ième itéré de π_1 et le $n^{\text{ième}}$ itéré de π_2 - d'après ii) cela est possible - on a

$$\forall n,m \in N \qquad f_{n,m} \equiv_L f.$$

Le couple C est dit de <u>type 1</u> si on a

$|\alpha_1 u_1 \beta_1 v_1| \leqslant |\alpha_2|$ c'est à dire si f peut se représenter schématiquement ainsi :

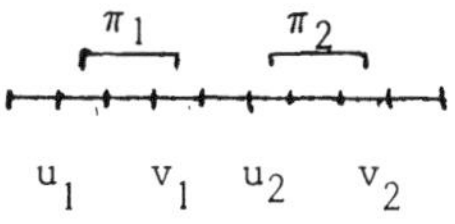

π_1 π_2

u_1 v_1 u_2 v_2

C est dit de <u>type 2</u> si on a

$$|\alpha_1 u_1| \leqslant |\alpha_2| \leqslant |\alpha_2 u_2| \leqslant |\alpha_1 u_1 \beta_1| \leqslant |\alpha_1 u_1 \beta_1 v_1| \leqslant |\alpha_2 u_2 \beta_2|$$

Soit schématiquement

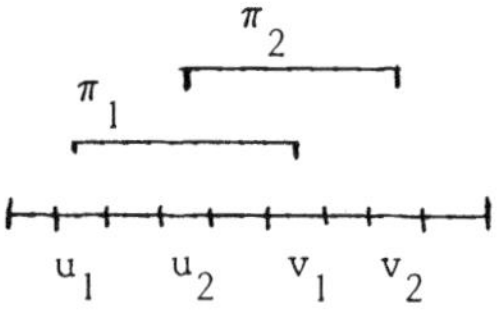

π_2 π_1

u_1 u_2 v_1 v_2

C est dit de type 3 si on a

$$|\alpha_1 u_1| \leqslant |\alpha_2 u_2 \beta_2 v_2| \leqslant |\alpha_1 u_1 \beta_1|$$

Soit schématiquement

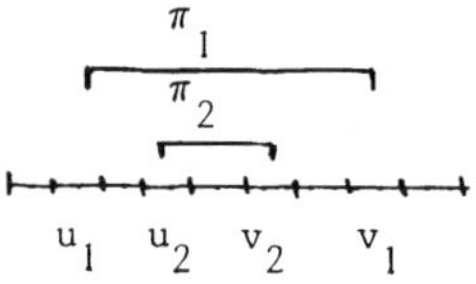

π_1 π_2

u_1 u_2 v_2 v_1

On appellera <u>éléments itérants</u> de C l'ensemble des occurrences des quatre facteurs $\{u_1, v_1, u_2, v_2\}$.

<u>Exemples</u> Soit $L_1 = \{a^p b^q c^r d^s \ / \ p,q,r,s \in N \qquad p + q = r + s\}$

Le mot f = abcd admet dans L_1 le couple de paires itérantes déterministes disjointes de type 2 $C = (\pi_1, \pi_2)$ avec $\pi_1 = (a, b, c, d, 1)$ et $\pi_2 = (1, a, b, c, d)$. Il admet aussi dans L_1 le couple de type 3

$C' = (\pi_1', \pi_2')$ avec $\pi_1' = (1, a, bc, d, 1)$ et $\pi_2' = (a, b, 1, c, d)$.

Soit $L_2 = \{a^p b^q c^r d^s \ / \ p,q,r,s \in N \quad p+r = q+s\}$. Le même mot $f = a\ b\ c\ d$ admet dans L_2 le couple $C = (\pi_1, \pi_2)$ précédent. Il n'admet pas dans L_2 le couple C' mais le couple de type 1 $C'' = (\pi_1'', \pi_2'')$ avec $\pi_1'' = (1, a, 1, b, cd)$ et $\pi_2'' = (ab, c, 1, d, 1)$.

Ces trois couples admettent les mêmes éléments itérants $\{a, b, c, d\}$

<u>Définition</u> Soient C un couple de paires itérantes déterministes disjointes d'un mot f dans un langage L et $\{u_1, v_1, u_2, v_2\}$ ses éléments itérants .

Soient $f_{n,m}$ un itéré de f et C' un nouveau couple de paires itérantes déterministes disjointes de $f_{n,m}$ dans L. C' est dit <u>déduit</u> de C si ses éléments itérants sont $\{u_1^h, v_1^h, u_2^k, v_2^k\}$ pour deux entiers h et k.

Dans les exemples précédents, si on considère le langage L_1, le couple C' est déduit de C (et réciproquement d'ailleurs) . Si on considère le langage L_2 les couples C et C'' sont déduits l'un de l'autre.

Nous pouvons maintenant donner la propriété annoncée :

Théorème 2 [7] <u>Soit L un langage algébrique déterministe et soit C un couple de paires itérantes déterministes disjointes de type 2 dans L. Alors il existe un couple C' , déduit de C et de type 1 ou de type 3</u>.

Ainsi on a trouvé C' déduit de C dans L_1 et C'' déduit de C dans L_2 dans nos exemples.

Soit $L_3 = \{a^p b^q c^r d^s \ / \ p, q, r, s \in N \quad p = r \quad \text{ou} \quad q = s\}$

Dans L_3 le mot f = abcd admet toujours le couple $C = (\pi_1, \pi_2)$

Il est facile de vérifier qu'il n'existe pas dans L_3 de couple de type 1 ou 3 . Il est d'ailleurs bien connu que L_3 n'est pas déterministe (puisqu'ambigu) .

d) <u>Groupes de rang $\geqslant 2$</u>

On peut écrire $G = Z^2 \times T$ avec $T = Z^{k-2} \times F$. Comme en b) nous choisissons $X = \{x, \bar{x}, y, \bar{y}\} \cup Y$ où Y est un alphabet quelconque ne contenant aucune des lettres $\{x, \bar{x}, y, \bar{y}\}$ et doté d'un homomorphisme ψ envoyant Y^* sur T et nous définissons $\varphi : X^* \to G$ par

$\varphi(x) = (1, 0, e_T)$ $\varphi(y) = (0, 1, e_T)$

$\varphi(\bar{x}) = (-1, 0, e_T)$ $\varphi(\bar{y}) = (0, -1, e_T)$

et $\varphi(y) = (0, 0, \psi(y))$ pour $y \in Y$ e_T désignant l'élément neutre de F.

Soient P une partie quelconque de G et $L = \varphi^{-1}(P)$.

On va supposer que L est une langage algébrique déterministe sur l'alphabet X et on va en déduire que P <u>n'est pas</u> une partie disjonctive de G ; et le théorème 1 sera enfin démontré. Comme G est un groupe, P n'est pas une partie disjonctive si, et seulement si, il existe un sous-groupe de G, nécessairement distingué puisque G est abélien, tel que P est union de cosets de ce sous-groupe.

Le mot $f = x\, y\, \bar{x}\, \bar{y}$ admet le couple $C = (\pi_1, \pi_2)$ de paires itérantes déterministes disjointes de type 2 dans L, avec $\pi_1 = (1, x, y, \bar{x}, \bar{y})$ et $\pi_2 = (x, y, \bar{x}, \bar{y}, 1)$. En effet

(1) $\forall n, m \in N \quad \forall v \in X^* \quad x\, y\, \bar{x}\, \bar{y}\, v \in L \Leftrightarrow x^n y^m \bar{x}^n \bar{y}^m v \in L$

puisque

(2) $\forall n, m \in N \quad \forall v \in X^* \quad \varphi(x\, y\, \bar{x}\, \bar{y}\, v) = \varphi(x^n y^m \bar{x}^n \bar{y}^m v) = \varphi(v)$

D'après le théorème 2 il existe un itéré $f_{n,m} = x^n y^m \bar{x}^n \bar{y}^m$ qui admet dans L un couple C' déduit de C, de type 1 ou de type 3 .

Supposons d'abord $C' = (\pi_1', \pi_2')$ de type 1 . On peut écrire

$\pi_1' = (x^{x-h}, x^h, 1, y^k, y^{m-k}\, \bar{x}^n\, \bar{y}^m),$

$\pi_2' = (x^n y^m \bar{x}^{n-h}, \bar{x}^h, 1, \bar{y}^k, \bar{y}^{m-k}).$

On a vu que $\forall w \in X^* \quad w \in L \Leftrightarrow f_{n,m}\, w \in L$

donc, d'après la définition d'un couple de paires itérantes déterministes disjointes de $f_{n,m}$ dans L on a

(3) $\forall p, q \in N \quad \forall w \in X^* \quad w \in L \Leftrightarrow x^{n+ph} y^{m+pk} \bar{x}^{n+qh} \bar{y}^{m+qk} w \in L$

Soit, en passant aux images dans G par φ,

(4) $\forall z \in Z \quad \forall (z_1, z_2, t) \in G \quad (z_1, z_2, t) \in P \Leftrightarrow (z_1+zh, z_2+zk, t) \in P$

c'est à dire que P est saturé modulo le sous-groupe de G engendré par l'élément (h, k, 0).

Le cas où C' est de type 3 se traite de manière analogue. On trouve alors que P est saturé modulo le sous-groupe de G engendré par l'élément (h, -k, 0).

Q.E.D.

Remarque : Dans cette démonstration, le fait que T est un groupe n'intervient pas. On peut également prouver la première partie du théorème sans cette hypothèse, par une technique différente de celle que nous avons donnée ici [7], d'où un résultat final plus général que celui que nous avons annoncé.

B I B L I O G R A P H I E

[1] L. BOASSON, Paires itérantes et langages algébriques, Thèse Sc. Math. , Univ. Paris VII, 1974.

[2] Y. COCHET et M. NIVAT, Une généralisation des ensembles de Dyck, Israël J. Math. 9 (1971) 389-395.

[3] S. GINSBURG et S. GREIBACH, Deterministic Context free Languages, Inf. and Control 9 (1966) 620-648.

[4] M. HARRISON et I. HAVEL, On the Parsing of Deterministic Languages, J. Assoc. Comput. Mach. 21 (1974) 525-548

[5] W. OGDEN, Intercalation Theorems for Push-down Store and Stack Languages, Ph. D. Thesis, Stanford 1968.

[6] J-F. PERROT, Monoïdes syntactiques des langages algébriques, à paraître dans les Actes de l'Ecole de Printemps sur les Langages algébriques, Bonascre 1973.

[7] J. SAKAROVITCH, Monoïdes syntactiques et langages algébriques, Thèse de 3ème cycle, Paris, à paraître en 1975.

[8] J. SMITH, Monoid acceptors and their relation to formal languages, Ph.D. Thesis, University of Pennesylvania, 1972.

[9] E. VALKEMA, Zur Charakterisierung formuler Sprachen durch Halbgruppen, Dissertation, Kiel 1974.

Best Possible Bounds on the Weighted Path Length of Optimum Binary Search Trees

by

Kurt Mehlhorn

Abstract :

We derive upper and lower bounds for the weighted path length P_{opt} of optimum binary search trees. In particular,

$$1/\log 3\ H \leq P_{opt} \leq 2 + H$$

where H is the entropy of the frequency distribution. We also present an approximation algorithm which constructs nearly optimal trees.

I. Introduction

"One of the popular methods for retrieving information by its 'name' is to store the names in a binary tree. We are given n names $B_1, B_2, \ldots, B_n$ and 2n+1 frequencies $\beta_1, \ldots, \beta_n, \alpha_o, \ldots, \alpha_n$ with $\Sigma\beta_i + \Sigma\alpha_j = 1$. Here β_i is the frequency of encountering name B_i, and α_j is the frequency of encountering a name which lies between B_j and B_{j+1}, (a name in the interval (B_j, B_{j+1})) α_o and α_n have obvious interpretations". ([5]).

Fachbereich 1o
Angewandte Mathematik und Informatik
Universität des Saarlandes, D 66 Saarbrücken

A binary search tree T is a tree with n interior nodes (nodes having two sons), which we denote by circles, and n + 1 leaves, which we denote by squares. The interior nodes are labelled by the B_i in increasing order from left to right and the leaves are labelled by the intervals (B_j, B_{j+1}) in increasing order from left to right. Let b_i be the distance of interior node B_i from the root and let a_j be the distance of leaf (B_j, B_{j+1}) from the root. To retrieve a name X, $b_i + 1$ comparisons are needed if $X = B_i$ and a_j comparisons are required if $B_j < X < B_{j+1}$. Therefore we define the weighted path lenght of tree T as :

$$P = \sum_{i=1}^{n} \beta_i (b_i+1) + \sum_{j=o}^{n} \alpha_j a_j$$

It is equal to the expected number of comparisons needed to retrieve a name.

The following two problems are among the most important in this area ([5]).

a) Prove good lower and upper bounds for the weighted path length of optimum binary search trees, i.e. the trees with minimal weighted path length. Such bounds would provide us with a simple a-priori test for the performance of binary search trees.

b) Design efficient algorithms for constructing optimal (or nearly so) binary search trees.

In this paper, we attempt to solve both problems.

II. Upper Bounds

In this section, we will show that $1 + \sum \alpha_j + H$ -- $H = -\sum \beta_i \log \beta_i - \sum \alpha_j \log \alpha_j$ is the entropy of the frequency distribution -- is an upper bound on the weighted path length P_{opt} of the optimum binary search tree. Furthermore this bound is best possible among the bounds of the form

$c_1 \sum \beta_i + c_2 \sum \alpha_j + c_3 \cdot H.$

We prove the upper bound by describing and analyzing an approximation algorithm. This algorithm constructs binary search trees in a top-down fashion. It uses bisection on the set

$$\{ s_i \; ; \; s_i = \sum_{p=o}^{i-1} (\alpha_p + \beta_p) + \beta_i + \alpha_i/2$$

$$\text{and } o \leq i \leq n \}, \text{ i.e.}$$

the root k is determined such that $s_{k-1} \leq 1/2$ and $s_k \geq 1/2$. It proceeds then recursively on the subsets $\{ s_i ; \; i \leq k - 1 \}$ and $\{ s_i ; \; i \geq k \}$.

The main program

begin

let $s_i \leftarrow \sum_{p=o}^{i-1} (\alpha_p + \beta_p) + \beta_i + \alpha_i/2$ for $o \leq i \leq n$;

construct-tree (0, n, 0, 1)

end

uses the recursive procedure construct-tree.

construct-tree (i, j, cut, ℓ) ;

comment we assume that the actual parameters of any call of construct-tree satisfy the following conditions.

(1) i and j are integers with $o \leq i < j \leq n$,

(2) ℓ is an integer with $\ell \geq 1$,

(3) cut $= \sum_{p=1}^{\ell-1} x_p \, 2^{-p}$ with $x_p \in \{0, 1\}$ for all p,

(4) cut $\leq s_i \leq s_j \leq$ cut $+ 2^{-\ell+1}$.

A call construct-tree (i, j, -, -,) will construct a binary search tree for the nodes (i+1) ,..., (j) and the leaves [i] ,..., [j] ;

<u>begin</u>

<u>if</u> i + 1 = j (case A)

<u>then</u> return the tree

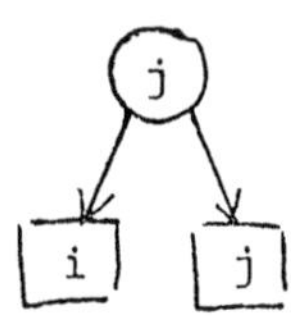

<u>else</u> <u>comment</u> we determine the root so as to bisect the interval

(cut, cut + $2^{-\ell+1}$)

<u>begin</u>

determine k such that

(5) $i < k \leq j$

(6) $k = i + 1$ or $s_{k-1} \leq$ cut $+ 2^{-\ell}$

(7) $k = j$ or $s_k \geq$ cut $+ 2^{-\ell}$

<u>comment</u> k exists because the actual parameters are supposed to satisfy condition (4);

<u>if</u> k = i + 1 (case B)

<u>then</u> return the tree

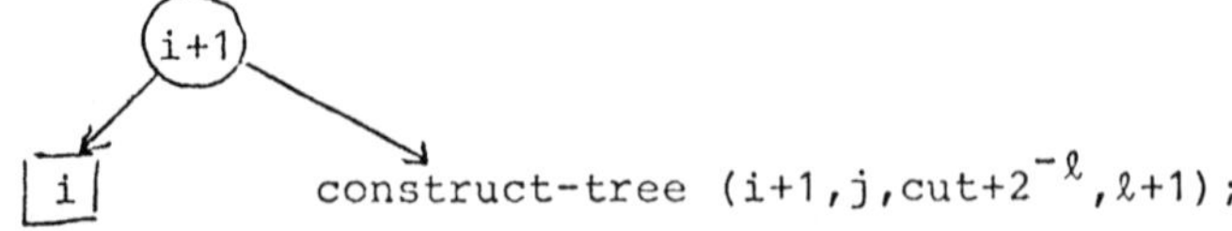

<u>if</u> k = j (case C)

<u>then</u> return the tree

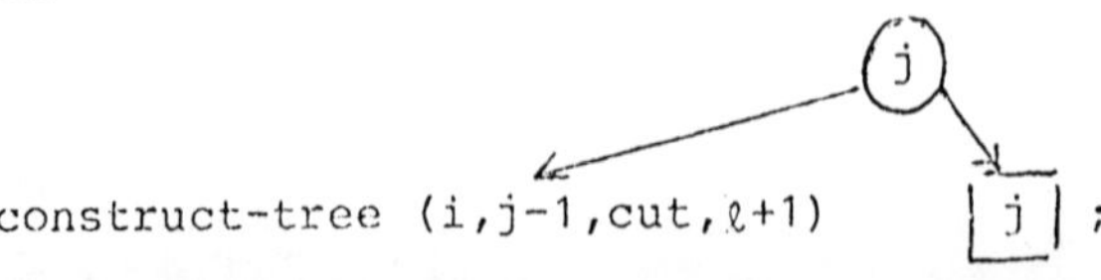

<u>if</u> i + 1 < k < j (case D)

<u>then</u> return the tree

k

construct-tree (i,k-1,cut,ℓ+1) construct-tree (k,j,cut+$2^{-\ell}$,ℓ+1)

<u>end</u>

<u>end</u>.

<u>Lemma :</u>

The approximation algorithm constructs a binary search tree whose weighted path length P_{approx} is bounded above by

$$1 + \sum \alpha_j + H.$$

The algorithm can be implemented to work in O (n log n) units of time and O (n) units of space.

<u>proof :</u>

We state several simple facts.

<u>Fact 1 :</u>

If the actual parameters of a call construct-tree (i, j, cut, ℓ) satisfy conditions (1) to (4) and i + 1 $\neq$ j then a k satisfying conditions (5) to (7) exists and the actual parameters of the recursive calls of construct-tree iniated by this call again satisfy conditions (1) to (4).

<u>Fact 2 :</u>

The actual parameters of every call of construct-tree satisfy conditions (1) to (4) (if the arguments of the top-level call do).

We say that node (h) (leaf [h] respectively) is constructed by call construct-tree (i, j, cut, ℓ) if h = j (h = i or h = j) and case A is taken or if h = i + 1 (h = i) and case B is taken or if h = j (h = j) and case C is taken or if h = k and case D is taken. Let b_i be the depth of node (i) and let a_j be the depth of leaf [j] in the tree returned by the call construct-tree (o, n, o, 1).

Fact 3 :

If node (h) (leaf [h]) is constructed by the call construct-tree (i, j, cut, ℓ) then $b_h + 1 = \ell$ ($a_h = \ell$).

Fact 4 :

If node (h) (leaf [h]) is constructed by the call construct-tree (i, j, cut, ℓ) then $\beta_h \leq 2^{-\ell+1}$ ($\alpha_h \leq 2^{-\ell+2}$).

Fact 5 :

The weighted path length P_{approx} of the tree constructed by the approximation algorithm is bounded above by $1 + \sum \alpha_j + H$.

We sketch now an efficient implementation of our approximation algorithm. The complexity of the algorithm is determined by the complexity of the search for k. If we search for k simultaneously from both ends, i.e. try k = i + 1, k = j, k = i + 2, k = j - 1, ... successively, then the complexity of this search is O (min (k - i, j - k + 1)). Hence we get the following recurrence relation for the complexity of construct-tree (as a function of j - i).

$$(*)\quad T(m) \leq \begin{cases} o & \underline{\text{if}}\ n = o \text{ (by definition)} \\ c_1 & \underline{\text{if}}\ n = 1 \\ \max\limits_{o<k<m/2} \left[T(k) + T(m-k+1) + c_2 (k+1) \right] & \text{otherwise} \end{cases}$$

for some constants c_1, c_2.

Fact 7 :

The recurrence relation ($*$) has a solution $T(n) \leq O(n \log n)$.

Fact 8 :

The approximation algorithm can be implemented to work in $O(n \log n)$ units of time and $O(n)$ units of space.

q. e. d.

Theorem 1 :

Let $\alpha_o, \beta_1, \alpha_1, \ldots, \beta_n, \alpha_n$ be any frequency distribution, let P_{opt} be the weighted path length of the optimum binary search tree for this distribution, let P_{approx} be the weighted path length of the tree constructed by the approximation algorithm, and let $H = -\sum \beta_i \log \beta_i - \sum \alpha_j \log \alpha_j$ be the entropy of the frequency distribution. Then

$$P_{opt} \leq P_{approx} \leq 1 + \sum \alpha_j + H.$$

Furthermore, this upper bounds is best possible in the following sense : If $c_1 \sum \beta_i + c_2 \sum \alpha_j + c_3 \cdot H$ is an upper bound on P_{opt} then $c_1 \geq 1$, $c_2 \geq 2$, and $c_3 \geq 1$.

proof :

The first part of the theorem follows from the preceding lemma. The second part is proven by exhibiting suitable frequency distributions.

$c_1 \geq 1$: Take $n = 1$, $\alpha_o = \alpha_1 = o$ and $\beta_1 = 1$.

$c_2 \geq 2$: Take $n = 2$, $\alpha_o = \alpha_2 = \beta_1 = \beta_2 = o$, $\alpha_1 = 1$.

$c_3 \geq 1$: Take $n = 2^k - 1$, $\beta_i = o$ for all i and $\alpha_j = 2^{-k}$ for all j. It is easy to see that the complete binary tree is the optimal binary search tree for this distribution. Thus

$$H = \log n + 1 = k = \sum_{\text{leaves}} 1/2^k \cdot k = P_{opt}.$$

q. e. d.

E.N. Gilbert and E.F. Moore (1) proved this theorem in the special case that all internal nodes have weight zero (i.e. $\beta_i = o$ for all i). Their proof suggest the approximation algorithm which we presented above. Other " rules of thumb " are discussed in [7, 8] ; we prove in [7] that the strategy " choose the root so as to equalize the total weights of the left and right subtree as much as poosible " yields trees whose weighted path length is bounded above by 2 + 1, 44 • H.

C.P. Schnorr improves this bound to 3 + 1, o7 • H in [8]. In the case that all internal nodes have weight o an algorithm due to T.C. Hu and A.C. Tucker [3] finds the optimum binary search tree in O (n log n) units of time and o (n) units of space. In the general case, D.E. Knuth shows how to find the optimum tree in O (n^2) units of time and O (n^2) units of space [5] .

III. Lower Bounds :

We turn now to lower bounds. Again we will exhibit bounds which are best possible. Upper and lower bounds differ only by a constant factor; thus they define a narrow interval containing the weighted path length of the optimum (and the nearly optimal) search tree. This permits a simple a-priori test for the performance of binary search trees.

Theorem 2 :

a) ([1]) : If all internal nodes have weight zero,

(all $\beta_i = o$) then

$H \leq P_{opt}$

b) Otherwise

$1/\log 3 \; H \leq P_{opt}$

c) Both bounds are best possible in the following sense :

If $c_1 \sum \beta_i + c_2 \sum \alpha_j + c_3 H$ is a lower bound on the weighted path length of optimum binary search trees then $c_3 \leq 1$ in case a) and $c_3 \leq 1/\log 3$ otherwise. Furthermore, if $c_3 = 1$ in case a) or $c_3 = 1/\log 3$ in case b) then $c_1, c_2 \leq o$.

d) Both bounds are sharp for infinitely many distributions.

Proof :

Let $\beta_o, \alpha_1, \ldots, \beta_n, \alpha_n$ be any frequency distribution and let T_{opt} be the optimum binary search tree for this distribution, let b_i (a_j) be the distance of node (i) (leaf [j]) from the root, and let $P_{opt} = \sum \beta_i (b_i + 1) + \sum \alpha_j a_j$ be the weighted path length of T_{opt}.

We define new frequency distributions. If all internal node have weight o (all $\beta_i = o$) then define

$$\beta'_i = o \text{ for } 1 \leq i \leq n$$

$$\alpha'_j = 2^{-a_j} \text{ for } o \leq j \leq n,$$

otherwise define

$$\beta''_i = 3^{-(b_i+1)} \quad \text{for } 1 \leq i \leq n$$

$$\alpha''_j = 3^{-a_j} \text{ for } o \leq j \leq n.$$

It is easy to see that $\sum \beta'_i + \sum \alpha'_j = \sum \beta''_i + \sum \alpha''_j = 1.$

The following inequality is well-known (cf. [4]). If $p_1, \ldots, p_n$ and $q_1, \ldots, q_n$ are two frequency distributions ($\sum p_i = \sum q_i = 1$) then

$$- \sum p_i \log p_i \le - \sum p_i \log q_i$$

with equality if and only if $p_i = q_i$ for all i.

It yields in our case :

$$\begin{aligned} H &= \sum \alpha_j \log 1/\alpha_j \\ &\le \sum \alpha_j \log 1/\alpha'_j \\ &\le \sum \alpha_j \log 2^{a_j} = P_{opt} \end{aligned}$$

if all internal nodes have weight zero and

$$\begin{aligned} H &= \sum \beta_i \log 1/\beta_i + \sum \alpha_j \log 1/\alpha_j \\ &\le \sum \beta_i \log 1/\beta''_i + \sum \alpha_j \log 1/\alpha''_j \\ &\le \sum \beta_i \log 3^{(b_i+1)} + \sum \alpha_j \log 3^{a_j} \\ &\le (\log 3) P_{opt} \end{aligned}$$

otherwise with equality if $\beta_i = \beta'_i$ (β''_i) and $\alpha_j = \alpha'_j$ (α''_j) for all i and j.

Assume now that $\beta_i = \beta'_i$ (β''_i) and $\alpha_j = \alpha'_j$ (α''_j) for all i and j. Then it is easy to see that the approximation algorithm of section II constructs T_{opt}. Thus $P_{opt} = H$ if all internal nodes have weight o and $P_{opt} = 1/\log 3\ H$ otherwise. The lower bounds stated above are hence sharp for infinitely many distributions.

Part c) of the theorem is now inferred easily. The details are left to the reader.

q.e.d.

IV. Conclusion

We proved that P_{opt}, the weighted path length of the optimum binary search tree, lies in the following interval

$1/\log 3\ H \le P_{opt} \le 1 + H$ if all leaves have weight o

$H \le P_{opt} \le 2 + H$ if all internal nodes have weight o

$1/\log 3\ H \le P_{opt} \le 1 + \sum \alpha_j + H$ otherwise.

All bounds are best possible. Furthermore, we exhibited an approximation algorithm which constructs trees, whose path legth lies in the intervals stated above, and which can be implemented to work in O (n log) units of time and O (n) units of space.

Acknowledgement :

I want to thank Prof. C.P. Schnorr for many extremely stimulating discussions on the subject of this paper.

Bibliography :

1. E.N. Gilbert and E.F. Moore : Bell System Techn. Journal 38 (1959), 933 - 968.
2. T.C. Hu and K.C. Tan : Least Upper Bound on the Cost of Optimum Binary Search Trees, Acta Informatica, 1, 3o7 - 31o (1972).
3. T.C. Hu and A.C. Tucker : Optimal Computer Search Trees and variable length alphabetic codes, Siam J. Applied Math. 21, 514 - 532, (1971).
4. T. Kameda and K. Weihrauch : Einführung in die Kodierungstheorie, B I Skripten zur Informatik, Vol. 7.
5. D.E. Knuth : Optimum Binary Search Trees, Acta Informatica, 1, 14 - 25, 1971.
6. D.E. Knuth : The Art of Computer Programming, Vol. 3.
7. K. Mehlhorn : Nearly Optimum Binary Search Trees, Preprint, Fachbereich 1o, Universität des Saarlandes, 1974.
8. C.P. Schnorr : Two Algorithms for Nearly Optimal Binary Search Trees, Preprint, Fachbereich Mathematik, Universität Frankfurt, 1974.

$E_n \setminus E_{n-1}$-entscheidbare Gruppen

J. Avenhaus und K. Madlener
Universität Kaiserslautern

Konstruiert man zu einer Turing-Maschine (TM), die eine unentscheidbare Menge erkennt, in bekannter Weise [4] die TM-Halbgruppe Γ, so ist das Wortproblem für Γ unentscheidbar. Boone [1] geht von einer TM aus, die eine Menge vom Unentscheidbarkeitsgrad D erkennt und zeigt, daß sich mit der zugehörigen TM-Halbgruppe Γ eine endlich dargestellte Gruppe G explizit angeben läßt, so daß das Wortproblem für G und das spezielle Wortproblem für Γ aufeinander reduzierbar sind. Es stellt sich nun die Frage, ob dieses Ergebnis auf den subrekursiven Bereich übertragbar ist.

Wir betrachten in dieser Arbeit die subrekursive Hierarchie der Grzegorczyk-Klassen E_n von Wortfunktionen und konstruieren zu jedem $n \geq 3$ eine TM-Halbgruppe Γ und eine endlich dargestellte Gruppe G, so daß das Wortproblem für G und das spezielle Wortproblem für Γ aufeinander reduzierbar sind und die Komplexität E_n haben. Geht man von einer TM aus, die eine $E_n \setminus E_{n-1}$-entscheidbare Menge erkennt, so erhält man eine endlich dargestellte Gruppe mit $E_n \setminus E_{n-1}$-entscheidbarem Wortproblem.

Dieses Ergebnis läßt sich auf beliebige Funktionenklassen $K' \subset K$ übertragen, falls K Rechenzeit-abgeschlossen und abgeschlossen gegenüber der Komposition und der beschränkten Rekursion ist und die Klasse E_3 enthält (siehe Meyer-Ritchie [7]). Außerdem läßt sich der Higman'sche Einbettungssatz übertragen: Zu jeder K-entscheidbaren rekursiv dargestellten Gruppe G läßt sich explizit eine K-entscheidbare endlich dargestellte Gruppe H angeben, in die G K-eingebettet ist. Diese beiden letzten Ergebnisse werden in einer späteren Arbeit bewiesen.

Die Existenz einer $E_n \setminus E_{n-1}$-entscheidbaren Gruppe wurde schon von Cannonito [2] und Gatterdam [3], [5] mit Hilfe der von Cannonito eingeführten E_n-berechenbaren Gruppen und dem von Gatterdam auf E_n-berechenbare Gruppen übertragenen Einbettungssatz von Higman auf anderem Wege für $n \geq 4$ bewiesen. Dabei liefert der Einbettungssatz von Higman zwar effektiv eine endlich dargestellte Gruppe, aber die Konstruktion ist in der Praxis nicht durchführbar und läßt im Gegensatz zur Boone-Konstruktion nicht erkennen, wie die endlich dargestellte Gruppe schließlich aussieht.

Die Arbeit ist in drei Paragraphen eingeteilt. Zunächst wird die

Boone-Konstruktion beschrieben, und es werden die Hauptergebnisse formuliert. Im zweiten Paragraphen werden die gruppentheoretischen Hilfsmittel bereitgestellt, und im letzten Teil werden die Hauptergebnisse bewiesen.

1. Die Konstruktion von Boone. Hauptergebnisse.

Sei S eine endliche Menge. S^* ist dann die Menge aller Wörter über S und e das leere Wort. Weiter ist $\equiv$ die Identität auf S^* und $|w|$ die Länge von $w \in S^*$. Man kann wie bei den arithmetischen Funktionen die Grzegorczyk-Hierarchie $E_n(S)$ in der Menge der Wortfunktionen über dem Alphabet S einführen. Eine Menge $A \subseteq S^*$ ist E_n-entscheidbar, falls für die charakteristische Funktionen $\chi_A \in E_n(S)$ gilt. Wir setzen voraus, daß der Leser mit dieser Theorie vertraut ist und benutzen einige Sätze von Weihrauch [9], [6] ohne weiteren Hinweis.

Satz 1. Sei $n \geq 3$.

a) Ist A eine E_n-entscheidbare Menge, so gibt es eine TM, die die charakteristische Funktion χ_A in einer Rechenzeitschranke $t \in E_n(S)$ berechnet.

b) Es gibt eine Menge $A \subset S^*$, die E_n- aber nicht E_{n-1}-entscheidbar ist.

Die TM T, die eine E_n-entscheidbare Menge A akzeptiert, läßt sich so modifizieren, daß die Menge der Konfiguration uq_iv ($u,v \in S^*$, q_i Zustand), von denen aus T den akzeptierenden Zustand erreicht, E_n-entscheidbar ist. Geht man nun zur TM-Halbgruppe über, so gilt:

Satz 2. Es sei S eine endliche Menge, $S_o = S \cup \{h\}$ und $n \geq 3$. Dann gibt es eine TM-Halbgruppe $\Gamma = (S_o \cup Q;\Pi)$ mit endlich vielen Erzeugenden $S_o \cup Q$, einem ausgezeichneten Element $q \in Q$ und endlich vielen Relationen Π, so daß das spezielle Wortproblem P von Γ

$$P(w) \iff w = q \text{ in } \Gamma \qquad w \in (S_o \cup Q)^*$$

E_n-entscheidbar ist. Geht man von einer $E_n \setminus E_{n-1}$-entscheidbaren Menge A aus, so ist P $E_n \setminus E_{n-1}$-entscheidbar.

Man überlegt sich leicht, daß P schon E_n-entscheidbar ist, wenn für alle $u,v \in S_o^*$, $q_j \in Q$, $uq_jv = q$ in Γ E_n-entscheidbar ist.

Sei S eine Menge, $\overline{S} = \{\overline{s} : s \in S\}$, $\underline{S} = S \cup \overline{S}$ und $\Delta \subseteq \underline{S}^*$. Mit $\langle S;\Delta \rangle$ bezeichnen wir die Gruppe, die durch die Erzeugenden S und die definierenden Relatoren Δ gegeben ist. Jedes Wort $w \in \underline{S}^*$ stellt ein Element aus $\langle S;\Delta \rangle$ dar, $\overline{s}$ stellt das zu s inverse Element und e das Einselement dar. Stellen $u,v \in \underline{S}^*$ gleiche Elemente von $\langle S;\Delta \rangle$ dar, so schreiben wir

$u = v$ in $<S;\Delta>$.

Eine Gruppe G hat eine Darstellung $<S;\Delta>$, falls $G \cong <S;\Delta>$ ist. G heißt endlich erzeugt (e.e.) bzw. endlich dargestellt (e.d.), falls S bzw. S und Δ endlich sind.

Im folgenden beschränken wir uns auf e.e. Gruppen.

Mit $\bar{}$ und $^{-1}$ bezeichnen wir die Funktionen aus $E_1(\underline{S})$, die durch $\overline{s_1 s_2 \ldots s_n} \equiv \bar{s}_1 \bar{s}_2 \ldots \bar{s}_n$, $\bar{\bar{s}}_i \equiv s_i$ und $(s_1 s_2 \ldots s_n)^{-1} \equiv \bar{s}_n \ldots \bar{s}_2 \bar{s}_1$, $s_i \in \underline{S}$ gegeben sind.

Definition 1. Sei $n \geq 1$. Die Gruppe $<S;\Delta>$ heißt E_n-entscheidbar, falls die Menge der Relatoren $R = \{w \in \underline{S}^* : w = e \text{ in } <S;\Delta>\}$ E_n-entscheidbar ist. Eine Gruppe G ist E_n-entscheidbar, wenn es eine E_n-entscheidbare Darstellung von G gibt.

Man überlegt sich leicht, daß die E_n-Entscheidbarkeit einer e.e. Gruppe unabhängig von der speziellen Darstellung ist und daß freie, en liche und allgemeiner alle Gruppen, für die Dehn's Algorithmus zur Lösung des Wortproblems anwendbar ist, E_1-entscheidbar sind.

Wir betrachten nur noch Gruppen, die durch Erzeugende und definiere de Relatoren gegeben sind. Hierbei verwenden wir definierende Relation statt Relatoren, wo dieses zweckmäßig erscheint, und benutzen die Bezeichnung $G' = <G,S';\Delta'>$, falls $G = <S;\Delta>$ und $G' = <S \cup S';\Delta \cup \Delta'>$ ist Wir führen nun wie Rotman [8] eine etwas modifizierte Boone-Konstruktion durch und erhalten eine Gruppe, deren Wortproblem die gleiche Komplexität hat wie das Problem P in Γ.

Sei $\Gamma = (S \cup Q;\Pi)$ eine TM-Halbgruppe mit den endlich vielen Relatic en $F_i q_{i_1} G_i = H_i q_{i_2} K_i$; $F_i, G_i, H_i, K_i \in S^*$, $q_{i_1}, q_{i_2} \in Q$ $(i = 1,\ldots,N)$. Ist $R = \{r_1,\ldots,r_N\}$ und sind x, t, k neue Symbole, so werden die Gruppen $G_o,\ldots,G_5$ wie folgt definiert:

$$G_o = <x;\emptyset>$$
$$G_1 = <G_o,S;\bar{s}xs = x^2, s \in S>$$
$$G_2 = <G_1,Q;\emptyset>$$
$$G_3 = <G_2,R;\bar{r}_i\bar{F}_i q_{i_1} G_i r_i = \bar{H}_i q_{i_2} K_i, \bar{r}_i s x r_i = s\bar{x}, 1 \leq i \leq N, s \in S>$$
$$G_4 = <G_3,t;\bar{t}xt = x, \bar{t}rt = r, r \in R>$$
$$G_5 = <G_4,k;\bar{k}ak = a, a \in \{x,\bar{q}tq\} \cup R>$$

Offenbar sind die Gruppen G_i $(i = 0,\ldots,5)$ endlich dargestellt. Es gilt der folgende zentrale Satz der Arbeit, der in Paragraph 3 bewies wird:

Satz 3. a) Die Gruppen G_o bis G_4 sind E_3-entscheidbar.

b) Das Wortproblem von G_5 hat die gleiche Komplexität wie das spezielle Wortproblem P von Γ, d.h. P ist genau dann E_n-entscheidbar, we

G_5 E_n-entscheidbar ist ($n \geq 3$).

Geht man bei dieser Konstruktion von einer TM-Halbgruppe Γ mit $E_n \setminus E_{n-1}$ entscheidbarem Problem P aus, so ist G_5 $E_n \setminus E_{n-1}$-entscheidbar.

Satz 4. Es gibt für $n \geq 3$ e.d. Gruppen, deren Wortproblem E_n-, aber nicht E_{n-1}-entscheidbar ist.

Auf Grund dieses Ergebnisses stellt sich die Frage nach der Existenz von e.d. Gruppen mit einer minimalen Anzahl von definierenden Relatoren, deren Wortproblem $E_n \setminus E_{n-1}$-entscheidbar ist. Es ist bekannt, daß Einrelatorengruppen entscheidbar sind; wir können sogar zeigen, daß Einrelatorengruppen mit definierendem Relator der Länge $\leq 2n - 1$ E_n-entscheidbar sind. Offen ist noch, ob es Einrelatorengruppen mit $E_n \setminus E_{n-1}$-entscheidbarem Wortproblem gibt.

Das verallgemeinerte Wortproblem für eine Gruppe $G = \langle S; \Delta \rangle$ und eine Untergruppe H von G besteht darin, zu entscheiden, ob ein Wort $w \in \underline{S}^*$ ein Element aus H darstellt oder nicht. Der Beweis zu Satz 3 liefert folgende Verschärfung des Resultates I von Boone [1].

Satz 5. Zu jedem $n \geq 3$ (zu jedem Unentscheidbarkeitsgrad D) gibt es eine E_3-entscheidbare e.d. Gruppe G mit einer e.e. Untergruppe H, so daß das verallgemeinerte Wortproblem $E_n \setminus E_{n-1}$-entscheidbar ist (den Unentscheidbarkeitsgrad D hat).

2. Gruppentheoretische Hilfsmittel

Es sei $G = \langle S; \Delta \rangle$ eine Gruppe. Eine Funktion $f : \underline{S}^* \longrightarrow \underline{S}^*$ heißt eine Entscheidungsfunktion für G, wenn für alle $w \in S^*$ gilt a) $f(w) = w$ in G und b) $f(w) \equiv e$, falls $w = e$ in G. Offenbar ist G genau dann E_n-entscheidbar, wenn es eine Entscheidungsfunktion $f \in E_n(\underline{S})$ für G gibt. Ist $A \subseteq \underline{S}^*$, so sei $\langle A \rangle$ die Menge der Wörter, die ein Element aus der von A erzeugten Untergruppe darstellen. Ist $G' = \langle G, S'; \Delta' \rangle$ eine weitere Gruppe, so schreiben wir $G \leq G'$, falls für alle $w \in \underline{S}^*$, $w = e$ in G' genau dann gilt, wenn $w = e$ in G gilt.

Das wesentliche gruppentheoretische Hilfsmittel dieser Arbeit ist das Konzept der Britton-Erweiterung. Wir stellen hier einige Fakten zusammen, die später benötigt werden. Für fehlende Beweise sei auf Rotman [8] verwiesen.

Definition 1. Es sei $G = \langle S; \Delta \rangle$ eine Gruppe und $P = \{p_i : i \in I\}$ eine Menge mit $P \cap \underline{S} = \emptyset$, es seien weiterhin für alle $i \in I$ Teilmengen $A_i = \{a_{ij} : j \in J_i\}$ und $B_i = \{b_{ij} : j \in J_i\}$ von $\underline{S}^*$ gegeben. Dann heißt $G' = \langle G, P; \overline{p_i} a_{ij} p_i = b_{ij}, i \in I, j \in J_i \rangle$ eine Britton-Erweiterung von G mit stabilen Buchstaben P, falls für jedes $i \in I$ die von A_i und B_i erzeugten

Untergruppen von G unter der Abbildung $a_{ij} \longmapsto b_{ij}$ isomorph sind.

Ist $u \in \underline{S}^*$, so heißt ein Wort der Form $p_i^{-\varepsilon}up_i^{\varepsilon}$ ein Pinch, falls $\varepsilon =$ und $u \in \langle A_i \rangle$ oder $\varepsilon = -1$ und $u \in \langle B_i \rangle$ gilt. Ist $\overline{p_i}up_i$ ein Pinch und si $\langle A_i \rangle$ und $\langle B_i \rangle$ unter ϕ_i isomorph, so gilt natürlich $\overline{p_i}up_i = \phi_i(u)$ in G' Ein Wort $w \in (S \cup P)^*$ heißt P-reduziert, falls es keinen Pinch als Tei wort enthält.

Satz 1. Ist G' eine Britton-Erweiterung von $G = \langle S; \Delta \rangle$ mit stabilen Buc staben P und $w \in (\underline{S} \cup \underline{P})^*$ mit $w = e$ in G', so gilt entweder $w \in \underline{S}^*$ und $w = e$ in G oder w enthält einen Pinch als Teilwort. Außerdem gilt $G \leq$

Aus Satz 1 folgt unmittelbar

Lemma 1. Sei G' eine Britton-Erweiterung von $G = \langle S; \Delta \rangle$ mit stabilen Buchstaben P, seien $u = u_o p_1^{\varepsilon_1} u_1 \ldots p_n^{\varepsilon_n} u_n$ und $v = v_o q_1^{\varepsilon_1} v_1 \ldots q_m^{\varepsilon_m} v_m$ $(u_i$, $v_i \in \underline{S}^*$, $p_i, q_i \in P$, $\varepsilon_i, \eta_i = \pm 1)$ P-reduzierte Wörter und gelte $u = v$ in G'. Dann gilt $n = m$, $p_i = q_i$ und $\varepsilon_i = \eta_i$ für $i = 1,2,\ldots,n$ und $p_1^{-\varepsilon_1} u_o^{-1} v_o p_1^{\varepsilon_1}$ ist ein Pinch.

Definition 2. a) Seien $G_i = \langle S_i; \Delta_i \rangle$, $i = 0,1,\ldots,m$, Gruppen mit $S_i = S_{i-1} \cup P_i$, so daß G_i eine Britton-Erweiterung von G_{i-1} mit stabilen Buchstaben P_i ist. Dann heißt $G_o \leq G_1 \leq \ldots \leq G_m$ ein Britton-Turm.

b) Ein Wort $w \in \underline{S}_i^*$ $(i \geq 1)$ heißt reduziert, falls es keinen Pinch $p^{-\varepsilon}up^{\varepsilon}$ in G_j $(j \leq i)$ als Teilwort enthält.

c) Eine Funktion $f_i : \underline{S}_i^* \longrightarrow \underline{S}_i^*$ $(i \geq 1)$ heißt eine Reduktionsfunkt für G_i, falls für alle $w \in \underline{S}_i^*$ gilt: (1) $f_i(w) = w$ in G_i, (2) $f_i(w)$ is reduziert, (3) $f_i(w) \equiv e$, falls $w = e$ in G_i und (4) $f_i(w) \equiv w$, falls w reduziert und nicht $w = e$ in G_i ist.

Eine Reduktionsfunktion f_i für G_i ist also auch eine Entscheidungs funktion von G_i. Wir untersuchen nun, wann eine Britton-Erweiterung e ner E_n-entscheidbaren Gruppe wieder E_n-entscheidbar ist.

Definition 3. a) Eine Britton-Erweiterung G' von $G = \langle S; \Delta \rangle$ mit stabil Buchstaben $P = \{p_i : i \in I\}$ heißt E_n-zulässig $(n \geq 3)$, falls für alle $i \in I$ gilt

(1) $\langle A_i \rangle$ und $\langle B_i \rangle$ sind in $\underline{S}^*$ E_n-entscheidbar.

(2) Es gibt linear beschränkte Funktionen ϕ_i, $\hat{\phi}_i \in E_n(\underline{S})$, die die Isomorphismen $\langle A_i \rangle \longrightarrow \langle B_i \rangle$ bzw. $\langle B_i \rangle \longrightarrow \langle A_i \rangle$ realisieren.

b) Ein Britton-Turm $G_o \leq G_1 \leq \ldots \leq G_m$ heißt E_n-zulässig, falls fü $i = 1,2,\ldots,m$ G_i eine E_n-zulässige Britton-Erweiterung von G_{i-1} ist.

Satz 2. Ist $G_o \leq G_1 \leq \ldots \leq G_m$ ein E_n-zulässiger Britton-Turm und ist G_o E_n-entscheidbar, so gibt es Reduktionsfunktionen $f_i \in E_n(\underline{S}_i)$ für G_i $(i = 1,2,\ldots,m)$. Die Gruppen G_i sind also E_n-entscheidbar.

Beweis: Wir betrachten nur den Fall $m = 1$. Sei f_o eine Entscheidungsfunktion für G_o. Wir definieren $h : \underline{S}_1^* \longrightarrow \underline{S}_1^*$ durch

$$h(e) \equiv e$$

$$h(ws) \equiv h(w)s \qquad \text{für } s \in \underline{S_o}$$

$$h(wp_i) \equiv \begin{cases} v\phi_i(u) & \text{falls } h(w) \equiv v\overline{p}_i u, v \in \underline{S}_1^*, u \in \underline{S}_o^*, u \in \langle A_i\rangle \\ h(w)p_i & \text{sonst} \end{cases}$$

$$h(w\overline{p}_i) \equiv \begin{cases} v\hat{\phi}_i(u) & \text{falls } h(w) \equiv vp_i u, v \in \underline{S}_1^*, u \in \underline{S}_o^*, u \in \langle B_i\rangle \\ h(w)\overline{p}_i & \text{sonst} \end{cases}$$

Dann ist $h \in E_n(\underline{S_1})$ und für alle $w \in \underline{S}_1^*$ gilt $h(w) = w$ in G_1 und $h(w)$ ist reduziert. Definiert man nun f_1 durch $f_1(w) \equiv f_o(w_o)p_1^{\varepsilon_1}f_o(w_1)\ldots$ $\ldots p_m^{\varepsilon_m}f_o(w_m)$, falls $h(w) \equiv w_o p_1^{\varepsilon_1}w_1\ldots p_m^{\varepsilon_m}w_m$ ($w_i \in \underline{S}_o^*$, $p_i \in P$, $\varepsilon_i = \pm 1$) gilt, so ist f_1 eine Reduktionsfunktion von G_1, die in $E_n(\underline{S_1})$ liegt.

3. Beweis von Satz 1.3

Zum Beweis von Teil a) des Satzes 1.3 zeigen wir, daß die in Paragraph 1 definierten Gruppen einen E_3-zulässigen Britton-Turm $G_o \leq G_1 \leq \leq \ldots \leq G_4$ bilden. Da G_o als freie Gruppe natürlich E_3-entscheidbar ist, sind dann auch G_1 bis G_4 E_3-entscheidbar. Rotman [8] zeigt, daß $G_o \leq \leq \ldots \leq G_4$ ein Britton-Turm ist; es bleibt also nur die E_3-Zulässigkeit nachzuweisen. Sei S_i die Menge der Erzeugenden von G_i $(i = 0,1,\ldots,5)$.

Lemma 1. Für $i = 1,2$ ist G_i eine E_3-zulässige Britton-Erweiterung von G_{i-1}. Es gibt also Reduktionsfunktionen $f_i \in E_3(\underline{S_i})$ für G_i.

Der Beweis ist einfach und wird übergangen.

Lemma 2. G_3 ist eine E_3-zulässige Britton-Erweiterung von G_2. Es gibt also eine Reduktionsfunktion $f_3 \in E_3(\underline{S_3})$ für G_3.

G_3 ist eine Britton-Erweiterung von G_2 mit stabilen Buchstaben $R = \{r_i : i = 1,2,\ldots,N\}$. In der Terminologie von Definition 2.1 ist $A_i = \{\overline{F}_i q_{i_1} G_i, s_1 x, \ldots, s_M x\}$ und $B_i = \{\overline{H}_i q_{i_2} K_i, s_1\overline{x}, \ldots, s_M\overline{x}\}$. Zum Beweis von Lemma 2 muß gezeigt werden, daß für alle $i = 1,2,\ldots,N$ $\langle A_i\rangle$ und $\langle B_i\rangle$ E_3-entscheidbare Untergruppen von G_2 sind und daß es linear beschränkte Abbildungen ϕ_i, $\hat{\phi}_i \in E_3(\underline{S_2})$ gibt, die die Isomorphismen $\langle A_i\rangle \longrightarrow \langle B_i\rangle$ und $\langle B_i\rangle \longrightarrow \langle A_i\rangle$ realisieren. Ein Beweis hierfür ergibt sich, wenn man den Beweis des folgenden Lemmas konstruktiv ausführt.

Lemma 3. Es sei $w \in \underline{S}_2^*$ und $1 \leq i \leq N$. Genau dann gilt $w \in \langle A_i\rangle$ (bzw. $w \in \langle B_i\rangle$), wenn es ein w'' in den Erzeugenden von $\langle A_i\rangle$ (bzw. $\langle B_i\rangle$) gibt mit $w = w''$ in G_2 und $|w''| \leq \alpha|w|$. Dabei ist $\alpha = 1 + \max\{|F_jG_j|, |H_jK_j| : j = 1,2,\ldots,N\}$.

Beweis: Die eine Richtung der Aussage ist trivial. Wir zeigen nur, daß es zu jedem $w \in \langle A_i \rangle$ ein w" in den Erzeugenden von $\langle A_i \rangle$ gibt mit w = w" in G_2 und $|w''| \leq \alpha |w|$.

Sei also $w \in \langle A_i \rangle$ und $w' \equiv f_2(w) \equiv u_o q_1^{\eta_1} u_1 \ldots q_m^{\eta_m} u_m$ mit $u_j \in \underline{S}_1^*$, $q_j \in Q$. Dann gilt auch $w' \in \langle A_i \rangle$, w' ist Q-reduziert, und die u_j sind S-reduziert. Es gibt also Wörter w_j in $s_1 x, \ldots, s_M x$ und $\varepsilon_j = \pm 1$ mit $u_o q_1^{\eta_1} u_1 \ldots q_m^{\eta_m} u_m = w_o (\overline{F}_i q_{i_1} G_1)^{\varepsilon_1} w_1 \ldots (\overline{F}_i q_{i_1} G_i)^{\varepsilon_n} w_n$ in G_2. Wählt man n minimal, so ist die rechte Seite Q-reduziert, und nach Lemma 2.1 gilt m = n, $\eta_j = \varepsilon_j$ und $q_j = q_{i_1}$ (j = 1,2,...,n) und $\overline{q_{i_1}} (w_o \overline{F}_i)^{-1} u_o q_{i_1}$ oder $q_{i_1} (w_o G_i)^{-1} u_o \overline{q_{i_1}}$ ist ein Q-Pinch, jenachdem, ob $\varepsilon_1 = +1$ oder $\varepsilon_1 = -1$ i Daraus folgt $(w_o \overline{F}_i)^{-1} u_o = e$ in G_1, bzw. $(w_o G_i)^{-1} u_o = e$ in G_1. Definier man $E_j, D_j \in \underline{S}_1^*$ durch $E_j q_{i_1}^{\varepsilon_j} D_j \equiv (\overline{F}_i q_{i_1} G_i)^{\varepsilon_j}$ für j = 1,2,...,n und $D_o \equiv E_o \equiv D_{n+1} \equiv E_{n+1} \equiv e$, so sind die $E_j \in \overline{S}^*$ (negative Wörter) und die $D_j \in S^*$ (positive Wörter). Durch Induktion nach j zeigt man $D_j^{-1} u_j E_{j+1}^{-1} = w_j$ in G_1, j = 0,1,...,n. Setzt man $u_j' \equiv f_1(D_j^{-1} u_j E_{j+1}^{-1})$, so ist u_j' S-reduziert, und es gilt $u_j' = w_j$ in G_1. Es gibt also frei reduzierte - und damit S-reduzierte - Wörter v_j in $s_1 x, \ldots, s_M x$ mit $v_j = u_j'$ in G_1, j = 0,1,...,n. Definiert man $w'' \equiv v_o (\overline{F}_i q_{i_1} G_i)^{\varepsilon_1} v_1 \ldots (\overline{F}_i q_{i_1} G_i)^{\varepsilon_n} v_n$, so gilt w = w' = w" in G_2. Es bleibt $|w''| \leq \alpha |w|$ zu zeigen. Es sei $|w|_Q$ die Q-Länge von w, d.h. die Anzahl der in w auftretenden Buchstaben au Q, und es sei $|w|_S$ die S-Länge von w. Dann gilt $|w'|_Q = |w''|_Q = n$. Wir zeigen, daß für die S-Längen $|v_j|_S \leq |u_j|_S$ gilt. Für $v_j \equiv e$ ist das tr vial. Sei also $v_j \not\equiv e$. D_j und E_j sind als positive bzw. negative Wörte S-reduziert und v_j ist S-reduziert. Wegen der speziellen Gestalt von D_j, v_j und E_{j+1} kann es in $D_j v_j E_{j+1}$ auch keinen Pinch auf der Grenze $D_j - v_j$ oder $v_j - E_{j+1}$ geben. Also ist $D_j v_j E_{j+1}$ S-reduziert und es gi $u_j = D_j v_j E_{j+1}$ in G_1. Da auch u_j S-reduziert ist, läßt sich Lemma 2.1 anwenden, und es gilt $|u_j|_S = |D_j v_j E_{j+1}|_S = |D_j|_S + |v_j|_S + |E_{j+1}|_S \geq |v_j|_S$. Wegen $\alpha \geq 2$ ergibt sich jetzt

$$|w''| = \textstyle\sum_{j=o}^{n} |v_j| + n \cdot |F_i q_{i_1} G_i| = 2 \sum_{j=o}^{n} |v_j|_S + n \cdot |F_i q_{i_1} G_i|$$
$$\leq \alpha \big(\textstyle\sum_{j=o}^{n} |u_j|_S + n\big) = \alpha (|w'|_S + |w'|_Q).$$

Wegen $w' \equiv f_2(w)$ gilt $|w'|_S \leq |w|_S$ und $|w'|_Q \leq |w|_Q$. Also folgt

$$|w''| \leq \alpha (|w'|_S + |w'|_Q) \leq \alpha (|w|_S + |w|_Q) \leq \alpha |w|.$$

Damit ist Lemma 3 bewiesen.

Dieser Beweis zeigt, daß $\langle A_i \rangle$ E_3-entscheidbar ist und daß man jede $w \in \langle A_i \rangle$ durch einen E_3-Prozeß in ein Wort w" in den Erzeugenden von $\langle A_i \rangle$ umschreiben kann. $\tilde{w}$ entstehe aus w", indem man $(sx)^{\varepsilon}$ durch $(s\overline{x})$ und $(\overline{F}_i q_{i_1} G_i)^{\varepsilon}$ durch $(\overline{H}_i q_{i_2} K_i)^{\varepsilon}$ ersetzt. Die Abbildung $\phi_i : w \longmapsto \tilde{w}$ realisiert dann den Isomorphismus $\langle A_i \rangle \longrightarrow \langle B_i \rangle$, liegt in $E_3(\underline{S_2})$ und ist linear beschränkt.

Bei der konstruktiven Ausführung des Beweises zu Lemma 3 ergibt si noch folgendes Lemma:

Lemma 4. Es gibt für i = 1,2,...,N Funktionen h_i, $\hat{h}_i \in E_3(\underline{S_2})$ mit

$$h_i(w) \equiv \begin{cases} x^j & wx^j \in \langle A_i \rangle \\ q_1 & \forall j \in \mathbb{Z} : wx^j \notin \langle A_i \rangle \end{cases} \qquad \hat{h}_i(w) \equiv \begin{cases} x^j & wx^j \in \langle B_i \rangle \\ q_1 & \forall j \in \mathbb{Z} : wx^j \notin \langle B_i \rangle \end{cases}$$

Lemma 5. G_4 ist E_3-zulässige Britton-Erweiterung von G_3. Es gibt also eine Reduktionsfunktion $f_4 \in E_3(\underline{S_4})$ für G_4.

Beweis: G_4 ist Britton-Erweiterung von G_3 mit einem stabilen Buchstaben t. Ist $A = R \cup \{x\} = B$, so muß gezeigt werden, daß $\langle A \rangle$ eine E_3-entscheidbare Untergruppe von G_3 ist. Die Identität auf $\underline{S_3^*}$ realisiert die Isomorphismen $\langle A \rangle \longrightarrow \langle B \rangle$ und $\langle B \rangle \longrightarrow \langle A \rangle$, sie ist natürlich linear beschränkt. Zu zeigen bleibt also nur die E_3-Entscheidbarkeit von $\langle A \rangle$.

Sei $R_x = R \cup \{x\}$. Zunächst sieht man leicht, daß ein frei reduziertes Wort aus $\underline{R_x^*}$ auch reduziert in G_3 ist. Ist $w \in \underline{S_3^*}$ und $w' \equiv f_3(w) \equiv u_o r_{i_1}^{\varepsilon_1} u_1 \ldots r_{i_n}^{\varepsilon_n} u_n$ ($u_j \in \underline{S_2^*}$), so liegt w - also auch w' - genau dann in $\langle A \rangle$, wenn es ein reduziertes Wort $v \equiv x^{j_n} r_{i_n}^{-\varepsilon_n} \ldots x^{j_1} r_{i_1}^{-\varepsilon_1} x^{j_o}$ gibt mit

$vw' = e$ in G_3, d.h. $x^{j_n} r_{i_n}^{-\varepsilon_n} \ldots x^{j_1} r_{i_1}^{-\varepsilon_1} x^{j_o} u_o r_{i_1}^{\varepsilon_1} u_1 \ldots r_{i_n}^{\varepsilon_n} u_n = e$ in G_3. Da v und w' R-reduziert sind, gilt dann (falls $\varepsilon_1 = 1$ ist), $x^{j_o} u_o \in \langle A_{i_1} \rangle$ oder $h_{i_1}(u_o^{-1}) \equiv x^{j_o}$. Dann kann man den Pinch $r_{i_1}^{-1} x^{j_o} u_o r_{i_1}$ durch $\phi_{i_1}(x^{j_o} u_o)$ ersetzen und hat dadurch die R-Länge verkleinert. Ist die R-Länge gleich Null, so muß für das verbliebene Wort $u \in \underline{S_2^*}$, $u = e$ in G_2, d.h. $f_2(u) \equiv e$ gelten. Mit diesen Überlegungen läßt sich leicht ein E_3-Algorithmus zur Entscheidung von $w \in \langle A \rangle$ angeben. Man erhält darüber hinaus

Lemma 6. Es gibt eine Funktion $g \in E_3(\underline{S_3})$, so daß für alle $w \in \underline{S_3^*}$ gilt

a) Es gibt ein $u \in \underline{R_x^*}$ mit $g(w) = uw$ in G_3.

b) Es gibt kein $u \in \underline{R_x^*}$, so daß $ug(w)$ einen Pinch $r_i^{-\varepsilon} v r_i^{\varepsilon}$ auf der Grenze $u - g(w)$ enthält.

Lemma 6 besagt, daß man durch einen E_3-Prozeß in einem Wort $w \in \underline{S_3^*}$ alle $r \in R$ eliminieren kann, die durch Multiplikation eines Wortes $u \in \underline{R_x^*}$ von links überhaupt eliminierbar sind. Analog lassen sich auch alle $r \in R$ eliminieren, die von rechts eliminierbar sind.

Es ist jetzt gezeigt, daß Teil a) von Satz 1.3 gilt. Um den Teil b) zu beweisen geben wir zunächst drei vorbereitende Lemmata an, die das auf $\underline{S_3^*}$ definierte Prädikat Q

$$Q(u) \Longleftrightarrow \exists w_o, w_1 \in \underline{R_x^*} : w_o u w_1 = q \text{ in } G_3$$

in Beziehung setzen zum speziellen Wortproblem P von Γ.

Lemma 7. Es sei $w_o, w_1 \in \underline{R_x^*}$, $u \in \underline{S_3^*}$, u, w_o und w_1 seien reduziert, und es gelte $w_o u w_1 = q$ in G_3. Dann gibt es $w_o', w_o'', w_1', w_1'' \in \underline{R_x^*}$ und $v \in \underline{S_2^*}$, so daß gilt

$$w_o'uw_1' = v \text{ in } G_3, \quad w_o''vw_1'' = q \text{ in } G_3.$$

Lemma 7 besagt, daß man in u zunächst durch Multiplikation mit w_o' und w_1' von links bzw. rechts alle $r \in R$ von u eliminieren kann. Mit Hilfe von g läßt sich v aus u in einem E_3-Prozeß bestimmen.

Lemma 8. Sind $v \in \underline{S_2^*}$, $w_o, w_1 \in \underline{R_x^*}$ reduzierte Wörter und gilt $w_o v w_1 = q$ in G_3, so hat v die Gestalt $v \equiv \overline{v_1} q_j v_2$ mit $v_1, v_2 \in (S \cup \{x,\overline{x}\})^*$, $q_j \in Q$. Entsteht X aus v_1 und Y aus v_2 $(X,Y \in S^*)$, indem man alle x's streicht, so gibt es $a,b \in \mathbb{Z}$ mit $v = x^a \overline{X} q_j Y x^b$ in G_2.

Lemma 9. Es sei $X,Y \in S^*$, $q_j \in Q$. Dann gilt $Xq_jY = q$ in Γ genau dann, wenn es reduzierte Wörter $w_o, w_1 \in \underline{R_x^*}$ gibt mit $w_o \overline{X} q_j Y w_1 = q$ in G_4, d.h. $P(Xq_jY) \iff Q(\overline{X}q_jY)$.

Den Beweis zu Lemma 9 findet man in Rotman [8] (Seite 299-33o und Lemma 12.18). Die Lemmata 7 bis 9 besagen, daß die Prädikate P in Γ und Q in G_4 von der gleichen Entscheidungskomplexität sind.

Wir nehmen jetzt an, daß das Prädikat P in Γ $E_n \setminus E_{n-1}$-entscheidbar ist.

Lemma 1o. G_5 ist eine E_n-zulässige Britton-Erweiterung von G_4. Es gibt also eine Reduktionsfunktion $f_5 \in E_3(\underline{S_5})$.

Beweis: G_5 ist eine Britton-Erweiterung von G_4 mit einem stabilen Buchstaben k. Setzt man $\tilde{A} = \tilde{B} = R \cup \{x, \overline{q}tq\}$, so braucht, wie bei Lemma 5, nur gezeigt zu werden, daß $\langle\tilde{A}\rangle$ eine E_n-entscheidbare Untergruppe von G_4 ist. Sei $w \in \underline{S_4^*}$ und $w' \equiv f_4(w) \equiv u_o t^{\varepsilon_1} u_1 \ldots t^{\varepsilon_m} u_m$ mit $u_i \in \underline{S_3^*}$. Es liegt w — also auch w' — genau dann in $\langle\tilde{A}\rangle$, wenn es ein Wort $v \equiv v_l(\overline{q}tq)^{\eta_l} \ldots v_1(\overline{q}tq)^{\eta_1} v_o$ $(v_i \in \underline{R_x^*})$ gibt mit $vw' = e$ in G_4. Wählt man l minimal, so ist v t-reduziert, und es gilt $m = l$ und $\eta_i = -\varepsilon_i$, $i = 1,2,\ldots,m$. Es gilt also $w \in \langle\tilde{A}\rangle$ genau dann, wenn es $v_o,\ldots,v_m \in \underline{R_x^*}$ gibt mit

$$v_m(\overline{q}tq)^{-\varepsilon_m} \ldots v_1(\overline{q}tq)^{-\varepsilon_1} v_o u_o t^{\varepsilon_1} u_1 \ldots t^{\varepsilon_m} u_m = e \text{ in } G_4.$$

Da v und w' t-reduziert sind, muß dann $qv_ou_o \in \langle A\rangle$ gelten, also auch $q = v'u_o^{-1}v_o^{-1}$ in G_3 mit $v_1'v_o^{-1} \in \underline{R_x^*}$. Dies ist äquivalent zu $Q(u_o^{-1})$ und somit E_n-entscheidbar. Gilt $Q(u_o^{-1})$, so kann man $(\overline{q}tq)^{-\varepsilon_1} v_o u_o t^{\varepsilon_1}$ durch v_ou_o ersetzen und hat damit die t-Länge verkleinert. Durch Induktion läßt sich zeigen

$$w \in \langle\tilde{A}\rangle \iff Q(u_o^{-1}) \wedge Q((u_ou_1)^{-1}) \wedge \ldots \wedge Q((u_ou_1\ldots u_m)^{-1}) \wedge u_ou_1\ldots u_m \in \langle A\rangle$$

Also ist $\langle\tilde{A}\rangle$ E_n-entscheidbar und Lemma 1o ist bewiesen.

Wir haben jetzt gezeigt, daß das Wortproblem von G_5 auf das spezielle Wortproblem von Γ reduzierbar ist. Das folgende Lemma von Boone liefert, daß umgekehrt das spezielle Wortproblem von Γ auf das Wortproblem von G reduzierbar ist.

Lemma 11 (Boone). Für $X,Y \in S^*$, $q_j \in Q$ gilt $Xq_jY = q$ in Γ genau dann, wenn $k(\overline{X}q_jY)^{-1}t(\overline{X}q_jY) = (\overline{X}q_jY)^{-1}t(\overline{X}q_jY)k$ in G_5.

Ist das spezielle Wortproblem in Γ also nicht E_{n-1}-entscheidbar, so ist auch G_5 nicht E_{n-1}-entscheidbar. G_5 ist damit eine e.d. $E_n \setminus E_{n-1}$-entscheidbare Gruppe.

Es bleibt noch Satz 1.5 zu beweisen. Dazu bemerken wir, daß G_4 E_3-entscheidbar ist und daß die Untergruppe $H = \langle\tilde{A}\rangle$ in G_4 E_n- aber nicht E_{n-1}-entscheidbar ist. Die Gruppe G_4 ist E_3-entscheidbar, unabhängig von der speziellen Wahl der TM-Halbgruppe. Geht man also aus von einer TM-Halbgruppe, in der das spezielle Wortproblem vom Unentscheidbarkeitsgrad D ist [1], so ist auch $\langle\tilde{A}\rangle$ in G_4 vom Unentscheidbarkeitsgrad D.

Literatur

[1] Boone W.W., Word problems and recursively enumerable degrees of unsolvability. A sequel on finitely presented groups. Ann. of Math. 84 (1966), 49-84.

[2] Cannonito F.B., Hierarchies of computable groups and the word problem. J. of Symb. Logic 31 (1966), 376-392.

[3] Cannonito F.B., Gatterdam R.W., The computability of group constructions, Part I, in Word problems. North-Holland (1973), 365-4oo.

[4] Davis M., Computability and unsolvability. Mac Graw Hill (1958).

[5] Gatterdam R.W., The Higman theorem for E_n(A) computable groups, in Lecture Notes Math. 319, Springer (1973), 71-74.

[6] von Henke, Weihrauch, Indermark, Hierarchies of primitive recursive wordfunctions and transductions defined by automata, in Nivat (Ed.), IRIA Symposium July 3-7 (1972).

[7] Meyer A., Ritchie D., A classification of the recursive functions, Z. math. Logik, Grundlagen d. Math. 18 (1972), 71-82.

[8] Rotman J.J., The theory of groups, 2. Edition, Allyn & Bacon (1973).

[9] Weihrauch K., Teilklassen primitiv-rekursiver Wortfunktionen, GMD Berichte, Bonn, Nr. 91 (1974).

STATISTICAL CHARACTERIZATION OF LEARNABLE SEQUENCES

P.H. Fuchs

Fachbereich Mathematik, Universität Frankfurt a.M.

Throughout this paper X denotes the binary alphabet $\{o,1\}$, X^* the set of (finite) words over X, X^∞ the set of infinite binary sequences; Λ denotes the empty word and $|x|$ denotes the length of $x \in X^*$.

First we present some informal considerations concerning learnability of infinite o-1-sequences. Let $R \subseteq X^* \times X^*$ be a rec. en. relation (an effective system of descriptions; sometimes called operator); we say y describes x iff yRx. We suppose that R is an universal rec. en. relation, i.e. if S is any rec. en. relation, there is $w \in X^*$ such that $\forall y,x$: $ySx \Rightarrow wyRx$. Now, if $z \in X^\infty$ is a recursive sequence, there is a "best" way to describe z: there is $v \in X^*$ such that $\forall n \in N$: vRz^n (where z^n denotes the initial segment $z_1 \ldots z_n$ of z). But usually (if z is not recursive) the length of the description of z^n will become larger as n grows, because more and more additional information must be provided b the description. We call z learnable, if there is a "best" way to describe all the initial segments z^n of z. The problem to characterize learnable sequences is due to R.P. Daley [1].

Let us pass to the formal definitions. Following Levin [3], we restric the systems of descriptions to monotonic operators. A rec. en. relatio $A \subseteq X^* \times X^*$ is called <u>monotonic operator</u> iff

(1) $\forall (y,x) \in A: \forall (v,u) \in A: \quad y \sqsubseteq v \rightarrow x \sqsubseteq u \vee u \sqsubseteq x$.

(We write $y \sqsubseteq v$ iff $v \in yX^*$)

There is an <u>universal</u> monotonic operator U; that means: if A is any mo tonic operator, then $w \in X^*$ can effectively be found such that $\forall (y,x) \in A$ $(wy,x) \in U$. We fix an universal monotonic operator U, a partial recursiv function $\varphi: X^* \times X^* \to X$ such that domain(φ) = U and a running time functi Φ for φ. For technical reasons we assume

(2) $\forall y,x$: $\Phi(y,x) \geq \log|y|$.

Notations:

(3) $Km(x) := \min \{|y| \mid y \in X^* \wedge yUx\}$; Km is called <u>monotonic operator complexity</u>.

(4) Let T be a growth function (i.e. T is recursive, isotonic, unbounded).

$M_x^T := \{y \in X^* \mid \forall i \leq |x| : \exists k \leq |y| : y^k U x^i \wedge \Phi(y^k, x^i) \leq T(i)\}$.

Condition (2) ensures that there is a finite set $\tilde{M}_x^T \subseteq X^*$ such that $M_x^T = \tilde{M}_x^T X^*$ and $y \in \tilde{M}_x^T \Rightarrow \log|y| \leq T(|x|)$.

(5) $Km^T(x) := \min \{|y| \mid y \in M_x^T\}$.

Km^T is recursive for sufficiently large functions T.

In order to give a short definition of learnability we introduce a relation $\leq^*$ for (arbitrary) functions $f_1, f_2 : N \to N$. We write $f_1 \leq^* f_2$ iff $\forall g$ growth funct.: $\forall^\infty n$: $f_1(n) \leq f_2(n) + g(n)$.

<u>Definition:</u>

$z \in X^\infty$ is called <u>learnable</u> iff there is a growth function T such that the function $n \to Km^T(z^n)$ is $\leq^*$-minimal among $(n \to Km^t(z^n) \mid t$ growth funct.).

An equivalent, but perhaps more intuitive definition of learnability makes use of the notion of a recursive coding. A recursive function $\psi : X^* \to X^*$ is called a <u>recursive coding</u>, iff $\forall x \in X^* : \psi(x) U x$. Thus $\psi(x)$ describes x; and $z \in X^\infty$ is learnable iff there is a recursive coding ψ such that $n \to |\psi(z^n)|$ is $\leq^*$-minimal among $(n \to |\psi'(z^n)| \mid \psi'$ rec. coding).

There is a rec. en. sequence z which is not learnable [2], [4]. Moreover this sequence z can be chosen such that it satisfies the following i.o. cut-down property.

For every growth function T there exists a growth function T' such that $\forall q < 1 : \exists^\infty n : Km^{T'}(z^n) \leq Km^T(z^n) - q \cdot n$.

The attempt to characterize learnable sequences statistically arises from the following idea. Consider random sequences with respect to the equiprobability distribution $\bar{\mu}$. These sequences are completely irregular; we suppose that the best way to describe their initial segments is to describe them by themselves. Recursive sequences are learnable but not at all μ-random. Therefore we first generalize the concept of randomness in order to cover both cases.

Let $p : X^* \to]o,1[\cap Q$ be a recursive function. p defines a recursive probability measure on X^∞ (i.e. on the σ-algebra generated by the sets xX^∞) as follows.

$$\bar{p}(xX^\infty) := \prod_{x_{i+1}=1} p(x^i) \cdot \prod_{x_{i+1}=o} (1 - p(x^i)).$$

We call p a recursive probability measure (r.p.m.), too. μ denotes the equiprobability distribution $\forall x \in X^*: \mu(x)=2^{-1}$.

A <u>recursive</u> <u>p-martingale</u> is a recursive function $V: X^* \to Q_+$ satisfying $\forall x \in X^*: V(x) = p(x)V(x1) + (1-p(x))V(xo)$. In analogy to the μ-case [5] we define p-randomness.

<u>Definition:</u>
Let p be a r.p.m.. $z \in X^\infty$ is not <u>p-random</u> iff $\exists V$ rec. p-martingale: $\exists h$ growth function: $\exists^\infty n$: $V(z^n) \geq h(n)$.

We call $\mathcal{K} := \{z \in X^\infty \mid \exists p$ r.p.m.: z is p-random$\}$ the set of <u>general</u> <u>random</u> <u>sequences</u>.

Let z be a recursive sequence. We define

$$p(z^{n-1}) = \begin{cases} (2^n+1)\cdot(2^n+2)^{-1} & , \text{ if } z_n=1 \\ (2^n+2)^{-1} & , \text{ if } z_n=o \end{cases}$$

It is easily seen that z is p-random. Thus, every recursive sequence i a general random sequence. Martingales and monotonic operator complexi are strongly related as the following theorem shows.

<u>Theorem 1.</u>
(a) Let T be a growth function. There is a recursive μ-martingale V > such that $\forall x \in X^*$: $\log V(x) \geq |x| - Km^T(x)$.
(b) Let V be a recursive μ-martingale, V > o. There is a growth functi T and a constant c such that $\forall x \in X^*$: $\log V(x) \leq |x| - Km^T(x) + c$.
<u>Proof:</u>
(a) Define $\overline{V}(x) := \overline{\mu}(M_x^T X^\infty)\cdot 2^{|x|}$. From condition (2) we conclude that $\overline{V}$ is recursive. $\overline{V}$ is a recursive μ-submartingale, i.e. $\forall x \in X^*$: $\overline{V}(x) \geq 2^{-1}\cdot(\overline{V}(xo)+\overline{V}(x1))$. Therefore we can construct a recursive μ-martingale $V \geq \overline{V}$. V satisfies (a): from $y \in M_x^T$, $|y| = Km^T(x)$ we conclude $\overline{\mu}(M_x^T X^\infty) \geq 2^{-|y|}$ and this implies $\log V(x) \geq |x| - Km^T(x)$.
(b) We define a r.p.m. p as follows: $p(x) := V(x1) / 2\cdot V(x)$. It suffic to find a growth function T such that $Km^T(x) \leq |\log \overline{p}(x)| + c$, for we have $V(x) = 2^{|x|}\overline{p}(x)(V(\Lambda))^{-1}$.
First we define a mapping $F: X^* \to X^*$ using the following notations. For i=1,2,3,... we divide the interval $[o,1]$ by 2^i-1 equidistant points into 2^i open intervals of length 2^{-i}; these intervals are denoted by I (k=1,...,2^i). To every interval of this kind we assoziate a finite bir ry sequence by the function B in the following way:

$B(I_k^i)$ = the (lexicographically) k-th sequence in X^i.

<u>Fact 1:</u> $I_k^i \supseteq I_r^i \Leftrightarrow B(I_k^i) \sqsubset B(I_r^i)$.

To define F at $x \in X^*$ we consider the interval $I_x =]\sum_{\substack{y<x \\ y \in X^n}} \bar{p}(y), \sum_{\substack{y \leq x \\ y \in X^n}} \bar{p}(y)[$,

where $x<y$ denotes the lexicographical ordering and $\bar{p}(y) := \bar{p}(yX^\infty)$.

Let I_k^i be an interval of maximal length contained in I_x, i.e. $I_k^i \subseteq I_x \wedge \forall j<i: \forall r(o<r\leq 2^j): I_r^j \not\subseteq I_x$. There is one and only one such I_k^i. Then we set $F(x) := B(I_k^i)$.

<u>Fact 2:</u> $\forall x: |F(x)| \leq \lceil -\log \bar{p}(x) \rceil + 1$.

The length of I_x is $\bar{p}(x)$; therefore $i \leq \lceil -\log \bar{p}(x) \rceil + 1$.

<u>Fact 3:</u> $F: X^* \to X^*$ is recursive.

<u>Fact 4:</u> F^{-1} is a monotonic operator.

Let $F(x) \sqsubset F(x')$. Applying fact 1 we conclude for the intervals $B^{-1}(F(x))$ and $B^{-1}(F(x'))$: $B^{-1}(F(x)) \supseteq B^{-1}(F(x'))$. Then $x' \sqsupset x$ must hold, for $x' \not\sqsupset x \wedge x \not\sqsupset x'$ would imply $I_{x'} \cap I_x = \emptyset$.

Choose $v \in X^*$ such that $\forall x,y \in X^*: y=F(x) \Rightarrow vyUx$. Define $T(n) := \max\{\Phi(vF(x),x) \mid x \in X^n\}$. Fact 3 implies that T is recursive. From fact 2 we conclude $\forall x \in X^*: Km^T(x) \leq |F(x)| + |v| \leq \lceil -\log \bar{p}(x) \rceil + 1 + |v|$.

Theorem 1 is a counterpart of Levin's theorem 2 [3]; in [4] theorem 1 is used to characterize p-randomness in terms of Km.

<u>Theorem 2.</u> (Statistical characterization of learnable sequences)
For every $z \in X^\infty$ the following conditions are equivalent.

(a) z is learnable

(b) z is a general random sequence.

<u>Proof:</u>

"(a)$\Rightarrow$(b)": Let T be a growth function which learns z. Apply thm.1(a) to T. We find a recursive μ-martingale $V>o$ s.th. $\log V(x) \geq |x| - Km^T(x)$. Define $p(x) := V(x1) / 2\cdot V(x)$. p is a r.p.m.. We claim that z is p-random.

Assume z is not p-random. Then there is a recursive p-martingale $\bar{V}$ and a growth function g s.th. $\exists^\infty n: \bar{V}(z^n) \geq g(n)$. We define a recursive μ-martingale $V'(x) := \bar{V}(x)\cdot\bar{p}(x)\cdot 2^{|x|}$. From thm.1(b) we get a growth function T' such that $\log V'(x) \leq |x| - Km^{T'}(x) + c$. Using the identity $\bar{p}(x) = (V(\Lambda))^{-1}\cdot V(x)\cdot 2^{-|x|}$ we obtain $\log \bar{V}(x) + Km^{T'}(x) \leq Km^T(x) + c + \log V(\Lambda)$; and this implies $\exists^\infty n: \log g(n) - c' + Km^{T'}(z^n) \leq Km^T(z^n)$, which is contradictory to the supposition that T learns z.

"(b) ⇒ (a)": Let z be p-random. Consider the μ-martingale $V(x)=2^{|x|}\bar{p}(x)$ and apply thm.1(b). We obtain T and c such that $o \leq |\log \bar{p}(x)| - Km^T(x)+c$ We show that T learns z. If not, there would be T' and a growth functio g such that $\exists^\infty n\colon Km^{T'}(z^n) + g(n) \leq Km^T(z^n)$. Applying thm.1(a) to T' we obtain a recursive μ-martingale V' such that $\exists^\infty n\colon g(n) \leq \log V'(z^n) + |\log \bar{p}(z^n)| - n + c$. But this is contadictory to the p-randomness of z, for $\bar{V}(x) := 2^{-|x|} \cdot V'(x) \cdot (\bar{p}(x))^{-1}$ is a recursive p-martingale.

A learnable sequence z may have many algorithmically recognizable regularities; but if T learns z, then all these regularities are found with in running time T. Beyond that, z must be quite irregular. The characterization theorem shows that all regularities of a learnable sequence can be completely condensed into a r.p.m. p.

The correspondence between growth functions and r.p.m.'s is effective in the sense that given T (which learns z), one can effectively find a r.p.m. p such that z is p-random and vice versa.

The set of non-learnable sequences, i.e. $X^\infty \setminus \mathcal{K}$ is rather small. In fact we have $\forall p$ r.p.m.: $\bar{p}(X^\infty \setminus \mathcal{K}) = o$.

References:

[1] R.P. Daley THE PROCESS COMPLEXITY AND THE UNDERSTANDING OF SEQUENCES. Proceedings of Symposium and Summer School MFCS, High Tatras, September 3-8, 1973.

[2] P.H. Fuchs PROGRAMMKOMPLEXITÄT,ZUFÄLLIGKEIT,LERNBARKEIT. Dissertation, Frankfurt 1975.

[3] L.A. Levin ON THE NOTION OF A RANDOM SEQUENCE. Soviet Math. Dokl. 14, 1973.

[4] C.P. Schnorr, P.H. Fuchs THE COINCIDENCE OF LEARNABLE, OF OPTIMALLY COMPRESSIBLE AND OF GENERAL RANDOM SEQUENCES. Preprint, Fachbereich Mathematik, Universität Frankfurt 1975.

[5] C.P. Schnorr ZUFÄLLIGKEIT UND WAHRSCHEINLICHKEIT. Lecture Notes in Math., vol 218, Berlin and New York, 1971.

ÜBER DEN MITTLEREN ZEITBEDARF
BEI DER LR(k) - ANALYSE KONTEXTFREIER SPRACHEN

von Herbert Kopp, Saarbrücken

I. EINLEITUNG

Ist $\mathcal{G}$ eine Chomskygrammatik, welche eine formale Sprache L definiert, dann besteht das Analyseproblem für $\mathcal{G}$ in der Aufgabe, zu gegebenen Worten w zu entscheiden, ob w ein Element der Sprache L ist und in diesem Fall die Ableitungen für w bezüglich $\mathcal{G}$ zu finden.

Ein einfaches Verfahren zur Lösung des Analyseproblems für die Klasse der kontextfreien Sprachen ist der LR(k) - Algorithmus von Knuth [3] . Für eine Untermenge der kontextfreien Sprachen, nämlich für die Klasse der LR(k) - Sprachen, läβt sich damit die Analyse sogar in Linearzeit durchführen. Im allgemeinen können aber während der Analyse Sackgassen auftreten, so daβ die Analyse im schlimmsten Fall sogar exponentiellen Zeitaufwand erfordert.

Um die Brauchbarkeit des LR(k) - Verfahrens für eine gegebene kontextfreie Grammatik beurteilen zu können , sind Antworten auf die folgenden Fragen interessant:

- Wie häufig treten Sackgassen bei der Analyse eines Wortes w durchschnittlich auf?
- Welche Analysezeit benötigt der LR(k) - Algorithmus im Mittel für ein Wort?

Es soll hier über eine Methode berichtet werden, mit der man die mittlere Analysezeit und die Wahrscheinlichkeit für das Auftreten von Sackgassen bei Vorgabe einer kontextfreien Grammatik abschätzen kann. Der Einfachheit halber beschränken wir uns auf die LR(0) - Analyse. Die Erweiterung auf den Fall $k > 0$ bereitet keine Schwierigkeiten.

Mit Hilfe dieser Abschätzungen kann man zeigen, daβ der LR(k) - Algorithmus auch für Grammatiken brauchbar ist, die nicht vom Typ LR(k) sind.

II. PRÄZISIERUNG DER PROBLEMSTELLUNG UND LÖSUNGSANSATZ

Wir betrachten eine Chomsky-reduzierte Grammatik $\mathcal{G} = \langle \mathcal{N}, \mathcal{T}, \mathcal{P}, \alpha \rangle$, wobei $\mathcal{N}$ das nichtterminale Alphabet, $\mathcal{T}$ das terminale Alphabet, $\mathcal{P}$ das Produktionensystem und α das Axiom ist.

Ist $f = x \to y$ eine Produktionsregel aus $\mathcal{P}$, dann bezeichnen wir mit $Q(f) = x$ und $Z(f) = y$ die linke bzw. die rechte Seite der Produktion f. Weiter betrachten wir zu $f \in \mathcal{P}$ die Menge

$$R(f) = \left\{ wq \;\middle|\; \begin{array}{l} w \in (\mathcal{N} \cup \mathcal{T})^{*} \;,\; Z(f) = q \;, \\ \text{und es gibt eine kanonische} \\ \text{Reduktion} \quad wqv \leftarrow wQ(f)v \xleftarrow[*]{} \alpha \end{array} \right\}$$

Zum Begriff der kanonischen Reduktion vergleiche man etwa [1] . Ist $wq \in R($ und $q = Z(f)$ und $v \in \mathcal{T}^{*}$, dann nennt man das Teilwort q ein Handle des Wortes wqv.

<u>Beispiel:</u> Wir betrachten die Grammatik $\mathcal{G}_1 = \langle \{Y\} \;,\; \{a,b\} \;,\; \{f_1, f_2\} \;,\; Y \rangle$.

mit den Produktionen

$$f_1 = \quad Y \to aY$$

$$f_2 = \quad Y \to b$$

$\mathcal{G}_1$ erzeugt die Sprache $\quad L_1 = \{a^n b \mid n \geq 0\}$

Außerdem gilt $\quad R(f_1) = \{a^n Y \mid n \geq 1\}$

$$R(f_2) = \{a^n b \mid n \geq 0\}$$

Die Mengen $R(f)$ sind also gerade diejenigen Anfangswörter, die man bei der LR(0) - Analyse gelesen haben muß, um ein Handle zu entdecken, das mit f reduziert werden kann.

Man kann nun zeigen, daß die Mengen $R(f)$ für kontextfreie Grammatiken stet[s] reguläre Sprachen sind, und darüber hinaus lassen sich LR(0) - Grammatiken damit folgendermaßen charakterisieren:

<u>Satz:</u> Eine kontextfreie Chomsky-reduzierte Grammatik ist genau dann vom Typ LR(0) , wenn für alle Produktionen $f, g \in \mathcal{P}$ gilt:

$$R(f) \cdot \mathcal{T}^{*} \cap R(g) = \emptyset \qquad \text{falls } f \neq g \text{ ist}$$

$$R(f) \cdot \mathcal{T}^{+} \cap R(g) = \emptyset \qquad \text{falls } f = g \text{ ist}$$

LR(0) - Grammatiken werden durch diesen Satz also gerade dadurch charakterisi[ert,] daß bei jedem Reduktionsschritt des LR(0) - Verfahrens höchstens ein Handle g[e]funden werden kann.

Ist nun $\mathcal{G}$ nicht vom Typ LR(0), dann kann es vorkommen, daß im Verlauf der Analyse ein Wort mit mehr als einem Handle auftritt. Es ist dann w von der Form $w = w_1 w_2$ mit $w_2 \in \mathcal{T}^{*}$ und :

$$w_1 \in M(\mathcal{P}) := \bigsqcup_{\substack{f,g \in \mathcal{P} \\ f \neq g}} \left[R(f)\cdot \mathcal{F}^* \cap R(g)\right] \cup \bigsqcup_{f} \left[R(f)\cdot \mathcal{F}^+ \cap R(f)\right]$$

In diesem Fall kann die Analyse in Sackgassen geraten, dann nämlich, wenn von den in Frage kommenden Handles ein falsches gewählt wird.

<u>Beispiel:</u> Wir betrachten die Grammatik $\mathcal{G}_2 = \langle \{X,Y\}, \{a,b,c\}, \{f_1,\ldots,f_4\}, X \rangle$ mit den Produktionen

$$f_1 = X \rightarrow aY$$
$$f_2 = X \rightarrow cc$$
$$f_3 = Y \rightarrow Xb$$
$$f_4 = Y \rightarrow aY$$

$\mathcal{G}_2$ erzeugt die Sprache $L_2 = \{ a^n ccb^m \mid n \geq m \geq 0 \}$. Weiter ist

$$R(f_1) = \{ a^n Y \mid n \geq 1 \}$$
$$R(f_2) = \{ a^n cc \mid n \geq 1 \}$$
$$R(f_3) = \{ a^n Xb \mid n \geq 1 \}$$
$$R(f_4) = \{ a^n Y \mid n \geq 2 \}$$

und daraus erhalten wir wie oben angegeben die Menge

$$M(\mathcal{P}) = \{ a^n Y \mid n \geq 2 \}$$

In $M(\mathcal{P})$ liegen also gerade diejenigen Anfangswörter, die bei der Analyse Konflikte verursachen, da sie sich sowohl mit f_1 als auch mit f_2 reduzieren lassen.

Es läßt sich nun vermuten, daß ein Zusammenhang besteht zwischen der Häufigkeit, mit der Sackgassen auftreten, und damit auch der durchschnittlichen Analysezeit und der "Größe" der Menge $M(\mathcal{P})$.

III. <u>RESULTATE</u>

Bezeichnungen: Ist L eine formale Sprache, dann definieren wir:

$$[L]_r := \left| \{ w \in L \mid |w| = r \} \right|$$

Weiter sei $\mathcal{G}$ eine kontextfreie Grammatik wie in II. mit $|Z(f)| = 2$ für alle Produktionen $f \in \mathcal{P}$. Diese Einschränkung dient nur zur Vereinfachung der fol -

genden Abschätzungen und hat keine grundsätzliche Bedeutung. Mit T bezeichnen wir die Anzahl der Terminalzeichen von $\mathcal{G}$ und mit k die maximale Anzahl von Produktionen mit gleicher Quelle, d.h.

$$k := \max_{f \in \mathcal{P}} \left| \left\{ g \in \mathcal{P} \mid Q(g) = Q(f) \right\} \right|$$

Damit kann man die folgenden Aussagen zeigen:

Theorem 1 : Für die Wahrscheinlichkeit $q(n)$, daß bei der LR(0) - Analyse eines Wortes $w \in \mathcal{T}^*$ mit $|w| = n$ keine Sackgassen auftreten, gilt:

$$q(n) > 1 - \frac{1}{T^n} \cdot \sum_{i=2}^{n} \left[M(\mathcal{P}) . \mathcal{T}^* \right]_i \cdot k^{n-i}$$

Theorem 2 : Die mittlere Analysezeit für ein Wort $w \in \mathcal{T}^*$ mit $|w| = n$ läßt sich folgendermaßen abschätzen :

1. falls $k < T$ ist :

$$\overline{t(n)} < \frac{n \cdot T \cdot |\mathcal{P}|}{T - k} \cdot \max \left\{ \frac{[R(f)]_r}{T^r} \;\middle|\; r \leq n \right\}$$

2. falls $k = T$ ist :

$$\overline{t(n)} < \frac{1}{2} \cdot |\mathcal{P}| \cdot (n^2 - 3n + 3) \cdot \max \left\{ \frac{[R(f)]_r}{T^r} \;\middle|\; r \leq n \right\}$$

Korollar : Für metalineare Grammatiken mit $k < T$ beträgt die mittlere Analysezeit höchstens

$$\overline{t(n)} < \frac{2 \cdot |\mathcal{N}| \cdot |\mathcal{P}| \cdot (n-1)}{T - k}$$

Wir skizzieren nun noch kurz den Beweis von Theorem 2 :

Eine R-Folge der Ordnung n zur Grammatik $\mathcal{G}$ ist eine Folge $\rho = (w_n, \ldots, w_r)$ wobei $w_i \in [(\mathcal{N} \cup \mathcal{T})^*]_i$ ist für $i = r, r+1, \ldots, n-1$ und $w_n \in \mathcal{T}^*$ und außerdem $w_n \leftarrow w_{n-1} \leftarrow \ldots \leftarrow w_r$ eine kanonische Reduktionsfolge, in der w_r nicht weiter reduzierbar ist.

Wir sagen, w komme auf der m-ten Ebene in der R-Folge ρ vor, wenn $w = w_m$ ist für einen Index m mit $r \leq m \leq n$.

Wir untersuchen nun zunächst das folgende Teilproblem: Gegeben sei eine Grammatik $\mathcal{G}$ wie oben und gesucht ist die Anzahl der Reduktionsschritte, die ein LR(O)-Automat durchführen muß, um alle R-Folgen der Ordnung n zu erzeugen.

Dazu komme w in einer R-Folge der Ordnung n auf der m-ten Ebene vor. Man kann dann w genau dann mit der Produktion $f \in \mathcal{P}$ reduzieren, wenn $w \in R(f)\cdot\mathcal{T}^*$ ist. Eine solche Reduktion ist eventuell auf mehrere Arten möglich und zwar auf

$$\sum_{r=2}^{m} \left| \left\{ R(f) \cap (\mathcal{N} \cup \mathcal{T})^r \right\} \cdot \mathcal{T}^* \cap \{w\} \right|$$

verschiedene Weisen. Variiert man nun noch über alle R-Folgen der Ordnung n, dann kann man auf der m-ten Ebene die Produktion f auf höchstens

$$\sum_{r=2}^{m} \left[R(f)\right]_r \cdot T^{m-r}$$

verschiedene Weisen anwenden. Jede dieser Reduktionsmöglichkeiten kann mehrfach angewandt werden, d.h. bei der Erzeugung verschiedener R-Folgen. Um abzuschätzen, wie oft dies möglich ist, ordnen wir den R-Folgen der Ordnung n einen Graphen zu:
Seine Knoten seien die Wörter $w \in (\mathcal{N} \cup \mathcal{T})^*$, die in irgendeiner dieser R-Folgen vorkommen.
Der Graph besitzt genau dann eine Kante $u \longrightarrow v$, wenn es eine R-Folge der Ordnung n gibt, in der v auf der m-ten und u auf der (m+1)-ten Ebene vorkommen. Da die R-Folgen kanonische Reduktionsfolgen sind, ist klar, daß höchstens k Kanten auf ein und denselben Knoten gerichtet sein können.

Daraus ergibt sich, daß der LR(O)-Algorithmus jede Anwendungsmöglichkeit der Produktion f auf der m-ten Ebene höchstens k^{n-m} mal benutzen kann. Es gibt daher höchstens

$$\sum_{r=2}^{m} \left[R(f)\right]_r \cdot T^{m-r} \cdot k^{n-m}$$

Möglichkeiten, ein Wort auf der m-ten Ebene einer R-Folge mit der Produktion f zu reduzieren.
Summiert man nun noch über alle möglichen Ebenen in den R-Folgen der Ordnung n, dann erhält man eine obere Schranke für die Anzahl S(n) der insgesamt auszuführenden Reduktionsschritte:

$$S(n) \leq \sum_{f \in \mathcal{P}} \sum_{m=2}^{n} \sum_{r=2}^{m} \left[R(f)\right]_r \cdot T^{m-r} \cdot k^{n-m}$$

Dies kann man leicht umformen zu

$$S(n) \leq \frac{1}{T-k} \cdot \sum_{f \in \mathcal{P}} \left\{ T^{n+1} \sum_{r=2}^{n} \frac{[R(f)]_r}{T^r} - k^{n+1} \sum_{r=2}^{n} \frac{[R(f)]_r}{k^r} \right.$$

Damit erhalten wir als eine obere Schranke für die mittlere Anzahl von Analyse schritten bei der Analyse von $w \in \mathcal{V}^n$:

$$\overline{t(n)} = \frac{S(n)}{T^n}$$

woraus die in Theorem 2 angegebenen Abschätzungen unmittelbar folgen.

IV. ANWENDUNGEN

Die in II. angegebene Grammatik $\mathcal{G}_2$ ist nicht eindeutig und somit für kein k vom Typ LR(k). Die Abschätzungen von Theorem 1 und Theorem 2 liefern für die Wahrscheinlichkeit q(n) und die mittlere Analysezeit:

$$q(n) > \frac{8}{9} + \frac{1}{4} \cdot \left(\frac{2}{3}\right)^n$$

$$\overline{t(n)} < 8(n-1)$$

Die folgende Grammatik $\mathcal{G}_3$ beschreibt arithmetische Ausdrücke mit unvollstädiger Klammerung und Vorrangregeln zwischen den Operatoren:

$$\mathcal{G}_3 = \left\langle \{\alpha, \tau, \varphi\} \;,\; \{V, (,), +, x\}, \{f_1, \ldots, f_6\}, \alpha \right\rangle$$

mit den Produktionen

$f_1 = \varphi \to V$ $\qquad$ $f_4 = \tau \to \tau \, x \, \varphi$

$f_2 = \varphi \to (\alpha)$ $\qquad$ $f_5 = \alpha \to \tau$

$f_3 = \tau \to \varphi$ $\qquad$ $f_6 = \alpha \to \alpha + \tau$

$\mathcal{G}_3$ ist vom Typ LR(1) und daher können bei der LR(0) - Analyse Sackgassen au treten. Wir erhalten für diese Grammatik:

$$q(2n) > 0{,}986 + 0{,}09 \cdot \left(\frac{6}{25}\right)^n + 0{,}06 \cdot \left(\frac{3}{25}\right)^n$$

$$\overline{t(n)} < 2$$

LITERATUR :

[1] G.Hotz, V.Claus : Automatentheorie und formale Sprachen III. BI - Hochschulskripten 823/823a

[2] R.Kemp : LR(k) - Analysatoren. Dissertation, Saarbrücken 1973

[3] D.E.Knuth: On the translation of languages from left to right. Information and Control 8, 607-639 (1965)

[4] H.Kopp: Über die Effizienz von LR(k)-Analysatoren. Berichte des Fachbereichs Angewandte Mathematik und Informatik A 74/13 , Universität des Saarlandes

ZUR ENDLICHEN APPROXIMIERBARKEIT SEQUENTIELLER SYSTEME

Rüdiger Valk

Institut für Informatik, Universität Hamburg

D-2000 Hamburg 13, Schlüterstraße 70

1. Einleitung

Ein wichtiges Anwendungsgebiet der Informatik ist die Simulation realer Systeme mit Hilfe von elektronischen Datenverarbeitungsanlagen. Bevor man jedo damit beginnen kann, eine geeignete Software für eine solche Simulation zu ers len, ist es notwendig, ein hinreichend genaues formales Modell des Systems zu entwickeln. Die Bereitstellung solcher Modelle ist Aufgabe der allgemeinen Sys theorie [MT] . Diese Modelle berücksichtigen im allgemeinen noch nicht Randbedingungen, die durch das Leistungsvermögen des zur Verfügung stehenden Rechner gegeben sind. In einem weiteren Schritt müssen also alle Mengen und Operatione des Modells an diese Randbedingungen angepaßt werden, d.h. das Modell muß möglicherweise vergröbert werden.

In [V1] wurden Topologien für den Zustandsraum eines solchen Modells ange geben. "Nähe" von Zuständen bezüglich dieser Topologien bedeutet - anschaulich interpretiert - "Ähnlichkeit" in ihrem Verhalten, d.h. "Ähnlichkeit" in der Au gabe bei gleicher Eingabe. In [V1] blieb jedoch die Frage offen, ob bei diese Topologien immer eine hinreichend genaue endliche Approximation möglich ist. I men wir an, eine der genannten Topologien sei durch eine Metrik d gegeben. Das angesprochene Problem der Approximation des Zustandsraumes läßt sich nun so fo mulieren : Gibt es zu jedem reellen positiven ε (dem gewünschten Genauigkeits grad der Approximation) eine endliche Menge von Zuständen $Z_1 = \{z_1, z_2, \dots, z_n\}$ aus der Zustandsmenge Z des Modells derart, daß jeder beliebige Zustand in de ε-Umgebung eines dieser Zustände z_i liegt ?

2. Allgemeine Definitionen

Die Menge der Zeitpunkte, bei denen ein reales System beobachtet wird, hei Zeitmenge. Als Zeitmenge bezeichnen wir jede linear geordnete Menge T, die ei kleinstes Element t_o besitzt. Außerdem soll T bezüglich einer zweistelligen V knüpfung + ein angeordnetes kommutatives Monoid mit Einselement t_o sein und f je zwei Punkte $t \leq t'$ sei eindeutig ein Element $t_1 =: t'-t \in T$ mit $t+t_1=t'$ ge ben. Beispiele von Zeitmengen sind die Mengen $\mathbb{N}_o$ und $\mathbb{R}^+_o$, aber auch Interva $[0,n]$ in diesen Mengen mit der Verknüpfung $t \oplus t' := \inf\{t+t',n\}$. Im Hinblick auf konkrete Anwendungen sind natürlich solche Zeitmengen von Bedeutung, die

die letzten beiden Beispiele beschränkt sind. Ein- und Ausgaben der betrachteten Systeme sind mit der Zeit veränderliche Größen, d.h. Abbildungen $x : T \longrightarrow A$. Intervalle $[t,t')$, $[t := \{t' \mid t \leq t'\}$ usw werden wie üblich bezeichnet und Einschränkungen von x auf solche Intervalle mit $x_{[t,t')}$, $x_{[t}$ usw. A^T bezeichnet die Menge aller Abbildungen von T nach A. Für $t \in T$ sei $\delta_t : A^T \longrightarrow A^T$ die Abbildung $\delta_t(x)(t') := x(t+t')$. $\delta_t(x)$ wird auch mit x_t bezeichnet. Für $x,x' \in A^T$ und $t \in T$ sei $x_{t)}x'(t')$ gleich $x(t')$ falls $t' < t$ und $x'(t'-t)$ falls $t' \geq t$.

Um die "Nähe" zweier Eingaben $x,x' \in A^T$ beschreiben zu können, werden ausgehend von einer uniformen bzw. metrischen Struktur auf A ebensolche Strukturen auf Teilmengen $D \subset A^T$ betrachtet. Ist $(A,\mathcal{U}_A)$ ein uniformer Raum, so bezeichne UPK bzw. UKK bzw. UGK die Uniformität der punktweisen bzw. kompakten bzw. gleichmäßigen Konvergenz auf $D \subset A^T$ ([BGT] ,X,1.3). Die UPK, UKK und UGK werden gemeinsam als Abbildungsuniformitäten bezeichnet. Ist (A,d_A) ein beschränkter metrischer Raum, so ist die UPK auf A^T durch eine Metrik erzeugbar, falls T abzählbar ist. Das gleiche gilt für die UKK falls $T = \mathbb{R}_0^+$ ist. Die UGK wird in jedem Falle von der Supremums-Metrik erzeugt.

Sind $f : M \longrightarrow N$, $f' : M' \longrightarrow N'$ Abbildungen, so bezeichnet $f \times f' : M \times M' \longrightarrow N \times N'$ die komponentenweise Produktabbildung, $\Delta_M : M \longrightarrow M \times M$ bezeichnet die Abbildung $m \longmapsto (m,m)$ und id_M die identische Abbildung auf M. pr_i ist die i-te Projektion eines kartesischen Produktes. Ist $f : M \times M' \longrightarrow N$ eine Abbildung und $m \in M$, so bezeichnet $f_m : M' \longrightarrow N$ die Abbildung $m' \longmapsto f(m,m')$.

. Systeme und Realisierungen

Die einzig exakt meßbaren Größen eines realen Systems sind im allgemeinen all die beobachteten Eingaben zusammen mit den zugehörigen Ausgaben. Aus diesem Grunde wird in der allgemeinen Systemtheorie [MT] jede solche Ein-Ausgabe-Relation $S \subset A^T \times B^T$ als T-System bezeichnet, wobei T eine Zeitmenge ist. $DS = pr_1(S)$ bezeichnet die Menge der zulässigen Eingabefunktionen von S. Ein Modell zur Erzeugung von S heißt Realisierung von S. Wir betrachten hier nur deterministische und sequentielle Realisierungen. Bei gegebener Zeitmenge T besteht eine Realisierung aus einem Tupel $R = (Z,A,B,D,I,f,h,Z_0)$, wobei Z bzw. $Z_0 \subset Z$ Mengen von Zuständen bzw. Anfangszuständen, A bzw. B Ein- bzw. Ausgabemengen, $I = [t_0,i] \subset$ ein Anfangsintervall mit $i > t_0$, $D \subset A^T$ die Menge der Eingabefunktionen und $f : Z \times D \times I \longrightarrow Z$ und $h : Z \longrightarrow B$ Transitions- und Ausgabeabbildungen bezeichnen, die den folgenden Axiomen genügen :

Für alle $z \in Z$, $x,x' \in D$, $t,t' \in I$ gilt :

Kausalität : $f(z,x,t_0) = z$ und falls $x_{t)} = x'_{t)}$ auch $f(z,x,t) = f(z,x',t)$

Transitivität : $x_{t)}x' \in D$ und falls $t+t' \in I$ auch $f(f(z,x,t),x',t) =$

$$f(z,x_{t)}x',t+t')$$

Kommutativität : $x_{t'} \in D$ und $f(f(z,x,t),x',t') = f(f(z,x_{t)}x',t'),(x_{t)}x')_{t'},t)$

Zeitmenge ist archimedisch bezüglich i : Für jedes Element $t \in T$ gibt es genau eine natürliche Zahl $n \in \mathbb{N}_0$ mit $ni \leq t < (n+1)i$. Dabei bedeutet $0i = t_0$

und $ni = \sum_{j=1}^{n} i$ für $n > 0$.

Die gerade definierte Realisierung ist vergleichbar mit der Definition eines Systems in [KAF]. Ein Unterschied besteht jedoch in der realitätsnäheren Beschränkung eines Zeitschrittes von einem Zustand zum nachfolgenden. Dies macht es andererseits notwendig, die Transitionsfunktion f rekursiv für jedes $n \in \mathbb{N}_o$ durch $f^{(o)} = pr_1$, $f^{(1)} = f_i$ und $f^{(n+1)} := f^{(1)} \circ (f^{(n)} \times \ell_{ni}) \circ (id_Z \times \Delta_D)$ zunächst auf $f^{(n)} : ZxD \to Z$ und schließlich auf $f^T : ZxD \to Z^T$ durch $f^T(z,x)(t) := f(f^{(n)}(z,x), x_{ni}, t-ni)$ zu erweitern, wobei $n \in \mathbb{N}_o$ eindeutig durch $ni \leq t < (n+1)i$ festgelegt ist. Als globale Ausgabe-Abbildung erhält man schließlich mit $Y = B^T$ $g^T : ZxD \to Y$, $g^T(z,x)(t) := h(f^T(z,x)(t))$. Die Menge $L(z) = \{(x,y) \mid x \in D \wedge y = g^T(z,x)\}$ heißt Leistung von z [BI]. g^T heißt Verhalten von R und $G := \{g_z^T : D \to Y \mid z \in Z\} \subset Y^D$ heißt Verhaltensmenge von R. Gelten für ein T-System $S \subset A^T \times B^T$ die Beziehungen $D = DS$ und $S = \{(x, g^T(z,x)) \mid z \in Z_o\}$, so heißt R eine Realisierung von S. Für ein System S existieren im Allgemeinen nur Realisierungen, bei denen alle Abbildungen partiell sind. Partielle Realisierungen und Kriterien zur Existenz von Realisierungen sind in [V2] untersucht worden. Die Leistung $L(z) \subset X \times Y$ eines Zustandes z ist für partielle Realisierungen gleichermaßen definiert. Durch Induktion zeigt man mit Hilfe der Funktionen $f^{(n)}$ und f^T den folgenden Satz [V4]:

Satz 1: Für das Verhalten g^T der Realisierung R und alle $z \in Z$, $x,x' \in D$ und $t \in I$ gilt: $g^T(f(z,x,t),x') = g^T(z,x_t)x')_t$

4. Gleichmäßig stetige Realisierungen und Uniformitäten für die Zustandsmenge

In diesem Abschnitt werden Uniformitäten für Z definiert, die die in der Einleitung geforderten Eigenschaften haben. Außerdem zitieren wir Ergebnisse über gleichmäßig stetige Realisierungen, welche wichtige Eigenschaften dieser Uniformitäten deutlich machen. Die Realisierung R heißt gleichmäßig stetig, wenn T,A,B und Z uniforme Räume sind und f und h gleichmäßig stetige Abbildungen sind. Dabei soll $D \subset A^T$ eine Abbildungsuniformität und $I \subset T$ die Spuruniformität tragen [V2,V4].

Satz 2: Das Verhalten g^T der gleichmäßig stetigen Realisierung R ist gleichmäßig stetig bezüglich der UPK oder UKK auf Y und die Verhaltensmenge G ist gleichmäßig gleichgradig stetig.

Ausgehend von einer beliebigen Uniformität auf Y definieren wir eine Uniformität für Z. Die initiale Uniformität auf Z bezüglich der Abbildung $V : Z \to G$, $z \mapsto g_z^T$ und der UGK auf der Verhaltensmenge G wird als Verhaltensuniformität $\mathcal{U}_V$ auf Z bezeichnet. Eigenschaften von $\mathcal{U}_V$ wurden in [V1] untersucht. Ist $T = \mathbb{N}_O$, so können wir $i = 1$ setzen und R im wesentlichen als Automaten auffassen. Trägt Y die UPK bezüglich der diskreten Uniformität auf B, so läßt sich für $\mathcal{U}_V$ eine Pseudometrik d_V derart angeben, daß $d_V(z,z') = 0$ genau dann gilt, wenn z und z' äquivalente Zustände sind und es gilt $d_V(z,z') \leq 1/2 \cdot 3^{-k}$ genau dann, wenn z ınd z' k-äquivalent sind, d.h. wenn sie für alle endlichen Eingabefolgen bis zur ,änge k gleiche Ausgaben produzieren [V3].

atz 3 : Die Mengen A und B der Realisierung R mögen uniforme Räume sein und D eine Abbildungsuniformität tragen. Dann sind f und h gleichmäßig stetig bezüglich der Verhaltensuniformität auf Z und der diskreten Uniformität auf I, wenn G gleichgradig gleichmäßig stetig ist.

rägt T eine nichtdiskrete Uniformität, dann muß G eine weitere Bedingung erfüllen, ie ebenfalls notwendig ist [V2,V4]. Daraus ergibt sich der folgende Satz.

atz 4 : Ersetzt man in der gleichmäßig stetigen Realisierung R die Uniformität $\mathcal{U}_Z$ des Zustandsraumes Z durch die Verhaltensuniformität $\mathcal{U}_V$, so wird R wieder eine gleichmäßig stetige Realisierung. Außerdem ist $\mathcal{U}_V$ gröber als $\mathcal{U}_Z$.

ieser Satz impliziert gleichzeitig einen Satz über die Existenz minimaler gleich-äßig stetiger Realisierungen. Wie in [V1] geben wir eine weitere Uniformität für an, die ähnliche Eigenschaften wie $\mathcal{U}_V$ hat, jedoch im Gegensatz zu $\mathcal{U}_V$ auch für artielle Realisierungen definierbar ist. Dazu seien die Mengen $X=A^T$ und $Y=B^T$ in uniforme Räume. Für die Potenzmenge P(XxY) des Produktraumes XxY ist in kano-ischer Weise eine Uniformität $\mathcal{U}_P$ definiert ([BGT],II,1,ex5). Die initiale niformität auf Z bezüglich der Abbildung L : Z $\longrightarrow$ P(XxY) , z $\longmapsto$ L(z) heißt Lei-tungsuniformität $\mathcal{U}_L$ der Zustandsmenge Z.

atz 5 : Die Leistungsuniformität $\mathcal{U}_L$ ist gröber als die Verhaltensuniformität. Beide sind jedoch gleich, wenn die Verhaltensmenge G gleichgradig gleich-mäßig stetig ist, also insbesondere dann, wenn R eine gleichmäßig ste-tige Realisierung ist.

Präkompaktheit der Zustandsmengen

Wir wenden uns nun der Frage zu, ob in der Zustandsmenge Z immer eine end-che Teilmenge Z_1 gefunden werden kann, die die am Ende der Einleitung geschil-rte Eigenschaft hat, d.h. ob Z präkompakt ist. Ein uniformer Raum $(Z,\mathcal{U}_Z)$ heißt äkompakt, wenn zu jeder Nachbarschaft $W \in \mathcal{U}_Z$ eine endliche Menge $Z_1 \subset Z$ derart istiert, daß $W[Z_1] := \{z \mid \exists\, z_1 \in Z_1 : (z_1,z) \in W\} = Z$ gilt. Mit dieser Defini-on zeigt man leicht, daß der oben genannte Potenzraum $(P(Z),\mathcal{U}_P)$ präkompakt ist, nn $(Z,\mathcal{U}_Z)$ präkompakt ist. Für die folgenden beiden Sätze nehmen wir an, daß X d Y präkompakte uniforme Räume sind. Dies gilt z.B. dann, wenn A und B präkom-kt (z.B. beschränkte reelle Intervalle) sind und $X=A^T$, $Y=B^T$ die UPK tragen.

tz 6 : Die Zustandsmenge Z der Realisierung R ist präkompakt bezüglich der Leistungsuniformität $\mathcal{U}_L$.

weis: Mit X und Y ist auch das Produkt XxY und der Potenzraum P(XxY) präkompakt. ist als initiale Uniformität der Abbildung L : Z $\longrightarrow$ P(XxY) präkompakt ([BGT], ,4.2).

die Präkompaktheit der Verhaltensuniformität zu zeigen, muß eine stärkere rausstzung gemacht werden.

Satz 7 : Die Zustandsmenge Z der Realisierung R ist präkompakt bezüglich der Verhaltensuniformität $\mathcal{U}_V$, wenn die Verhaltensfamilie G von R gleichgradig gleichmäßig stetig ist, also insbesondere dann, wenn R gleichmäßig stetig ist. Die Bedingung ist sogar notwendig, wenn alle Abbildungen $g_z^T : D \to Y$ aus G gleichmäßig stetig sind.

Beweis: $\mathcal{U}_V$ ist als initiale Uniformität bezüglich der Abbildung $V : Z \to G$ gen dann präkompakt, wenn (G,UGK) präkompakt ist ([BGT],II,4.3). Daraus folgt di Behauptung mit dem Satz von Ascoli ([BGT],X,2.5).

Sind X und Y präkompakt, so besagen die Sätze 4 und 7 gerade, daß man die Uniformität $\mathcal{U}_Z$ jeder gleichmäßig stetigen Realisierung R zu der präkompakten Uniformität $\mathcal{U}_V$ vergröbern kann. Eine Richtung von Satz 7 folgt auch aus Satz 5 und Satz 6.

Aus ähnlichen Gründen wie hier wird in [KW] eine Topologie für die Zustan menge eines Dialogsystems definiert. Das Dialogsystem kann als Automat mit Zustandsmenge Z und globaler Ausgabeabbildung $h^* : Z \times A^* \to B^*$ dargestellt werde Definiert man für beliebige Worte $v \in A^*$, $w \in B^*$ die Menge 'verification-scope VSK(v,w) = $\{z \in Z \mid h^*(z,v) = w\}$, so erhält man eine Subbasis der in [KW] def nierten Topologie τ_{VSK} für Z. Es gilt die folgende äquivalente Definition.

Satz 8 : Es sei $T = \mathbb{N}_o$, $X = A^T$, $Y = B^T$ und $g^T(z,x)(t) := h^*(z,x(0)\ldots x(t))$ fü alle $z \in Z$ und $x \in X$. Versieht man B mit der diskreten Topologie, Y u $G = \{g_z^T : X \to Y \mid z \in Z\}$ jeweils mit der Produkttopologie, so ist d initiale Topologie auf Z bezüglich der Abbildung $V : Z \to G$ gleich d Topologie τ_{VSK}.

Beweis : Die angegebene Subbasis für τ_{VSK} ist gleich der aus den Mengen $\langle x,O_w$ $:= \{z \mid g^T(z,x) \in O_w\}$ ($x \in X$, $w \in B^*$) gebildeten Subbasis, wobei $O_w := \{y \in$ $\exists t \in T : y_{t]} = w\}$ ist.

Satz 9 : Der Raum (Z,τ_{VSK}) ist

a) genau dann hausdorff'sch, wenn A reduziert ist,

b) genau dann diskret, wenn A reduziert und G diskret in Y^X liegt,

c) diskret, wenn A reduziert und Z endlich ist,

d) uniformisierbar durch eine Uniformität $\mathcal{U}_{VSK}$, und

e) präkompakt bezüglich $\mathcal{U}_{VSK}$, wenn B endlich ist.

Beweis : A ist genau dann reduziert, wenn V injektiv ist. Ist B diskret, dann sind Y und G hausdorff'sch. Daraus folgen a) bis c) mit der Charakterisierung von τ_{VSK} in Satz 8. Weiterhin wird die Produkttopologie auf Y von der UPK bez lich der diskreten Uniformität auf B erzeugt, also τ_{VSK} von der initialen Uni mität bezüglich der Abbildung V und der UPK auf G. Schließlich ist die endlic Menge B präkompakt, was sich auf die UPK von $Y=A^T$ und $G \subset Y^X$ und auf Z übertr

Das Ausgabealphabet B des Dialogsystems A in [KW] besteht aus Sätzen über einem endlichen Grundalphabet B_o. Zur Approximation von Z genügt es wegen Sat e) daher zu fordern, daß B nur aus Sätzen beschränkter Länge besteht.

6. Approximative Realisierungen

Die Präkompaktheit der Zustandsmenge einer Realisierung gestattet die Konstruktion einer approximativen endlichen Realisierung, d.h. einer Realisierung mit endlicher Zustandszahl. Dazu nehmen wir an, daß die Zeitmenge T eines Systems S abzählbar 'gerastert' ist, d.h. S wird über einer abzählbaren Teilmenge $T' \subset T$ betrachtet. Zur Konstruktion einer Realisierung R für dieses T'-System vergleiche man [V2] . Die Approximation des Systems wird nun bezüglich einer endlichen Rasterung $T'' \subset T'$ durchgeführt.

Satz 10 : Gegeben sei ein (abzählbar gerastertes) T-System $S \subset A^T \times B^T$ (d.h. o.B.d.A. $T = \mathbb{N}_o$), bei dem (B,d_B) ein durch 1 beschränkter metrischer Raum ist und eine Realisierung $R = (Z,A,B,DS,I,f,h,Z_o)$ von S, deren Zustandsraum Z präkompakt bezüglich der Verhaltensuniformität $\mathcal{U}_V$ ist. Zu jedem $\varepsilon > 0$ und zu jeder endlichen Rasterung $T' = [0,\dots,n] \subset T$ existiert eine endliche Realisierung R' mit endlicher Zustandszahl eines T-Systems S' derart, daß für alle $(x,y) \in S$ ein Paar $(x,y') \in S'$ mit $d_B(y(t),y'(t)) < \varepsilon$ für alle $t \in T'$ existiert.

Beweis: Die UPK auf $Y = B^T$ werde durch die Metrik $d_Y(y,y') := \sum_{t\in T} 2^{-t} d_B(y(t),y'(t))$ und $\mathcal{U}_V$ werde durch die Pseudometrik $d_V(z,z') := \sup\{ d_Y(g^T(z,x),g^T(z',x)) \mid x \in DS\}$ erzeugt, wobei g^T das Verhalten von R ist. Wegen $T = \mathbb{N}_0$ können wir $i = 1$ setzen und für alle $x \in DS$ folgt aus Satz 1 : $d_V(f(z,x,i),f(z',x,i)) \leq 2d_V(z,z')$ (I). Zu $\varepsilon' := 2^{-(n+2)}\varepsilon$ gibt es wegen der Präkompaktheit von (Z,d_V) eine endliche Teilmenge $Z_1 := \{z_1,\dots,z_m\} \subset Z$ und eine Partition $K = \{K_1,\dots,K_m\}$ von Z mit $z_k \in K_k \subset \overline{B}(z_k,\varepsilon') = \{z' \mid d_V(z_k,z') \leq \varepsilon'\}$ für alle $1 \leq k \leq m$. Wir setzen $A_j^k := \{x(o) \mid x \in DS \wedge f(z_k,x,i) \in K_j\}$ für $j,k \in \{1,\dots,m\}$ und definieren $f' : Z' \times DS \times I \rightarrow Z'$ durch $f'(z_k,x,o) = z_k$ und $f'(z_k,x,i) = z_j :\Longleftrightarrow x(o) \in A_j^k$, $Z_o' := \{z_k \in Z' \mid K_k \cap Z_o \neq \emptyset\}$ und h' als Einschränkung von h auf Z'. Für alle $x \in DS$ und $z_k \in Z'$ gilt dann $d_V(f(z_k,x,i),f'(z_k,x,i)) \leq \varepsilon'$ (II), denn aus $f(z_k,x,i) \in K_j$ folgt $x(o) \in A_j^k$ und $f'(z_k,x,i) = z_j$. Haben zwei Zustände $z,z' \in Z$ den Abstand $d_V(z,z') \leq \varepsilon''$, so gilt $d_B(h(z),h(z')) = d_B(g^T(z,x)(0),g^T(z',x)(0)) \leq d_Y(g^T(z,x), g^T(z',x)) \leq d_V(z,z') \leq \varepsilon''$ (III) wobei x irgendein Element von DS ist. Wir zeigen nun, daß das durch die Realisierung $R' = (Z',A,B,DS,f',h',Z_o')$ erzeugte T-System S' die gewünschte Eigenschaft hat. Dazu sei $(x,y) \in S$ d.h. $y = g^T(z_o,x)$ für ein $z_o \in Z_o$. Zu z_o existiert ein $z_o' \in Z_o'$ mit $d_V(z_o,z_o') \leq \varepsilon'$. Wir zeigen durch Induktion über t : $d_V(f^T(z_o,x)(t),f'^T(z_o',x)(t)) \leq (2^{t+1}-1)\varepsilon'$. Für $t = 0$ gilt $d_V(f^T(z_o,x)(o),f'^T(z_o',x)(o)) = d_V(z_o,z_o') \leq \varepsilon'$ und für $t > 0$ und $z := f^T(z_o,x)(t-1)$,

$z' := f'^T(z'_o,x)(t-1)$ gilt nach Induktionsvoraussetzung $d_V(z,z') \leq (2^t-1)\varepsilon'$ d.h. mit (I) $d_V(f(z,x_t,i),f(z',x_t,i)) \leq 2(2^t-1)\varepsilon'$. Aus (II) folgt $d_V(f(z',x_t,i),f'(z',x_t,i)) \leq \varepsilon'$, d.h. insgesamt $d_V(f^T(z_o,x)(t),f^T(z'_o,x)(t)) = d_V(f(z,x_t,i),f'(z',x_t,i) \leq 2(2^t-1)\varepsilon' + \varepsilon' = (2^{t+1}-1)\varepsilon'$. Aus (III) ergibt sic schließlich für alle $t \in T'$: $d_B(y(t),g'^T(z'_o,x)(t)) = d_B(h(f^T(z_o,x)(t)), h'(f'^T(z'_o,x)(t))) \leq (2^{t+2}-1)\varepsilon' \leq (2^{n+2}-1)\varepsilon' < \varepsilon$.

7. Literatur

[BGT] BOURBAKI,N., General Topology, Hermann, Paris 1966

[BI] BÖHLING,K.H., INDERMARK,K., Endliche Automaten I, BI, Mannheim 1969

[KAF] KALMAN,R.E., ARBIB,M.A., FALB,P.L., Topics in Mathematical Systems Theory, McGraw Hill, New York 1969

[KW] KUPKA,I., WILSING,N., A formal framework for dialog languages, Bericht Nr.2, Institut für Informatik, Hamburg 1972

[MT] MESAROVIC,M.D., TAKAHARA,Y., General Systems Theory : Mathematical Foundations, Academic Press, New York 1975

[V1] VALK,R., The Use of Metric and Uniform Spaces for the Formalization of Behavioral Proximity of States, in 1.GI-Fachtagung Automatentheorie un formale Sprachen, Lecture Notes in Computer Science No 2, Springer, Be 1973

[V2] VALK,R., Realisierungen allgemeiner Systeme, erscheint als GMD-Berich

[V3] VALK,R., On some Elementary Properties of Uniform Automata, erscheint in Revue Francaise d'Automatique Informatique Recherche Operationnell

[V4] VALK,R., Zeitkontinuierliche topologische Automaten, zur Veröffentlich vorbereitet,

The Complexity of Negation-Limited Networks - A Brief Survey

Michael J. Fischer[†]
Massachusetts Institute of Technology
Cambridge, Massachusetts U.S.A.

1. Introduction

Let $B = \{0,1\}$, $F_n = \{f \mid f: B^n \to B\}$, and let $\Omega \subseteq \bigcup_{m\geq 1} F_m$. The combinational complexity $C^{\Omega}(F)$ of a set of Boolean functions $F \subseteq F_n$ is the least size network over the basis Ω which computes each of the functions in F. Combinational complexity provides a meaningful measure of the difficulty of finite functions and has been widely studied. Our definitions are similar to those of Savage [20,21] and are formalized in Section 2.

Combinational complexity is interesting for both practical and theoretical reasons. The practical motivation comes from its correspondence with the cost of actual digital hardware. Theoretical interest derives both from its clean mathemati-structure and its connection with computation time on Turing machines [17]. Namely, if $g: B^* \to B^*$ can be computed in time $T(n)$ on a multitape Turing machine, then the restriction $g_n = g \mid B^n$ of g to length n inputs can be computed by a network over any complete basis of size $O(T(n) \log T(n))$.[††] (Schnorr strengthens this bound to $cp \cdot T(n) \log S(n)$ where p is the number of instructions of the Turing machine, and $S(n)$ is the number of storage cells visited [22].)

It follows that a lower bound greater than $cn \log n$ on the combinational complexity of g_n implies a non-linear lower bound on the Turing machine time complexity of g. Such lower bounds on Turing machine time have never been obtained for particular concrete functions g except by diagonal techniques.

[†] This research was supported in part by the National Science Foundation under research grant GJ-43634X to M.I.T. The author did some of this work at the University of Toronto and the University of Frankfurt.

[††] The lengths of $g_n(x)$ may differ for different $x \in B^n$. Since a network has a fixed number of outputs, we must assume appropriate conventions for representing the values of g_n. For example, if $m = \max_{x\in B^n} |g_n(x)|$, then the network might have m pairs of outputs encoding one of the three symbols 0, 1 or blank.

Unfortunately, few techniques exist for proving lower bounds on the combinational complexity of specific functions of interest, even though the following theorem shows that "most" functions are hard.

Theorem 1 (Lupanov [8]). $C(f) \sim \frac{2^n}{n}$ for all but a vanishing fraction of functions $f \in F_n$.†

For certain natural problems, diagonal techniques can be applied to obtain large lower bounds [2,25]. A sample of such a result is the following:

Theorem 2 (Meyer [11]). Let D_n be the decision problem for length n sentences of Presburger arithmetic [5,19]. Then $C(D_n) \geq c^n$, where $c > 1$ is independent of n.

These techniques, however, do not apply to concrete problems, for example, to any Boolean function whose truth-table can be generated by a multitape Turing machine in time polynomial in the length of the truth-table. Examples of concrete problems are binary integer multiplication, Boolean matrix product, Boolean convolution product, transitive closure of a Boolean matrix, context-free language recognition, and numerous other problems from automata and language theory, combinatorics, and other branches of discrete mathematics and computer science.

Recently, attention has been directed toward developing new techniques for proving lower bounds on concrete problems [6,15,23,24]. To date, only linear lower bounds have been obtained, but with a coefficient of linearity greater than one. An example of such a theorem is the following:

Theorem 3 (Schnorr [23]). Let $f = (x_1 \wedge x_2 \wedge \ldots \wedge x_n) \vee (\neg x_1 \wedge \neg x_2 \wedge \ldots \wedge \neg x_n)$. Then $C(f) = 2n - 3$.

The largest lower bound of this kind is 2.5n, obtained recently by Paul [15].

2. Basic Definitions

Let $B = \{0,1\}$. For each $n \in \mathbb{N}$, let $F_n = \{f \mid f: B^n \to B\}$. Let $\Phi = \bigcup_{n \geq 1} F_n$. For $f \in F_n$, let $\rho(f) = n$, the number of arguments of f.

A logical network $\mathfrak{N}$ over the basis $\Omega \subseteq \Phi$ and initial functions $A \subseteq F_n$ is a directed acyclic graph $G = (V,E)$ with labelled vertices such that the arcs entering each vertex are ordered. The vertices of indegree zero are called source nodes and are denoted by V_s. The remaining vertices, V_g, are called gates. The labels are specified by a function $\nu: V \to \Omega \cup A$ such that (1) if $v \in V_s$, then $\nu(v) \in A$; and (2) if $v \in V_g$, then $\nu(v) \in \Omega$ and the indegree of $v = \rho(\nu(v))$.

We associate with each $v \in V$ a function $\xi_v \in F_n$. If $v \in V_s$, then $\xi_v = \nu(v)$.

---

† $r(n) \sim s(n)$ iff $\lim \frac{r(n)}{s(n)} = 1$, where $r,s: \mathbb{N} \to \mathbb{R}$.

If $v \in V_g$, then

$$\xi_v = \nu(v)(\xi_{w_1}, \ldots, \xi_{w_k})$$

where $k = \rho(\nu(v))$ and $(w_1,v), \ldots, (w_k,v)$ are the arcs incident on v, in order. The fact that $\mathfrak{h}$ is acyclic insures that each ξ_v is well-defined. Let $F \subseteq F_n$. We say $\mathfrak{h}$ computes F if $F \subseteq \{\xi_v \mid v \in V\}$.

The cost $C(\mathfrak{h})$ of a network $\mathfrak{h}$ is the number of gates it contains. The combinational complexity of $F \subseteq F_n$ relative to the basis $\Omega \subseteq \Phi$ and the initial functions $A \subseteq F_n$ is

$$C^{\Omega,A}(F) = \min\{C(\mathfrak{h}) \mid \mathfrak{h} \text{ is a network over basis } \Omega \text{ and initial functions A, and } \mathfrak{h} \text{ computes F}\}.$$

When considering n-argument functions, we will always assume the initial functions $A_n = \{x_1, \ldots, x_n, 0, 1\}$, where x_i is the ith projection function of n arguments $\lambda y_1 \ldots y_n \cdot y_i$, and 0 and 1 are the constant functions of n arguments with values 0 and 1, respectively. We generally omit explicit mention of the initial functions. If the basis is also not specified, the full binary basis $F_1 \cup F_2$ is assumed.

3. Monotone Networks

In an effort to understand better the difficulties in proving lower bounds on combinational complexity and hopefully to develop new proof techniques applicable to the general case, various restrictions on networks have been considered which enable non-trivial lower bounds to be proved.

Let $M = \{\wedge, \vee\} \subseteq F_2$. We call a network over M a monotone network, and we denote $C^M(F)$ by MC(F), the monotone complexity of F. A function $f \in F_n$ is monotone increasing (or monotone for short) if for all $x, y \in B^n$, $x \leq y \Rightarrow f(x) \leq f(y)$, where $x \leq y$ iff $x_j \leq y_j$ for all j, $1 \leq j \leq n$. It is clear by induction that a monotone network can compute only monotone increasing functions. Conversely, every monotone function can be computed by a monotone network.

A close relationship between monotone functions and general Boolean functions allows Theorem 1 to be used to establish the existence of hard monotone functions.

Definition. Let $f \in F_n$, $g \in F_{2n}$. g is a monotone cover of f if (i) g is monotone increasing, and (ii) $f(x_1, \ldots, x_n) = g(x_1, \neg x_1, \ldots, x_n, \neg x_n)$.

Lemma 4. Every $f \in F_n$ has a monotone cover $g \in F_{2n}$.

Proof. Take

$$g(x_1,y_1, \ldots, x_n,y_n) = \begin{cases} 1 & \text{if } \Sigma(x_i + y_i) > n; \\ 0 & \text{if } \Sigma(x_i + y_i) < n; \\ f(x_1, \ldots, x_n) & \text{otherwise.} \end{cases}$$

□

Theorem 5. Let $MC^{max}(n) = \max\{MC(g) \mid g \in F_n \text{ and } g \text{ is monotone}\}$. Then $MC^{max}(n) \gtrsim \sqrt{2} \cdot \frac{2^{n/2}}{n}$.†

Proof. Let $m = \lfloor n/2 \rfloor$. Choose a function $f \in F_m$ maximizing $C(f)$. Let g be a monotone cover of f. Then using Theorem 1,

$$\frac{2^{(n-1)/2}}{n/2} \le \frac{2^m}{m} \lesssim C^{max}(m) = C(f) \le C(g) + m \le MC^{max}(n) + m,$$

where $C^{max}(m) = \max\{C(f) \mid f \in F_n\}$. The theorem follows since $m = o(\frac{2^{n/2}}{n})$. □

A stronger result can be obtained by looking into the proof of Theorem 1. The lower bound of Theorem 1 is established by counting the number N_q of n-input networks of size at most q and showing that $N_q \le (cq)^q$ for some constant c. (Cf. Fischer [3] or Strassen [26].) Comparing this number with 2^{2^n}, the number of functions in F_n, yields the bound. For monotone functions we need only compare N_q with the number of monotone functions in F_n. While this number is not known exactly, it is at least $2^{\binom{n}{\lfloor n/2 \rfloor}}$, for the set $S = \{s \in B^n \mid \#\text{ 1's in } S = \lfloor n/2 \rfloor\}$ has cardinality $\binom{n}{\lfloor n/2 \rfloor}$, and a monotone function can assume arbitrary values on S. Taking $q = (1-\varepsilon)\sqrt{\frac{2}{\pi}} \cdot \frac{2^n}{n^{3/2}}$ it follows that

$$\frac{N_q}{\#\text{ monotone functions in } F_n} \to 0 \text{ as } n \to \infty.$$

This proves the following:

Theorem 6. All but a vanishing fraction of monotone functions f in F_n have $MC(f) \ge C(f) \gtrsim \sqrt{\frac{2}{\pi}} \cdot \frac{2^n}{n^{3/2}}$.

As with general networks, no non-trivial lower bounds are known on the monotone complexity of particular concrete single functions. However, for sets of monotone functions, considerable success has been achieved. Several such results follow from a general theorem about graphs due to Pippenger and Valiant [16,27].

Theorem 7. Let $G = (V,E)$ be an undirected graph with vertices V and edges E. Let $X,Y \subseteq V$, $X \cap Y = \emptyset$, and let $\mathcal{P} = \{P_1, \ldots, P_k\}$, where each P_i is a set of vertex-disjoint paths from X to Y. Assume further that for every $x \in X$, $y \in Y$, there is a path from x to y in $P = \bigcup_i P_i$. Then $|E| \ge \frac{c|X| \cdot |Y|}{|\mathcal{P}|} \log(|X| + |Y|)$.

To apply this theorem, we must show the existence of sets of disjoint paths with the required properties. This is where we make use of the assumption of monotonicity

† $r(n) \lesssim s(n)$ $(s(n) \gtrsim r(n))$ iff $\limsup_{n\to\infty} \frac{r(n)}{s(n)} \le 1$, where $r,s: \mathbb{N} \to \mathbb{R}$.

<u>Definition</u>. Let $\tau_k^n(x_1, \ldots, x_n) = \begin{cases} 1 \text{ if } \sum_i x_i (= |\{x_i \mid x_i = 1\}|) \geq k; \\ 0 \text{ otherwise.} \end{cases}$

τ_k^n is the <u>threshold-k</u> function of n arguments. <u>Boolean sorting</u> of n arguments is the set

$$BS_n = \{\tau_k^n \mid 1 \leq k \leq n\} \subseteq F_n.$$

The following corollary to Theorem 7 was originally proved directly by Lamagna and Savage [7].

<u>Corollary 8</u>. $MC(BS_n) \geq cn \log n$ for some $c > 0$.

<u>Proof</u>. Let η compute BS_n. Let $X = \{x_0, \ldots, x_{n-1}\}$ be the source vertices of η and let $Y = \{y_0, \ldots, y_{n-1}\}$ be vertices of η such that $\xi_{y_k} = \tau_{k+1}^n$, $0 \leq k \leq n-1$.

We define a family $\mathcal{P} = \{P_0, \ldots, P_{n-1}\}$ of sets of vertex-disjoint paths. Intuitively, each set P_k is obtained by initially setting all inputs to zero and then turning them on one at a time. Since η computes BS_n, the outputs also turn on one at a time. Clearly, if an output changes as a result of a change in a single input, there must be a path in the network connecting the input to the output on which every vertex changes value. By monotonicity, every vertex on that path changes from zero to one when the input is turned on. Thus, each such path is distinct from those previously obtained. These paths comprise the set P_k. By varying the order of turning on the inputs, we obtain in this way each of the sets in $\mathcal{P}$.

More precisely, for $0 \leq k \leq n-1$, $0 \leq j \leq n$, let $\alpha_{k,j} \in B^n$ be the input vector whose i^{th} component is given by

$$(\alpha_{k,j})_i = \begin{cases} 1 & \text{if } i = k + \ell (\text{mod } n) \text{ for some } \ell,\ 0 \leq \ell < j; \\ 0 & \text{otherwise.} \end{cases}$$

Let $G_{k,j} = \{v \in \text{vertices}(\eta) \mid \xi_v(\alpha_{k,j}) = 1\}$. Since $\alpha_{k,j+1} \geq \alpha_{k,j}$, then $G_{k,j+1} \supseteq G_{k,j}$ by the monotonicity of η. Let $D_{k,j} = G_{k,j+1} - G_{k,j}$, $0 \leq j < n$. Clearly, the sets $D_{k,0}, \ldots, D_{k,n-1}$ are pairwise disjoint. Since $\xi_{y_j}(\alpha_{k,j+1}) = 1$ and $\xi_{y_j}(\alpha_{k,j}) = 0$, $y_j \in D_{k,j}$. Also, $x_{k+j(\text{mod } n)} \in D_{k,j}$. An easy induction shows that to every node in $D_{k,j}$ there is a path from $x_{k+j(\text{mod } n)}$ consisting entirely of nodes in $D_{k,j}$. Let $p_{k,j}$ be such a path from $x_{k+j(\text{mod } n)}$ to y_j, and let $P_k = \{p_{k,j} \mid 0 \leq j < n\}$. Then P_k is the desired set of vertex-disjoint paths from X to Y.

It is easily verified that $\mathcal{P}$ satisfies the hypotheses of Theorem 7, and the lower bound immediately follows. □

For another application of this theorem, we consider networks which rotate a subset of their inputs under control of the remaining variables.

Definition. Let $R = \{g_0, \ldots, g_{n-1}\} \subseteq F_{n+p}$, $\beta \in B^p$. β causes an (n,r)-rotation in R if

$$g_j(x_0, \ldots, x_{n-1}, \beta_0, \ldots, \beta_{p-1}) = x_{j+r(\text{mod } n)}$$

for all $x_0, \ldots, x_{n-1} \in B$ and all $0 \le j \le n - 1$, where $(\beta_0, \ldots, \beta_{p-1}) = \beta$. R is an n-rotation set if for all r, $0 \le r \le n - 1$, there exists $\beta_r \in B^p$ which causes an (n,r)-rotation in R.

Corollary 9. There exists $c > 0$ such that for all n-rotation sets R, $MC(R) > cn \log$

Proof. The proof is identical to that of Corollary 8 except that we define

$$(\alpha_{k,j})_i = \begin{cases} 1 & \text{if } 0 \le i < n \text{ and } i = k + \ell(\text{mod } n) \text{ for some } \ell,\ 0 \le \ell < j; \\ 0 & \text{if } 0 \le i < n \text{ and } i \ne k + \ell(\text{mod } n) \text{ for any } \ell,\ 0 \le \ell < j; \\ \beta_{k,i-n} & \text{if } n \le i < n + p \end{cases}$$

where $\beta_r = (\beta_{r,0}, \ldots, \beta_{r,p-1})$ causes an (n,r)-rotation. □

Still a third application of Theorem 7 is to Boolean matrix product.

Definition. The Boolean matrix product of two n x n matrices $A = (a_{ij})$ and $B = (b_{ij})$ is the set $MP_n = \{c_{ij} \mid c_{ij} = \bigvee_{k=1}^{n} a_{ik} \wedge b_{kj},\ 1 \le i,j \le n\} \subseteq F_{2n^2}$.

Corollary 10. $C(MP_n) > cn^2 \log n$ for some $c > 0$ independent of n.

This bound was greatly improved using more refined techniques developed originally by Pratt [18].

Theorem 11 (Mehlhorn [10] and Paterson [14]). $MC(MP_n) = 2n^3 - n^2$. Moreover, the straightforward network obtained from the definition of MP_n is uniquely optimal to within the associativity and commutativity of the basic operations in M.

The lower bound techniques we have discussed so far depend critically on the monotone restriction, for asymptotically smaller networks are known using a full basis.

Theorem 12 (Muller and Preparata [12]). $C(BS_n) = O(n)$.

Theorem 13 (Fischer and Meyer [4]). $C(MP_n) = O(n^{\log_2 7} \cdot (\log n)^{1+\epsilon})$, for any $\epsilon > 0$.

The combinations of Corollary 8 with Theorem 12, and Theorem 11 with Theorem 13 establish that a considerable savings in the complexity of a network for a set of monotone functions can be realized by using negations. To discuss the extent of su savings, we define the gap between monotone and general combinational complexity.

Definition. Let $F \subseteq F_n$, F monotone. Then $GAP(F) = MC(F)/C(F)$. (If $C(F) = 0$, let $GAP(F) = 0$).

<u>Question</u>. How big is $\max\{\mathrm{GAP}(F) \mid F \subseteq F_n,\ F \text{ monotone}\}$ as a function of n?

It follows from Theorem 11 and 13 that $\mathrm{GAP}(MP_n) \gtrsim n^{\alpha}$ for any $\alpha < 3 - \log_2 7 \approx .19$. Just how much larger the maximum can be is not known -- it is not even known if the maximum grows exponentially in n. If a good upper bound on GAP(F) could be obtained, then a lower bound on MC(F) would translate into a lower bound on C(F), giving a new technique for obtaining lower bounds on combinational complexity.

4. Inversion Complexity

An obvious way to generalize the class of monotone functions is to consider those functions that can be realized by a network over the complete basis $\Delta = \{\wedge,\vee,\neg\}$ but using only a limited number of negations. The monotone functions are the extreme case in which no negations are permitted.

For a network η over Δ, let $I(\eta)$ = the number of negations in η. For $F \subseteq F_n$, define $I(F) = \min\{I(\eta) \mid \eta \text{ computes } F\}$.

I(F) can be characterized quite simply. Let $|F| = m$ and treat F as a function $B^n \to B^m$. A sequence $C = (\zeta_1,\zeta_2, \ldots, \zeta_k)$ of vectors $\zeta_i \in B^n$ is called a <u>chain</u> of length k. For such a chain, define

$$\mathrm{alt}_F(C) = |\{i \mid 1 \le i < k \text{ and } F(\zeta_i) \nleq F(\zeta_{i+1})\}|.$$

Let $A(F) = \max\{\mathrm{alt}_F(C) \mid C \text{ is a chain}\}$, and let $b(n) = \lceil \log_2(n+1) \rceil$.

<u>Theorem 14</u>. $I(F) = \lceil \log_2(A(F) + 1) \rceil$.

<u>Corollary 15</u>.

(a) $\max_{f \in F_n} I(f) = \lfloor \log_2(n+1) \rfloor$;

(b) $\max_{F \subseteq F_n} I(F) = \lceil \log_2(n+1) \rceil = b(n)$.

Theorem 14, stated for singleton sets F, and Corollary 15 are due to Markov and appear in [9]. Nakamura, Tokura and Kasami [13] and this author [3] give algorithms for finding a network for F with only $\lceil \log_2(A(F) + 1) \rceil$ negations. A proof that $I(F) \ge \lceil \log_2(A(F) + 1) \rceil$ also appears in [3].

We now define the <u>negation-restricted</u> complexity of a set $F \subseteq F_n$ such that $I(F) \le k$ to be

$$NC_k(F) = \min\{C^{\Delta}(\eta) \mid \eta \text{ is a network over } \Delta,\ \eta \text{ computes } F, \text{ and } I(\eta) \le k\}.$$

Note that $NC_0 = MC$.

As mentioned in the last section, little is known about the behavior of GAP(F), or even if it is bounded by a polynomial in the number of arguments of F. A natural generalization of GAP is to let $\mathrm{GAP}_k(F) = NC_k(F)/C(F)$. (If $C(F) = 0$, let $\mathrm{GAP}_k(F) = 0$.) Thus, $\mathrm{GAP}_k(F)$ is defined only for those F which can be realized with at most k negations and is an expression of the increase in network size when the number of negations is restricted to k. Note that $GAP_0(F)$ agrees with our previous definition of GAP(F).

In view of our inability to bound GAP(F) nontrivially from above, the following theorem and its corollary come as somewhat of a surprise.

Theorem 16. $NC_{b(n)}(F) \le 2 \cdot C^{\Delta}(F) + O(n^2 \log^2 n) \le 6 \cdot C(F) + O(n^2 \log^2 n)$ for all $F \subseteq F_n$.

Corollary 17. $GAP_{b(n)}(F) \le O(n \log^2 n)$ for all $F \subseteq F_n$.

Proof of Corollary 17. We say a function $f \in F_n$ depends on its ith argument if there exist $a_1, \ldots, a_{i-1}, a_{i+1}, \ldots, a_n \in B$ such that

$$f(a_1, \ldots, a_{i-1}, 0, a_{i+1}, \ldots, a_n) \ne f(a_1, \ldots, a_{i-1}, 1, a_{i+1}, \ldots, a_n).$$

Let $F \subseteq F_n$, let X be the set of argument positions upon which some function in $F-A_n$ depends, and let $m = |X| \le n$. (Recall that A_n is the set of initial functions, so the functions in $F-A_n$ must be computed by gates.) Let $F' \subseteq F_m$ be the restriction of $F-A_n$ to the argument positions in X. It is easily shown that $C(F') = C(F)$ and $NC_k(F') = NC_k(F)$. Also, $C(F') \ge m/2$ since we permit only gates of at most two inputs, and F' depends on all of its arguments. By Theorem 16,

$$GAP_{b(n)}(F') \le 6 + \frac{cm^2 \log^2 m}{C(F')}$$

for a fixed constant c. Hence,

$$GAP_{b(n)}(F) = GAP_{b(n)}(F') \le 6 + 2cm \log^2 m \le 6 + 2cn \log^2 n = O(n \log^2 n).$$

Note that $GAP_{b(n)}(F)$ can only be as large as $O(n \log^2 n)$ for F of low complexity; if $o(C(F)) = n^2 \log^2 n$, then $GAP_{b(n)}(F) \lesssim 6$. The behavior of $GAP_k(F)$ is not well-understood, however, for any $k < b(n)$.

Before proving Theorem 16, we generalize and strengthen Lemma 4. A monotone cover of a set of functions $F \subseteq F_n$ is a set $G \subseteq F_{2n}$ that contains a monotone cover of each function in F.

Lemma 18. Every $F \subseteq F_n$ has a monotone cover $G \subseteq F_{2n}$ such that $MC(G) \le 2 \cdot C^{\Delta}(F)$.

Proof. We proceed by induction on $C^{\Delta}(F)$.

Base: If $C^{\Delta}(F) = 0$, then F is monotone, so G is trivially constructed.
Induction: Let $s > 0$ and assume the lemma holds for all F' such that $C^{\Delta}(F') < s$. Let $C^{\Delta}(F) = s$ and let η be a network over Δ of cost s which computes F. By choosing an initial gate of η, F may be decomposed in one of three ways, depending on the label of the gate, for some $F' \subseteq F_{n+1}$:

1. $F(x_1, \ldots, x_n) = F'(x_i \vee x_j, x_1, \ldots, x_n)$;
2. $F(x_1, \ldots, x_n) = F'(x_i \wedge x_j, x_1, \ldots, x_n)$;
3. $F(x_1, \ldots, x_n) = F'(\neg x_i, x_1, \ldots, x_n)$.

$C^{\Delta}(F') \leq s - 1$ since a network for F' is obtained from $\mathfrak{h}$ by deleting the chosen gate. By the induction hypothesis, there is a monotone cover $G'(y,y',x_1,x_1',\ldots,x_n,x_n')$ of F' such that $MC(G') \leq 2\cdot C^{\Delta}(F')$. Define G according to the case that obtained above:

1. $G(x_1,x_1', \ldots, x_n,x_n') = G'(x_i \vee x_j, x_1' \wedge x_j', x_1,x_1', \ldots, x_n,x_n')$;
2. $G(x_1,x_1', \ldots, x_n,x_n') = G'(x_i \wedge x_j, x_i' \vee x_j', x_1,x_1', \ldots, x_n,x_n')$;
3. $G(x_1,x_1', \ldots, x_n,x_n') = G'(x_i',x_i,x_1,x_1', \ldots, x_n,x_n')$.

It follows easily using DeMorgan's law that G is a monotone cover for F. Also, $MC(G) \leq 2 + MC(G') \leq 2 + 2\cdot C^{\Delta}(F') \leq 2\cdot C^{\Delta}(F)$, proving the lemma for $C^{\Delta}(F) = s$. That the lemma holds for all s follows by induction. □

From Lemma 18 we see that any F can be realized with no negations and with only a factor 2 increase in complexity if the negations of the variables are available as inputs.

<u>Definition</u>. $V_n = \{x_1, \neg x_1, \ldots, x_n, \neg x_n\}$.

<u>Lemma 19</u>. $NC_{b(n)}(V_n) \leq O(n^2\log^2 n)$.

<u>Proof</u>. Let

$$\tau^n_{k,i}(x_1,\ldots,x_n) = \begin{cases} 1 & \text{if } \sum_{j\neq i} x_j \geq k; \\ 0 & \text{otherwise.} \end{cases}$$

Note that $\tau^n_{k,0}$ is the function τ^n_k defined previously in connection with Boolean sorting. We use the fact that

$$\begin{aligned} \neg x_i = 1 &\Leftrightarrow x_i = 0 \\ &\Leftrightarrow \forall k[\tau^n_{k,0}(x) = \tau^n_{k,i}(x)] \\ &\Leftrightarrow \forall k[\tau^n_{k,0}(x) \rightarrow \tau^n_{k,i}(x)] \\ &\Leftrightarrow \bigwedge_k[\neg \tau^n_{k,0}(x) \vee \tau^n_{k,i}(x)]. \end{aligned}$$

Thus, $\neg x_i$ can be computed from the functions $\neg \tau^n_{k,0}$ and $\tau^n_{k,i}$ using only $2n-1$ $\wedge$- and $\vee$-gates. It remains to compute $U^n_i = \{\tau^n_{k,i} \mid 1 \leq k \leq n\}$, $0 \leq i \leq n$, and $V^n = \{\neg \tau^n_{k,0} \mid 1 \leq k \leq n\}$.

<u>Fact</u> (Batcher [1]). $MC(U^n_i) \leq O(n \log^2 n)$.

It follows immediately that $MC(\bigcup_{i=0}^{n} U^n_i) \leq O(n^2\log^2 n)$.

To compute V^n, it suffices to find a network $\mathfrak{M}_n$ for any set of functions $\Gamma_n = \{\gamma^n_1, \ldots, \gamma^n_n\} \subseteq F_n$ with the property that

$$\gamma^n_i(\tau^n_{1,0}(x), \ldots, \tau^n_{n,0}(x)) = \neg \tau^n_{i,0}(x);$$

that is, when the inputs are sorted in decreasing order, γ_i^n is the complement of the ith input.

Let $n = 2^r - 1$. We define Γ_n inductively on r.

$r = 1$: $\gamma_1^1(x_1) = \neg x_1$.

$r > 1$: Let $m = 2^{r-1}$. For $1 \le j \le m - 1$, let

$$\delta_j^n(x_1, \ldots, x_n) = (x_j \wedge \neg x_m) \vee x_{j+m}.$$

Now define

$$\gamma_i^n(x_1, \ldots, x_n) = \begin{cases} \gamma_i^{m-1}(\delta_1^n(x), \ldots, \delta_{m-1}^n(x)) \wedge \neg x_m & \text{if } 1 \le i \le m-1; \\ \neg x_m & \text{if } i = m; \\ \gamma_{i-m}^{m-1}(\delta_1^n(x), \ldots, \delta_{m-1}^n(x)) \vee \neg x_m & \text{if } m+1 \le i \le n. \end{cases}$$

A network $\mathfrak{M}_n$ for Γ_n is pictured in Figure 1.

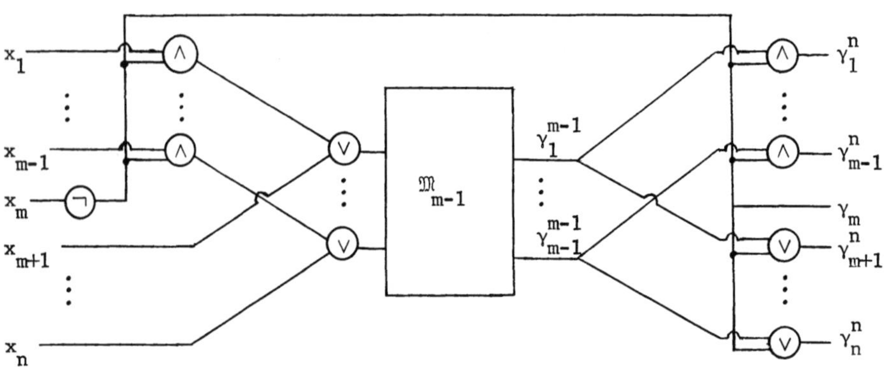

Figure 1. A network for Γ_n.

To see that Γ_n has the desired properties, we consider separately the two cases $x_m = 0$ and $x_m = 1$. Note that if the inputs are sorted in decreasing order, $x_m = 0$ implies that $x_k = 0$ for all $k > m$, and $x_m = 1$ implies $x_k = 1$ for all $k < m$. The remaining details are left to the reader. □

Proof of Theorem 16. Let $F \subseteq F_n$. By Lemma 18, there is a monotone cover G of F such that $MC(G) \le 2 \cdot C^{\Delta}(F)$. By Lemma 19, $NC_{b(n)}(V_n) \le O(n^2 \log^2 n)$. Since F can be realized as the composition of G with V_n, $NC_{b(n)}(F) \le 2 \cdot C^{\Delta}(F) + O(n^2 \log^2 n)$.

To complete the proof, we must show that $C^{\Delta}(F) \le 3 \cdot C(F)$. But that is immediate since for every $f \in F_1 \cup F_2$, $C^{\Delta}(f) \le 3$. Hence, each gate in a general network for F can be replaced by a sub-network of at most three gates from Δ.

5. Conclusion

Proving lower bounds on the combinational complexity of concrete functions is a difficult and challenging problem. Previous successes in establishing lower bounds for monotone networks and the known gaps between the monotone and general combinational complexity indicate the key role that negations play in determining combinational complexity.

We have investigated the way in which the complexity of a set of functions F decreases with the use of additional negations beyond the minimum number necessary to realize F. For sets F of maximum inversion complexity, at most a factor of 2 and an additive term of order $n^2\log^2 n$ is saved. However, for sets of lower inversion complexity, no interesting bounds are known on the amount of savings possible. Good upper bounds on the amount of such savings would enable lower bounds on combinational complexity to be concluded from lower bounds on the negation-restricted complexity.

Acknowledgment

The author is grateful to A.R. Meyer, M.S. Paterson, and N. Pippenger for several helpful discussions.

References

1. Batcher, K.E., Sorting networks and their applications, Proc. AFIPS Spring Joint Computer Conference, Vol. 32, AFIPS Press, Montvale, N.J.,(1968), 296-291.

2. Ehrenfeucht, A., Practical decidability, Report CU-CS-008-72, Dept. of Computer Science, Univ. of Colorado, Boulder, Colo., (1972), 14 pp.

3. Fischer, M.J., Lectures on network complexity, University of Frankfurt, Germany, June 1974, 25 pp.

4. Fischer M.J., and A.R. Meyer, Boolean matrix multiplication and transitive closure, Proc. 12th IEEE Symp. on Switching and Automata Theory (1971), 129-131.

5. Fischer, M.J. and M.O. Rabin, Super-exponential complexity of Presburger arithmetic. In Complexity of Computation, SIAM-AMS Proceedings, Vol. 7 (1974), 27-41.

6. Hsieh, W.N., L.H. Harper and J.E. Savage, A class of Boolean functions with linear combinational complexity, MAC Technical Memorandum 55, M.I.T. Project MAC, Cambridge, Mass. (1974), 38 pp.

7. Lamagna, E.A. and J.E. Savage, Combinational complexity of some monotone functions, Proc. 15th IEEE Symp. on Switching and Automata Theory (1974), 140-144.

8. Lupanov, O.B., A method of circuit synthesis, Izvestia v.u.z. Radiafizike, No. 1 (1958), 120-140.

9. Markov, A.A., On the inversion complexity of a system of functions, J. ACM 5, 4 (1958), 331-334.

10. Mehlhorn, K., On the complexity of monotone realizations of matrix multiplication, Technical report A74-11, Fachbereich Angewandte Mathematik und Informatik, Universität des Saarlandes, Saarbrucken, Germany (1974), 17 pp.

11. Meyer, A.R., Private communication.

12. Muller, D.E. and F.P. Preparata, Bounds to complexities of networks for sorting and for switching, J. ACM 22, 2 (1975), 195-201.

13. Nakamura, K., N. Tokura, and T. Kasami, Minimal negative gate networks, IEEE Trans. Comp., Vol. C-21, No. 1 (1972), 5-11.

14. Paterson, M.S., Complexity of monotone networks for Boolean matrix product, Theoretical Computer Science 1, 1 (1975), to appear.

15. Paul, W.J., A 2.5 N-lower bound on the combinational complexity of Boolean functions, Proc. 7th ACM Symp. on Theory of Computing (1975), 27-36.

16. Pippenger, N., Private communication.

17. Pippenger, N., and M.J. Fischer, Relationships among complexity measures, in preparation.

18. Pratt, V.R., The power of negative thinking in multiplying Boolean matrices, Proc. 6th ACM Symp. on Theory of Computing (1974), 80-83.

19. Presburger, M., Über die Vollständigkeit eines gewissen Systems der Arithmetic ganzer Zahlen in welchem die Addition als einzige Operation hervortritt. Comptes-rendus du I Congrès des Mathématiciens des Pays Slaves, Warsaw (1930), 92-101, 395.

20. Savage, J.E., Computational work and time on finite machines, J. ACM 19, 4 (197 660-674.

21. Savage, J.E., The Complexity of Computing, manuscript, 1974.

22. Schnorr, C.P., The network complexity and the Turing machine complexity of finite functions, manuscript, University of Frankfurt, Germany (1975), 18 pp.

23. Schnorr, C.P., The combinational complexity of equivalence, Theoretical Compute Science, to appear.

24. Schnorr, C.P., Zwei lineare untere Schranken fur die Komplexität Boolescher Funktionen, Computing 13 (1974), 155-171.

25. Stockmeyer, L.J., The complexity of decision problems in automata theory and logic, Project MAC Technical Report 133, M.I.T., Cambridge, Mass. (1974), 224 p

26. Strassen, V., Berechnungen in partiellen Algebren endlichen Typs, Computing 11 (1973), 181-196.

27. Valiant, L.G., On non-linear lower bounds in computational complexity, Proc. 7th ACM Symposium on Theory of Computing (1975), 45-52.

The Network-Complexity of Equivalence and Other Applications of the Network Complexity

(Extended Abstract)

C. P. Schnorr
Fachbereich Mathematik
Universität Frankfurt

1. Introduction

Let $B = \{0,1\}$ be the set of Boolean values, let $V = \{x_i \mid i \in N\}$ be a countable set of Boolean variables and let Ω be the set of Boolean polynomials with variables in V.

We consider Boolean computations (i.e. logical networks) that are based on the set of all 16 binary Boolean operations $\sigma : B^2 \to B$.

A logical network β is a finite, directed, acyclic graph with labelled nodes such that

(1) every node ν has either 0 (i.e. ν is an entry) or 2 (i.e. ν is a non-entry) entering edges,

(2) every entry ν is labelled either with a variable or with a constant Boolean function,

(3) every non-entry ν is labelled with some binary Boolean operation $op(\nu)$ such that the entries of ν correspond to the arguments of $op(\nu)$.

In a natural way we associate with every node ν of β an output function $res_\beta^\nu \in \Omega$. We say β computes res_β^ν for all $\nu \in \beta$. Let cost(β) be the number of non-entries of β. We define the Network-Complexity of a set $F \subset \Omega$ of Boolean functions as

$$L(F) = \min \{cost(\beta) \mid \beta \text{ computes } F\}.$$

We believe that the network complexity is a natural measure for the complexity of Boolean functions. Observe that the asymptotical behaviour of the network complexity does not depend on the choice of the finite base of Boolean operations provided that this base is complete in the sense that every Boolean function can be computed from this base. The choice of the complete finite base only influences the network complexity up to a constant factor.

2. Network Complexity and Turing Machine Complexity

We compare the network complexity and the Turing Machine complexity of finite functions. In the following we consider programs on multitape Turing machines with binary input-output alphabet. In an efficient program p for a function f at least some of the following complexity measures should be rather small with respect to all other programs for f:

1) the time bound T_p of the program
2) the storage requirement S_p of the program, i.e. the total number of all tape squares that are handled by the heads during the computation on inputs of f.
3) the size $\|p\|$, i.e. the number of instructions of the program p.

Experience indicates that we cannot always minimize each of these measures by a unique program. So we expect some trade-off's between these measures. Much attention has been paid to the asymptotical behaviour of S_p and T_p for large inputs. However, the size of the program might also be considerably interesting for the computation of finite functions. It is usually rather hard to write and to check large programs. Therefore, a "table look up"-program for a finite function might be fast and might use little space but it might nevertheless be inefficient. In particular it might be very difficult to find such a "table look up"-program.

In the following we relate the above complexity measures for programs p to the network complexity of the Boolean functions that are computed by p. M. Fischer [2] proved that the network complexity L(f) of $f \in \Omega$ yields a lower bound on the product $c_p\ T_p\ \lg T_p$ for every Turing program p for f. However, his proof gives no information on the constant c_p that obviously depends on the program p. We improve this result by involving the size $\|p\|$ and the space requirements S_p of program p.

We shall also generalize previous results in that we consider Turing-Machines with oracles. Our concept of an <u>oracle-Turing-Machine</u> is as follows. There is an additional input tape with some finite or infinite inscription A. A is called the oracle. Relative to a fixed oracle A a Turing program acts like a standard Turing program. There are no special oracle-instructions. Let A be an oracle and let p be a Turing-program then we use the following notations:

$res_p^A : B^* \to B$ is the partial 0-1 valued function which is computed by program p with oracle A. Let $res_p^A(n)$ be the restriction $res_p^A|_{B^n}$.

$T_p^A(n)$ is the minimal running time of program p with oracle A on inputs $x \in B^n$

$S_p^A(n)$ is the total number of tape squares that are used in the computation of p on inputs $x \in B^n$

$\|p\|$ is the number of instructions of program p.

Theorem 1 [7]

$\exists c \in N: \forall \text{programs } p: \forall \text{oracles } A: \forall n:$

$L(res_p^A(n)) \leq c \cdot \|p\| \cdot T_p^A(n) \cdot \lg(S_p^A(n))$

Hereby c depends on the number of tapes and the size of the alphabet. c also depends on how the set of possible Turing-instructions is defined.

There is a converse to Theorem 1:

Theorem 2 [7]

$\forall f \in \Omega$ (depending on n variables): $\exists$ program p with oracle A for f:

$\|p\| \cdot T_p^A(n) \cdot \lg S_p^A(n) \leq O(L(f) \lg L(f))^2$

The complete proofs of Theorems 1,2 can be found in [7].

3. The Network Complexity of Equivalence

Consider the functions $and(n) = \bigwedge_{i=1}^{n} x_i$, $nor(n) = \bigwedge_{i=1}^{n} \neg x_i$,

$Eq(n) = and(n) \vee nor(n)$

Theorem 3

$L(Eq(n)) = 2n-3$

$L\{and(n), nor(n))\} = 2n-2 = L(and(n)) + L(nor(n))$

(i.e. and(n), nor(n) are independent).

One interesting feature of this theorem is that there exist many structurally different optimal computations for Eq(n) as for instance

$$\bigwedge_{i=1}^{n-1} [x_i = x_{i+1}] \quad , \quad \bigwedge_{i=1}^{n-1} [x_i = x_n]$$

We believe that in such a case there are particular difficulties to evaluate the exact value of the network complexity.
Theorem 3 also implies that the operations $\ominus$ and $\oplus$ do not help in the computation of {and(n),nor(n)} since $\bigwedge_{i=1}^{n} x_i$, $\bigwedge_{i=1}^{n} \neg x_i$ is an optimal computation.

The proof of Theorem 3 uses an inductive argument. The different cases of the induction step are covered by 3 Lemmata. The complete proof of these Lemmata will appear in [5].

Lemma 1

Let ß be an optimal computation for Eq(n). Suppose that there is a variable x_i in ß which is input to exactly one gate ν and this gate is either a $\ominus$ -gate or a $\oplus$ -gate. Then we can compute Eq(n-1) by fixing $res_{ß}^{\nu}$ either to 0 or to 1 and by eliminating at least 2 nodes in ß.

An (x_i,x_j)-path in a logical network is a pair of edge-disjoint paths (w,v) such that w starts at an x_i-variable and v starts at an x_j-variable and w,v have the same head:

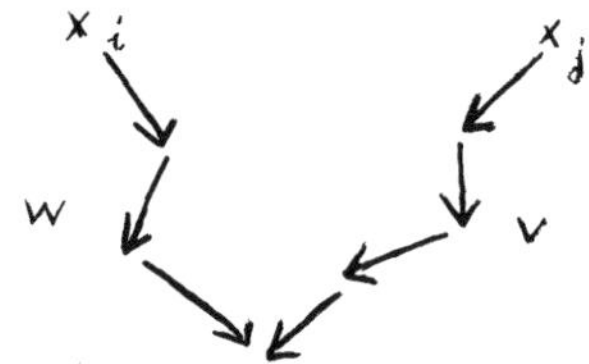

The length of an (x_i,x_j)-path is the total number of edges. Let $\Gamma_ß(x_i,x_j)$ be the minimal length of an (x_i,x_j)-path in ß.

Lemma 2

Suppose ß satisfies (1) - (3): (1) ß computes Eq(n), (2) there is a unique (x_i,x_j)-path in ß, (3) x_i,x_j are not entry of any $\ominus$ -gate and of any $\oplus$ -gate. Then there is a computation ß for Eq(n) which satisfies (1) - (3) such that $\Gamma_{\bar{ß}}(x_i,x_j) < \Gamma_ß(x_i,x_j)$ and $\text{cost}(\bar{ß}) = \text{cost}(ß)$.

Observe that the reduction

$$ß \mapsto \bar{ß} \mapsto \bar{\bar{ß}} \mapsto \bar{\bar{\bar{ß}}} \cdots\cdots$$

according to Lemma 2 can only be applied finitely often since each ste reduces $\Gamma_ß(x_i,x_j)$.

Lemma 3

Let ß be a Boolean computation depending on the variables in V(ß). Suppose that for all $x_i,x_j \in V(ß)$ there exist at least 2 different (x_i,x_j)-paths. This implies $\text{cost}(ß) \geq 2\cdot\|V(ß)\|-2$.

It can easily be seen that Lemmata 1-3 cover all cases of an inductive proof for L(Eq(n)) = 2n-3. The same kind of arguments can be used to prove L{and(n),nor(n)} = 2n-2.

The Boolean functions and(n),nor(n) are independent in the sense that

$$L\{\text{and}(n),\text{nor}(n)\} = L(\text{and}(n)) + L(\text{nor}(n))$$

and we conjecture that this independence holds for any choice of a co lete base of Boolean operations. Independence seems to be a basic notion of complexity theory. It should be observed that many fast algorithms which improve standard algorithms are based on hidden dependencies of certain functions. For example, Strassen's fast matrix multiplication yields a particularly interesting example of such a hidden dependence:

Theorem 4

There exist sets $F,G \subset \Omega$ of Boolean functions such that (1) F,G depend on disjoint sets of variables and (2) $L(F \cup G) < L(F) + L(G)$.

Proof Let A_n be an (n,n)-Boolean matrix and let x be a vector of n Boolean variables. We associate with A_n and x the Boolean function $\tilde{A}_n : B^n \to B$ as follows: $\tilde{A}_n : x \mapsto A_n \cdot x$ where $A_n \cdot x$ is the Boolean matrix product with respect to addition mod(2) and multiplication mod(2). There exist 2^{n^2} different Boolean (n,n)-matrices. Therefore, a standard counting argument implies that for all n there exists A_n such that $L(A_n) \geq c\, n^2/\lg n$ where $c > 0$ is some fixed real number. Let $x^1, x^2, \ldots, x^n$ be a set of n-vectors that consist of disjoint sets of Boolean variables. Let $\tilde{A}_n^i$ be the function $\tilde{A}_n^i : x^i \mapsto A_n \cdot x^i$. If Theorem 4 does not hold then

$$L(A_n^1, A_n^2, \ldots., A_n^n) \geq c\, n^3 \lg n$$

However, $A_n x^1, A_n x^2, \ldots., A_n x^n$ is the matrix product of A_n and the matrix with column vectors $x^1, \ldots., x^n$. Therefore, Strassen's fast algorithm for matrix multiplication yields

$$L(A_n^1, \ldots, A_n^n) \leq O(n^{\lg 7})$$

This proves Theorem 4 by contradiction.

. Satisfiability is quasi-linear complete in NQL

fundamental problem of computer science is the power of non-determin- stic machines. Cook raised the question whether the classes P (NP,resp.) f all decision problems that can be solved within polynomially bounded time on deterministic (non-deterministic, resp.) Turing-machines coincide. Cook proved that Satisfiability (i.e. the problem to decide whether a given conjunctive Boolean normal form is satisfiable) is polynomial complete in NP. This means that Satisfiability is in NP and for every problem A in NP there is a polynomially time bounded reduction of A to Satisfiability. Cook, Karp and others established a long list of polynomial complete problems in NP.

These results are improved by the following Theorem 5 which shows that Satisfiability is one of the most hardest polynomial complete problems in NP. In order to formulate this result we restrict the class of pol nomially time bounded reductions.

A time bound T(n) is called <u>quasi-linear</u> in n if $T(n) = O(n(\lg n)^k)$ fo some fixed k. Consider the following classes of functions and problem

Let QL^f be the class of functions that are computable on Turing machin in quasi-linear time. Let QL be the class of decision problems that c be solved on Turing-machines in deterministid quasi-linear time.

Let NQL be the class of decision problems that can be solved on Turing machines in non-deterministic quasi-linear time.

Then we can prove that Satisfiybility is quasi-linear complete in NQL

<u>Theorem 5</u> [8]

(1) Satisfiability is in NQL

(2) $\forall A \in NQL : \exists \psi \in QL^f$:

$[\forall x : x \in A : \iff \psi(x)$ is satisfiable$]$

(i.e. ψ is a quasi-linear reduction of A to Satisfiability)

An immediate consequence of Theorem 5 is the following

<u>Corollary</u> QL = NQL <=> Satisfiability $\in$ QL

The main step in the proof of part (2) in Theorem 5 is an application of the simulation of Turing-machines by logical networks according to Theorem 1.

The question whether QL = NQL? is very much like the famous P = NP?-problem. However, a proof for QL $\neq$ NQL seems to be not as hard as for P $\neq$ NP. Using Theorem 1 it would satisfy to prove a slightly higher than quasi-linear lower bound on the network complexity of Satisfiability. However, a proof for P $\neq$ NP by this way requires a superpolynomial lower bound on the network complexity of Satisfiability.

References

1. Cook, S.A.: The Complexity of Theorem-Proving Procedures. Symposium on Theory of Computing 1971. 151-158

2. Fischer, M.J.: Lectures on Network Complexity. Preprint Universität Frankfurt, 1974

3. Karp, R.M.: Reducibility among Combinatorial Problems. in: Complexity of Computer Computations. R.E. Miller and J.W. Thatcher, Eds., Plenum Press, New York (1972) 85-1o4

4. Paul, W.J.: 2.25N - Lower Bound on the Combinational Complexity of Boolean Functions. Symposium on Theory of Computing, 1975

5. Schnorr, C.P.: The Combinational Complexity of Equivalence. Preprint Universität Frankfurt 1975, to appear in Theoretical Computer Science

6. Schnorr, C.P.: Zwei lineare untere Schranken für die Komplexität Boolescher Funktionen. Computing 13, (1974)

7. Schnorr, C.P.: The Network Complexity and the Turing Machine Complexity of Finite Functions. Preprint Universität Frankfurt, 1975

8. Schnorr, C.P.: Satisfiability is Quasi-Linear Complete in NQL. Preprint Universität Frankfurt, 1975.

TEST D'ISOMORPHIE D'HYPERGRAPHES PLANAIRES

Max FONTET
Institut de Programmation
UNIVERSITE PIERRE ET MARIE CURIE
PARIS

1. INTRODUCTION

Le test d'isomorphie de deux graphes ou de deux hypergraphes est un problème dont on ignore s'il est polynomial complet ou non au sens de la classification des problèmes combinatoires introduite par Karp [10] .

Notre approche de ce problème consiste à utiliser les liens profonds entre le groupe d'automorphismes d'un graphe ou d'un hypergraphe et leurs représentations sur une surface de genre minimum [9]. Ces liens sont particulièrement faciles à mettre en évidence lorsque les hypergraphes sont planaires . En effet, toute représentation planaire d'un hypergraphe connexe est équivalente à la donnée d'une hypercarte [2,8].

Nos résultats fournissent une nouvelle caractérisation des hypercartes planaires (théorème 1) et une formulation algébrique des propriétés de la congruence d'automorphismes de ces hypercartes (théorème 2). Le problème du calcul de cette congruence se réduit alors, au sens de Karp [10], au calcul d'une partition d'imprimitivité associée à une équivalence.

Nous retrouvons ainsi le résultat de Hopcroft et Tarjan [6] sur l'existence d'un test d'isomorphie de deux graphes planaires 3 - connexes en un temps $O(n \log_2 n)$ où n est le nombre de sommets de chaque graphe.

Nous montrons que la même méthode permet de calculer explicitement le groupe d'automorphismes d'un hypergraphe planaire 3-connexe en un temps $O(n^2)$ où n est le nombre de sommets de l'hypergraphe (théorème 3).

2. GENERALITES - DEFINITIONS

Nous rappelons qu'une carte C est un triplet (B, α, σ) formé d'un ensemble B dont les éléments sont appelés brins et d'un couple de permutations (α, σ) de $\mathfrak{S}_B$ engendrant un groupe de permutations transitif sur B tel que α soit une involution sans point fixe.

Edmonds [3] en établissant l'identité entre cette notion combinatoire de carte et la notion de carte topologique définie sur une surface orientée a permis une approche de ces problèmes topologiques.

Cori [2] a étendu ces résultats aux hypergraphes en introduisant la notion d'hypercarte qui est une carte pour laquelle on supprime la restriction sur la permutation α.

Etant donné un hypergraphe [1] $\mathcal{H}=(X,\mathcal{E})$ avec $\mathcal{E}=\{E_y ; y \in y,\ E_y \subset X\}$, on peut lui associer son graphe d'incidence $\mathcal{G} = (X \cup Y, R)$ défini par : $(x,y) \in R$ ssi $x \in E_y$. On constate alors que l'hypergraphe $\mathcal{H}$ et le graphe $\mathcal{G}$ ont les mêmes propriétés algébriques. En particulier, il existe une correspondance canonique entre les hypercartes de $\mathcal{H}$ et les cartes de $\mathcal{G}$ [2,14].

Pour énoncer nos résultats, définissons une notion de cheminement sur les cartes qui s'étend aux hypercartes par l'intermédiaire de la correspondance précédente. Etant donné une carte C = (B, α, σ), on appelle chemin une suite de brins $(b_1, b_2, \ldots, b_n)$ telle que $b_i = b_{i-1}\alpha\,\sigma^{k_i}$ $(k_i \in Z)$. Un circuit sera un chemin tel que $b_1 = b_n$ et une face un circuit tel que soit $k_i = 1$ $(2 \leq i \leq n)$, soit $k_i = -1$ $(2 \leq i \leq n)$.

3. RESULTATS

3.1. Caractérisation des hypercartes planaires

Notre premier théorème donne une caractérisation des hypercartes planaires par un théorème équivalent au théorème de Mac Lane pour les graphes planaires [10].

THEOREME I : Une hypercarte 2 - connexe est planaire ssi pour tout circuit c, il existe une face f telle que $c \cap f$ soit un chemin.

La preuve de ce théorème se fait par réduction du problème à un problème analogue sur les cartes que l'on prouve être équivalente à une formulation du théorème de Mac Lane adaptée aux cartes [5].

3.2. Caractérisation de la congruence d'automorphismes d'une hypercarte.

A tout brin b d'une hypercarte H, on associe le quadruplet d'entiers (t, u, v, w) où t (resp. u, v, w) est la longueur du cycle de α (resp. σ, $\sigma\alpha$, $\alpha\sigma$) contenant b.

Nous définissons comme Hopcroft et Tarjan [6] une équivalence d'indiscernabilité I_H sur les brins de l'hypercarte H par :

$b\ I_H\ b' \Leftrightarrow (t, u, v, w) = (t', u', v', w')$

Soit $\hat{I}_H$ la congruence la plus grossière contenue dans I_H. Soit ρ_H la congruence d'automorphismes de l'hypercarte H.

THEOREME 2 : Soit H une hypercarte planaire 2-connexe, on a alors $\hat{I}_H = \rho_H$.

La preuve de ce théorème se trouve en appendice.

On déduit du théorème les deux corollaires suivants :

COROLLAIRE 1 : Pour un hypergraphe $\mathcal{H}$ planaire 3-connexe, le calcul de la congruence d'automorphismes se réduit, au sens de Karp [10], au calcul de $\hat{I}_H$ pour l'une de ses représentations H.

COROLLAIRE 2 : Pour tester l'isomorphisme de deux hypergraphes planaires 3-connexes $\mathcal{H}$ et $\mathcal{H}'$, il suffit de calculer $\hat{I}$ pour une représentation de $\mathcal{H} \cup \mathcal{H}'$ où l'un des deux hypergraphes est représenté entièrement dans une face de la représentation de l'autre.

Le calcul de $\hat{I}_H$ se fait en étendant aux hypergraphes, selon la méthode de Penaud [12], l'algorithme de Hopcroft et Tarjan [6] convenablement adapté.

3.3. Calcul du groupe d'automorphismes d'un hypergraphe planaire 3-connexe.

Les représentations d'un hypergraphe $\mathcal{H}$ planaire 3-connexe sont données par deux hypercartes $H = (B, \alpha, \sigma)$ et $H^{-1} = (B, \alpha^{-1}, \sigma^{-1})$. Le groupe d'automorphismes de $\mathcal{H}$ est induit par l'ensemble des permutations de $\mathfrak{S}_B$ qui commutent avec les permutations α et σ ou qui les inversent. Ces permutations se caractérisent par leurs décompositions en produit d'involutions [4]. On obtient ainsi le résultat suivant:

THEOREME 3 : Le calcul effectif des éléments du groupe d'automorphismes d'un hypergraphe planaire 3-connexe peut se faire en un temps proportionnel au carré du nombre de sommets de l'hypergraphe .

4. CONCLUSION

Nos résultats donnent une justification simple de l'algorithme de Hopcroft et Tarjan et nous en obtenons une extension et une application. L'intérêt de cet algorithme reste entier bien que Hopcroft et Wong aient fourni un algorithme de test de l'isomorphie de deux graphes planaires en un temps linéaire [6]. De leur avis même, cet algorithme n'est pas efficace à cause d'une constante très élevée et n'a donc qu'un intérêt théorique.

Nous venons d'obtenir un nouvel algorithme effectuant le test de l'isomorphie de deux hypergraphes planaires en temps linéaire ; nous en testons actuellement l'efficacité.

APPENDICE

PREUVE DU THEOREME 2

La première étape de la preuve consiste à réduire le problème à un problème identique sur les cartes. Pour cela, on associe à l'hypercarte $H = (B, \alpha, \sigma)$ une carte bipartie $C = (B', \alpha' \ \sigma')$ définie comme suit :

$B' = B \times \{0, 1\}$

$(b, 0)\ \sigma' = (b\sigma, 0) \qquad (b,0)\ \alpha' = (b,1)$

$(b, 1)\ \sigma = (b\alpha, 1) \qquad (b,1)\ \alpha' = (b,0)$

L'hypercarte H est planaire ssi la carte C l'est [14] ; de même, l'hypercarte H est 2-connexe ssi la carte C l'est.

Les congruences d'automorphismes et d'indiscernabilité de H et de C sont reliées par la proposition suivante :

PROPOSITION 1 :

$$b\ \hat{I}_H\ b' \Leftrightarrow (b,1)\ \hat{I}_C\ (b',1) \Leftrightarrow (b,0)\ \hat{I}_C\ (b',0)$$

$$b\ \rho_H\ b' \Leftrightarrow (b,1)\ \rho_C\ (b',1) \Leftrightarrow (b,0)\ \rho_C\ (b',0)$$

PREUVE : Etant donné un brin b de l'hypercarte H, on note (t, u, v, w) le quadruplet associé définissant I_H. Le quadruplet associé au brin (b, 0) de la carte C est alors (2, u, 2v, 2w) et celui associé au brin (b,1) (2, t, 2w, 2v) . On a donc

$$b\ I_H\ b' \Leftrightarrow \begin{cases}(b,0)\ I_C\ (b',0)\\(b,1)\ I_C\ (b',1)\end{cases}$$

On en déduit la caractérisation de $\hat{I}_H$ en regardant l'action de α, σ (resp. α', σ') sur les classes ainsi définies.

La caractérisation de ρ_H traduit le fait qu'un automorphisme de H définit un automorphisme de C et qu'inversement un automorphisme de C respectant la coloration des brins définit un automorphisme de H.

On en déduit le corollaire suivant :

COROLLAIRE 1 :

$$\hat{I}_H = \rho_H \Leftrightarrow \hat{I}_C = \rho_C$$

Introduisons quelques définitions supplémentaires sur le cheminement dans une carte.

Un circuit est élémentaire ssi les brins extrêmes sont les seuls brins égaux.

Un circuit (resp. chemin) est propre ssi aucuns brins ne se correspondent dans l'involution α .

Un circuit est complétement impropre ssi tous les brins se correspondent deux à deux dans l'involution α.

Deux chemins $C = (b_1, \ldots, b_n)$ et $C' = (b'_1, \ldots b'_{n'})$ se correspondent ssi $n = n'$ et $k_i = k'_i$ $(2 \leqslant i \leqslant n)$.

On a immédiatement le lemme suivant :

Lemme : Dans une carte C , tout circuit se décompose en circuits élémentaires propres et en circuits élémentaires complétement impropres.

Nous avons une première caractérisation de la congruence d'automorphismes d'une carte par la proposition suivante :

PROPOSITION 2 :

Etant donnée une carte C, ρ_C est la congruence θ la plus grossière telle que si deux brins sont congrus modulo θ, tout circuit contenant l'un des brins correspond à un circuit contenant l'autre.

PREUVE : On note G le groupe engendré par les permutations α et σ, et G_b le sous-groupe de G fixant le brin b .

Cette proposition est la traduction d'un résultat classique sur les automates [13] affirmant que ρ_C est la congruence θ la plus grossière telle que

$$b \equiv b' \quad \mod \theta \Leftrightarrow G_b = G_{b'}$$

On obtient l'énoncé donné en remarquant qu'il y a une bijection entre les éléments de G_b et les circuits contenant b ou $b\alpha$.

Il est maintenant possible de terminer la preuve du théorème 2 :

Preuve du théorème 2

Un automorphisme de carte échange respectivement les sommets, les arêtes et les faces de la carte ; il conserve en particulier leur cardinalité. On a donc : $\rho_C \subseteq \hat{I}_C$

Pour avoir l'inclusion dans l'autre sens, il suffit de montrer d'après la proposition 2 que si deux brins sont indiscernables, tout circuit contenant l'un correspond à un circuit contenant l'autre. On peut ne considérer que des circuits élémentaires propres ou des circuits élémentaires complétement impropres en vertu du lemme sur la décomposition des circuits.

Un circuit élémentaire complétement impropre contenant un brin b se décompose en deux chemins propres disjoints l'un contenant b et l'autre contenant $b\alpha$. On est donc ramené exclusivement à des chemins ou des circuits propres.

Il suffit alors de montrer que si deux brins sont indiscernables, tout circuit élémentaire propre contenant l'un correspond à un circuit contenant l'autre.

Le théorème 1 fournit une décomposition en faces de tout circuit élémentaire propre. D'après la définition de l'indiscernabilité, si deux brins b et b' sont indiscernables, une face contenant l'un correspond à une face contenant l'autre. On montre alors par récurrence sur le nombre de faces définissant une décomposition d'un circuit élémentaire propre que si deux brins b et b' sont indiscernables, un circuit élémentaire propre contenant l'un correspond à un circuit élémentaire propre contenant l'autre.

BIBLIOGRAPHIE

[1] BERGE, C. : Graphes et hypergraphes Dunod 1970.

[2] CORI, R. : Un code pour les graphes planaires et ses applications Thèse PARIS 1973 .

[3] EDMONDS, J.R. : A combinatorial representation for oriented polyhedral surfaces M.A. Thesis University of Maryland (U.S.A.) 1960.

[4] FONTET, M. : Un résultat en théorie des groupes de permutations et son application au calcul effectif du groupe d'automorphismes d'un automate fini dans 2nd Colloquium on Automata, languages and programming Saarbrücken (1974) 335-341.

[5] FONTET, M. : Une caractérisation des hypercartes planaires (en préparation)

[6] HOPCROFT, J.E., R.E. TARJAN : A V log V algorithm for isomorphism of triconnected planar graphs J C S S 7 323-331 (1973)

[7] HOPCROFT, J.E., WONG : Linear time algorithm for isomorphism of planar graphs (Preliminary report) 6th ACM SIGACT (1974)

[8] JACQUES, A. : Sur le genre d'une paire de substitutions, C.R. Acad. Sci. PARIS 267 625-627 (1968)

[9] JACQUES, A. : Constellations et propriétés algébriques des graphes topologique Thèse 3ème cycle PARIS 1969.

[10] KARP, R.M. : Reducibility among combinatorial problems in Complexity of computer computations Plenum Press IBM Symposium (1972)

[11] MAC LANE, S. : A structural characterisation of planar combinatorial graphs Duke Math. 3 460-472 (1937)

[12] PENAUD, J.G. : Quelques propriétés des hypergraphes planaires - Thèse Docteur Ingénieur Bordeaux 1974.

[13] PERRIN, D., PERROT, J-F. : Congruences et automorphismes des Automates finis Acta Informatica 1 159-172 (1971)

[14] WALSH, R.S. : Hypermaps versus bipartite maps , J. Comb. Theory (B) 18 155-163 (1975)

OBERE UND UNTERE SCHRANKE FÜR DIE KOMPLEXITÄT VON BOOLESCHEN FUNKTIONEN

Hanke Bremer
Institut für angewandte Mathematik
Joh. Wolfg. Goethe Univ. Frankfurt

Eine Menge Boolescher Funktionen heiße n - stellig , wenn alle enthaltenen Funktionen auf den gleichen n Variablen definiert sind. Alle n-stelligen Mengen der Mächtigkeit t werden zu

$$M_{t,n} = \{ F \mid |F| = t,\ F \text{ ist n-stellig} \}$$

zusammengefaßt. Im folgenden soll eine obere und eine untere Schranke für die Komplexität von F in Abhängigkeit von n und t angegeben werden. Zur Berechnung von F seien als o - stellige Operationen mit den Kosten o die Konstanten o und 1 und die Projektionen $x_1, \ldots, x_n$ zugelassen, als 2-stellige Operationen die Multiplikation und die Addition mod 2 mit den Kosten 1.

Lemma 1

Für die Komplexität L(F) einer Menge Boolescher Funktionen F aus $M_{t,n}$ gilt

$$L(F) \leq \frac{t2^n}{\mathrm{ldt}} \left(1 + c \frac{\mathrm{ldldt}}{\mathrm{ldt}} \right) .$$

Darin ist c eine von n und t unabhängige Konstante.

Der Beweis ist in [1] angegeben , jedoch ohne Abschätzung des Fehlergliedes. Dazu werden erst alle Produkte aus Variablen und negierten Variablen berechnet. Diese 2^n Produkte werden in $\lceil 2^n/p \rceil$ Gruppen zu je p Stück geteilt. In jeder Gruppe werden alle Linearkombinationen berechnet , aus denen dann durch Addition die t Ergebnisse zusammengesetzt werden. Es kommt die Schranke des Lemmas heraus, die jedoch nur für große t gut ist. Deshalb der folgende Satz.

Satz 2

Für die Komplexität L(F) einer Menge Boolescher Funktionen F aus $M_{t,n}$ gilt

$$L(F) \leq \frac{t2^n}{\mathrm{ld}\, t2^n} \left(1 + c \, \frac{\mathrm{ld}\,\mathrm{ld}\, t2^n}{\mathrm{ld}\, t2^n} \right) .$$

Darin ist c eine von n und t unabhängige Konstante.

Der Beweis ist für eine Funktion ohne Abschätzung des Fehlergliedes in [1] gegeben. Es muß jedoch der Parameter m genauer gewählt und schärfer abgeschätzt werden, damit das Verfahren für Mengen F kleiner Mächtigkeit zum Ziel führt. Für große F reicht schon Lemma 1 aus. Eine Berechnung von $F = \{f_1,\ldots,f_t\} \in M_{t,n}$ ist gegeben durch die Zerlegung

$$f_i(x_1,\ldots,x_n) = \sum_{e_{m+1},\ldots,e_n \in \{0,1\}} g^{(i)}_{e_{m+1},\ldots,e_n}(x_1,\ldots,x_m) \cdot x_{m+1}^{e_{m+1}} \ldots x_n^{e_n} ,$$

worin die Funktionenmenge $G = \{g^{(i)}_{\ldots}(\ldots)\}$ in $M_{s,m}$ mit $s \leq t2^{n-m}$ liegt. G wird nach dem Lemma 1 berechnet und F aus G und den restlichen Variablen gemäß der Zerlegung.

Nun soll eine untere Schranke für L(F) von der gleichen Größenordnung gezeigt werden, wozu jedoch zwei Ausnahmen zu machen sind. Einmal müssen allzu einfache Funktionen ausgenommen werden, die aber nur selten auftreten. Außerdem führt die angewendete Abzählung der Berechnungen nur für relativ kleine Mengen F zum Ziel. Deshalb die zwei folgenden Definitionen.

$$M = \bigcup_{t \leq 2^{2^{n/4}}} M_{t,n}$$

$N \subset M$ heißt Nullmenge, wenn

$$\lim_{t2^n \to \infty} \frac{|M_{t,n} \cap N|}{|M_{t,n}|} = 0 .$$

Satz 3

Für fast alle F aus M , d. h. für alle außerhalb einer Nullmenge N , gilt

$$L(F) \geq \frac{t2^n}{\mathrm{ld}\,t2^n} \left(1 - \frac{\mathrm{ld}\,\mathrm{ld}\,t2^n}{\mathrm{ld}\,t2^n} \right) ,$$

falls F aus $M_{t,n}$.

Zum Beweis des Satzes werden alle F aus M , für die die Ungleichung nicht gilt zur Menge N zusammengefaßt. Es bleibt zu zeigen , daß N eine Nullmenge ist , wozu die normalen Berechnungen mit vorgegebener Länge wie in [1] abgezählt werden.

Nun ist eine obere und eine untere Schranke für die Komplexität von Mengen Boolescher Funktionen angegeben. Weiterhin ist die Lücke zwischen diesen beiden Schranken klein und bekannt , so daß es nun möglich ist, Ersparnisse bei gemeinsamer Berechnung anzugeben. Definiert man etwa die Ersparnis durch

$$E = \frac{L(f_1)+\ldots+L(f_t) - L(f_1,\ldots,f_t)}{t2^n/n}$$

so kommt

$$E \gtrless \frac{\mathrm{ld}\,t}{n+\mathrm{ld}\,t} \mp 2c \frac{\mathrm{ld}\,n}{n}$$

heraus. Genaue Angaben über die Ersparnis sind also nur möglich, wenn ldt $\gg$ ldn ist. So erhält man etwa bei gemeinsamer Berechnung von 2^n Funktionen , die nicht in der Nullmenge liegen , für große n eine Ersparnis von genau 50%. Selbst bei Berechnung von relativ wenig Funktionen im Vergleich zu allen kann man also erheblich sparen.

[1] V. STRASSEN:
Berechnungen in partiellen Algebren endlichen Typs
Computing 11/3

[2] D. E. MULLER:
Complexity in Electronic Switching Circuits
IRE Transactions on Electronic Computers, March 1956

[3] H. BREMER:
Berechnungskomplexität von Mengen Boolescher Funktionen
und von Polynomen über endlichen Körpern
Diplomarbeit, Institut für angewandte Mathematik an der
Johann Wolfgang Goethe Universität in Frankfurt

ON THE ENTROPY OF A FORMAL LANGUAGE

by

A. de Luca

Laboratorio di Cibernetica del C.N.R.,Arco Felice ,Napoli.

and

Istituto di Scienze dell'Informazione dell'Università di Salerno.

0.Introduction

The problem of transmission of information over a communication channel can be studied in two ways which are conceptually different.The first was originated by the fundamental work of C.E.Shannon [16].The source of information is a probabilistic ergodic source.It satisfies the following property [8] (E-property) which is very important in information theory:the sequences of large length n generated by an ergodic source of entropy H(S) can be divided in two groups.The sequences of the first group,called also standard,have a probability close to $2^{-H(S)n}$ and are in number approximately equal to $2^{H(S)n}$.The remaining sequences of length n have a total probability which vanishes for n diverging.The E-property makes it possible then,to separate from the initial language a sub-language formed by the "high-probability group" of the approximately equiprobable standard sequences,which play the essential role in the coding of Shannon's theorems.

Another approach to information theory that we call "linguistic" exists.This in some respects equivalent to the previous one,consists in considering directly a language L described by the so-called stucture-function f of Mandelbrot [12].For all n, f(n) gives the number of distinct words of length n contained in the language L.The entropy H(L) of the language L can be,then,defined in a purely combinatorial fashion,as the $\lim_{n\to\infty} (1/n)\ln_2 f(n)$ [or,more generally,as $\limsup_{n\to\infty}(1/n)\ln_2 f(n)$] .It can be regarded as the number of [or the least upper bound to] bits per symbol required,on the average , to specify a word of the language.This concept of entropy was initially introduced by Shannon himself [16] in the case of languages consisting of all "messages" generated by a finite-state communication channel,and was named channel-capacity.This definition of entropy was successively extended by Chomsky and Miller [3] to any finite-state language and by other authors [1,10,17] to wider classes of formal languages. The main problem considered by these authors was, essentially, that of giving for some classes of formal languages (as, for instance, some subclasses of context-free languages) genera computation methods of the entropy of a language of the class by knowing an underlyi grammar generating it. Recently Kaminger [7] proved that there cannot exist a general computation method of the entropy of languages generated by context-sensitive gramma

The aim of this paper is that of making a preliminary analysis of the problem of transmission of information in the context of the linguistic approach. We shall consider sources of information generating, in the general case, recursively enumerabl (r.e.) languages (which can be always produced by type-0 grammars [14]) initially desc ibed by the structure function only. We are not much interested in the underlying gra mar generating a language L, but exclusively in its entropy H(L). The main problem tha we shall consider is the one of efficient coding for the words of L relative to a gi ven "effective-decoder" of it. This problem can be faced in a natural way by making u of the Kolmogorov program-complexity [2,9,11,15]. In fact the program-complexity $K_\psi(\xi$ of a word ξ, relative the partial recursive (p.r.) function (or decoder) $\psi : Y^* \to X^*$, ca be regarded as the minimal length of a "code-word" of ξ in a "communication-schema" where the "receiver" is an algorithm computing ψ and a "code-word" of a string is a "computer-program" for it (*). Moreover the program-complexity $K(\xi)$ relative to a univ sal p.r. function (or universal decoder) of the words of L gives a measure of their structural-complexity, since $K(\xi)$ represents the minimum number of bits, to within an additive constant, required to define ξ in an effective manner. The function K allows therefore, an analysis of the structure of a r.e. language L deeper than those obtain by means of the structure function f. However, as we shall see in the following, the overwhelming majority of the words of L of large length $|\xi|$ has a "compression-coeff cient" $\mu(\xi) := K(\xi)/|\xi|$ approximately equal to $(1/|\xi|)\ln_2 f(|\xi|)$ (in the case of a binar code-alphabet). The entropy H(L) can be, then, redefined in terms of Kolmogorov's com xity of the words of L.

1. Entropy of a formal language and Kolmogorov complexity

Let X be a finite (non empty) alphabet of cardinality $\|X\|$, and X^* the free-mo noid generated by X, that is the set of all finite sequences or words ξ of symbols o X including the empty word λ. The length of a word ξ will be denoted by $|\xi|$. A langu

(*) A generalization of this schema in which the "receiver" is a formal system has been proposed by the author [4-6]

L over the alphabet X is any subset of X^*.Let X^n be the set of all the words over X of length n.For any language L we denote by L_n its subset $L_n := L \cap X^n$.The entropy H(L) of L is the quantity $H(L) := \lim_{n\to\infty} \sup (1/n) \ln_2 f(n)$,where f is the structure-function of L defined as $f(n) := \| L_n \|$,for all n.From the definition one has that H(L) is finite iff L is an infinite language.In this latter case $0 \leq H(L) \leq \ln_2 \|X\|$.

In the following we shall mainly consider recursively enumerable languages.A language L is recursive iff L and its complement $\sim L$ are recursively enumerable [14]. Moreover a r.e. language is recursive iff its structure function is computable.We want now describe a r.e.language in terms of the Kolmogorov program-complexity of its words.We recall that for any p.r.function $\psi : Y^* \to X^*$,the program-complexity $K_\psi(\xi)$ relative to ψ is defined as $K_\psi(\xi) := \min \{ |p| \mid \psi(p) = \xi \}$,where,conventionally $\min \emptyset = +\infty$.The quantity $K_\psi(\xi)$ depends in an essential way on the p.r.function ψ.However a basic theorem due to Solomonoff [18] and Kolmogorov [9] shows that there are asymptotically optimal p.r.functions with respect to which to evaluate the program-complexity.More precisely,a universal p.r.function $U : Y^* \to X^*$ exists with the property that for any other p.r.function $\psi : Y^* \to X^*$ one has that $K_U(\xi) \leq K_\psi(\xi) + c_{U,\psi}$ with $\xi \in X^*$ and $c_{U,\psi} \in N$ (N is the set of nonnegative integers).For any such two universal p.r.functions U_1 and U_2 , $|K_{U_1}(\xi) - K_{U_2}(\xi)| \leq$ cost.for all $\xi \in X^*$.Therefore,for all $\xi \in X^*$, $K_{U_1}(\xi)$ and $K_{U_2}(\xi)$ are equal to within an additive constant which can be neglected for high values of the complexity.The program-complexity of a string $\xi \in X^*$ relative to a fixed universal p.r.function U,will be simply denoted by $K(\xi)$.The following theorem,that generalizes a result of Kolmogorov and Martin-Lof [13],shows the relationship existing between the program-complexity of the words of a r.e.language and its structure function.

Theorem1.1.For all n,such that $L_n \neq \emptyset$,one has that

i. $K(\xi) \leq \ln_d f(n) + O(\ln_d n)$,for all $\xi \in L_n$,where $d = \|Y\|$ and $O(\ln_d n)$ denotes a quantity of the order of $\ln_d n$ when n diverges.

ii.The number of words of L_n for which $K(\xi) \geq \lfloor \ln_d f(n) \rfloor - \delta$,with $\delta \in N$ ($\lfloor x \rfloor$ is the greatest integer $\leq x$) is greater than $f(n)(1 - d^{-\delta}/d-1)$.

iii.There is a lower bound to the number of words of L_n for which $K(\xi) <$ $\lfloor \ln_d f(n) \rfloor - \delta$ given by $f(n)\, d^{-\delta}\; {}^{-c}/d^3 (d-1)((d-1)n+d)^2 - 1/d-1$,with $c \in N$.

For any r.e.language L the elements of the sublanguage $V(\delta) \equiv \{ \xi \in L \mid K(\xi) \geq \lfloor \ln_d f(n) \rfloor - \delta \}$,whose entropy equals H(L),are called the (f,δ)-random elements of L.With the only exception when $H(L) = \ln_2 \|X\|$ the (f,δ)-random elements of L_n are,for large n,a very small fraction of the set of all sequences of length n .A consequence of theorem 1.1

is that if $L_n \neq \emptyset$ then $V_n(\delta) \neq \emptyset$ since there is at least a word $\xi \varepsilon L_n$ such that $K(\xi) \geq |\ln_d f(n)|$. Furthermore, when $H(L) > 0$ a p.r.function $r: N \to X^*$ cannot exist such that $r(n) \varepsilon V_n(\delta)$ for all n for which $L_n \neq \emptyset$. From this it is easy to derive that if L is recursive and $H(L) > 0$, then $V(\delta)$ cannot be recursively enumerable and K is not computable in L.

2. Effective coding

Let $\psi : Y^* \to X^*$ be a p.r. function. A word $p \varepsilon Y^*$ such that $\psi(p) = \xi$ with $\xi \varepsilon X^*$ can be regarded as a code-word (or coding), in the alphabet Y, of ξ relative to ψ. The function ψ will be referred to as an effective-decoder (e.d.) for any language $L \subsetneq$ Range ψ.

Definition 2.1 . For any given language L ($L \subseteq X^*$) an |effective| -decoder of L is any |p.r.| -function $\psi : Y^* \to X^*$, such that Range $\psi \supseteq L$.

The alphabet Y is called the code-alphabet (Y can be equal to X). For all $\xi \varepsilon L$ the inverse-image $\psi^{-1}(\xi) \subsetneq Y^*$ is formed by all code-words of ξ. The quantity $C(\psi) :=$ H(Range ψ) will be named the capacity of ψ. For any |effective| -decoder ψ, $C(\psi)$ equa the maximum of the entropy of any |r.e.| language contained in Range ψ.

Definition 2.2 .For any given |effective| -decoder ψ of L an |effective| -encoder of L, relative to ψ, is any |p.r.| -function $\psi_{-1} : X^* \to Y^*$ such that Dom $\psi_{-1} \supseteq L$ and $\psi_{-1}(\xi) \varepsilon \psi^{-1}(\xi)$, for all $\xi \varepsilon L$.

It is easy to derive, from recursive function theory, the following:

Lemma 2.1 .Given an arbitrary r.e. language L and an e.d. ψ of it there exists alw an effective encoder ψ_{-1} of L.

For any partial function $\rho : X^+ \to R$ ($X^+ = XX^*$ and R is the set of real numbers) such that Dom $\rho \supseteq L - \{\lambda\}$, let us denote by $\rho(L)$, $\langle\rho\rangle(n)$ and $\langle\rho\rangle(L)$ respectively the quantities $\rho(L) := \lim_{n\to\infty} \sup\{\rho(\xi) \mid \xi \varepsilon L \,\&\, |\xi| \geq n\}$, $\langle\rho\rangle(n) := \sum_{\xi \varepsilon L_n} \rho(\xi)/f(n)$ for $L_n \neq \emptyset$, $\langle\rho\rangle(L) :=$ $\lim_{n\to\infty} \sup \langle\rho\rangle(n)$.

With respect to any encoder ψ_{-1}, relative to the decoder ψ of L the compression-coefficient $\Psi_{-1}(\xi)$ of a nonempty string ξ of L is defined as $\Psi_{-1}(\xi) := |\psi_{-1}(\xi)|/|\xi|$. Furthermore $\Psi_{-1}(L)$, $\langle\Psi_{-1}\rangle(n)$ and $\langle\Psi_{-1}\rangle(L)$ will be called, respectively, the compressic coefficient of L, the average compression-coefficient of L_n ($L_n \neq \emptyset$) and the average comp ression-coefficient of L. For any effective decoder ψ of a r.e. language L the quanti $\mu_\psi(\xi) := K_\psi(\xi) / |\xi|$, where ξ is a nonempty word of L and $K_\psi(\xi)$ the program-complexit of ξ relative to ψ, represents the minimal value of the compression coefficient of ξ

with respect to all encoders ψ_{-1} of L relative to ψ.Moreover,one has that $\Psi_{-1}(L) \geqq \mu_{\psi}(L)$, $\langle\Psi_{-1}\rangle(n) \geqq \langle\mu_{\psi}\rangle(n)$ and $\langle\Psi_{-1}\rangle(L) \geqq \langle\mu_{\psi}\rangle(L)$.

An encoder ψ_{-1} such that $|\psi_{-1}(\xi)| = K_{\psi}(\xi)$ in L is called absolutely-optimal.Such an encoder is effective iff K_{ψ} is computable in L.Therefore,the existence of an effective absolutely-optimal encoder of a r.e.language depends in an essential way on the effective decoder ψ.For an infinite r.e.language L there exists always a recursive injection $\psi^{0} : Y^{*} \to X^{*}$ such that $L \equiv \text{Range}\ \psi^{0}$.An effective encoder ψ^{0}_{-1} (which certainly exists by Lemma 2.1) relative to ψ^{0} is absolutely optimal since $\{\psi^{0}_{-1}(\xi)\} \equiv (\psi^{0})^{-1}(\xi)$. On the contrary,from what we said at the end of the previous section,it follows that an absolutely-optimal effective encoder of a recursive language L,with $H(L)>0$,relative to a universal e.d. U does not exist.

It is easy to prove that the e.d. U,whose capacity equals $\ln_2 \|X\|$,is such that any word $\xi \varepsilon X^{*}$ has an infinite number of code-words.This fact justifies our definition of $|$effective$|$-decoder which is a more general one than the usual.Furthermore the basic Solomonoff-Kolmogorov theorem can be restated,in terms of compression-coefficients,in the following form:there exists an effective decoder U of any r.e.language L (that is U is a universal e.d.)which is asymptotically-optimal with respect to all effective-decoders ψ of L,in the sense that for any $\varepsilon>0$, $\mu_{U}(\xi) \leq \mu_{\psi}(\xi)+\varepsilon$,when $\xi \varepsilon L_{n}$ with n sufficiently large.It follows that $\mu_{U}(L) \leq \mu_{\psi}(L)$ and $\mu_{U_1}(L) = \mu_{U_2}(L)$ for any such two universal decoders U_1 and U_2 .Therefore the quantity $\mu(L) := \mu_{U}(L)$,which depends only on the r.e.language L,represents the minimal compression-coefficient of L with respect to all e.d.of it.

A corollary of theorem 2.1 of the previous section is the following proposition concerning the compression-coefficient $\mu(\xi) := K(\xi)/|\xi|$ of the words of an infinite r.e. language L.

Proposition 2.1 .Given any $\varepsilon>0$,the (f,δ)-random elements of L of length n,for a fixed δ,are such that $|\ \mu(\xi) - (1/n)\ln_{d} f(n)\ | < \varepsilon$,when n diverges.The fraction of the remaining words of L_n ,for which $\mu(\xi) \leq (1/n)\ln_{d} f(n) - \varepsilon$,becomes as small as one wishes for a sufficiently large δ.

If there exists $\lim_{n\to\infty} (1/n)\ln_2 f(n) = H(L)$ one has that $|\ \mu(\xi) - H(L)/\ln_2 d\ | < \varepsilon$ for $\xi \varepsilon V_{n}(\delta)$ when n diverges.A consequence of proposition 2.1 and of theorem 1.1 is that $\langle\mu\rangle(L) = \mu(L) = H(L)/\ln_2 d$. Furthermore,for any r.e.language L,of entropy $H(L)$,there is always an e.d.ψ which is optimal in the sense that $\mu_{\psi}(L) = \langle\mu_{\psi}\rangle(L) = H(L)/\ln_2 d$,relative to which there exists an absolutely-optimal effective encoder ψ_{-1}.

A class of decoders very important from a theoretical and practical point of view is those of <u>sequential-decoders</u> which are such that if a word ξ of a language L can be factorized in subwords ξ_i (i=1,..,k) still belonging to L, then a code-word (or program) for ξ can be obtained by making the juxtaposition of the code-words of ξ_i's. This condition is very important in information theory since one is interested in transmitting sequences of words (or messages) of a given language.

Definition 2.3 . Let $\psi: Y^* \to X^*$ be an [effective]-decoder of a language L. It is called sequential if for all $k \in N$:

$$\psi(p_{i_1}),\ldots,\psi(p_{i_k}) \in L \text{ and } \psi(p_{i_1})\cdot\cdot\cdot\psi(p_{i_k}) \in L \Rightarrow \psi(p_{i_1}..p_{i_k}) = \psi(p_{i_1})\ldots\psi(p_{i_k})$$

From the definition it follows that if ψ is a sequential decoder of L and $\xi = \xi_{i_1}\ldots\xi_{i_k}$ with $\xi, \xi_{i_1},..\xi_{i_k} \in L$ then one has $K_\psi(\xi) \leq \sum_{i=1}^{k} K_\psi(\xi_i)$. It is possible to show that for any r.e. language L of entropy H(L) there is an effective sequential decoder ψ of L^* (L^* denotes the monoid generated by L) and therefore of L, which is optimal in the sense that $\mu_\psi(L) = \langle\mu_\psi\rangle(L) = H(L)/\ln_2 d$.

3. Concluding remarks

In the setting of the communication-schema described in the introduction we have seen in the previous section some results on coding which are obtained by means of the Kolmogorov program-complexity theory. However we stress that the "efficiency" of such a coding does not depend only on the compression-coefficient of the words which one wishes to transmit, but also on the <u>time of computation</u> required to obtain them. In fact it can occur that one can keep "small" the amount of program but increasing the computation resources (time, space, etc) beyond any realistic limitation. Therefore also the "dynamic" aspects of the computation have to play a relevant role in this theory. Moreover we believe that the previous approach in which the receiver is schematized by an algorithm (or, more generally, by a formal system) can be a good frame to analyze higher levels of the communication as, for instance, how to transmit in order that the message affects the conduct of the receiver in the desidered way (<u>pragmatic level</u>).

References

1 . Banerji, R.B. - Phrase structure languages, finite machines and channel capacity. <u>Information and Control</u>, <u>6</u>, 153-162, 1963.

2 . Chaitin, G.J. - On the length of programs for computing finite binary sequences. <u>J.ACM</u>, <u>13</u>, 547-569, 1966.

3 .Chomsky,N.and G.A.Miller,Finite state languages.Information and Control,1,91-112, 1958.

4 .De Luca,A.,Complexity and information theory.Proc.of summer school on"Coding and complexity".CISM,Udine,July 15-26,1974.

5 . " " .,Some information-theoretic aspects of the complexity theory,Proc.of the informal meeting on "Computational complexity,codes and formal languages".Laboratorio di Cibernetica,Naples,March 13-14,1975.

6 .De Luca A.and E.Fischetti,Outline of a new logical approach to information theory. In "New concepts and technologies in parallel information processing". (E.R.Caianiello ed.).Proc.of NATO summer school,Capri,June,17-30,1973. Noordhoff,Series E,n.9,1975.

7 .Kaminger,F.P.,The non computability of the channel capacity of context-sensitive languages".Information and Control,17,175-182,1970.

8 .Khinchin,A.I.,"Mathematical foundations of information theory".Dover Publ.1950

9 .Kolmogorov,A.N.,Three approaches to the quantitative definition of information. Problemy Pederachi Informatsii,1,3-11,1965.

10.Kuich,W.,On the entropy of context-free languages.Information and Control,16,173-200,1970.

11.Levin,L.A.and A.K.Zvonkin,The complexity of finite objects and the development of the concepts of information and randomness by means of the theory of algorithms,Usphehi Mat.Nauk,25,85-127,1970

12.Mandelbrot,B.,On recurrent noise limiting coding,Proc.Symp.on Inf.Networks,Polytechn.Inst.of Brooklyn,205-221,1954.

13.Martin-Löf,P.,The definition of random sequences,Information and Control,6,602-619, 1966.

14.Salomaa,A."Formal languages".Academic Press.New York and London,1973.

15.Schnorr,C.P.,"Zufälligkeit und Wahrscheinlichkeit".Springer Verlag Lecture Notes in Mathematics,n.218,1970.

16.Shannon,C.E.,A mathematical theory of communication,Bell Syst.Tech.J.27,379-423, 1948.

17.Siromoney,R.,Channel capacity of equal matrix languages.Information and Control, 14,507-511,1969.

18.Solomonoff,R.J.,A formal theory of inductive inference.Part 1,Information and Control,7,1-22,1964.

On the Complexity of Computations under Varying Sets of Primitives†

David P. Dobkin and Richard J. Lipton
Department of Computer Science
Yale University
New Haven, Connecticut 06520 USA

1. Introduction

The principal goal of research in computational complexity is the determination of tight lower bounds on the complexity, in terms of primitive operation executions, of solving problems or performing larger operations. While algorithms now exist that yield better than naive upper bounds for various operations (e.g. [1,9,11,12]), finding lower bounds for the solution of a problem using a general model has proved to be more difficult. In order to circumvent these difficulties, many authors (e.g. [3,5,6,8,13]) have chosen to work with models that place some restriction on the primitive operations that can be used or on the flow of output that can occur. Typical of the restrictions that have been placed on models are: allowing the use of only a monotone basis of functions [6,8] or requiring that all circuits be restricted to fan-out one [3,5,13]. The value of using such models is in the insights they produce into the general process of finding lower bounds; many of the actual lower bounds they produce are shown, however, to be invalid for more general models.

The goal of the current research is the study of lower bounds on the complexity of a set of searching problems under various restrictions on the nature of the primitive operation used to determine each branch within a search tree. Our model, to be described in more detail in the next section, has programs consisting of two types of statements, query statements of the form:

L_k: *if* f(x) R 0 *then* *goto* L_m *else* *goto* L_n

where R is one of the relations (> or =) and f is a function of restricted form on the input of x. An output statement of the form

L_s: *accept* (or *reject*)

† Portions of the research of the first author were supported by ONR Grant N00014-75-C-0450.

occurs for each possible outcome of the problem.

The problems we consider all involve searching a set of geometric objects in Euclidean space to determine in which region of their partition of space a given point lies or whether the point lies in any of the given regions. Among the new results obtained are exponential lower bounds for searching for solutions to a knapsack problem, viewed as a hyperplane search problem, for various models involving restrictions on the primitive operations allowed. A non-linear (in the number of hyperplanes) lower bound is given for a generalized hyperplane search problem along with an O(n log n) bound for a problem in the plane.

2. Basic Model

Our model of computation is based on the notion of a search program. A search program P with input $(x_1,\ldots,x_n)$ is a finite list of instructions of the following three types:

1) L_k: if $f(x_1,\ldots,x_n)$ R 0 then goto L_m $(R \in \{>,=\})$
else goto L_p

2) L_k: accept

3) L_k: reject

Control initially starts at the first instruction. An instruction of type (1) determines whether or not the indicated test is true: If it is true, then control passes to the statement with label L_m; otherwise, control passes to the statement with label L_p. An instruction of type (2) denotes that the program has halted and it has accepted the input. Correspondingly, an instruction of type (3) denotes that the program has halted and it has rejected the input.

We will restrict search programs in two distinct ways. The functions allowed in instructions of type (1) are called primitives. Often we will restrict the class of allowed primitives. We will also restrict at times the relations R allowed in instructions of type (1). Thus an equality search program can have R equal only to =. On the other hand, a linear search program can have only functions f that are linear.

The complexity measure we will use on our search programs is "time." Each possible input $(x_1,\ldots,x_n)$ determines a computation through the search program. The length of this computation is the number of steps associated with the input $(x_1,\ldots,x_n)$. We are always interested in the worst-case behavior, i.e. the maximum number of steps required by a given search program.

3. Restricted Linear Programs

In this section we will investigate the n-dimensional knapsack problem (KS_n). We can view this problem as follows: Given a point $(x_1,\ldots,x_n,b) \in E^{n+1}$ we are to determine whether or not there exists an index set I such that

$$\sum_{i\in I} x_i - b = 0.$$

The first question we ask is: If we restrict our search programs to queries of the form

$$\sum_{i\in I} x_i \gtreqless b$$

can we show that they must take exponential time? The answer is yes:

Theorem 1. Any search program having as its primitive operation functions of the form

$$\sum_{i\in I} x_i - b$$

for some index set I and any tests >, =, or < must require $O(2^n)$ primitive steps to solve the n-dimensional Knapsack Problem.

Proof. We adopt an adversary approach and provide a set of data such that if less than $\binom{n}{n/2}$ primitive operations are executed the data can be altered so as to make it possible for the solution to the problem to change without changing previous results.

Our adversary will return answers to queries according to the following plan

i) if $|I| < n/2$, then $\sum_{i\in I} x_i < b$

ii) if $|I| > n/2$, then $\sum_{i\in I} x_i > b$

iii) if $|I| = n/2$ and less than $\binom{n}{n/2} - 1$ tests on index sets of exactly n/2 elements have been done, then $\sum_{i\in I} x_i > b$.

We now make the claim that it is possible to provide three sets of data satisfying conditions (i), (ii), and (iii) such that each set yields a different result on the final query. From this claim, the theorem follows since although an algorithm knowing this adversary's strategy could eliminate all tests of index sets with cardinality not equal to n/2 the $\binom{n}{n/2} \simeq O(2^n)$ tests of index sets of cardinality n/2 must all be performed.

Claim. Assume the last test performed on an index set of exactly n/2 elements compares $x_1 + x_2 + \ldots + x_{n/2}$ to b; then there are choices of $x_1 = \gamma$, $x_2 = x_3 = \ldots = x_{n/2} = \alpha$ and $x_{(n/2)+1} = x_{(n/2)+2} = \ldots = x_n = \beta$ for $0 < \gamma \leq \alpha \leq \beta$ satisfying the three conditions of the adversary and yielding any of the three possible results $x_1 + \dots + x_{n/2} \lesseqgtr b$.

Proof. The conditions (i), (ii), and (iii) can be restated as

i) $((n/2)-1)\cdot\beta < b$

ii) $\gamma + ((n/2)-1)\cdot\alpha + \beta > b$

iii) $\gamma + ((n/2)-2)\cdot\alpha + \beta > b$

and we observe that (iii) implies (ii), so that we need show only that conditions (i) and (iii) can be met along with the result of one of the cases:

Case I: $\gamma + ((n/2)-1)\cdot\alpha > b$

Case II: $\gamma + ((n/2)-1)\cdot\alpha < b$

Case III: $\gamma + ((n/2)-1)\cdot\alpha = b$.

In the first case, the choice $\gamma = \alpha = \beta = 2b/(n-1)$ works since

i) $((n/2)-1)\cdot(2b/(n-1)) = ((n-2)/(n-1))\cdot b < b$

iii) $(2b/(n-1)) + ((n/2)-2)\cdot(2b/(n-1)) + (2b/(n-1)) = (n/(n-1))\cdot b > b$

and $(2b/(n-1)) + ((n/2)-1)\cdot(2b/(n-1)) = (n/(n-1))\cdot b > b$.

The second case is handled by the choice $\gamma = b\cdot(\frac{2n-5}{(n-(1/2))^2})$,

$\alpha = 2b\cdot(\frac{1}{n-2} + \frac{2}{(n-(1/2))^2})$, $\beta = 2b\ (\frac{1}{n-2} - \frac{1}{(n-(1/2))^2})$ since

i) $((n/2)-1)\cdot(2b\ (\frac{1}{n-2} - \frac{1}{(n-(1/2))^2})) = b\cdot(1 - \frac{n-2}{(n-(1/2))^2}) < b$

iii) $b\cdot(\frac{2n-5}{(n-(1/2))^2}) + ((n/2)-2)\cdot 2b\cdot(\frac{1}{n-2} + \frac{2}{(n-(1/2))^2}) + 2b\cdot(\frac{1}{n-2} - \frac{1}{(n-(1/2))^2})$
$= b\cdot(\frac{4n-11}{(n-(1/2))^2} + 1) > b$

and $b\cdot(\frac{2n-5}{(n-(1/2))^2}) + ((n/2)-1)\cdot 2b\cdot(\frac{1}{n-2} + \frac{2}{(n-(1/2))^2}) = b\cdot(\frac{4n-9}{(n-(1/2))^2} + 1) > b$

Finally, the choices $\gamma = \frac{2b(n-2)}{n^2-4}$, $\alpha = \frac{2bn}{n^2-4}$, $\beta = \frac{2b(n+1)}{n^2-4}$ settle the third case via

i) $((n/2)-1)\cdot(\frac{2b(n+1)}{n^2-4}) = \frac{b(n+1)}{n+2} < b$

iii) $\frac{2b(n-2)}{n^2-4} + ((n/2)-2)\cdot(\frac{2bn}{n^2-4}) + \frac{2b(n+1)}{n^2-4} = b\cdot(\frac{n^2-2}{n^2-4}) > b$

and $\frac{2b(n-2)}{n^2-4} + ((n/2)-1)\cdot(\frac{2bn}{n^2-4}) = b$. □

The result of this theorem is that any polynomial-time algorithm for solving the knapsack problem must use comparisons to hyperplanes not in the original set but generated from the original set. While such an algorithm is possible, it is unlikely to exist as a general procedure but might rather exist as a set of procedures $\{P_i\}_{i=1}^{\infty}$ such that solving the n-dimensional knapsack problem involves using procedure P_n to generate new hyperplanes and solving the n+1-dimensional knapsack problem involves using (possibly different) procedure P_{n+1} to generate new hyperplanes. Examples of such procedures as well as a brief discussion of the implications of such a system for the question "P = NP?" are contained in [2]. The present result in conjunction with those discussions makes it extremely unlikely that P and NP are the same.

4. Linear Programs

Next we will study linear programs. That is, we will allow any tests of the form

$$f(x_1,\ldots,x_n) \gtreqless 0$$

where f is a linear function. The next theorem allows us to obtain lower bounds for the complexity of various membership problems:

Theorem 2. Any linear search tree that solves the membership problem for a disjoint union of a family $\{A_i\}_{i\in I}$ of open subsets of R^n requires at least $\log_2 |I|$ queries in the worst case.

Proof. We prove that any such search tree T with leaves $D_1,\ldots,D_r$ has $r \geq |I|$ and hence a path of depth $\geq \log_2 |I|$. The leaves partition R^n and, for each j, D_j is a accepting leaf if $D_j \subseteq \bigcup_{i\in I} A_i$ and a rejection leaf otherwise. The theorem then follows from the observation that the function $Y: I \to \{1,\ldots,r\}$ defined by Y(i)'s being the least i such that $A_i \cap D$ is non-empty is an injective function. This observation is true since if $Y(i) = Y(j) = \ell$ for $i \neq j$ then there exist distinct points x and y such that $x \in A_i \cap D_\ell$ and $y \in A_j \cap D_\ell$. By the convexity of D_ℓ, each point on the line joining x and y lies in D_ℓ and hence is accepted as a point of $\bigcup_{i\in I} A_i$. Defining the function $g: L \to I$ by $g(Z) = k$ whenever $Z \in A_k$ yields the contradiction that g is the constant function i, since A_i is open and I is finite. □

Let us now generalize the knapsack problem (KS_n) to the generalized knapsack problem (GKS_n): We are given 2^n hyperplanes $H_1,\ldots,H_{2^n}$ in E^{n+1} space that form a simple arrangement, i.e. no n+2 hyperplanes have a common point. For each new point x we are to determine whether or not x lies in any of these hyperplanes. Note, we do <u>not</u> insist that the search tree determine which hyperplane x lies in, only that it determine whether or not x lies in some hyperplane.

From this result we obtain the following corollaries:

Corollary 1. The membership problem for GKS_n takes at least $O(n^2)$ queries for any search tree.

Proof. Since the hyperplanes of this problem form a simple arrangement, we can fi a family $\{A_i\}_{i\in I}$ of open subsets of R^n such that

$$x \in \bigcup_{i\in I} A_i \leftrightarrow x \in GKS_n$$

and $|I| \geq O(2^{n^2})$ [4]. The corollary then follows from the theorem. □

This result improves a lower bound of O(n) due to Spira [10].

Corollary 2. (Element Uniqueness Problem.) Let E_n be the set of points in R^n that have two coordinates equal; then any algorithm for determining membership in E_n requires at least O(n log n) queries.

Proof. Solving the membership problem for E_n corresponds to solving the membership problem for the family $\bigcup_{\pi\in S_n} \{A_\pi\}$ where

$$A_\pi = \{(x_1,\ldots,x_n) \in R^n \mid x_{\pi(1)} < x_{\pi(2)} < \ldots < x_{\pi(n)}\}$$

and S_n is the set of permutations on n objects. The result then follows from $|S_n| = n!$. □

5. Equality Programs

In the previous section, we considered the problem of determining whether a point belonged to the union of a family of open sets allowing linear search programs. Here, we extend our methodology to the problem of determining whether a point belongs to the union of a family of varieties allowing search programs that determine at each step whether the point is the root of an irreducible polynomial. Before proceeding, we state some results from algebraic geometry [7] that will be necessary to our development.

Definition. A variety $V(f_1,\ldots,f_m)$ is a subset of R^n defined by

$$V(f_1,\ldots,f_m) = \{(x_1,\ldots,x_n) \in R^n \mid f_1(x_1,\ldots,x_n) = \ldots = f_m(x_1,\ldots,x_n) = 0\}$$

for polynomials $f_1,\ldots,f_m$.

Definition. The polynomials f and g are said to be equivalent iff there exists a non-zero constant λ such that $f = \lambda g$.

Fact 1. If the dimension of $V(f_1,\ldots,f_n)$ is denoted by $\dim(V(f_1,\ldots,f_n))$ then

i) $\dim(A) = 0$ if and only if A is empty

ii) if $R^n = \bigcup_{i=1}^{k} V(f_i)$, then one of the polynomials f_i is trivial

iii) if f and g are non-trivial irreducible polynomials that are not equivalent, then $\dim(V(f,g)) < \dim(V(f))$.

Theorem 3. If $f_1,\ldots,f_m$ are irreducible polynomials of n real variables that are not equivalent, then any equality search program for

$$\bigcup_{i=1}^{m} V(f_i)$$

using only irreducible polynomials requires at least m queries.

Proof. Let T be a search program of depth k that determines for any $x \in R^n$ whether $x \in \bigcup_{i=1}^{m} V(f_i)$. Suppose that a path through T makes queries as to whether $g_i(x) = 0$ for $i = k$ if $x \in \bigcup_{i=1}^{m} V(f_i)$ and $\neq 0$ for $i = k$ if $x \notin \bigcup_{i=1}^{m} V(f_i)$. We will show by dimension arguments that this is possible only if $k \geq m$.

To begin, we define the sets $F = \bigcup_{i=1}^{m} V(f_i)$ and $G_i = (\bigcup_{j=1}^{i} V(g_j))^c$ (A^c is the complement of the set A) and observe that $x \in G_{t-1}$ if and only if $k \geq t$. Furthermore, either $G_k \subseteq F$ or $G_k \subseteq F^c$ since after k queries we can determine for each x whether x belongs to F or not. Now, if $k < m$, then for some i $V(f_i)$ is not one of the sets $V(g_1),\ldots,(V(g_k)$ and $\dim(V(g_j) \cap V(f_i)) < \dim(V(f_i))$. Thus the set $G_k \cap V(f_i)$ is of the same dimension as the variety $V(f_i)$ and is non-empty. Hence $G_k \cap F \neq 0$. Assume next that $G_k \subseteq F$; then $G_k^c \cup F = R^n$. But this implies that R^n can be written as the union of non-trivial varieties, which is not true, and thus $G_k \cap F^c \neq 0$ and so k queries are insufficient for $k < m$. □

Corollary 3. Any equality search program for KS_n that uses only irreducible polynomials requires at least 2^n queries.

References

[1] Blum, Floyd, Pratt, Rivest, Tarjan. Linear time bounds for selection. JCSS 7:448-461, 1973.

[2] Dobkin, Lipton. On some generalizations of binary search. ACM Symposium on the Theory of Computing, Seattle, Washington, May 1974.

[3] Fischer, Meyer, Paterson. Lower bounds on the size of Boolean formulas. ACM Symposium on the Theory of Computing, Albuquerque, New Mexico, May 1975.

[4] Grünbaum. Convex Polytopes. Interscience Publishers, 1967.

[5] Harper, Savage. On the complexity of the marriage problem. Advances in Mathematics 9:299-312, 1972.

[6] Kerr. The effect of algebraic structure on the computational complexity of matrix multiplication. PhD thesis, Cornell University, Ithaca, New York, 197

[7] Lefschetz. Algebraic Geometry. Princeton University Press, 1953.

[8] Schnorr. A lower bound on the number of additions in monotone computations o monotone rational polynomials. Unpublished manuscript.

[9] Schönhage, Strassen. Fast multiplication of large numbers (in German). Computing 1:182-196, 1966.

[10] Spira. On the number of comparisons necessary to rank an element. Computational Complexity Symposium, Courant Institute, 1973.

[11] Strassen. Gaussian elimination is not optimal. Numerische Mathematik 13: 354-6, 1969.

[12] Tarjan. Depth-first search and linear graph algorithms. SIAM Journal on Computing 1, 1972.

[13] Vilfan. The complexity of finite functions. Technical Report 97, Project MAC, MIT, 1972.

About the deterministic simulation of nondeterministic (log n)-tape bounded Turing machines

BURKHARD MONIEN
Universität Dortmund
Abteilung Informatik

1. Introduction

One of the oldest problem in the theory of automata and languages is the so-called LBA problem, that is the question whether deterministic linear bounded automata are as powerful as nondeterministic linear bounded automata. This problem can be formulated also in the terminology of computational complexity. Let us denote by TAPE(f(n)) the class of all languages which are acceptable by deterministic multi-tape Turing machines operating with tape bound f(n). Correspondingly NTAPE(f(n)) is defined taking the nondeterministic Turing machine as the underlying machine model. Then the LBA problem is just the question whether TAPE(n) is equal to NTAPE(n).

It is not difficult to see that equality results which hold for some tape functi do hold also for every tape function which grows more rapidely. That means:

Let $g: \mathbb{N} \to \mathbb{N}$ be some function such that NTAPE(log n) $\subset$ TAPE(g(log n)) holds. Then NTAPE(f(n)) $\subset$ TAPE(g(f(n))) holds for all functions $f: \mathbb{N} \to \mathbb{N}$ such that $f(n) \geq \log n$ for all n.

In particular we have: If NTAPE(log n) = TAPE(log n) then also NTAPE(n) = TAPE(n

Therefore we can restrict our study to the behaviour of (log n)-tape bounded non-deterministic Turing machines. This has been done before by J. Hartmanis [2] and I.H. Sudborough [8] . First we define a subclass of NTAPE(log n).

Definition: Let C be the class of all languages accepted by nondeterministic one-way one-counter automata. Such an automaton consists of a finite control, an input tape where one head is moving from the left to the right and of a counter. The next move function is nondeterministic.

It is not difficult to see that C $\subset$ NTAPE(log n) because every string accepted by such an automaton is accepted also by a sequence of moves such that the numbers stored by the counter are always lineary bounded by the lenght of the input. Furthe more it is clear that all elements of C are context-free languages. In section 2 we prove the following theorem.

Theorem 1: Let $\alpha \geq 1$ be some rational number. Then NTAPE(log n) $\subset$ TAPE($(\log n)^{\alpha}$) is equivalent to C $\subset$ TAPE($(\log n)^{\alpha}$).

Because of the results of P.M.Lewis, R.E. Stearns and J. Hartmanis [4] we know that every context-free language can be accepted by a deterministic Turing machine with tape bound $(\log n)^2$. Therefore we get the result of W.J. Savitch [6] as a corollary of our theorem.

Corollary 1: NTAPE(log n) $\subset$ TAPE($(\log n)^2$)

Furthermore theorem 1 shows that the simulation of (log n)-tape bounded nondeterministic Turing machines by deterministic Turing machines is simpler (that means that the deterministic Turing machine needs at most the same amount of space) than the deterministic acceptance of context-free languages. As an immediate consequence of theorem 1 we get the following result.

Corollary 2: NTAPE(log n) = TAPE(log n) $\Leftrightarrow$ C $\subset$ TAPE(log n)

In order to get an idea of the difference between determinism and nondeterminism, we now consider the usual closure operations. It is obvious that both classes, TAPE(log n) and NTAPE(log n), are closed under union, intersection, concatenation and inverse homomorphism. To the author's knowledge nothing is known about the closure of either of these classes against ε-free homomorphism, but it is easy to show that TAPE(log n) is equal to NTAPE(log n) if TAPE(log n) is closed under ε-free homomorphism. The most interesting operation in this context is Kleene's $*$-operator. The $*$-operator is defined in the following way: Let L be some language. Then $L^* = \{v_1 \ldots v_k \mid k \in \mathbb{N} \cup \{0\}, v_i \in L \text{ for all } i = 1,\ldots,k\}$. It is obvious that NTAPE(log n) is closed under the application of the $*$-operator and we show in section 3 that this property is characteristic for the nondeterminism. We prove the following result.

Theorem 2: NTAPE(log n) = TAPE(log n) holds if and only if TAPE(log n) is closed under the application of the $*$-operator.

This theorem makes clear that in the case of the tape function log n the difference between nondeterministic and deterministic machines is just the ability to compute an admissible decomposition of the given input string. We even get the following, more general result.

Theorem 2a: Let $\alpha \geq 1$ be some rational number such that TAPE($(\log n)^\alpha$) is closed under the application of the $*$-operator. Then NTAPE(log n) $\subset$ TAPE($(\log n)^\alpha$).

It is not difficult to see (by means of the methods of [4]) that TAPE($(\log n)^2$) is closed under the application of the $*$-operator, and therefore again we get Savitch's result. Furthermore if we could prove an analogon of theorem 2 for any tape function growing faster than log n, then most probably we would get the corresponding analogon of theorem 2a too and this would imply a better result for the deterministic simulation of nondeterministic machines.

The results of this paper are proved by means of transformational methods. These methods have been used extensively by R.V. Book in [1] and in other papers. Further results are proved in [5] .

2. Proof of theorem 1

We use the notion of many-one reducibility as it is defined in recursive function theory (due to D. Knuth [3] we will speak of transformability).

Definition Let $\mathcal{C}$ be a class of functions (on strings).

(i) Let $f: \Sigma^* \to \Gamma$ be a function in $\mathcal{C}$. A set $L_1 \subset \Sigma^*$ is f-transformable to $L_2 \subset \Gamma^*$ if for every $w \in \Sigma^*$. $w \in L_1$ if and only if $f(w) \in L_2$.

(ii) A class $\mathcal{L}_1$ of sets is $\mathcal{C}$-transformable to a class $\mathcal{L}_2$ of sets if for every $L_1 \in \mathcal{L}_1$ there exist $L_2 \in \mathcal{L}_2$ and $f \in \mathcal{C}$ such that L_1 is f-transformable to L_2.

(iii) A class $\mathcal{L}$ of sets is closed under $\mathcal{C}$-transformabilities if for every set L_1, L_1 is $\mathcal{C}$-transformable to some set $L_2 \in \mathcal{L}$ implies $L_1 \in \mathcal{L}$.

The following lemma follows immediately from the definitions above:

Lemma 1: Let $\mathcal{L}_1, \mathcal{L}_2, \mathcal{L}_3$ be classes of sets and let $\mathcal{C}$ be a class of functions. Suppose that $\mathcal{L}_1$ is $\mathcal{C}$-transformable to $\mathcal{L}_2$ and that $\mathcal{L}_3$ is closed under $\mathcal{C}$-transformabilities. Then $\mathcal{L}_2 \subset \mathcal{L}_3$ implies $\mathcal{L}_1 \subset \mathcal{L}_3$.

The method of trnaformabilities was used explicitly by R.V. Book in [1] and implicitly by J. Hartmanis who showed in [2] that NTAPE(log n) $\subset$ TAPE(log n) is equivalent to $N_3 \subset$ TAPE(log n). N_3 is defined below.

Definition: A k-head two-way automaton consists of a finite control and an input tape where k heads may move independently in both directions (k-head two-way finite automata). The input is placed between two endmarkers ($\dashv$ and $\vdash$). The automaton starts in a distinguished starting state with its k heads on the left endmarker. It accepts the input if it stops in an accepting state. The automaton is called deterministic if its nextmove function is deterministic, otherwise it is called nondeterministic. Let $D_k(N_k)$, $k \in \mathbb{N}$, be the class of all sets accepted by deterministic (nondeterministic) k-head two-way automata.

It is obvious that $\bigcup_{k \in \mathbb{N}} N_k =$ NTAPE(log n).

In 1973 I.H. Sudborough [8] improved the result of Hartmanis and showed that $\bigcup_{k \in \mathbb{N}} N_k \subset$ TAPE(log n) is equivalent to $1\text{-}N_2 \subset$ TAPE(log n), where $1\text{-}N_k$, $k \in \mathbb{N}$, is the class of all languages accepted by nondeterministic k-head one-way finite automata (that means, the k heads are only allowed to move from the left to the right between the two endmarkers). We will show in this paper that it is also equivalent to consider the problem whether C is contained in TAPE(log n).

This result looks similar to Sudborough's result but it seems that this result can't be proved by using his methods, and the fact that C is a subclass of the context-free languages may be useful to get further results. Furthermore we get our results by using only transformational methods whereas Sudborough uses Savitch's language of threadable mazes [7].

We use a class π of functions which is defined in the following way:

(i) Let Σ be an alphabet, let $\dashv, \vdash$ be elements not in Σ and let k be a natural number. Let $f_{\Sigma,k}: \dashv\Sigma^*\vdash \rightarrow ((\Sigma \cup \{\dashv,\vdash\})^k)^*$ be the following function. For all $m \in \mathbb{N}$ and all $a_i \in \Sigma$, $i = 1,\ldots,m$,

$f_{\Sigma,k}(\dashv a_1\ldots a_m\vdash) = \alpha_0\alpha_1\ldots\alpha_{n^k-1}$ where $n = m+2$ and

$\alpha_j = (a_{i_1}, a_{i_2}, \ldots, a_{i_k})$ for $j = i_1 + i_2 n + \ldots + i_k n^{k-1}$ with

$0 \leq i_\nu \leq n-1$ for all $\nu = 1,..,k$. For the sake of simplicity we set $a_0 = \dashv$ and $a_{n-1} = \vdash$.

As an example let us consider the case $k = 3$ and $n = 3$.

Then $f_{\Sigma,3}(a_0a_1a_2) = \alpha_0\alpha_1\ldots\alpha_{26}$, where

$$\begin{array}{lllll}
\alpha_0 = (a_0,a_0,a_0) & \alpha_3 = (a_0,a_1,a_0) & \ldots & \alpha_9 = (a_0,a_0,a_1) \\
\alpha_1 = (a_1,a_0,a_0) & \alpha_4 = (a_1,a_1,a_0) & \ldots & \alpha_{10} = (a_1,a_0,a_1) \\
\alpha_2 = (a_2,a_0,a_0) & \alpha_5 = (a_2,a_1,a_0) & \ldots & \alpha_{11} = (a_2,a_0,a_1)
\end{array}$$

Note that $(\dashv,\dashv,\ldots,\dashv)$ and $(\vdash,\vdash,\ldots,\vdash)$ enclose the new string and don't occur inside, therefore they can be regarded as endmarkers.

(ii) Let d be a natural number and let

$g_{\Sigma,k,d}: \dashv\Sigma^*\vdash \rightarrow \dashv((\Sigma \cup \{\dashv,\vdash\})^k)^*$ be defined by

$g_{\Sigma,k,d}(\dashv w\vdash) = \dashv(f_{\Sigma,k}(\dashv w\vdash) \cdot f_{\Sigma,k}(\dashv w\vdash)^R)^{d \cdot 1(\dashv w\vdash)^k}\vdash \quad \forall w \in \Sigma^*$.

We denote by π the class of all functions which are defined in (ii).

<u>Lemma 2:</u> $\bigcup_k N_k$ is π-transformable to

$\{L \mid \exists\, L_1 \in C,\ L_2 \in \text{TAPE}(\log n) \text{ such that } L = L_1 \cap L_2\}$.

<u>Proof:</u> Let $L \subset \Sigma^*$ be an arbitrary element of N_k for some k. We will show that there exists a $d \in \mathbb{N}$ such that $g_{\Sigma,k,d}(L) = \tilde{L} \cap g_{\Sigma,k,d}(\dashv\Sigma^*\vdash)$ where $\tilde{L} \in C$. Therefore we first have to show that $g_{\Sigma,k,d}(\dashv\Sigma^*\vdash) \in \text{TAPE}(\log n)$. This is not difficult to be proved and we refer the reader to [5] where a detailed proof of a slightly stronger result is given.

Now we will construct a nondeterministic 1-counter automaton $\tilde{M}$ which accepts an input string of the form $g_{\Sigma,k,d}(\dashv w \vdash)$ if and only if $\dashv w \vdash \varepsilon L$. We don't care about the behavior of $\tilde{M}$ on input strings which are not of this form.

Let M_k be a nondeterministic k-head two-way automaton accepting L. Then there exists a $d \varepsilon \mathbb{N}$ such that every computation of M on an input of lenght n needs at most $2 \cdot d \cdot n^k$ moves. In the following let d be this number. M simulates on the input string $g_{\Sigma,k,d}(\dashv w \vdash)$ all the moves performed by M_k on the input string $\dashv w \vdash$. When M is simulating the t-th step, $1 \leq t \leq 2 \cdot d \cdot n^k$, of M_k, then its head is located in the t-th block (a block is a string $f_{\Sigma,k}(\dashv w \vdash)$ or $f_{\Sigma,k}(\dashv w \vdash)^R$, respectively) of $g_{\Sigma,k,d}(\dashv w \vdash)$. Let $i_1, i_2, \ldots, i_k$ be the positions of the k head of M_k before M_k performs its t-th step. Then the head position of $\tilde{M}$ is given by

$i = i_1 + i_2 n + \ldots + i_k n^{k-1} + tn^k$ if $t \equiv 1 \bmod 2$, and

$i = (t+1)n^k - (i_1 + i_2 n + \ldots + i_k n^{k-1})$ if $t \equiv 0 \bmod 2$.

Note that the head of $\tilde{M}$ is located in a block of the form $f_{\Sigma,k}(\dashv w \vdash)$ if $t \equiv 1 \bmod 2$ and in a block of the form $f_{\Sigma,k}(\dashv w \vdash)^R$ if $t \equiv 0 \bmod 2$.

Therefore the i-th symbol of $g_{\Sigma,k,d}(\dashv w \vdash)$ is just $(a_{i_1}, a_{i_2}, \ldots, a_{i_k})$ when $\dashv w \vdash = a_0 \ldots a_{n-1}$. That means that $\tilde{M}$ reads with its single head just the symbols read by the k heads of M_k and so $\tilde{M}$ has all the information necessary to simulate the next move of M_k.

Let us suppose that $\tilde{M}$ is simulating the t-th step of M_k and let i be the head position of $\tilde{M}$. Then M has to move its head to the position $i' = t \cdot n^k + (t \cdot n^k - \tilde{i}$ where

$$\tilde{i} = i + \sum_{j=0}^{k-1} \beta_j n^j$$ and $\beta_j \varepsilon \{-1,0,+1\}$, $j = 1, \ldots, k$, are determined by the moves performed by the k heads of M_k in its t-th step.

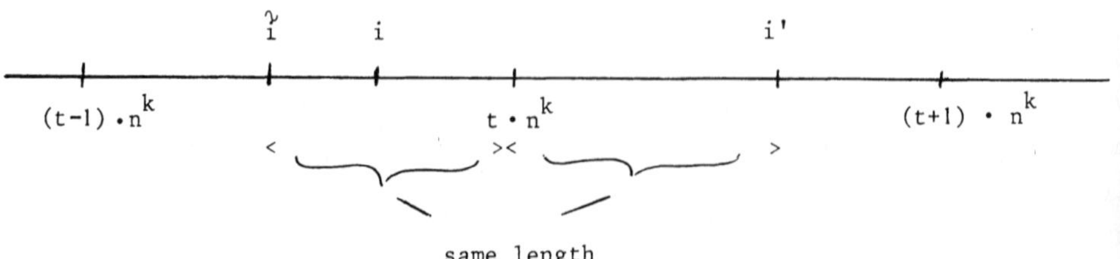

$\tilde{M}$ performs the following operations (note that the head of $\tilde{M}$ is not allowed to move to the left).

Its head moves to the right and the number of these moves are stored by its counter. During this process $\tilde{M}$ subtracts all numbers n^j such that $\beta_j = +1$. That means, if $\tilde{M}$ reads a symbol of the form $(\underbrace{\dashv, \dashv, \ldots, \dashv}_{m}, a, \ldots)$, $a\varepsilon\Sigma$, on the input tape, it looks for the greatest $j \leq m$ such that it still has to subtract n^j. Then $\tilde{M}$ moves to the next cell containing a symbol of the form $(\underbrace{\dashv, \dashv, \ldots, \dashv}_{j}, a, \ldots), a\varepsilon\Sigma$. The distance of these two cells is just n^j. During these moves the counter remains unchanged. Therefore the counter stores the number

$(t \cdot n^k - i) - \sum_{j,\beta_j=1} n^j$ when the head reaches the $(t \cdot n^k)$-th cell.

Now $\tilde{M}$ adds to its headposition all numbers n^j such that $\beta_j = -1$ one after the other beginning with the largest one. Again the movement of the head is controlled by symbols of the form $(\underbrace{\dashv, \dashv, \ldots, \dashv}_{j}, a, \ldots)$, $a\varepsilon\Sigma$. During this process the head moves to the position $t \cdot n^k + \sum_{j,\beta_j=-1} n^j$. Now $\tilde{M}$ reaches the head position i' by adding the contents of the counter.

$\tilde{M}$ accepts the input string when it notices that M_k reaches a final state. Therefore $\tilde{M}$ accepts $g_{\Sigma,k,d}(\dashv w \vdash)$ if and only if M_k accepts $\dashv w \vdash$. Let $\tilde{L}$ be the language accepted by $\tilde{M}$, then $g_{\Sigma,k,d}(L) = \tilde{L} \cap g_{\Sigma,k,d}(\dashv \Sigma^* \vdash)$. q.e.d.

It is not difficult to see that the class TAPE($(\log n)^\alpha$) is closed under π-transformabilities.

<u>Lemma 3:</u> For any rational number $\alpha \geq 1$ the class TAPE($(\log n)^\alpha$) is closed under π-transformabilities.

<u>Proof:</u> We have to show that $L\varepsilon$TAPE($(\log n)^\alpha$) implies

$f^{-1}(L) = \{w \mid f(w)\varepsilon L\}\varepsilon$TAPE($(\log n)^\alpha$) for all $f\varepsilon\pi$.

Let M be some deterministic $(\log n)^\alpha$-tape bounded Turing machine accepting L. We will define a Turing machine $\tilde{M}$ accepting $f^{-1}(L)$. $\tilde{M}$ simulates on the input w all moves performed by M on the input f(w). Since there exists a $k\varepsilon\mathbb{N}$ such that $l(f(w)) \leq l(w)^k$, $\tilde{M}$ needs not more that $(\log n)^\alpha$ cells to store in each step of the simulation the contents of the working tape of M. Furthermore $\tilde{M}$ has to store the head position of M. This can be done in log n cells. It is clear that $\tilde{M}$ can decode the head position of M in order to read just the symbols necessary to simulate one step of M.

Our transformational lemma 1 implies together with lemma 2 and lemma 3 our first main result.

Theorem 1: Let $\alpha \geq 1$ be some rational number. Then
$NTAPE(\log n) \subset TAPE((\log n)^{\alpha})$ is equivalent to $C \subset TAPE((\log n)^{\alpha})$.

Proof: Because of lemma 1,2,3 the following relation holds:
$NTAPE(\log n) \subset TAPE((\log n)^{\alpha})$
$\Leftrightarrow \mathcal{L} = \{L_1 \cap L_2 \mid L_1 \varepsilon C, L_2 \varepsilon TAPE(\log n)\} \subset TAPE((\log n)^{\alpha}$.
Since $C \subset TAPE((\log n)^{\alpha})$ implies $\mathcal{L} \subset TAPE((\log n)^{\alpha})$ the theorem follows.

3. Proof of theorem 2

Let $L \subset \Sigma^*$ be an arbitrary element of NTAPE(log n). We showed in the proof of lemma 2 that there exist $k,d \varepsilon \mathbb{N}$ and a set $\tilde{L} \varepsilon C$ such that $g_{\Sigma,k,d}(L) = \tilde{L} \cap g_{\Sigma,k,d}(\dashv \Sigma^* \vdash)$. Furthermore we constructed a nondeterministic 1-counter automaton $\tilde{M}$ accepting $\tilde{L}$ whose head is moving one cell to the right in each step and which has the following property:

If its counter stores a number not equal to zero then the next move of $\tilde{M}$ is determined deterministically.

That means that $\tilde{M}$ can act nondeterministerically only if its counter stores zero Now let $S = \{s_o,\ldots,s_r\}$ be the set of states, $F \subset S$ the set of final states and $s_o \varepsilon$ the starting state of $\tilde{M}$. We define sets $L_{ij} \subset \Sigma^*$, $0 \leq i,j \leq r$.

Let $\tilde{M}$ start its computation with the state s_i, $v \varepsilon \Sigma^*$ on its input tape and its counter storing zero. v is an element of L_{ij} if and only if the following two condition are fulfilled: (1) After $\tilde{M}$ has read the whole string v, that means after its head has left the input string, the state of $\tilde{M}$ is s_j and its counter stores zer (2) During the whole computation (except of the first step) the contents of the counter are always greater than zero.

Because of this definition $\tilde{M}$ can act nondeterministically only in its first step when it is accepting an element of L_{ij}. Therefore each L_{ij}, $0 \leq i,j \leq r$, is a finite union of elements of C_D, where C_D is the class of all languages accepted by deterministic one-way one-counter automata. This implies $L_{ij} \varepsilon TAPE(\log n)$ for all $0 \leq i,j \leq r$, because $C_D \subset TAPE(\log n)$ and TAPE(log n) is closed under union.

Now let $w \varepsilon \Sigma^*$ be an arbitrary element of $\tilde{L}$. Then there exists a decomposition $w = v_1 v_2 \ldots v_t$ such that the contents of the counter of $\tilde{M}$ are zero if and only if the head of $\tilde{M}$ is located on the first symbol of one of the v_i, $i \varepsilon \{1,\ldots,t\}$. This shows us that $w \varepsilon \tilde{L}$ holds if and only if there exist a $t \varepsilon \mathbb{N}$ and $i_1,\ldots,i_t \varepsilon \{0,\ldots,r\}$

such that $w \varepsilon L_{oi_1} \circ L_{i_1 i_2} \circ \dots \circ L_{i_{t-1} i_t}$ and $s_{i_t} \varepsilon F$

We set now

$$L_{ij}^k = \bigcup_{t \varepsilon \mathbb{N}} \; \bigcup_{i_1,\dots,i_t \varepsilon \{0,\dots,k-1\}} L_{ij_1} \circ L_{i_1 i_2} \circ \dots \circ L_{i_t j} \;.$$

The L_{ij}^k are also defined by the wellknown recursive formula

$$L_{ij}^o = L_{ij}$$

$$L_{ij}^{k+1} = L_{ij}^k \cup L_{i,k+1}^k \circ \left(L_{k+1,k+1}^k\right)^{*} \circ L_{k+1,j}^k$$

Intuitively L_{ij}^k consists of all words which lead from the state s_i to the state s_j such that during this computation only states s_ν with $0 \leq \nu \leq k-1$ are reached.

We have seen above that $\tilde{L} = \bigcup_{j, s_j \varepsilon F} L_{oj}^r$.

Now let $\alpha \geq 1$ be some rational number such that TAPE($(\log n)^\alpha$) is closed under the application of the $*$-operator. We have shown already that $L_{ij} \varepsilon$TAPE(log n) for all $i,j \varepsilon \{0,\dots,r\}$ and therefore the recursion formula above and the closure of TAPE(log n) against π-transformabilities (Lemma 3) lead to the following conclusions:

$$L_{ij} \varepsilon \text{TAPE}(\log n) \qquad \forall i,j \varepsilon \{0,\dots,r\}$$

$$\Rightarrow L_{ij}^k \varepsilon \text{TAPE}((\log n)^\alpha) \qquad \forall i,j,k \varepsilon \{0,\dots r\}$$

$$\Rightarrow \tilde{L} = \bigcup_{j,s_j \varepsilon F} L_{oj}^r \varepsilon \; \text{TAPE}(\log n)^\alpha)$$

$$\Rightarrow g_{\Sigma,k,d}(L) = \tilde{L} \cap g_{\Sigma,k,d}(\dashv \Sigma^{*} \vdash) \varepsilon \; \text{TAPE}((\log n)^\alpha).$$

$$\Rightarrow L \varepsilon \text{TAPE}((\log n)^\alpha)$$

Because L was arbitrarely chosen this completes the proof of theorem 2 and theorem 2a.

References

1. Book, R.V.: On the structure of complexity classes, 2 nd Colloquium: Automata, Languages and Programming, 1974, 437-445.

2. Hartmanis, J., On Non-Determinacy in Simple Computing Devices, Acta Informatica 1 (1972), 336-344.

3. Knuth, D.E., Postscript about NP-hard problems, SIGACT News 6, 2 (1974), 15-16.

4. Lewis, P.M. Stearns, R.E. and Hartmanis, J., Memory bounds for recognition of context-free and context-sensitive languages, IEEE conf.rec. 7-th ann. symp. Switch.Cir.Th.Log. Des., 1965, 191-202.

5. Monien, B., Transformational Methods and their Application to Complexity Problems, submitted for publication

6. Savitch, W.J., Relationships between nondeterministic and deterministic tape complexity, J. Comp. Syst. Sci. 4 (1970), 177-192.

7. Savitch, W.J. Maze Recognizing Automata and Nondeterministic Tape Complexity, J. Comp. Syst. Sci. 7 (1973), 389-403.

8. Sudborough, I.H., On Tape-Bounded Complexity Classes and Multi-Head Finite Automata, IEEE conf. rec. 14-th ann.symp. Switch.Aut.Th., 1973, 138-144.

ZUR ENTSCHEIDBARKEIT DER FUNKTIONALEN ÄQUIVALENZ

H. Beck
Institut für Informatik I, Universität Karlsruhe
D-7500 Karlsruhe 1, Postfach 6380

Abstract: *In this paper we consider the equivalence problem for several classes of programs. We show that it is unsolvable for all "acceptable" program classes of the Grzegorczyk class* $\mathcal{E}_0$ *and of the polynominals over the integers formed with* $\dot{-}$ *instead of* $-$. *Furthermore we show that the equivalence problem is solvable for the class* $L_1(\dot{-}1)$ *of loop programs with the additional instruction* $X := X\dot{-}1$, *but again unsolvable for the class* $L_1(\dot{-}1,+)$ *and the Cleave-Ritchie-classes* $L_2^2 \subsetneqq L_2$ *and* $L_2^1(\dot{-}1)$.

1. Einführung

Will man Programme verifizieren oder optimieren, so stellt sich oft die Frage: "gibt es einen Algorithmus, der für zwei beliebige Programme einer Programmklasse Γ entscheidet, ob diese Programme dieselbe Funktion berechnen ?"; mit anderen Worten: "ist die (funktionale) Äquivalenz entscheidbar ?"

Tsichritzis (1970) hat für die Klasse L_1 der Loophierarchie einen solchen Algorithmus angegeben. Weiterhin zeigt er mit Resultaten von Meyer und Ritchie (1967), daß für die Klasse L_2 (diese Klasse berechnet gerade die elementaren Funktionen $\mathcal{E} = \mathcal{E}_3$ der Grzegorczykhierarchie) kein solcher Algorithmus existieren kann. Dabei lautet Lemma 1: "The equivalence problem is recursively unsolvable for primitive recursive functions". Man kann aber Programmklassen für die primitiv rekursiven Funktionen mit entscheidbarem Äquivalenzproblem angeben (siehe 2.6). Um diesen Widerspruch zu lösen, definieren wir in Abschnitt 2 in Analogie zu den Gödelnumerierungen (vgl. Rogers (1958)) die "akzeptablen" Programmklassen für subrekursive Funktionenklassen und übertragen dann das Äquivalenzproblem auf Klassen von Funktionen.

Im 3. Abschnitt zeigen wir mit Hilfe von Ergebnissen von Grzegorczyk (1953) und Matijasevič (1970), daß für alle Klassen der Grzegorczykhierarchie und für die mit $+,\dot{-},\cdot$ gebildeten Polynome über den natürlichen Zahlen die Äquivalenz unentscheidbar ist. Im 4. Abschnitt erweitern wir die Klasse L_1 der Loophierarchie durch Hinzunahme der Befehle $X := X\dot{-}1$ und $X := Y+Z$ zu den Klassen $L_1(\dot{-}1)$ und $L_1(\dot{-}1,+)$. Für die zugehörigen Funktionenklassen gilt: $\mathcal{L}_1(\dot{-}1,+) \supsetneqq \mathcal{L}_1(\dot{-}1) \supsetneqq \mathcal{L}_1$ und in $\mathcal{L}_1(\dot{-}1)$ ist die Äquivalenz entscheidbar, während sie in $\mathcal{L}_1(\dot{-}1,+)$ nicht entscheidbar ist.

Im letzten Abschnitt untersuchen wir die "Cleave-Ritchie-Hierarchien" zwischen L_1 und L_2 bzw. $L_1(\dot{-}1)$ und $L_2(\dot{-}1)$ und zeigen, daß für L_2^2 und $L_2^1(\dot{-}1)$ die Äquivalenz nicht entscheidbar ist.

2. Definitionen und Schreibweisen

Sei $PR^{(n)}$ die Menge der n-stelligen partiell rekursiven Funktionen und sei $PR = \bigcup_n PR^{(n)}$. Seien i,j,k,n,m immer aus $\mathbb{N} = \{0,1,\dots\}$. Seien C_k^n, U_i^n, s die Funktionen mit $\forall x_1 \dots x_n (C_k^n(x_1,\dots,x_n) = k,\ U_i^n(x_1,\dots,x_n) =$ und $\forall x\ s(x) = x+1$. Sei $\mathcal{K} = \{x \mid$ x-te Turingmaschine angesetzt auf x hält$\}$.

Def. 2.1: A sei ein endliches Alphabet. Ist $\mathbb{P} \subset A^*$ mit $\mathbb{P} = \bigcup_n \mathbb{P}^{(n)}$ und $\mathbb{P}^{(n)} \cap \mathbb{P}^{(m)} = \emptyset$ für $n \neq m$ und ist φ eine partiell rekursive Abbildung $A^* \times \mathbb{N}^* \to \mathbb{N}$, dann heiße $(\mathbb{P},\varphi)$ Programmklasse mit dem Sprachschatz $\mathbb{P}$ und dem Interpreter φ. Die Menge $\mathcal{F} = \bigcup_n \mathcal{F}^{(n)}$, wobei $\mathcal{F}^{(n)} = \{\varphi_P \mid \exists P (P \in \mathbb{P}^{(n)} \wedge \varphi_P : \mathbb{N}^n \to \mathbb{N} \wedge \forall \underline{x} \in \mathbb{N}^n (\varphi_P(\underline{x}) = \varphi(P,\underline{x}))\}$ heiße die zugehörige Funktionenklasse.

Def. 2.2: Eine Programmklasse $(\mathbb{P},\varphi)$ heiße akzeptabel, falls sie das uniforme S_n^m-Theorem erfüllt, das heißt, falls es eine partiell rekursive Abbildung $S: A^* \times \mathbb{N}^* \to A^*$ gibt, so daß $\forall n \forall m \forall P \in \mathbb{P}^{(n+m)} \forall \underline{x} \in \mathbb{N}^m$

$$\forall \underline{y} \in \mathbb{N}^n : S(P,\underline{x}) \in \mathbb{P}^{(n)} \wedge \varphi_P(\underline{x},\underline{y}) = \varphi_{S(P,\underline{x})}(\underline{y}).$$

Def. 2.3: Eine Programmklasse $(\mathbb{P},\varphi)$ heiße entscheidbar, falls es eine totale berechenbare Abbildung $t: A^* \to \mathbb{N}$ gibt, so daß

$$\forall \omega \in A^* : (t(\omega) = k+1 \text{ falls } \omega \in \mathbb{P}^{(k)}) \wedge (t(\omega) = 0 \text{ sonst})).$$

Durch Gödelisierungen lassen sich (akzeptable, entscheidbare) Programmklassen rekursiv auf (akzeptable, entscheidbare) Programmklassen mit $A^* = \mathbb{N}$ und zurück übersetzen. Ist $(\mathbb{P},\varphi)$ eine akzeptable entscheidbare Programmklasse mit $A^* = \mathbb{N}$ für PR, dann bilden die Listen $\{\varphi_P\}$ mit $P \in \mathbb{P}^{(n)}$ Gödelnumerierungen für $PR^{(n)}$; weiterhin läßt sich jede Gödelnumerierung mit geeignetem $(\mathbb{P},\varphi)$ so gewinnen.

Def. 2.4: Die Äquivalenz ist für eine Programmklasse $(\mathbb{P},\varphi)$ entscheidbar genau dann, wenn es eine partiell rekursive Abbildung $E: A^* \times A^* \to \mathbb{N}$ gibt, so daß $\forall n \forall P,Q \in \mathbb{P}^{(n)} : (E(P,Q) = 0$ falls $\varphi_P \equiv \varphi_Q) \wedge (E(P,Q) = 1$ sonst$)$.

Lemma 2.5: Sind $(\mathbb{P},\varphi)$ und $(\mathbb{P}',\varphi')$ akzeptable Programmklassen und ist τ eine rekursive Übersetzung von $(\mathbb{P},\varphi)$ nach $(\mathbb{P}',\varphi')$, dann überträgt sich die Entscheidbarkeit der Äquivalenz von $(\mathbb{P}',\varphi')$ auf $(\mathbb{P},\varphi)$.

Lemma 2.6: Die Äquivalenz ist für eine entscheidbare Programmklasse der primitiv rekursiven Funktionen entscheidbar.

Beweisskizze: Man wähle die üblichen Definitionsschemen für die primi rekursiven Funktion. Es gibt einen Algorithmus, der die kleinsten Definitionsschemen und somit für jede Funktion genau ein Schema aufzählt. Wählt man die Urbilder einer solchen Aufzählung als Programme, so hat man eine entscheidbare Programmklasse, die das Äquivalenzproblem löst. Um solche etwas pathologischen Programmklassen auszuschließen definieren wir:

Def. 2.7: Die Äquivalenz ist genau dann für eine Funktionenklasse entscheidbar, wenn sie für eine akzeptable Programmklasse einer Obermenge $\mathcal{F}'$ von $\mathcal{F}$ entscheidbar ist.

Folgerung 2.8: Nach Def. 2.7 überträgt sich die Entscheidbarkeit der Äquivalenz auf die Teilmengen und die Unentscheidbarkeit auf Obermengen einer Funktionenklasse. Außerdem kann man sich wegen Lemma 2.5 beim Führen der Entscheidbarkeits- oder Unentscheidbarkeitsbeweise auf Programmklassen mit $A^* = \mathbb{N}$ beschränken.

Lemma 2.9: Ist für eine Funktionenklasse $\mathcal{F}$ $f \leq g$ entscheidbar, so ist auch die funktionale Äquivalenz entscheidbar.

Beweis: $f \equiv g \Leftrightarrow f \leq g \wedge g \leq f$.

3. Die Grzegorczykhierarchie und modifizierte Polynome

In Grzegorczyk (1953) werden die Klassen $\mathcal{E}_i$ eingeführt, welche bezüglich der Substitution und der beschränkten Rekursion abgeschlossen sind.

Satz 3.1: Die Äquivalenz ist für keine Grzegorczykklasse $\mathcal{E}_i$ entscheidbar.

Beweis: Wegen Folgerung 2.8 genügt es zu zeigen, daß es für kein $\mathcal{F} \supset \mathcal{E}_0$ eine akzeptable Programmklasse $(\mathbb{P}, \varphi)$ mit $A^* = \mathbb{N}$ und entscheidbarer Äquivalenz geben kann. Sei $(\mathbb{P}, \varphi)$ eine Programmklasse für $\mathcal{F} \supset \mathcal{E}_0$ mit $A^* = \mathbb{N}$. Nach Grzegorczyk (1953) (theorem 5.3) gibt es für jede rekursiv aufzählbare Menge also auch für $\mathcal{K}$ ein $f \in \mathcal{E}_0$ mit $\mathcal{K} = \{x \mid \exists y f(x,y) = 0\}$. Da die Signumfunktion sig aus $\mathcal{E}_0$ ist, ist auch $\mathrm{sig}(f) \in \mathcal{E}_0$. Sei $k \in \mathbb{P}^{(2)}$ ein Programm für sig(f) und $j \in \mathbb{P}^{(1)}$ für C_1^1. Dann gilt:

$$\forall x (x \notin \mathcal{K} \Leftrightarrow \neg(\exists y \varphi_k(x,y) = 0) \Leftrightarrow \forall y (\varphi_k(x,y) = 1)$$

$$\Leftrightarrow \forall y (\varphi_{S(k,x)}(y) = \varphi_j(y)) \Leftrightarrow \varphi_{S(k,x)} \equiv \varphi_j \Leftrightarrow E(S(k,x),j) = 0$$

Da $k,j \in \mathbb{P}$, sig(f) total und $(\mathbb{P}, \varphi)$ akzeptabel ist, ist $\lambda x E(S(k,x),j)$ eine totale Funktion. Somit folgt aus der Entscheidbarkeit des Äquivalenzproblems für $\mathcal{E}_0$ die Lösbarkeit des Halteproblems für Turingmaschinen. Als Folgerung aus diesem Satz können wir mit Lemma 2.9 schließen, daß $f \leq g$ und damit auch die Frage: "definieren drei Funktionen durch beschränkte Rekursion eine neue Funktion ?" in allen $\mathcal{E}_i$ nicht entscheid-

bar ist. Die Definition von Grzegorczyk führt deshalb zu nicht entscheidbaren akzeptablen Programmklassen. Durch Modifikation der beschränkten Rekursion lassen sich aber auch akzeptable entscheidbare Programmklassen für $\mathcal{E}_o$ finden. Als weitere Folgerung dieses Satzes ergibt sich, daß für die primitiv rekursiven, die elementaren und die subelementaren Funktionen die Äquivalenz nicht entscheidbar ist.
Als nächstes zeigen wir, daß es zwei Funktionenklassen gibt, deren Funktionen höchstens polynomiales Wachstum besitzen und für die die funktionale Äquivalenz nicht entscheidbar ist.

<u>Def. 3.3 a:</u> Sei <u>Polm</u> die Klasse von Funktionen, die aus den folgenden Funktionen durch Komposition entsteht: $C_k^n, U_i^n, s, +, \cdot, \dot{-}$ $(x_1 \dot{-} x_2 = x_1 - x_2$ falls $x_1 \geq x_2$ und gleich null sonst).

<u>Def. 3.3 b:</u> Sei <u>Polg</u> definiert wie Polm nur statt $\dot{-}$ werde $\chi_=$ $(\chi_=(x_1,x_2) = 0$, falls $x_1 = x_2$ und gleich eins sonst) als als Ausgangsfunktion gewählt.

<u>Satz 3.4</u>: Für Polm und Polg ist die Äquivalenz nicht entscheidbar.

<u>Beweis</u>: Da $\forall x \forall y (\chi_=(x,y) = 1 \dot{-} (1 \dot{-} ((1 \dot{-} x) + (1 \dot{-} y))))$ ist, gilt Polm $\supset$ Polg, so daß der Beweis wegen Folgerung 2.9 nur für Polg geführt werden muß.

Nach Matijasevič (10-Hilbert'sches Problem) gibt es ein Polynom f_1 (dieses habe m+2-Stellen) und zu jedem einstelligen rekursiv aufzählbaren Prädikat T ein t, so daß gilt:
$\forall x (Tx \leftrightarrow \exists y_1 \dots \exists y_m [f_1(t,x,y_1,\dots,y_m)=0]$ mit $x,t,y_1,\dots,y_m \in \mathbb{N}$.
Sei t so gewählt, daß $T = \mathcal{K}$ und sei f das Polynom, welches aus f_1 durch Einsetzung von diesem t entsteht.
Ein Polynom f ist gleich der Differenz zweier Polynome p und q, welch keine Subtraktion und nur positive Koeffizienten enthalten. Damit gilt $\forall \underline{z} \in \mathbb{N}^{m+1} (f(\underline{z}) = 0 \leftrightarrow \chi_=(p(\underline{z}), q(\underline{z})) = 0)$. Sei nun $(\mathbb{P}, \varphi)$ eine akzeptable Programmklasse für $\mathcal{F} \supset$ Polg, dann gibt es $i \in \mathbb{P}^{(m+1)}$, so daß $\varphi_i \equiv \chi_=(p,q)$, da $\chi_=(p,q) \in$ Polg ist. Weiter sei $j \in \mathbb{P}^{(m)}$, so gewählt, daß $\varphi_j \equiv C_1^m$. Nun können wir schließen:

$$\forall x (x \notin K \leftrightarrow \neg \exists y_1 \dots \exists y_m f_1(k,x,y_1,\dots,y_m)=0 \leftrightarrow \neg \exists y_1 \dots y_m \varphi_i(x,y_1,\dots,y_m) = 0$$

$$\leftrightarrow \forall y_1 \dots \forall y_m \varphi(x,y_1,\dots,y_m)=1 \leftrightarrow \varphi_{S(i,x)} \equiv \varphi_j \leftrightarrow E(S(i,x),j) = 0$$

Die Lösbarkeit des Äquivalenzproblems bedingt also auch hier die Lösbarkeit des Halteproblems für Turingmaschinen.
Für die Klasse Pol der Polynome über $\mathbb{Z}$ ist die funktionale Äquivalenz dagegen durch Koeffizientenvergleich lösbar.

4. Loopprogramme

Die Klasse L der Loopprogramme wurde von Meyer und Ritchie (1967) eingeführt. Wir wollen diese und zwei Erweiterungen im Folgenden (der Kürze wegen nur informal) definieren. Durch Loopprogramme werden natürliche Zahlen, die in beliebig vielen Registern X_i abgespeichert sind manipuliert. Der Sprachschatz der Loopprogramme lautet:

Def. 4.1: Ein Loopprogramm $P \in L$ ist eine endliche Folge von Befehlen, die mit $In(X_1,\ldots,X_n)$ beginnt und mit $Out(X_o)$ endet. Die übrigen Befehle haben die Form $X_i := X_j$, $X_i := X_i+1$, $X_i := 0$, $Loop(X_i)$ oder End. Für $P \in L(\dot{-}1)$ sind außerdem noch die Befehle $X_i := X_i \dot{-} 1$ und für $P \in L(\dot{-}1,+)$ die Befehle $X_i := X_i \dot{-} 1$ und $X_i := X_j+X_k$ erlaubt. Die Befehle $Loop(X_i)$ und End müssen immer wie öffnende und schließende Klammern angeordnet sein.

Def. 4.2: Ein Loopprogramm wird interpretiert, indem die Befehle der Reihe nach abgearbeitet und die Registerinhalte entsprechend verändert werden. Zu Beginn seien alle Registerinhalte gleich 0. Dann liest $In(X_1,\ldots,X_n)$ das Argument n-Tupel ein. Die Interpretation der Befehle $X_i := X_i+1$, $X_i := 0$, $X_i := X_j$ und $X_i = X_j+X_k$ ist offensichtlich. $X_i := X_i \dot{-} 1$ wird abgearbeitet indem der Inhalt des Registers X_i um 1 erniedrigt wird, falls er größer null ist, und sonst gleich null bleibt. Ist als nächster Befehl $Loop(X_i)$ abzuarbeiten, so suche man das zugehörige End und arbeite das Programmstück, welches zwischen $Loop(X_i)$ und diesem End liegt so oft ab, wie der Inhalt des Registers X_i beim Eintritt in diese Schleife angibt. Anschließend führe man die Interpretation des diesem End folgenden Befehls aus. $Out(X_o)$ gibt schließlich den Inhalt des Registers X_o als Ergebnis aus. Jedem Loopprogramm P wird durch diese Interpretation φ eine Funktion φ_P zugeordnet.
Zur Abkürzung stehe $L(\sim)$ für $L, L(\dot{-}1)$ oder $L(\dot{-}1,+)$.

Def. 4.3: Für alle n sei $L_n(\sim)$ die Klasse von Programmen aus $L(\sim)$, deren $Loop(X_i)$-End-Paare höchstens n-mal geschachtelt sind, das heißt $L_o(\sim)$ enthalte kein $Loop(X_i)$-End-Paar, $L_1(\sim)$ nur einfache Schleifen etc.

Def. 4.4: $\mathcal{L}(\sim)$ bzw. $\mathcal{L}_n(\sim)$ seien die zu $L(\sim)$ bzw. $L_n(\sim)$ und der Interpretation φ gehörenden Funktionenklassen. $\mathcal{L}(\sim)$ sind gerade die primitiv rekursiven Funktionen.

Lemma 4.5: Die Klassen $(L_n(\sim),\varphi)$ sind entscheidbare akzeptable Programmklassen.

Beweisskizze: Der einzige nicht offensichtliche Punkt ist das

S_n^m-Theorem. Wie man die Funktion S erhält, sei hier am Beispiel S_1^1 gezeigt. Ist P :≡ In(X_1,X_2);P', dann lautet S_1^1(P,x) = In(X_1);X_2 := X_1; X_1 := 0; $\underbrace{X_1 := X_1+1;\ldots,X_1 := X_1+1}_{x\text{-mal}}$;P'.

Für den Beweis des nächsten Satzes benötigen wir die Presburger Arithmetik. Dies ist die Theorie, die zu dem üblichen Axiomensystem für 0, ' (Nachfolger) und + in der Logik der 1. Stufe mit Gleichheit gehört. Die n+1-stelligen rechtseindeutigen Ausdrücke definieren n-stellige berechenbare Funktionen.

Satz 4.6: Für $\mathcal{L}_1(\dot{-}1)$ ist die funktionale Äquivalenz entscheidbar.

Beweis: Wie wir im nächsten Satz zeigen, läßt sich $L_1(\dot{-}1)$ rekursiv in die Presburgerarithmetik übersetzen. Da die Presburgerarithmetik entscheidbar ist (vgl. Presburger (1930)), ist das Äquivalenzproblem dort lösbar und somit nach Lemma 2.5 auch in $L_1(\dot{-}1)$.

Def. 4.7: Eine Funktion heiße "partiell linear", wenn sie durch Komposition aus den Ausgangsfunktion C_o^n,U_i^n,s,+,$\dot{-}$,w(w(x_1,x_2)=x_1 für $x_2 \neq 0 \wedge$= sonst), [x/k] und [x,k] (abgeschnittene Division bzw. Rest bei Division durch eine Konstante) gewonnen werden kann. Dies sind gerade um $\dot{-}$ als Ausgangsfunktion erweiterten "simple functions".

Satz 4.8: a) Die Klasse $L_1(\dot{-}1)$ läßt sich in die Klasse der "partiell linearen" Funktionsausdrücke übersetzen. b) Die "partiell linearen" Funktionsausdrücke lassen sich in die Presburgerarithmetik übersetzen

Beweisskizze: Zu a) Hierzu kann der Beweis des Theorems 4 von Tsichritzis (1970) so erweitert werden, daß auch der Befehl X:=X$\dot{-}$1 miterfaßt wird. Zu b) Zunächst werden für die Grundfunktionen der "partiell linearen" Funktionen äquivalente Presburgerausdrücke angegeben. So kann z.B. $y=x_1\dot{-}x_2$ in $x_1=y+x_2 \vee (y=0 \wedge \exists z(x_1+z=x_2))$ und $y=[x/k]$ in $\exists v(\exists w(v+w+1=k) \wedge x=\underbrace{y+\ldots+y}_{k\text{-mal}}+v)$ übersetzt werden.

Sei f aus g,h_1 und h_2 durch Substitution gewonnen, also f(x) = g(h_1(x),h_2(x)) und seien H_1,H_2 bzw. G Presburgerausdrücke für h_1,h_2 und g, dann ist

$F \equiv \exists y_1 \exists y_2 (H_1(x,y_1) \wedge H_2(x,y_2) \wedge G(y_1,y_2,y))$ ein Ausdruck für f. Somit kann zu jedem partiell linearen Funktionsausdruck durch Induktion über seinen Aufbau ein äquivalenter Presburger Ausdruck gefunden werden.

5. Cleave-Ritchie-Hierarchien

Die bisher betrachteten Loophierarchien $L_i(\sim)$ werden nun weiter verfeinert, indem der Bereich zwischen zwei benachbarten Loopklassen in unendliche Hierarchien aufgeteilt wird. Dabei seien die $L_i^k(\sim)$-Programme gerade die Programme aus $L_{i+1}(\sim)$, die höchstens k-verschiedene Loop-End Paare der Schachtelungstiefe i+1 besitzen. $\mathcal{L}_i^k$ seien die zugehörigen Funktionenklassen. Diese sind nun im allgemeinen nicht mehr gegenüber der Komposition von Funktionen abgeschlossen. Daß sie aber gegenüber der Substitution von Konstanten abgeschlossen sind, zeigt:

Lemma 5.1: Die Klassen $L_i^k[\sim]$ sind akzeptable entscheidbare Programmklassen.

Beweis: Der Beweis geht wie für Lemma 4.5.

Satz 5.2: Für die Klassen $\mathcal{L}_1^2$ und $\mathcal{L}_2^1(\dot{-}1)$ ist die Äquivalenz nicht entscheidbar.

Beweisskizze: Sind p und q beliebige Polynome ohne Subtraktionen, so läßt sich $\chi_=(p,q)$ mit L_2^2 bzw. $L_2^1(\dot{-}1)$-Programmen berechnen. Damit ergibt sich dann wie beim Beweis des Satzes 3.4 ein Widerspruch zwischen der Unlösbarkeit des 10. Hilbert'schen Problems und der Entscheidbarkeit der Äquivalenz.

Schluß: Insgesamt zeigt sich also, daß die funktionale Äquivalenz nicht erst in der Klasse $\mathcal{E}$ der elementaren Funktionen, die exponentiell-wachsende Funktionen enthält, sondern schon in kleineren Klassen, deren Funktionen höchstens polynomial oder linear wachsen unentscheidbar werden kann. Andernseits lassen sich die "simple functions" noch ohne Verlust der Entscheidbarkeit etwas erweitern.

Literaturverzeichnis

Grzegorczyk, A.: "Some classes of recursive functions", Rozprawy Mathematyczne 4. (1953)

Matijasevič, J.V.: "Enumerable sets are Diophantine", Soviet Math. Dokl. 11, 354-358. (1970)

Meyer, A.R., D.M. Ritchie: "The complexity of loop programs", Proc. 22nd Nat. Conf. ACM, 1967, ACM Pub P-67, pp. 465-469

Presburger, M.: "Über die Vollständigkeit eines gewissen Systems der Arithmetik ganzer Zahlen, in welchen die Addition als einzige Operation hervortritt", Comptes-rendus du I Congrès des Mathématiciens des Pays Slaves, Warsaw (1930) pp. 92-101, 395

Tsichritzis, D.: "The equivalence problem of simple programs", Journal of the Association for Computing Machinery 17: 729-738. (1970)

Quantifier Elimination for Real Closed Fields by Cylindrical Algebraic Decomposition

George E. Collins*
University of Wisconsin, Madison
University of Kaiserslautern

1. Introduction. Tarski in 1948, [18] published a quantifier elimination method for the elementary theory of real closed fields (which he had discoverd in 1930). As noted by Tarski, any quantifier elimination method for this theory also provides a decision method, which enables one to decide whether any sentence of the theory is true or fals Since many important and difficult mathematical problems can be expressed in this theory, any computationally feasible quantifier elimination algorithm would be of utmost significance.

However, it became apparent that Tarski's method required too muc computation to be practical except for quite trivial problems. Seidenberg in 1954, [17], described another method which he thought would be more efficient. A third method was published by Cohen in 1969, [3]. Some significant improvements of Tarski's method have been made by W. Böge, [20], which are described in a thesis by Holthusen, [21].

This paper describes a completely new method which I discoverd in February 1973. This method was presented in a seminar at Stanford University in March 1973 and in abstract form at a symposium at Carnegie-Mellon University in May 1973. In August 1974 a full presentation of the method was delivered at the EUROSAM 74 Conference in Stockholm and a preliminary version of the present paper was published in the proceedings of that conference, [8].

*This research was partially supported by National Science Foundation grants GJ-30125X and DCR74-13278.

The method described here is much more efficient than the previous methods, and therefore offers renewed hope of practical applicability. In fact, it will be shown that, for a prenex input formula $\emptyset$, the maximum computing time of the method is dominated, in the sense of [5], by $(2n)^{2^{2r+8}} m^{2^{r+6}} d^3 a$, where r is the number of variables in ϕ, m is the number of polynomials occurring in ϕ, n is the maximum degree of any such polynomial in any variable, d is the maximum length of any integer coefficient of any such polynomial, and a is the number of occurrences of atomic formulas in ϕ. Thus, for fixed r, the computing time is dominated by a polynomial function $P_r(m,n,d,a)$. In contrast, it can be shown that the maximum computing times of the methods of Tarski and Seidenberg are exponential in both m and n for every fixed r, including even r=1, and this is likely the case for Cohen's method also. (In fact, Cohen's method is presumbly not intended to be efficient.) Böge's improvement of Tarski's method eliminates the exponential dependency on m, but the exponential dependency on n remains.

Fischer and Rabin, [9], have recently shown that every decision method, deterministic or non-deterministic, for the first order theory of the additive group of the real numbers, a fortiori for the elementary theory of a real closed field, has a maximum computing time which dominates 2^{cN} where N is the length of the input formula and c is some positive constant. Since m, n, d, r and a are all less than or equal to N (assuming that x^n must be written as $x \cdot x \cdot \ldots \cdot x$), the method of this paper has a computing time dominated by $2^{2^{kN}}$ where in fact $k \leq 8$. The result of Fischer and Rabin suggests that a bound of this form is likely the best achievable for any deterministic method.

In a letter received from Leonard Monk in April 1974, I was informed that he and R. Solovay had found a decision method, but not a quantifier elimination method, with a maximum computing bound of the form $2^{2^{2^{kN}}}$. However, the priority and superiority of the method described below are easily established.

The most essential observation underlying the method to be described is that if $\mathfrak{A}$ is any finite set of polynomials in r variables with real coefficients, then there is a decomposition of r-dimensional real space into a finite number of disjoint connected sets called cells, in each of which each polynomial in $\mathfrak{A}$ is invariant in sign. Moreover, these cells are cylindrically arranged with respect to each of the r variables, and they are algebraic in the sense that their boundaries are the zeros of certain polynomials which can be derived from the polynomials in $\mathcal{A}$. Such a decomposition is therefore called an $\mathcal{A}$-invariant cylindrical algebraic decomposition. The sign of a polynomial in $\mathcal{A}$ in a cell of the decomposition can be determined by computing its sign at a sample point belonging to the cell. In the application of cylindrical algebraic decomposition to quantifier elimination, we assume that we are given a quantified formula ϕ in prenex form, and we take $\mathcal{A}$ to be the set of all polynomials occurring in ϕ. From a set of sample points for a decomposition, we can decide in which cells the unquantified matrix of the formula ϕ is true. The decomposition of r-dimensional space induces, and is constructed from, a decomposition of each lower-dimension space. Each cylinder is composed of a finite number of cells, so universal and existential quantifiers can be treated like conjunctions and disjunctions, and one can decide in which cells of a lower-dimension space the quantified formula is true. The quantifier elimination can be completed by constructing formulas which define these cells.

The polynomials whose zeros form the boundaries of the cells are the elements of successive "projections" of the set $\mathcal{A}$. The projection of a set of polynomials in r variables is a set of polynomials in r-1 variables. The cylindrical arrangement of cells is ensured by a condition called delineability of roots, which is defined in Section 2. Several theorems giving sufficient conditions for delineability are proved, culminating in the definition of projection and the fundamental theorem that if each element of the projection of a set $\mathcal{A}$ is invariant on a connected set S then the roots of A are delineable on S. This theorem implicitly defines an $\mathcal{A}$-invariant cylindrical algebraic decomposition. Section 2 also defines the "augmented projection", a modification of the projection which is applied in certain contexts in order to facilitate the construction of defining formulas for cells. Section 2 is concluded with the specification of the main algebraic algorithms which are required as subalgorithms of the quantifier elimination algorithm described in Section 3. These algebraic algorithms include algorithms for various operations on real algebraic numbers and on polynomials with rational integer or real algebraic number coefficients.

Section 3 describes the quantifier elimination algorithm, ELIM, and its subalgorithms, which do most of the work. ELIM invokes successively its two subalgorithms, DECOMP (decomposition) and EVAL (evaluatio

DECOMP produces sample points and cell definitions, given a set of polynomials. EVAL uses the sample points and cell definitions, together with the prenex formula ϕ, to produce a quantifier-free formula equivalent to ϕ. DECOMP itself uses a subalgorithm, DEFINE, to aid in the construction of defining formulas for cells. These algorithms are described in a precise but informal style with extensive interspersed explanatory remarks and assertions in support of their validity.

Section 4 is devoted to an analysis of the computing time of the quantifier elimination algorithm. Since some of the required algebraic subalgorithms have not yet been fully analyzed, and since in any case improved subalgorithms are likely to be discovered from time to time, the analysis is carried out in terms of a parameter reflecting the computing times of the subalgorithms.

Section 5 is devoted to further discussion of the algorithm, including possible modifications, examples, special cases, and the observed behavior of the method.

It should be noted that the definition of the projection operator has been changed in an important way since the publication of the preliminary version of this paper. This change is justified by a new definition of delineability in Section 3 and a new proof of what is now Theorem 5. This change in the projection operator contributes greatly to the practical feasibility of the algorithm.

2. Algebraic Foundations. In this section we make some needed definitions, prove the basic theorems which provide a foundation for the quantifier elimination algorithm to be presented in Section 3, and define and discuss the main subalgorithms which will be required.

By an integral polynomial in r variables we shall mean any element of the ring $I[x_1,\ldots,x_r]$, where I is the ring of the rational integers. As observed by Tarski, any atomic formula of elementary algebra can be expressed in one of the two forms $A = 0$, $A > 0$, where A is an integral polynomial. Also, any quantifier-free formula can be easily expressed in disjunctive normal form as a disjunction of conjunctions of atomic formulas of these two types. However, for the quantifier elimination algorithm to be presented in this paper, there is no reason to be so restrictive, and we define a <u>standard atomic formula</u> as a formula of one of the six forms $A = 0$, $A > 0$, $A < 0$, $A \neq 0$, $A \geq 0$, and $A \leq 0$. A <u>standard formula</u> is any formula which can be constructed from standard atomic formulas using propositional connectives and quantifiers. A <u>standard prenex formula</u> is a standard formula of the form

$$(Q_k x_k)(Q_{k+1} x_{k+1}) \ldots (Q_r x_r)\phi(x_1,\ldots,x_r), \tag{1}$$

where $\phi(x_1,\ldots,x_r)$ is a quantifier-free standard formula, $1 \leq k \leq r$, and each $(Q_i x_i)$ is either an existential quantifier $(\exists x_i)$ or a universal quantifier $(\forall x_i)$.

The variables x_i range over the ordered field R of all real numbe[rs] or over any other real closed field. For additional background informa[-]tion on elementary algebra, the reader is referred to Tarski's excellent monograph, [18], and van der Waerden, [19], has an excellent chapter on real closed fields.

The quantifier elimination algorithm to be described in the next section accepts as input any standard prenex formula of the form (1), with $1 \leq k \leq r$, and produces as output an equivalent standard quantifier-free formula $\psi(x_1,\ldots,x_{k-1})$.

$\mathcal{R}$ will denote an arbitrary commutative ring with identity. Unles[s] otherwise specified, we will always regard a polynomial $A(x_1,\ldots,x_r) \varepsilon$ $\mathcal{R}[x_1,\ldots,x_r]$ as an element of $\mathcal{R}[x_1,\ldots,x_{r-1}][x_r]$; that is, A is rega[rded] as a polynomial in its <u>main variable</u>, x_r, with coefficients in the pc[ly]nomial ring $\mathcal{R}[x_1,\ldots,x_{r-1}]$. Thus, for example, the <u>leading coefficie[nt]</u> of A, denoted by ldcf(A), is an element of $\mathcal{R}[x_1,\ldots,x_{r-1}]$. Similarly deg(A) denotes the degree of A in x_r. If $A(x_1,\ldots,x_r) = \Sigma_{i=0}^{n} A_i(x_1,\ldots x_{r-1})\cdot x_r^i$ and deg(A)=n, then ldcf(A)=A_n and ldt(A)=$A_n(x_1,\ldots,x_{r-1})\cdot x_r^n$, <u>leading term</u> of A. Following Tarski, red(A), the <u>reductum</u> of A is the difference A-ldt(A). By convention, deg(0)=ldcf(0)=0, and hence also ldt(0)=red(0)=0. A' will denote the derivative of A.

R^k will denote the k=fold Cartesian product $R \times \ldots \times R$, $k \geq 1$. If f and g are real-valued functions defined on a set $S \subseteq R^k$, we write _f > 0 on S_ in case $f(x) > 0$ for all $x \in S$, _f = 0 on S_ in case $f(x) = 0$ for all $x \in S$; _f < 0 on S_, $f \neq 0$ on S, _f < g on S_ and other such relations are similarly defined. We say that _f is invariant on S_ in case $f > 0$ on S, $f = 0$ on S, or $f < 0$ on S. These definitions are also applied to real polynomials, which may be regarded as real-valued functions.

The field of complex numbers will be denoted by C. We will regard R as a subset, and hence a subfield, of C. A polynomial $A(x_1, \ldots, x_r)$ belonging to $R[x_1, \ldots, x_r]$ will be called a _real polynomial_.

Let $A(x_1, \ldots, x_r)$ be a real polynomial, $r \geq 2$, S a subset of R^{r-1}. We will say that $f_1, \ldots, f_m$, $m \geq 1$, _delineate the roots_ of A on S in case the following conditions are all satisfied:

(1) $f_1, \ldots, f_m$ are distinct continuous functions from S to C.

(2) There is a positive integer e_i such that $f_i(a_1, \ldots, a_{r-1})$ is a root of $A(a_1, \ldots, a_{r-1}, x)$ of multiplicity e_i for $(a_1, \ldots, a_{r-1}) \in S$ and $1 \leq i \leq m$.

(3) If $(a_1, \ldots, a_{r-1}) \in S$, $b \in C$ and $A(a_1, \ldots, a_{r-1}, b) = 0$ then for some i, $1 \leq i \leq m$, $b = f_i(a_1, \ldots, a_{r-1})$.

(4) For some k, $0 \leq k \leq m$, $f_1, \ldots, f_k$ are real-valued with $f_1 < f_2 < \ldots < f_k$ and the values of $f_{k+1}, \ldots, f_m$ are all non-real.

e_i will be called the multiplicity of f_i. If $k \geq 1$, we will say that $f_1, \ldots, f_k$ _delineate the real roots_ of A on S. The roots of A are _delineable_ on S in case there are functions $f_1, \ldots, f_m$ which delineate the roots of A on S.

Note that if the roots of A are delineable on S then $A(a_1, \ldots, a_{r-1}, x)$ is a non-zero polynomial for $(a_1, \ldots, a_{r-1}) \in S$, and the number of distinct roots of $A(a_1, \ldots, a_{r-1}, x)$ is independent of the choice of $(a_1, \ldots, a_{r-1})$ in S. The number of roots, multiplicities counted, $\Sigma_{i=1}^m e_i = n$, must also be invariant on S. Hence $\deg(A) = n$ is also invariant on S, so $\mathrm{ldcf}(A) \neq 0$ on S. The following basic theorem shows that if these necessary conditions are satisfied and additionally S is connected, then the roots of A are delineable on S.

Theorem 1. Let $A(x_1, \ldots, x_r)$ be a real polynomial, $r \geq 2$. Let S be a connected subset of R^{r-1}. If $\mathrm{ldcf}(A) \neq 0$ on S and the number of distinct roots of A is invariant on S, then the roots of A are delineable on S.

Proof. We may assume S is non-empty and $\deg(A) = n > 0$ since otherwise the theorem is trivial. Let $(a_1,\ldots,a_{r-1})=a \in S$ and let $\alpha_1,\ldots,\alpha_m$ be the distinct roots of $A(a_1,\ldots,a_{r-1},x)$. We may assume that $\alpha_1 < \alpha_2 < \ldots < \alpha_k$ are real and $\alpha_{k+1},\ldots,\alpha_m$ are non-real. If m=1 let $\delta=1$ and otherwise let $\delta=\frac{1}{2}\min_{i<j}|\alpha_i-\alpha_j|$. Let C_i be the circle with center α_i and radius δ. Let $A(x_1,\ldots,x_r)=\Sigma_{i=0}^{n} A_i(x_1,\ldots,x_{r-1})x_r^i$. Since the A_i are continuous functions on S and $A_n \neq 0$ on S, by Theorem (1,4) of [7] there exists $\epsilon>0$ such that if $a'=(a'_1,\ldots,a'_{r-1}) \in S$ and $||a-a'||<\epsilon$ then $A(a',x)$ has exactly e_i roots, multiplicities counted, inside C_i, where e_i is the multiplicity of α_i. Since by hypothesis $A(a',x)$ has exactly m distinct roots and the interiors of the m circles C_i are disjoint, each circle must contain a unique root of $A(a',x)$, whose multiplicity is e_i. Since the non-real roots of $A(a,x)$ occur in conjugate pairs, the interiors of the circles $C_{k+1},\ldots,C_m$ contain no real numbers and hence the roots of $A(a',x)$ in $C_{k+1},\ldots,C_m$ are non-real. If $i \leq k$ and C_i contained a non-real root of $A(a',x)$ then its conjugate would also be a non-real root of $A(a',x)$ in C_i since the center of C_i is real. So the roots of $A(a',x)$ in $C_1,\ldots,C_k$ are real.

Let $N=\{a':a' \in S \& ||a-a'||<\epsilon\}$. For $a' \in N$ define $f_i(a')$ to be the unique root of $A(a',x)$ inside C_i. Then $f_1<f_2<\ldots<f_k$ are real functions and $f_{k+1},\ldots,f_m$ are non-real valued. By another application of Theorem (1,4) of [7], the f_i are continuous functions on N, which is an open neighborhood of a in S. Hence if $0 \leq k \leq m$ and S_k is the set of all $a \in S$ such that $A(a,x)$ has exactly k distinct real roots, then S_k is open in S. Since a connected set is not a union of two disjoint non-empty subsets, there is a unique k such that $S=S_k$.

We can now define $f_i(a)$ to be the ith real root of $A(a,x)$ for $a \in S$ and $1 \leq i \leq k$, so that $f_1<f_2<\ldots<f_k$ on S. By the preceding paragraph it is immediate that $f_1,\ldots,f_k$ are continuous. By another application of the connectivity, the multiplicity of f_i as a root of A is an invariant throughout S since, as we have already shown, the multiplicity is locally invariant.

The proof of the existence of the non-real functions $f_{k+1},\ldots,f_m$ is somewhat more difficult because the topology of C is not induced by a linear order. Choose a fixed point a of S and arbitrarily denote the non-real roots of $A(a,x)$ by $\alpha_{k+1},\ldots,\alpha_m$. For any $a' \in S$ there is a path P in S from a to a' since S is connected. For any point a'' of P there is an open neighborhood N of a'' and m-k continuous functions defined on ich are non-real roots of A. These open neighborhoods for all points ´of P constitute an open cover of the set P. Since P is compact, this over has a finite subcover. Since P is connected, the elements of the nite subcover can be arranged into a chain $N_1,\dots,N_h$ such that $a\epsilon N_1$, ϵN_h and $N_i \cap N_{i+1}$ is non-empty for $1\le i<h$. The functions defined on N_1 n be designated by $f^{(1)}_{k+1},\dots,f^{(1)}_m$ in such a manner that $f^{(1)}_j(a)=\alpha_j$. The nctions on N_{i+1} can be uniquely designated by $f^{(i+1)}_j$ so that $f^{(i+1)}_j(a'')$ $f^{(i)}_j(a'')$ for all $a''\epsilon N_i \cap N_{i+1}$. Finally we can set $\alpha'_j=f^{(h)}_j(a')$ for k+1 $\le m$. In this way we can define the jth root of $A(a',x)$ for $k+1\le j\le m$ and ϵS. Then we define $f_j(a')$ to be the jth root of $A(a',x)$ and easily prove at f_j is continous, non-real valued, and of invariant multiplicity. ∎

We say that the polynomials $A,B,\epsilon\mathcal{R}[x]$ are <u>similar</u>, and write $A\approx B$, case there exist non-zero $a,b\epsilon\mathcal{R}$ such that $aA = bB$.

We define $\mathrm{red}^k(A)$, the kth reductum of the polynomials A, for $k\ge 0$, induction on k as follows: $\mathrm{red}^0(A)=A$ and $\mathrm{red}^{k+1}(A)=\mathrm{red}(\mathrm{red}^k(A))$ for). We say that B is <u>a reductum</u> of A in case $B=\mathrm{red}^k(A)$ for some $k\ge 0$.

We repeat some definitions from [4]. Let A and B be polynomials over ith $\deg(A)=m$ and $\deg(B)=n$. The <u>Sylvester matrix</u> of A and B is the by m+n matrix M whose successive rows contain the coefficients of polynomials $x^{n-1}A(x),\dots,A(x),x^{n-1}B(x),\dots,xB(x),B(x)$, with the fficients of x^i occuring in column m+n-i. We allow either m=0 or . As is well known, res(A,B), the resultant of A and B, is det(M), determinant of M. (We adopt the convention det(N)=0 in case N is a o by zero determinant.) For $0\le i\le j\le \min(m,n)$ let $M_{j,i}$ be the matrix obned from M by deleting the last j rows of A coefficients, the last j s of B coefficients, and all of the last 2j+1 columns except column -i-j. The <u>jth subresultant</u> of A and B is the polynomial $S_j(A,B)$ $=_0 \det(M_{j,i})\cdot x^i$, a polynomial of degree j or less. We define also the <u>principal subresultant coefficient</u> of A and B by $\mathrm{psc}_j(A,B)=\det(M_{j,j})$. s $\mathrm{psc}_j(A,B)$ is the coefficient of x^j in $S_j(A,B)$. We note, for subsequent lication, that if $\deg(A)=m>0$ then $\mathrm{psc}_{m-1}(A,A')=m\cdot \mathrm{ldcf}(A)$.

<u>Theorem 2.</u> Let A and B be non-zero polynomials over a unique facization domain. Then $\deg(\gcd(A,B))=k$ if and only if k is the least j that $\mathrm{psc}_j(A,B)\neq 0$.

Proof. Let $k=\deg(\gcd(A,B))$. By the fundamental theorem of polynomial remainder sequences, [2], $\mathcal{S}_j(A,B)=0$ for $0\leq j<k$, and $\gcd(A,B)\approx\mathcal{S}_k(A,B)$. Hence $\mathrm{psc}_j(A,B)=0$ for $0\leq j<k$, $\deg(\mathcal{S}_k(A,B))=k$, and $\mathrm{psc}_k(A,B)\neq 0$. ∎

Theorem 3. Let $A(x)$ be a real univariate polynomial with $\deg(A)=m\geq 1$ and let $k=\deg(\gcd(A,A'))$. Then $m-k$ is the number of distinct roots of A.

Proof. Let A have the distinct roots $\alpha_1,\ldots,\alpha_n$ with respective multiplicities $e_1,\ldots,e_n$. By a familiar argument, α_i is a root of A' with multiplicity e_i-1 (meaning that α_i is not a root of A' if $e_i=1$). Hence α_i is a root of $\gcd(A,A')$ with multiplicity e_i-1. Since every root of $\gcd(A,A')$ is some α_i, $k=\deg(\gcd(A,A'))=\Sigma_{i=o}^{h}(e_i-1)=\Sigma_{i=o}^{h}e_i-h=m-h$ and $m-k=h$. ∎

Using reducta and principal subresultant coefficients, we now obtain a more useful sufficient condition for the delineability of the roots of a polynomial.

Theorem 4. Let $A(x_1,\ldots,x_r)$ be a real polynomial, $r\geq 2$, S a connected subset of R^{r-1}. Let $\mathcal{B}=\{\mathrm{red}^k(A):k\geq 0\ \&\ \deg(\mathrm{red}^k(A))\geq 1\}$, $\mathcal{L}=\{\mathrm{ldcf}(B):B\varepsilon\mathcal{B}\}$, $\mathcal{S}=\{\mathrm{psc}_k(B,B'):B\varepsilon\mathcal{B}\ \&\ 0\leq k<\deg(B')\}$ and $\mathcal{P}=\mathcal{L}\cup\mathcal{S}$. If every element of $\mathcal{P}$ is invariant on S, then the roots of A are delineable on S.

Proof. If $\deg(A)\leq 1$ then the theorem is obvious, so let $A(x_1,\ldots,x_r)=\Sigma_{i=o}^{n}A_i(x_1,\ldots,x_{r-1})x_r^i$ with $\deg(A)=n\geq 2$. If $i\geq 1$ and $A_i\neq 0$ then $A_i\varepsilon\mathcal{L}$ so A_i is invariant on S for $1\leq i\leq n$. If $A_i=0$ on S for $1\leq i\leq n$ then the theorem is obvious, so let $m\geq 1$ be maximal such that $A_m\neq 0$ on S and let k be such that $\mathrm{red}^k(A)=\Sigma_{i=o}^{m}A_i(x_1,\ldots,x_{r-1})x_r^i=B$. Then $A=B$ on S so it suffices to show tha the roots of B are delineable on S. $B\varepsilon\mathcal{B}$ so $\mathrm{psc}_j(B,B')$ is invariant on S for $0\leq j<m-1$. Also $\mathrm{psc}_{m-1}(B,B')=mA_m\neq 0$ on S. By Theorem 2, $\deg(\gcd(B,B'))$ is invariant on S, that is, for some k, $\deg(\gcd(B(a,x),B'(a,x)))=k$ for all $a\varepsilon S$. By Theorem 3, the number of distinct roots of B on S is the invariant $m-k$. By Theorem 1, the roots of B are delineable on S. ∎

Let $\mathcal{A}$ be a set of real polynomials in r variables, $r\geq 2$. Let $\mathcal{B}=\{\mathrm{red}^k(A):A\varepsilon\mathcal{A}\ \&\ k\geq 0\ \&\ \deg(\mathrm{red}^k(A))\geq 1\}$, $\mathcal{L}=\{\mathrm{ldcf}(B):B\varepsilon\mathcal{B}\}$, $\mathcal{S}_1=\{\mathrm{psc}_k(B,B'):B\varepsilon\mathcal{B}$ $0\leq k<\deg(B')\}$, $\mathcal{S}_2=\{\mathrm{psc}_k(B_1,B_2):B_1,B_2\varepsilon\mathcal{B}\ \&\ 0\leq k<\min(\deg(B_1),\deg(B_2))\}$ and $\mathcal{P}=\mathcal{L}\cup\mathcal{S}_1\cup\mathcal{S}_2$. Then $\mathcal{P}$ will be called the projection of $\mathcal{A}$. If $\mathcal{A}=\{A_1,\ldots,A_n\}$ a non-empty finite set of non-zero polynomials, we will say that the root of $\mathcal{A}$ are delineable on a set S in case the roots of the product $A=\Pi_{i=1}^{n}A_i$ are delineable on S. Note that the roots of each A_i could be delineable on S without the roots of $\mathcal{A}$ being delineable on S. The next theorem shows how the inclusion of the set $\mathcal{S}_2$ in the projection $\mathcal{P}=\text{proj}(\mathcal{A})$ helps to ensure the delineability of the roots of $\mathcal{A}$.

Theorem 5. Let $\mathcal{A}=\{A_1,\ldots,A_n\}$ be a non-empty set of non-zero real polynomials in r real variables, $r\geq 2$. Let S be a connected subset of R^{r-1}. Let $\mathcal{P}$ be the projection of $\mathcal{A}$. If every element of $\mathcal{P}$ is invariant on S, then the roots of $\mathcal{A}$ are delineable on S.

Proof. By Theorem 4, the roots of A_i are delineable on S for $1\leq i\leq n$. Let $\mathcal{F}_i$ be the set of delineating functions for A_i and let $\mathcal{F}=\bigcup_{i=1}^{n}\mathcal{F}_i$. If $f_1,\ldots,f_m$ are the distinct elements of $\mathcal{F}$, with $f_1< f_2<\ldots<f_k$ real valued, $f_{k+1},\ldots,f_m$ non-real valued, and if $f_i(a)\neq f_j(a)$ for $i\neq j$ and $a\varepsilon S$, then $f_1,\ldots,f_m$ delineate the roots of $\mathcal{A}$. For if $A=\Pi_{i=1}^{n}A_i$ then (1), (2) and (4) of the definition of delineation are obviously satisfied. Also, if $f_i(a)$ is a root of A_j of multiplicity $e_{i,j}$ then $f_i(a)$ is a root of A of multiplicity $e_i=\Sigma_{j=1}^{m}e_{i,j}$. Hence if $f_i(a)\neq f_j(a)$ for $i\neq j$ then $e_{i,j}>0$ just in case f_i is a delineating function of A_j. So if $f_i(a)\neq f_j(a)$ for all $a\varepsilon S$ then the multiplicity of f_i as a root of A on S is the invariant $e_i=\Sigma_j e_{i,j}$ where the sum is taken over all j such that f_i is a delineating function of A_j.

Hence it suffices to show that if $f_i\neq f_j$ then $f_i(a)\neq f_j(a)$ for all $a\varepsilon S$. Without loss of generality we may assume that f_i is a delineating function of A_1 and g_j is a delineating function of A_2. Let $g_1,\ldots,g_s$ be the delineating functions of A_1, $h_1,\ldots,h_t$ the delineating functions of A_2. Let M be any s by t matrix of zeros and ones and let S_M be the set of all $a\varepsilon S$ such that $g_i(a)=h_j(a)$ if $M_{i,j}=0$ and $g_i(a)\neq h_j(a)$ if $M_{i,j}=1$ for all i and all j. Assume S_M is non-empty, and let $a\varepsilon S_M$. By continuity there is an open neighborhood N of a in S such that if $M_{i,j}=1$ then $g_i(a')\neq h_j(a')$ for all $a'\varepsilon N$. Since S_M is non-empty, there is for each i at most one j such that $M_{i,j}=0$. Let $(i_1,j_1),\ldots,(i_l,j_l)$ be all the distinct pairs (i,j) such that $M_{i,j}=0$. Let d_i be the multiplicity of f_i as a root of A_1, e_j the multiplicity of g_j as a root of A_2. Then $\deg(\gcd(A_1(a,x), A_2(a,x))$ $=\Sigma_{k=1}^{l}\min(d_k,e_k)$. Since $psc_h(A_1,A_2)$ is in $\mathcal{P}$ for $0\leq h<\min(\deg(A_1), \deg(A_2))$, $\deg(\gcd(A_1(a',x),A_2(a',x)))$ is invariant for all $a'\varepsilon S$. Hence if $a'\varepsilon N$ and $g_{i_1}(a')\neq h_{j_1}(a')$ then $\deg(\gcd(A_1(a',x),A_2(a',x)))=\Sigma_{k=2}^{l}\min(d_k,e_k)$ $<\Sigma_{k=1}^{l}\min(d_k,e_k)$, a contradiction.

So $a' \in S_M$ for all $a' \in N$. It follows that each S_M is an open subset of S. Since S is connected and the sets S_M are disjoint, there is a unique M such that $S=S_M$, which M must obviously satisfy $M_{i,j}=0$ if and only if $g_i=h_j$. Hence if $a \in S$ and $g_i \neq h_j$ then $g_i(a) \neq h_j(a)$, completing the proof. ∎

Let us write der(A) for A′, the derivative of A. We define $der^0(A) = A$ and, inductively, $der^{k+1}(A) = der(der^k(A))$ for $k \geq 0$.

Let $\mathcal{A}$ be a set of real polynomials in r variables, $r \geq 2$. Let $\mathcal{B} = \{red^k(A) : A \in \mathcal{A} \& k \geq 0 \& deg(red^k(A)) \geq 1\}$, $\mathcal{D} = \{der^k(B) : B \in \mathcal{B} \& 0 < k < deg(B)\}$ and $\mathcal{P}' = \{psc_k(D, D') : D \in \mathcal{D} \& 0 \leq k < deg(D')\}$. Then $\mathcal{P} \cup \mathcal{P}'$, where $\mathcal{P}$ is the projection of $\mathcal{A}$, will be called the <u>augmented projection</u> of $\mathcal{A}$.

<u>Theorem 6.</u> Let $\mathcal{A}$ be a set of real polynomials in r variables, $r \geq 2$. Let S be a connected subset of R^{r-1}. Let $\mathcal{P}^*$ be the augmented projection of $\mathcal{A}$. If every element of $\mathcal{P}^*$ is invariant on S then the roots of $der^j(A$ are delineable on S for every $A \in \mathcal{A}$ and every $j \geq 0$.

<u>Proof.</u> Let $A \in \mathcal{A}$, $j \geq 0$, $A^* = der^j(A)$, $\mathcal{B} = \{red^k(A^*) : k \geq 0 \& deg(red^k(A^*)) \geq 1\}$ $\mathcal{L} = \{ldcf(B) : B \in \mathcal{B}\}$, $\mathcal{S} = \{psc_h(B, B') : 0 \leq h < deg(B')\}$, and $\mathcal{P} = \mathcal{L} \cup \mathcal{S}$. By Theorem 4, it suffices to show that each element of $\mathcal{P}$ is invariant on S. If $k \geq 0$ and $deg(red^k(A^*)) \geq 1$ then $red^k(A^*) = red^k(der^j(A)) = der^j(red^k(A))$ so $ldcf(red^k(A^*)) = ldcf(der^j(red^k(A)) = a \cdot ldcf(red^k(A))$ for some positive integer a. Also $deg(red^k(A)) \geq deg(red^k(A^*)) \geq 1$ so $ldcf(red^k(A))$ is in the projecti of $\mathcal{A}$. Hence every element of $\mathcal{L}$ is invariant on S. If $j=0$ then the roots of $A = der^j(A)$ are delineable on S by Theorem 5, so assume $j>0$. If $j \geq deg(red^k(A))$ then $der^j(red^k(A))$ is an integer and hence invariant on S. Otherwise, $0 < j < deg(red^k(A))$ so if $B = red^k(der^j(A)) = der^j(red^k(A))$ then ps (B, B') belongs to the augmented projection of $\mathcal{A}$ and is invariant on S for $0 \leq h < deg(B')$. Hence every element of $\mathcal{S}$ is invariant on S. ∎

We now complete this section with discussion and specification of more important subalgorithms which will be needed for the quantifier el mination algorithm.

The quantifier elimination algorithm of the next section will requ computation of the projection or augmented projection of $\mathcal{A}$ just in case $\mathcal{A}$ is finite and $\mathcal{P} = I[x_1, \ldots, x_{r-1}]$, $r \geq 2$. Thus we assume the availability of an algorithm with the following specifications.

B = PROJ(A)

Input: $\mathcal{A}=(A_1,\ldots,A_m)$ is a list of distinct integral polynomials in r variables, $r\geq 2$.

Output: $\mathcal{B}=(B_1,\ldots,B_n)$ is a list of distinct integral polynomials in r-1 variables, such that $\{B_1,\ldots,B_n\}$ is the projection of $\{A_1,\ldots,A_m\}$.

Another like algorithm, APROJ, is assumed for computing the augmented projection.

Now let $\mathcal{U}$ be a unique factorization domain, abbreviated u.f.d. If $a,b\in\mathcal{U}$ we say that a and b are associates, and write $a\sim b$, in case a=ub for some unit u. An ample set for $\mathcal{U}$ (see [10]) is a set $A\subseteq\mathcal{R}$ which contains exactly one element from each equivalence class of associates. Relative to $\mathcal{A}$ we can define a function gcd on $\mathcal{U}\times\mathcal{U}$ into $\mathcal{U}$ such that $\gcd(a,b)\in\mathcal{A}$ and gcd(a,b) is a greatest common divisor of a and b for all $a,b\in\mathcal{U}$. We will assume, moreover, that $\mathcal{A}$ is multiplicative, i.e. closed under multiplication, from which $1\in\mathcal{A}$. Whenever $\mathcal{U}$ is a field we will have $\mathcal{A}=\{0,1\}$. For $\mathcal{U}=I$, we set $\mathcal{A}=\{0,1,2,\ldots\}$. $\mathcal{U}[x]$ is also a u.f.d and if $\mathcal{A}$ is an ample set for $\mathcal{U}$ we take $\{A:\mathrm{ldcf}(A)\in\mathcal{A}\}$ as ample set for $\mathcal{U}[x]$ (see [14]).

If $A(x)=\Sigma_{i=0}^{n}a_ix^i$ is a non-zero polynomial over $\mathcal{U}$, we set cont(A) $\gcd(a_n,a_{n-1},\ldots,a_0)$, the content of A, and we set cont(0)=0. If $A\neq 0$ we define pp(A), the primitive part of A, to be the ample associate of A/cont(A), and we set pp(0)=0. The polynomial A is primitive in case cont(A)=1. Clearly pp(A) is primitive and $A\sim\mathrm{cont}(A)\cdot\mathrm{pp}(A)$ for all $A\neq 0$.

Let $\mathcal{A}$ be a set of primitive polynomials of positive degree over $\mathcal{U}$. A basis for $\mathcal{A}$ is a set $\mathcal{B}$ of ample primitive polynomials of positive degree over $\mathcal{U}$ satisfying the following three conditions:

a) If $B_1,B_2\in\mathcal{B}$ and $B_1\neq B_2$ then $\gcd(B_1,B_2)=1$.

b) If $B\in\mathcal{B}$, then $B|A$ for some $A\in\mathcal{A}$.

c) If $A\in\mathcal{A}$, there exist $B_1,\ldots,B_n\in\mathcal{B}$ and positive integers $e_1,\ldots,e_n$ such that

$$A\sim\prod_{i=1}^{n}B_i^{e_i}\text{ (with } n=0 \text{ if } A\sim 1).$$

If $\mathcal{A}$ is an arbitrary set of polynomials over $\mathcal{U}$, then a basis for $\mathcal{A}$ is a set $\mathcal{B}=\mathcal{B}_1\cup\mathcal{B}_2$ where $\mathcal{B}_1=\{\mathrm{cont}(A):A\in\mathcal{A}\ \&A\neq 0\}$ and $\mathcal{B}_2$ is a basis for $\{\mathrm{pp}(A):A\in\mathcal{A}\ \&\deg(A)>0\}$.

If $\mathcal{A}$ is a set of primitive polynomials of positive degree then the set $\mathcal{P}$ of ample irreducible divisors of elements of $\mathcal{A}$ is clearly a basis for $\mathcal{A}$. If $\mathcal{B}_1$ and $\mathcal{B}_2$ are bases for $\mathcal{A}$, we say that $\mathcal{B}_1$ is a refinement of $\mathcal{B}_2$ in case every element of $\mathcal{B}_1$ is a divisor of some element of $\mathcal{B}_2$. $\mathcal{P}$ is the finest basis for $\mathcal{A}$ in the sense that it is a refinement of every other basis.

Every set $\mathcal{A}$ also has a coarsest basis, $\mathcal{C}$, in the sense that every basis for $\mathcal{A}$ is a refinement of $\mathcal{C}$, as we will now see. Let $\mathcal{P}$ be the set of all ample irreducible divisors of positive degree of elements of $\mathcal{A}$. For $P \in \mathcal{P}$, let $\sigma(P)$ be the set of all positive integers i such that, for some $A \in \mathcal{A}$, $P^i | A$ but not $P^{i+1} | A$. Let $e(P)$ be the greatest common divisor of the elements of $\sigma(P)$. For P,Q in $\mathcal{P}$, define $P \equiv Q$ in case, for every $A \in \mathcal{A}$, the orders of P and Q in A are identical. Let $\mathcal{C}$ be the set of all products $\{\Pi_{Q \equiv P} Q^{e(P)}\}$ with $P \in \mathcal{P}$. Then it can be shown that $\mathcal{C}$ is a coarsest basis for $\mathcal{A}$.

If $\mathcal{A}$ is finite, its coarsest basis can be computed by g.c.d. calculation. Set $\mathcal{C} = \mathcal{A}$. If A and B are distinct elements of $\mathcal{C}$, set $C = \gcd(A,B)$, $\bar{A} = A/C$, $\bar{B} = B/C$. If $C \neq 1$, replace A and B in $\mathcal{C}$ by the non-units from among $C, \bar{A}$ and $\bar{B}$. Eventually the elements of $\mathcal{C}$ will be pairwise relatively prime and $\mathcal{C}$ will be a coarsets basis for $\mathcal{A}$.

A squarefree basis for $\mathcal{A}$ is a basis each of whose elements is squarefree. If A is any primitive element of $\mathcal{U}[x]$ of positive degree, there exist ample, squarefree, relatively prime polynomials $A_1, \ldots, A_k$ and integers $e_1 < \ldots < e_k$ such that $A \sim \Pi_{i=1}^{k} A_i^{e_i}$. $(A_1, \ldots, A_k)$ and $(e_1, \ldots, e_k)$ constitute the squarefree factorization of A. Musser, [14] and [15], discusses algorithms for squarefree factorization, which require if $\mathcal{U}$ has characteristic zero, only differentiation, division and greatest common divisor calculations. We assume the availability of an algorithm for squarefree factorization in $\mathcal{U}[x]$ for the cases $\mathcal{U} = I[x_1, \ldots, x_{r-1}]$, $r \geq$ and $\mathcal{U} = Q(\alpha)$, where $Q(\alpha)$ is the real algebraic number field resulting from adjoining the real algebraic number α to the field Q of the rational numbers. For the case $\mathcal{U} = Q(\alpha)$ we assume the following specificati

SQFREE$(\alpha, A, \mathcal{A}, e)$

Inputs: α is a real algebraic number. A is a primitive element of $Q(\alpha)[x]$ of positive degree.

Outputs: $\mathcal{A} = (A_1, \ldots, A_k)$ and $e = (e_1, \ldots, e_k)$ constitute the squarefree factorization of A.

A similar algorithm for the case $\mathcal{U}=I[x_1,\ldots,x_{r-1}]$ is needed in order to compute a coarsest squarefree basis for integral polynomials, as follows.

If $A \sim \prod_{i=1}^{k} A_i^{e_i}$ is the squarefree factorization of A, then $\{A_1,\ldots,A_k\}$ is clearly a coarsest squarefree basis for {A}. Let $\bar{\mathcal{A}}=\{A_1,\ldots,A_m\}$ be a squarefree basis for $\mathcal{A}$, $\bar{\mathcal{B}}=\{B_1,\ldots,B_n\}$ a squarefree basis for $\mathcal{B}$. Consider the following algorithm proposed by R. Loos:

(1) For j=1,...,n set $\bar{B}_j \leftarrow B_j$.

(2) For i=1,...,m do $[\bar{A}_i \leftarrow A_i$; for j=1,...,n do $(C_{i,j} \leftarrow \gcd(\bar{A}_i,\bar{B}_j)$; $\bar{A}_i \leftarrow \bar{A}_i/C_{i,j}$; $\bar{B}_j \leftarrow \bar{B}_j/C_{i,j})]$.

(3) Exit.

Upon termination, the distinct nonunits among the $\bar{A}_i$, the $\bar{B}_j$ and the $C_{i,j}$ constitute a squarefree basis $\bar{\mathcal{C}}$ for $\mathcal{C}=\mathcal{A}\cup\mathcal{B}$. Moreover, if $\bar{\mathcal{A}}$ and $\bar{\mathcal{B}}$ are coarsest squarefree bases, then so is $\bar{\mathcal{C}}$. Thus by squarefree factorization and application of Loos' algorithm we can successively obtain coarsest squarefree bases for $\{A_1\}$, $\{A_1,A_2\}$,..,$\{A_1,A_2,\ldots,A_m\}$. Thus we assume the availability of the following basis algorithm.

$\mathcal{B}$ = BASIS($\mathcal{A}$)

<u>Input:</u> $\mathcal{A}=(A_1,\ldots,A_m)$ is a list of distinct integral polynomials in r variables, $r \geq 1$.

<u>Output:</u> $\mathcal{B}=(B_1,\ldots,B_n)$ is a list of distinct integral polynomials in r variables such that $\{B_1,\ldots,B_n\}$ is a coarsest squarefree basis for $\{A_1,\ldots,A_m\}$.

A similar algorithm, ABASIS, with an additional input α, a real algebraic number, will be assumed for computing the coarsest squarefree basis when $\mathcal{A}$ is a finite list of univariate polynomials over $Q(\alpha)$.

A recent Ph.D. thesis by Rubald, [16], provides algorithms for the arithmetic operations in the field $Q(\alpha)$ and in the polynomial domain $Q(\alpha)[x]$. Rubald also provides an efficient modular homomorphism algorithm for g.c.d. calculation in $Q(\alpha)[x]$. An important feature of Rubald's work is that the minimal polynomial of α is not required. Instead, α is represented by any pair (A,I) such that A is a primitive squarefree integral polynomial of positive degree with $A(\alpha)=0$, and $I=(r,s)$ is an open interval with rational number endpoints such that α is the unique zero of A in I. This feature is important because as yet (see [6]) no algorithm with polynomial-dominated maximum computing time is known for factoring a primitive univariate integral polynomial into its irreducible factors. A non-zero element β of $Q(\alpha)$ is then represented by any polynomial $B(x) \in Q[x]$ such that $\deg(B) < \deg(A)$ and $B(\alpha) = \beta$. Although this representation fails to be unique whenever A is reducible, no difficulties arise.

The next algorithm is easily obtained using Sturm's theorem, since Rubald's work provides an efficient algorithm for determining the sign of any element of $Q(\alpha)$, and because his algorithm for g.c.d. calculation in $Q(\alpha)[x]$ can be extended to the computation of Sturm sequences.

ISOL(α, $\mathfrak{a}$, I, ν)

<u>Inputs:</u> α is a real algebraic number. $\mathfrak{a} = (A_1, .., A_m)$ is a list of non-zero squarefree and pairwise relatively prime polynomials over $Q(\alpha)$.

<u>Outputs:</u> $I = (I_1, ..., I_n)$ is a list of open intervals with rational endpoints with $I_1 < I_2 < ... < I_n$ such that each I_j contains exactly one real zero of $A = \Pi_{i=1}^{m} A_i$, and every real zero of A belongs to some I_j. $\nu = (\nu_1, ..., \nu_n)$ is such that the zero of A in I_j is a zero of A_{ν_j}.

The Algorithm ISOL can be easily obtained by application of Sturm's theorem and repeated interval bisection. Heindel, [11], presents an algorithm of this type for the case of a single univariate integral polynomial. If the real zeros of each A_i are separately isolated, then the resulting intervals can be refined until they no longer overlap, while retaining the identity of the polynomials from which they came.

In the quantifier elimination algorithm, occasion will arise to reduce a multiple real algebraic extension of the rationals, $Q(\alpha_1, ..., \alpha$ to a simple extension $Q(\alpha)$. This can be accomplished by iterating an algorithm of Loos, [12], based on resultant theory, with the following specifications.

SIMPLE(α, β, γ, A, B)

<u>Inputs:</u> α and β are real algebraic numbers.
<u>Outputs:</u> γ is a real algebraic number. A and B are polynomials which represent α and β respectively as elements of $Q(\gamma)$.

Finally, one additional subalgorithm, also provided in [12], is the following.

NORMAL$(\alpha, A, I, \bar{A}, \bar{I})$

<u>Inputs:</u> α is a real algebraic number. A is a non-zero polynomial over $Q(\alpha)$. $I=(I_1,\ldots,I_m)$ is a list of rational isolating intervals, $I_1<I_2<\ldots<I_m$, for the real zeros of A.

<u>Outputs:</u> $\bar{A}$ is a non-zero squarefree primitive integral polynomial such that every real zero of A is a real zero of $\bar{A}$.
$\bar{I}=(\bar{I},\ldots,\bar{I}_m)$ is a list of rational intervals with $\bar{I}_j \subseteq I_j$ such that if α_j is the zero of A in I_j then α_j is the unique zero of $\bar{A}$ in $\bar{I}_j$, $1 \leq j \leq m$.

3. <u>The Main Algorithms.</u> We define, by induction on r, a <u>cylindrical</u> <u>lgebraic decomposition</u> of R^r, abbreviated c.a.d. For r=1, a c.a.d. of is a sequence $(S_1, S_2, \ldots, S_{2\nu+1})$, where either $\nu=0$ and $S_1=R$, or $\nu>0$ nd there exist ν real algebraic numbers $\alpha_1<\alpha_2<\ldots<\alpha_\nu$ such that S_{2i} $\{\alpha_i\}$ for $1\leq i\leq\nu$, S_{2+1} is the open interval (α_i, α_{i+1}) for $1\leq i<\nu$, $S_1=(-\infty, \alpha_1)$ nd $S_{2\nu+1}=(\alpha_\nu, \infty)$. Now let $r>1$, and let $(S_1,\ldots,S_\mu)$ be any c.a.d. of R^{r-1}. or $1\leq i\leq\mu$, let $f_{i,1}<f_{i,2}<\ldots<f_{i,\nu_i}$ be continuous realvalued algebraic unctions on S_i. If $\nu_i=0$, set $S_{i,1}=S_i \times R$. If $\nu_i>0$ set $S_{i,2j}=f_{i,j}$, that is, $_{i,2j}=\{(a,b): a\in S_i \& b=f_{i,j}(a)\}$ for $1\leq j\leq\nu_i$, set $S_{i,2j+1}=\{(a,b): a\in S_i \& f_{i,j}(a)$ $b<f_{i,j+1}(a)\}$ for $1\leq j<\nu_i$, set $S_{i,1}=\{(a,b): a\in S_i \& b<f_{i,1}(a)\}$, and set $_{i,2\nu_i+1}=\{(a,b): a\in S_i \& f_{i,\nu_i}(a)<b\}$. A c.a.d. of R^r is any sequence $(S_{1,1}$, $\ldots, S_{1,2\nu_1+1}, \ldots, S_{\mu,1}, \ldots, S_{\mu,2\nu_\mu+1})$ which can be obtained by this conruction from a c.a.d. of R^{r-1} and functions $f_{i,j}$ as just described.

It is important to observe that the cylinder $S_i \times R$ is the disjoint ion $\bigcup_{j=1}^{2\nu_i+1} S_{i,j}$ for $1\leq i\leq\mu$. If $S=(S_1,\ldots,S_\mu)$ is any c.a.d. of R^r, the will be called the <u>cells</u> of S. Clearly every cell of a c.a.d. is a nnected set. If $\mathcal{A}$ is a set of real polynomials in r variables, the c.a.d. S or R^r is <u>$\mathcal{A}$-invariant</u> in case each A in $\mathcal{A}$ is invariant on each cell of S.

A <u>sample</u> of the c.a.d. $S=(S_1,\ldots,S_\mu)$ is a tuple $\beta=(\beta_1,\ldots,\beta_\mu)$ such that $\beta_i \varepsilon S_i$ for $1 \le i \le \mu$. The sample β is <u>algebraic</u> in case each β_i is an algebraic point, i.e. each coordinate of β_i is an algebraic number. A <u>cylindrical</u> <u>sample</u> is defined by induction on r. For r=1, any sample is cylindrical. For r>1, let $S=(S_{1,1},\ldots,S_{1,2\nu_1+1},\ldots,S_{\mu,1},\ldots,S_{\mu,2\nu_\mu+1})$ a c.a.d. of R^r constructed from a c.a.d. $S^*=(S_1,\ldots,S_\mu)$ of R^{r-1}, and let $\beta^* =(\beta_1,\ldots,\beta_\mu)$ be a sample of S^*. The sample $\beta=(\beta_{1,1},\ldots,\beta_{1,2\nu_1+1},\ldots,\beta_{\mu,1},\ldots,\beta_{\mu,2\nu_\mu+1})$ of S is cylindrical if the first r-1 coordinates of $\beta_{i,j}$ are, respectively, the coordinates of β_i, for all i and j, and β^* is cylindrical. Cylindrical algebraic sample will be abbreviated c.a.s.

Since a c.a.d. of R^r can be constructed from a unique c.a.d of R^{r-1}, any c.a.d. S of R^r determines, for $1 \le k < r$, a c.a.d. S^* of R^k, which will be called the c.a.d. of R^k <u>induced</u> by S. Similarly any c.a.s. β of S induces a unique c.a.s. β^* of S .

If S is an arbitrary subset of R^r, the standard formula $\phi(x_1,\ldots,x_r)$ containing just $x_1,\ldots,x_r$ as free variables, <u>defines</u> S in case $S=\{(a_1,\ldots,a_r):a_1,\ldots,a_r \varepsilon R \& \phi(a_1,\ldots,a_r)\}$. A <u>standard definition</u> of the c.a.d. $S=(S_1,\ldots,S_\mu)$ is a sequence $(\phi_1,\ldots,\phi_\mu)$ such that, for $1 \le i \le \mu$, ϕ_i is a standard quantifier-free formula which defines S_i.

We are now prepared to describe a decomposition algorithm, DECOMP. The inputs to DECOMP are a finite set $\mathcal{A}$ of integral polynomials in r variables, $r \ge 1$, and an integer k, $0 \le k \le r$. The outputs of DECOMP are a c.a.s. β of some $\mathcal{A}$-invariant c.a.d. S of R^r and, if $k \ge 1$, a standard definition ψ of the c.a.d. S^* of R^k induced by S.

Before proceeding to describe DECOMP we first explain its intended use in the quantifier elimination algorithm, ELIM, which will be describ[ed] subsequently. ELIM has two distinct stages. Given as input a standard prenex formula ϕ, namely $(Q_{k+1}x_{k+1})\ldots(Q_r x_r)\hat{\phi}(x_1,\ldots,x_r)$, ELIM applies DECOMP to the set $\mathcal{A}$ of all non-zero polynomials occurring in $\hat{\phi}$, and the integer k. The outputs β and ψ of DECOMP, together with the formula ϕ, are then input to an "evaluation" algorithm, EVAL, which produces a standard quantifier-free formula $\phi^*(x_1,\ldots,x_k)$ which is equivalent to ϕ. Thus, ELIM does little more than to successively invoke DECOMP and

EVAL.

DECOMP uses a subalgorithm, DEFINE, for construction of the standard definition. The inputs to DEFINE are an integral polynomial $A(x_1,\ldots,x_r), r\geq 2$, such that for some connected set $S\subseteq R^{r-1}$ the real roots of A and of each derivative of A are delineable on S, and an algebraic point $\beta\varepsilon S$. The output of DEFINE is a sequence $(\phi_1,\ldots,\phi_{2m+1})$ of standard quantifier-free formulas ϕ_i such that if ϕ is any formula which defines S, then the conjunction $\phi\wedge\phi_i$ defines the ith cell of the cylinder SxR determined by the m real roots of A on S, as in the definition of a c.a.d. The description of DEFINE will be given following that of DECOMP.

DECOMP($\mathfrak{A}$,k,β,ψ)

Inputs: $\mathfrak{A}=(A_1,\ldots,A_m)$ is a list of distinct integral polynomials in r variables, $r\geq 1$. k is an integer such that $0\leq k\leq r$.

Outputs: β is a c.a.s. for some $\mathfrak{A}$-invariant c.a.d. S of R^r. ψ is a standard definition of the c.a.d. S of R^k induced by S if k>0, and ψ is the null list if k=0.

Algorithm Description

(1) If r>1, go to (4). Apply BASIS to $\mathfrak{A}$, obtaining a coarsest squarefree basis $\mathfrak{B}=(B_1,\ldots,B_h)$ for $\mathfrak{A}$. Apply ISOL to $\mathfrak{B}$, obtaining outputs $I=(I_1,\ldots,I_n)$ and $\nu=(\nu_1,\ldots,\nu_n)$. (Each I_j contains a unique zero, say α_j, of B_{ν_j}, and $\alpha_1<\alpha_2<\ldots<\alpha_n$ are all the real zeros of elements of $\mathfrak{A}$. Thus the α_j determine an $\mathfrak{A}$-invariant c.a.d. S of R, and (B_{ν_j},I_j) represents α_j).

(2) For j=1,...,n, where $I_j=(r_j,s_j)$, set $\beta_{2j-1}\leftarrow r_j$ and $\beta_{2j}\leftarrow\alpha_j$. If n=0, set $\beta_{2n+1}\leftarrow 0$ and if n>0, set $\beta_{2n+1}\leftarrow s_n$. Set $\beta\leftarrow(\beta_1,\ldots,\beta_{2n+1})$. ($\beta$ is now a c.a.s. of S.)

(3) If k=0, set $\psi\leftarrow()$ and exit. If n=0, set $\psi_1\leftarrow$"0=0",$\psi\leftarrow(\psi_1)$ and exit. For i=1,...,h do [$\sigma_{i,n}\leftarrow\text{sign}(\text{ldcf}(B_i))$; for j=n-1,...,0 set $\sigma_{i,j}\leftarrow(-\sigma_{i,j+1}$ if $i=\nu_{j+1}$, $\sigma_{i,j+1}$ otherwise)]. (Now $\sigma_{i,j}$ is the sign of B_i in S_{2j+1}, where $S=(S_1,\ldots,S_{2n+1})$.) For j=1,...,n, where $r_j=a_j/b_j$ and $s_j=c_j/d_j$ with $b_j>0$ and $d_j>0$, set $\psi_{2j}\leftarrow$"$B_{\nu_j}=0\&b_jx_1-a_j>0\&d_jx_1-c_j<0$". (Now ψ_{2j} defines $S_j=\{\alpha_j\}$.)

For j=1,...,n-1, set $\psi_{2j+1} \leftarrow$ "$\sigma_{\nu_j,j} B_{\nu_j} > 0 \& \sigma_{\nu_{j+1},j} B_{\nu_{j+1}} > 0 \& b_j x_1 - a_j > 0 \& d_{j+1} x_1 - c_{j+1} < 0$". (If $\nu_j = \nu_{j+1}$ then the first two conjuncts are identical, so one can be omitted.) Set $\psi_1 \leftarrow$ "$\sigma_{\nu_1,0} B_{\nu_1} > 0 \& d_1 x_1 - c_1 < 0$" and $\psi_{2n+1} \leftarrow$ "$\sigma_{\nu_n,n} B_{\nu_n} > 0 \& b_n x_1 - a_n > 0$". Set $\psi \leftarrow (\psi_1, \ldots, \psi_{2n+1})$. ($\psi$ is now a standard definition of S.) Exit.

(4) Apply BASIS to $\mathcal{A}$, obtaining $\mathcal{B}$, a coarsest squarefree basis for $\mathcal{A}$. (This action is inessential; we could set $\mathcal{B} \leftarrow \mathcal{A}$. But the algorithm is likely more efficient if the coarsest squarefree basis is used, and it may be still more efficient, on the average, if the finest basis is computed here.) If k<r, apply PROJ to $\mathcal{B}$, obtaining the projection, $\mathcal{P}$, of $\mathcal{B}$. If k=r, apply APROJ to $\mathcal{B}$, obtaining the augmented projection, $\mathcal{P}$, of $\mathcal{B}$.

(5) If k=r, set $k' \leftarrow k-1$; otherwise, set $k' \leftarrow k$. Apply DECOMP (recursively) to $\mathcal{P}$ and k', obtaining outputs β' and ψ'. (For some $\mathcal{P}$-invariant c.a.d. S' of R^{r-1}, β' is a c.a.s. of S' and ψ' is a standard definition of the c.a.d. S^* of $R^{k'}$ induced by S', except that $\psi' = ()$ if k'=0. Since $\mathcal{P}$ contains the projection of $\mathcal{B}$ and S' is $\mathcal{P}$-invariant the real zeros of $\mathcal{B}$ are delineable on each cell of S' by Theorem 5. Hence S', together with the real algebraic functions defined by elements of $\mathcal{B}$ on the cells of S', determines a c.a.d. S of R^r. S is $\mathcal{B}$-invariant and therefore also $\mathcal{A}$-invariant since $\mathcal{B}$ is a basis for $\mathcal{A}$. Also, S^* is induced by S .)

(6) (This step extends the c.a.s. β' of S' to a c.a.s. β of S. Let $\beta' = (\beta'_1, \ldots, \beta'_l)$ and $\beta'_j = (\beta'_{j,1}, \ldots, \beta'_{j,r-1})$. We assume, inductively, that there is associated with each algebraic point β'_j an algebraic number α'_j such that $Q(\beta'_{j,1}, \ldots, \beta'_{j,r-1}) = Q(\alpha'_j)$ and polynomials $B'_{j,k}$ which represent the $\beta'_{j,k}$. The basis for this induction is trivial since the polynomial x represents $\beta'_{j,1} = \alpha'_j$ as an element of $Q(\alpha'_j)$ if α'_j is irrational, and if α'_j is rational it represents itself as an element of $Q = Q(\alpha'_j)$.) Let $\mathcal{B} = (B_1, \ldots, B_h)$. For j=1,..., l do [For i=1,...,h set $B^*_{j,i}(x) \leftarrow B_i(\beta'_{j,1}, \ldots, \beta'_{j,r-1}, x)$. ($B^*_{j,i}$ is a polynomial over $Q(\alpha'_j)$.) Apply ABASIS to α'_j and $(B^*_{j,1}, \ldots, B^*_{j,h})$, obtaining $\hat{\mathcal{B}}_j = (\hat{B}_{j,1}, \ldots, \hat{B}_{j,m_j})$ a coarsest squarefree bas[is]. Apply ISOL to α'_j and $\hat{B}_j$, obtaining outputs $I_j = (I_{j,1}, \ldots, I_{j,n_j})$ and $\nu_j = (\nu_{j,1}, \ldots, \nu_{j,n_j})$. ($\hat{B}_{j,\nu_{j,k}}$ has a unique real zero $\gamma_{j,k}$ in $I^j_{j,k}$, and $\gamma_{j,1} < \ldots < \gamma_{j,n_j}$ are all the real zeros of elements of $\hat{\mathcal{B}}_j$. For k=1,..., m_j do [Set $\hat{I}_{j,k}$ to the subsequence of I_j consisting of those $I_{j,l}$ such that $\nu_{j,l} = k$. (Then $\hat{I}_{j,k}$ is a list of rational isolating intervals for th[e] real roots of $\hat{B}_{j,k}$.) Apply NORMAL to α'_j, $\hat{B}_{j,k}$ and $\hat{I}_{j,k}$, obtaining as out-

ts $\bar{B}_{j,k}$ and $I^*_{j,k}$.] Merge the sequences $I^*_{j,k}$ into a single sequence $=(\bar{I}_{j,1},\ldots,\bar{I}_{j,n_j})$ with $\bar{I}_{j,1}<\bar{I}_{j,2}<\ldots<\bar{I}_{j,n_j}$. (Now $\gamma_{j,k}$ is represend by $(\bar{B}_{j,k},\bar{I}_{j,k})$.) If $n_j=0$, set $\delta_{j,1}\leftarrow 0$. If $n_j>0$, for $k=1,\ldots,n_j$, where $_{,k}=(r_{j,k},s_{j,k})$, set $\delta_{j,2k-1}\leftarrow r_{j,k}$ and $\delta_{j,2k}\leftarrow\gamma_{j,k}$; also set $\delta_{j,2n_j+1}\leftarrow s_{j,n_j}$. r $k=1,\ldots,2n_j+1$, set $\beta_{j,k}\leftarrow(\beta'_{j,1},\ldots,\beta'_{j,r-1},\delta_{j,k})$. For $k=1,\ldots,2n_j+1$ ply SIMPLE to α'_j and $\delta_{j,k}$, obtaining outputs $\alpha_{j,k}$, $A_{j,k}$ and $B_{j,k}$. (Now $\beta'_{j,1},\ldots,\beta'_{j,r-1},\delta_{j,k})=Q(\alpha'_j,\delta_{j,k})=Q(\alpha_{j,k})$, $A_{j,k}$ represents α'_j in $Q(\alpha_{j,k})$, d $B_{j,k}$ represents $\delta_{j,k}$ in $Q(\alpha_{j,k})$.) For $h=1,\ldots,r-1$ and $k=1,\ldots,2n_j+1$, ere $\alpha_{j,k}$ is represented by $(C_{j,k},I'_{j,k})$, set $D_{j,h,k}(x)\rightarrow B'_{j,h}(A_{j,k}(x))$ dulo $C_{j,k}(x)$. ($\alpha'_j=A_{j,k}(\alpha_{j,k})$, $\beta'_{j,h}=B'_{j,h}(\alpha'_j)$ and $C_{j,k}(\alpha_{j,k})=0$, so $D_{j,h,k}$ presents $\beta'_{j,h}$ in $Q(\alpha_{j,k})$.)] Set $\beta\leftarrow(\beta_{1,1},\ldots,\beta_{1,2n_1+1},\ldots,\beta_{1,1},\ldots,$ $_{,2n_1+1})$. (Now β is a c.a.s. of S.)

) If $k<r$, set $\psi\leftarrow\psi'$ and exit. (If $k<r$, then $k'=k$ so ψ' is a standard finition of the c.a.d. S^* of R^k induced by S', and hence induced also by Otherwise $k=r$, $k'=r-1$ and we next proceed to extend the standard denition ψ' of S' to a standard definition ψ of S. Since $k=r$, $\mathcal{P}$ is the gmented projection of $\mathcal{B}$ and, by Theorem 6, the real roots of every derivative of every element of $\mathcal{B}$ are delineable on every cell of S' because is $\mathcal{P}$-invariant.) For $j=1,\ldots,l$ do [For $i=1,\ldots,h$ apply DEFINE to and β'_j, obtaining as output a sequence $\mathcal{X}_{i,j}=(\mathcal{X}_{i,j,1},\ldots,\mathcal{X}_{i,j,2n_{i,j}+1})$. $_{i,j,k}$ is a standard quantifier-free formula such that $\psi'_j\&\mathcal{X}_{i,j,k}$ dees the kth cell of the cylinder $S'_j\times R$ as determined by the real zeros B_i on S'_j. We next proceed to use the $\mathcal{X}_{i,j,k}$ to define the cells of the inder $S'_j\times R$ as determined by the real zeros of $B=\Pi_{i=1}^h B_i$, that is, the ls of the jth cylinder of S, using the results of step (6). Observe t B has n_j real zeros on S_j and that the kth real zero is a zero of $_{\nu_{j,k}}$.) For $i=1,\ldots,h$ and $k=1,\ldots,n_j$, set $\delta_{i,j,k}=1$ if $\hat{B}_{j,\nu_{j,k}}$ is a isor of $B^*_{j,i}$, and $\delta_{i,j,k}=0$ otherwise. (Now $\delta_{i,j,k}=1$ just in case $_i(\gamma_{j,k})=0$. For $k=1,\ldots,n_j$, set $\lambda_{j,k}$ to the least i such that $\delta_{i,j,k}=1$. w $\gamma_{j,k}$ is a root of $B^*_{j,\lambda_{j,k}}$.) For $k=1,\ldots,n_j$, set $\mu_{j,k}\leftarrow\Sigma_{i=1}^{\lambda_{j,k}}\delta_{i,j,k}$. w $\gamma_{j,k}$ is the $\mu_{j,k}$th real root of $B^*_{j,\lambda_{j,k}}$. Hence the kth real root of n S'_j is the $\mu_{j,k}$th real root of $B_{\lambda_{j,k}}$ on S'_j.) For $k=1,\ldots,n_j$ set $\psi_{j,2k}$ $\&\mathcal{X}_{\lambda_{j,k},j,2\mu_{j,k}}$. For $k=1,\ldots,n_j-1$ set $\psi_{j,2k+1}\leftarrow\psi'_j\&\mathcal{X}_{\lambda_{j,k},j,2\mu_{j,k}+1}\&$ $_{\lambda_{j,k+1},j,2\mu_{j,k+1}-1}$. If $\nu_{j,k}=\nu_{j,k+1}$ then the last two conjuncts of $\psi_{j,2k+1}$ ncide so one may be omitted.) If $n_j>0$, set $\psi_{j,1}\leftarrow\psi'_j\&\mathcal{X}_{\lambda_{j,1},j,1}$ and $_{2n_j+1}\leftarrow\psi'_j\&\mathcal{X}_{\lambda_{j,n},j,2\mu_{j,n_j}+1}$. If $n_j=0$, set $\psi_{j,1}\leftarrow\psi'_j$.]

Set $\psi \leftarrow (\psi_{1,1},\ldots,\psi_{1,2n_1+1},\ldots,\psi_{1,2n_1+1})$. (Now ψ is a standard definition of S.) Exit.

Next we describe the algorithm DEFINE.

$$\phi = \text{DEFINE}(B,\beta)$$

Inputs: B is an integral polynomial in r variables, $r \geq 2$, such that for some connected set $S \subseteq R^{r-1}$ the real roots of B and of each derivative of B are delineable on S. β is an algebraic point of S.

Output: $\phi = (\phi_1,\ldots,\phi_{2m+1})$ is a sequence of standard quantifier-free formulas ϕ_i such that if ψ defines S then $\psi \& \phi_i$ defines the ith cell of the cylinder SxR as determined by the m real roots of B on S.

Algorithm Description

(1) (We let $\beta = (\beta_1,\ldots,\beta_{r-1})$. As in DECOMP, we may assume that we are given an algebraic number α such that $Q(\beta_1,\ldots,\beta_{r-1}) = Q(\alpha)$, and polynomia[ls] B_i which represent β_i as elements of $Q(\alpha)$. Set $B^*(x) = B(\beta_1,\ldots,\beta_{r-1},x)$. Apply SQFREE to α and B^*, obtaining the list $\mathcal{B}^* = (B_1^*,\ldots,B_h^*)$ of squarefre[e] factors of B^* and the list $(e_1,\ldots,e_h)$ of corresponding exponents. Apply ISOL to α and $\mathcal{B}^*$, obtaining as outputs the lists $(I_1,\ldots,I_m)$ and $(\nu_1,\ldots,\nu_m)$. (I_j isolates the jth real zero, γ_j, of the elements of $\mathcal{B}^*$, and γ_j is a zero of B_{ν_j}.) If m=0, set $\phi_1 \leftarrow$"0=0", $\phi \leftarrow (\phi_1)$, and exit. For $i=1,\ldots,m$ set $\mu_i \leftarrow e_{\nu_i}$. (Now γ_i is a zero of $B^*_{\nu_i}$ of multiplicity μ_i.) Set $\sigma_m \leftarrow$sign (ldcf(B^*)). For $j=m-1,\ldots,0$ set $\sigma_j \leftarrow (-1)^{\mu_{j+1}}\sigma_{j+1}$. (Now σ_j is the sign of B in the (2j+1) th cell of the B-invariant decomposition of the cylinder SxR.) If m=1 and μ_1 is odd, set $\phi_1 \leftarrow$"σ_0B>0", $\phi_2 \leftarrow$"B=0", $\phi_3 \leftarrow$"σ_1B>0", $\phi \leftarrow (\phi_1,\phi_2,\phi_3)$, and exit.

(2) Set $B^{*\prime} \leftarrow \text{der}(B^*)$, $G \leftarrow \gcd(B^*,B^{*\prime})$ and $H \leftarrow B^{*\prime}/G$. (Now $H(\delta)=0$ if and only if $B^{*\prime}(\delta)=0$ and $B^*(\delta) \neq 0$.) Set $\bar{H} \leftarrow \gcd(H,H')$. ($\bar{H}$ is squarefree and has the same roots as H.) Apply ISOL to α and the list $(\bar{H})$, obtaining as output the list $I' = (I_1',\ldots,I_n')$ of isolating intervals for the roots of $B^{*\prime}$ which are not roots of B . For $j=1,\ldots,m$ and $k=1,\ldots,n$, if I_j and I_k' are non-disjoint, replace I_j by its left or right half, whichever contains a root of B^*, and replace I_k' by its left or right half, whichever contains a root of B ′, and repeat until I_j and I_k' are disjoint. Set n_0 to the number of intervals I_k' such that $I_k' < I_1$. For $j=1,\ldots,m-1$, set n_j

to the number of intervals I'_k such that $I_j<I'_k<I_{j+1}$. Set n_m to the number of intervals I'_k such that $I_m<I'_k$. Set $\lambda_1\leftarrow n_o$. For j=1,...,m set $\lambda_{2j}\leftarrow\{\lambda_{2j-1}$ if $\mu_j=1$; $\lambda_{2j-1}+1$ if $\mu_j>1\}$, and $\lambda_{2j+1}\leftarrow\lambda_{2j}+n_j$. (Now λ_{2j-1} is the number of zeros of $B^{*\prime}$ less than γ_j, λ_{2j} is the number less than or equal to γ_j, and λ_{2m+1} is the number of all the zeros.)

(3) Set B'←der(B). Apply DEFINE to B' and ß, obtaining $(\phi'_1,\dots,\phi'_l)$ as output. (Thus DEFINE is a recursive algorithm; its termination is assured because deg(B')<deg(B).)

(4) (This step computes ϕ_{2i} for $1\le i\le m$.) For i=1,...,m if $\mu_i>1$ set $\phi_{2i}\leftarrow\phi'_{2\lambda_{2i}}$. (If $\mu_i>1$ then the ith real zero of B is the λ_{2i}-th real zero of B'.) For i=1,...,m if $\mu_i=1$ set $\phi_{2i}\leftarrow$"$B=0\&\phi'_{2\lambda_{2i-1}+1}$". (There are λ_{2i-1} zeros of B less than the ith zero of B, so the ith zero of B is in the $2\lambda_{i-1}+1$-th cell of the B' decomposition. By Rolle's theorem, any two real zeros of B are separated by a zero of B' so there is only one zero of B in this cell.)

(5) (This step defines ϕ_{2i+1} for $1\le i<m$. There are four cases.) For i=1,...,m-1 if $\mu_i>1$ and $\mu_{i+1}>1$ set $\phi_{2i+1}\leftarrow\bigvee_{2\lambda_{2i}+1\le j\le 2\lambda_{2i+2}-1}\phi'_j$. (In this case the ith zero of B is the λ_{2i}th zero of B' and the (i+1)th zero of B is the λ_{2i+2}th zero of B'.) For i=1,...,m-1 if $\mu_i=1$ and $\mu_{i+1}>1$ set $\phi_{2i+1}\leftarrow\{\sigma_iB>0\&\phi'_{2\lambda_{2i}+1}\}\vee\{\bigvee_{2\lambda_{2i}+2\le j\le 2\lambda_{2i+2}-1}\phi'_j\}$. (There are λ_{2i} zeros of B' less than the ith zero of B. By Rolle's theorem the ith zero of B is only zero of B in the $(2\lambda_{2i}+1)$th cell of the B' decomposition. Since $\mu_i=1$, B changes sign from σ_{i-1} to σ_i at this zero.) For i=1,...,m-1 if $\mu_i>1$ and $\mu_{i+1}=1$ set $\phi_{2i+1}\leftarrow\{\sigma_iB>0\&\phi'_{2\lambda_{2i+2}+1}\}\vee\{\bigvee_{2\lambda_{2i}+1\le j\le 2\lambda_{2i+2}}\phi'_j\}$. (This case is similar to the preceding case.) For i=1,...,m-1 if $\mu_i=1$ and $\mu_{i+1}=1$ set $\phi_{2i+1}\leftarrow\{\sigma_iB>0\&\sigma'_{2\lambda_{2i}+1}\}\vee\{\sigma_iB>0\&\phi'_{2\lambda_{2i+2}+1}\}\vee\{\bigvee_{2\lambda_{2i}+2\le j\le 2\lambda_{2i+2}}$ $\}$.

(6) (This step defines ϕ_1 and ϕ_{2m+1}.) If $\mu_1>1$ set $\phi_1\leftarrow\bigvee_{1\le j\le 2\lambda_2-1}\phi'_j$. If $\mu_1=1$ set $\phi_1\leftarrow\{\sigma_oB>0\&\phi'_{2\lambda_2+1}\}\vee\{\bigvee_{1\le j\le 2\lambda_2}\phi'_j\}$. If $\mu_m>1$ set $\phi_{2m+1}\leftarrow\bigvee_{2\lambda_{2m}+1\le 2\lambda_{2m+1}+1}\phi'_j$. If $\mu_m=1$ set $\phi_{2m+1}\leftarrow\{\sigma_mB>0\&\phi'_{2\lambda_{2m}+1}\}\vee\{\bigvee_{2\lambda_{2m}+2\le j\le 2\lambda_{2m+1}+1}\phi'_j\}$. Set $\phi\leftarrow(\phi_1,\dots,\phi_{2m+1})$ and exit.

Let ϕ be any formula in r free variables and let $S \subseteq R^r$. ϕ is <u>invariant on</u> S in case either $(a_1,\ldots,a_r)$ is true for all $(a_1,\ldots,a_r)\varepsilon S$ or $(a_1,\ldots,a_r)$ is false for all $(a_1,\ldots,a_r)\varepsilon S$. If S is a c.a.d. of R^r, we say that S is <u>ϕ-invariant</u> in case ϕ is invariant on each cell of S. If ϕ is a standard quantifier-free formula in r variables, $\mathcal{A}$ is the set of all non-zero polynomials which occur in ϕ, and S is an $\mathcal{A}$-invariant c.a.d. of R^r, then clearly S is also ϕ-invariant.

If ϕ is a sentence, we will denote by $v(\phi)$ the truth value of ϕ, with "true" represented by 1, "false" by 0. Accordingly, if $(v_1,\ldots,v_n)$ is a vector of zeros and ones, then we define $\bigwedge_{i=1}^n v_i=1$ if each $v_i=1$ and $\bigwedge_{i=1}^n v_i=0$ otherwise. Similarly, we define $\bigvee_{i=1}^n v_i=0$ if each $v_i=0$ and $\bigvee_{i=1}^n v_i=1$ otherwise. If ϕ is a formula in r free variables and $a=(a_1,\ldots,a_r)\varepsilon R^r$, we set $v(\phi,a)=v(\phi(a_1,\ldots,a_r))$. If ϕ is invariant on S, we set $v(\phi,S) =v(\phi,a)$ for any $a\varepsilon S$.

The following theorem is fundamental in the use of a c.a.d. for quantifier elimination.

<u>Theorem 7.</u> Let $\phi(x_1,\ldots,x_r)$ be a formula in r free variables and let ϕ^* be $(\forall x_r)\phi$ or $(\exists x_r)\phi$. If $r>1$, let S be a ϕ-invariant c.a.d. of R^r, S^* the c.a.d. of R^{r-1} induced by S. Then S^* is ϕ -invariant. If $S^*=(S_1,\ldots,S_m)$ and $S=(S_{1,1},\ldots,S_{1,n_1},\ldots,S_{m,1},\ldots,S_{m,n_m})$ where $(S_{i,1},\ldots, S_{i,n_i})$ is the <u>ith</u> cylinder of S, then $v((\forall x_r)\phi,S_i)=\bigwedge_{j=1}^{n_i} v(\phi,S_{ij})$ and $v((\exists x_r)\phi,S_i)=\bigvee_{j=1}^{n_i} v(\phi,S_{i,j})$. If $r=1$ and $S=(S_1,\ldots,S_n)$ is a c.a.d. of R, then $v((\forall x_1)\phi)=\bigwedge_{i=1}^n v(\phi,S_i)$ and $v((\exists x_1)\phi)=\bigvee_{i=1}^n (\phi,S_i)$.

<u>Proof.</u> We will prove this theorem only for $r>1$, and only for the case that ϕ^* is $(\forall x_r)\phi$. The omitted cases are similar. So let $S=(S_{1,1}, \ldots,S_{1,n_1},\ldots,S_{m,1},\ldots,S_{m,n_m})$ be a ϕ-invariant c.a.d. of R^r, $S^*=(S_1,\ldots,$ the c.a.d. of R^{r-1} induced by S. Let $1\leq i\leq m$ and choose $(a_1,\ldots,a_{r-1})\varepsilon S_i$. Assume $\phi^*(a_1,\ldots,a_{r-1})$ is true. Let $(b_1,\ldots,b_{r-1})\varepsilon S_i$. Let $b_r\varepsilon R$. Then for some j, $(b_1,\ldots,b_r)\varepsilon S_{i,j}$. Choose a_r so that $(a_1,\ldots,a_r)\varepsilon S_{i,j}$. Since $\phi^*(a_1,\ldots,a_{r-1})$ is true, $\phi(a_1,\ldots,a_{r-1},a)$ is true for all $a\varepsilon R$. In particular, $\phi(a_1,\ldots,a_r)$ is true. Since S is ϕ-invariant, ϕ is invariant on $S_{i,j}$ So $\phi(b_1,\ldots,b_r)$ is true. Since b_r is an arbitrary element of R, $\phi^*(b_1,\ldots,b_{r-1})$ is true. Since $(b_1,\ldots,b_{r-1})$ is an arbitrary element of S_i ϕ^* is invariant on S_i. Since S_i is an arbitrary element of S, ϕ^* is

-invariant. This completes the proof of the first part.

Now assume $v(\phi^*, S_i)=1$. Let $1\leq j\leq n_i$. Choose $(a_1,\ldots,a_{r-1})\varepsilon S_i$. By e first part, ϕ^* is S-invariant so $\phi^*(a_1,\ldots,a_{r-1})$ is true. Hence $(a_1,\ldots,a_r)$ is true for all $a_r\varepsilon R$. Choose a_r so that $(a_1,\ldots,a_r)\varepsilon S_{i,j}$. the ϕ-invariance of S, $v(\phi,S_{i,j})=1$. Since j is arbitrary, $\bigwedge_{j=1}^{n_i} v(\phi,S_{i,j})$.

Next assume $v(\phi^*,S_i)=0$. Choose $(a_1,\ldots,a_{r-1})\varepsilon S_i$. Since ϕ^* is S-in- riant, $\phi^*(a_1,\ldots,a_{r-1})$ is false. Hence for some $a_r\varepsilon R$, $\phi(a_1,\ldots,a_r)$ is lse. Let $(a_1,\ldots,a_r)\varepsilon S_{i,j}$. By the ϕ-invariance of S, $v(\phi,S_{i,j})=0$. Hence $_{j=1}^{n_j} v(\phi,S_{i,j})=0$. ▮

Let $a,b,\varepsilon R^r$ with $a=(a_1,\ldots,a_r)$ and $b=(b_1,\ldots,b_r)$. We define $a\sim_k b$ case $a_i=b_i$ for $1\leq i\leq k$. Note that $a\sim_r b$ if and only if $a=b$, while $a\sim_0 b$ r all $a,b\varepsilon R_r$. We define $a<b$ in case $a\sim_k b$ and $a_{k+1}<b_{k+1}$ for some k, $k<r$. The relation $a<b$ is a linear order on R^r, which we recognize as e lexicographical order on R^r induced by the usual order on R. We note at if $(\beta_1,\ldots,\beta_m)$ is a cylindrical sample of a c.a.d. S, then $\beta_1<\beta_2< \ldots<\beta_m$.

The cylindrical structure of a c.a.d. S is obtainable from any .s. β of S. We define a grouping function g. Let $\beta=(\beta_1,\ldots,\beta_m)$ by any quence of elements of R^r. Then for $0\leq k\leq r$, $g(k,\beta)=((\beta_1,\ldots,\beta_{n_1}),(\beta_{n_1+1},\ldots,\beta_{n_2}),\ldots,(\beta_{n_{l-1}+1},\ldots,\beta_{n_l}))$ where $1\leq n_1<n_2<\ldots<n_{l-1}<n_l=m$, $\beta_j\sim_k\beta_{j+1}$ for $j<n_{i+1}$, and $\beta_{n_i}\not\sim_k\beta_{n_i+1}$. Note that $g(0,\beta)=((\beta_1,\ldots,\beta_m))$ and $g(r,\beta)$ $(\beta_1),\ldots,(\beta_m))$. Also, if S is a c.a.d. of R^r, $S^*=(S_1,\ldots,S_m)$ is the c.a.d. R^k induced by S, and β is a c.a.s. of S, then $g(k,\beta)=(\beta_1^*,\ldots,\beta_m^*)$ where is the list of those points in β which belong to $S_i^* x R^{r-k}$.

We define now an evaluation function e. Let $\phi(x_1,\ldots,x_r)$ be a stan- d quantifier-free formula, S a ϕ-invariant c.a.d. of R^r, β a c.a.s. of and let $\phi^*(x_1,\ldots,x_k)$ be $(Q_{k+1}x_{k+1})\ldots(Q_r x_r)\phi(x_1,\ldots,x_r)$, $0\leq k\leq r$. $S^*=(S_1^*,\ldots,S_m^*)$ be the c.a.d. of R^k induced by S, $\beta^*=(\beta_1^*,\ldots,\beta_m^*)$ $k,\beta)$. Then we define $e(\phi^*,\beta_i^*)$ by induction on r-k, as follows. If then ϕ^* is ϕ, $\beta_i^*=(\beta_i)$, and we define $e(\phi^*,\beta_i^*)=v(\phi,\beta_i)$. If $k<r$, let $+1,\beta_i^*)=(\hat\beta_1,\ldots,\hat\beta_n)=\hat\beta$. Then each $\hat\beta_j$ is in the sequence $g(k+1,\beta)$. Let $,\ldots,x_{k+1})$ be $(Q_{k+2}x_{k+2})\ldots(Q_r x_r)\phi(x_1,\ldots,x_r)$. Then we define

$$e(\phi^*, \beta_i^*) = \bigwedge_{j=1}^{n} e(\hat{\phi}, \hat{\beta}_j), \text{ if } Q_{k+1} = \forall,$$

$$e(\phi^*, \beta_i^*) = \bigvee_{j=1}^{n} e(\phi, \beta_j), \text{ if } Q_{k+1} = \exists.$$

<u>Theorem 8.</u> Let $\phi(x_1,\ldots,x_r)$ be a standard quantifier-free formula, S a ϕ-invariant c.a.d. of R^r, β a cylindrical algebraic sample o: S. Let $\phi^*(x_1,\ldots,x_k)$ be $(Q_{k+1}x_{k+1})\ldots(Q_r x_r)\phi(x_1,\ldots,x_r)$, $0 \le k \le r$. If $k>0$ let $S^* = (S_1^*,\ldots,S_m^*)$ be the c.a.d. of R^k induced by S and let $g(k,\beta) = \beta^* = (\beta_1^*,\ldots,\beta_m^*)$. Then $e(\phi^*,\beta_i^*) = v(\phi^*, S_i^*)$ for $1 \le i \le m$. If $k=0$, then $e(\phi^*, \beta) = v(\phi^*)$.

<u>Proof.</u> By an induction on $r-k$, paralleling the definition of e and using Theorem 7. ∎

By Theorem 8, if $k=0$, then $e(\phi^*,\beta)$ is the truth value of ϕ^*. If $k>0$, let $\psi = (\psi_1,\ldots,\psi_m)$ be a standard definition of the c.a.d. S^*, as produced by DECOMP, and let ψ^* be the disjunction of those ψ_i such that $e(\phi^*, \beta_i^*) = 1$. Then ψ^* is a standard quantifier-free formula equivalent to ϕ^*.

The function e can be computed by an algorithm based directly on the definition of e. $e(\phi^*, \beta_i^*)$ is ultimately just some Boolean functi of the truth values of ϕ at the sample points β_j in the list β_i^*, that is, of the $v(\phi,\beta_j)$. It is important to note, however, that usually no all $v(\phi,\beta_j)$ need be computed. For example, if $Q_{k+1} = \forall$ then the comput tion of $e(\phi^*,\beta_i^*)$ can be terminated as soon as any j is found for whic $e(\hat{\phi},\beta_j)=0$. Similarly, the computation of $v(\phi,\beta)$, β an algebraic point, is Boolean-reducible to the case in which ϕ is a standard atomic formula. This case itself amounts to determining the sign of $A(\beta_1,\ldots,\beta_r$ where A is an integral polynomial and $\beta = (\beta_1,\ldots,\beta_r)$ is a real algebra point. With β we are given an algebraic number α such that $Q(\beta_1,\ldots,\beta$ $=Q(\alpha)$ and rational polynomials B_i such that $\beta_i = B_i(\alpha)$. We then obtain s $(A(\beta_1,\ldots,\beta_r)) = \text{sign}(A(B_1(\alpha),\ldots,B_r(\alpha))) = \text{sign}(C(\alpha))$ using an algorithm of [16]

Since a standard formula ϕ may contain several occurences of the same polynomial, we assume that the polynomials occurring in ϕ are st uniquely in a list $\mathfrak{a}$ inside the computer, and that the formula ϕ is stored so that the atomic formulas of ϕ contain references to this list in place of the polynomials themselves. Note also that the list $\mathfrak{a}$ need not contain two different polynomials whose ratio is a non-zero rational number. In computing $v(\phi,\beta)$, a list σ should be maintained, containing $\text{sign}(A(\beta))$ for various polynomials $A\epsilon\mathcal{A}$. Whenever the computation of $v(\phi,\beta)$ requires the computation of $\text{sign}(A(\beta))$ the list σ should be searched to determine whether $\text{sign}(A(\beta))$ was previously computed; if not, $\text{sign}(A(\beta))$ should be computed and placed on the list. Thus the computation of $v(\phi,\beta)$ will require at most one computation of $\text{sign}(A(\beta))$ for each $A\epsilon\mathcal{A}$, and in some cases $\text{sign}(A(\beta))$ will not be computed for all $A\epsilon\mathcal{A}$.

In terms of the funetions g and e, the evaluation algorithm can now be described as follows.

$$\psi^* = \text{EVAL}(\phi^*,\beta,\psi)$$

Inputs: ϕ^* is a standard prenex formula $(Q_{k+1}x_{k+1})\dots(Q_r x_r)\phi(x_1,\dots,x_r)$ where $0\leq k\leq r$ and ϕ is quantifier-free. β is a c.a.s. of some ϕ-invariant c.a.d. S of R^r. ψ is a standard definition of the c.a.d. S^* of R^k induced by S if $k>0$, the null list if $k=0$.

Output: $\psi^* = \psi\ (x_1,\dots,x_k)$ is a standard quantifier-free formula equivalent to ϕ^*.

Algorithm Description

(1) If $k>0$ go to (2). Set $v=e(\phi^*,\beta)$. If $v=0$ set $\psi^*\leftarrow$"1=0". If $v=1$, set $\psi^*\leftarrow$"0=0". Exit.
(2) Set $\beta^*\leftarrow g(k,\beta)$. Let $\beta^*=(\beta_1^*,\dots,\beta_m^*)$ and $\psi=(\psi_1,\dots,\psi_m)$. Set $\psi^*\leftarrow$"1=0". For $i=1,\dots,m$ if $e(\phi^*,\beta_i^*)=1$ set $\psi^*\leftarrow\psi_i\vee\psi$. Exit.

Finally we have the following quantifier elimination algorithm.

$$\psi^* = \text{ELIM}(\phi^*)$$

Input: ϕ^* is a standard prenex formula $(Q_{k+1}x_{k+1})\dots(Q_r x_r)\phi(x_1,\dots,x_r)$ where $0\leq k\leq r$ and ϕ is quantifier-free.

Output: ψ^* is a standard quantifier-free formula equivalent to ϕ^*.

Algorithm Description

(1) Determine k. Extract from ϕ the list $\mathcal{A}=(A_1,\dots,A_m)$ of distinct non-zero polynomials occurring in ϕ.

(2) Apply DECOMP to $\mathcal{A}$ and k, obtaining β and ψ as outputs.

(3) Set $\psi^* \leftarrow \mathrm{EVAL}(\phi^*, \beta, \psi)$ and exit.

4. Algorithm Analysis. Step (4) of the algorithm DECOMP provides for the optional computation of a basis $\mathcal{B}$ for a set $\mathcal{A}$ of integral polynomials. Experience with the algorithm provides a strong indication that this basis calculation is very important in reducing the total computing time of the algorithm. If the set $\mathcal{A}$ is the result of two or more projections, as in general it will be, then it appears that the polynomials in $\mathcal{A}$ have a considerable probability of having factors, common factors, and multiple factors. This will be discussed further in Section 5. But, as remarked in Section 3, the basis calculation of step (4) is not essential to the validity of the algorithm. In order to simplify the analysis of the algorithm, we will assume that this basis calculation is not performed. In general, the polynomials in the basis $\mathcal{B}$ will have smaller degrees than the polynomials of $\mathcal{A}$, but the number of polynomials in $\mathcal{B}$ may be either greater or less than the number in $\mathcal{A}$.

In Section 3 we gave conceptually simple definitions of projectio and augmented projection, which definitions can be improved somewhat order to reduce the sizes of these sets. It is easy to see that in th definition of the projection we can set $\mathcal{S}_2 = \{\mathrm{psc}_k(\mathrm{red}^i(A), \mathrm{red}^j(B)) :$ $A, B \in$ $\& A < B \& i \geq 0 \& j \geq 0 \& 0 \leq k < \min(\deg(\mathrm{red}^i(A)), \deg(\mathrm{red}^j(B)))\}$, where "<" is an arbitrary linear ordering of the elements of $\mathcal{A}$. Also, in the definition of the augmented projection, we can set $\mathcal{P}' = \{\mathrm{psc}_k(\mathrm{der}^j(\mathrm{red}^i(A)),$ $\mathrm{der}^{j+1}(\mathrm{red}^i(A))) : A \in \mathcal{A} \; \& i \geq 0 \& j \geq 0 \& 0 \leq k < \deg(\mathrm{der}^{j+1}(\mathrm{red}^i(A)))\}$. Then the set $\mathcal{S}_1$ in the definition of the projection is contained in $\mathcal{P}'$, and the augmented projection of $\mathcal{A}$ is $\mathcal{L} \cup \mathcal{S}_2 \cup \mathcal{P}'$.

Now suppose that the set $\mathcal{A}$ contains m polynomials, with the degree of each polynomial in each variable at most n. Assume $m \geq 1$ and $n \geq$ Then the set $\mathcal{L}$ contains at most mn elements. In the set $\mathcal{S}_2$, the pair

A,B) can be chosen in $\binom{m}{2}$ ways. Since $k<\min(\deg(\mathrm{red}^i(A)),\deg(\mathrm{red}^j(B)))$ $\min(n-i,n-j)=n-\max(i,j)$, we have $0\le i,j\le n-k-1$. Hence for given k, $0\le k\le n-1$, he pair (i,j) can be chosen in at most $(n-k)^2$ ways. Hence (i,j,k) can be hosen in $\Sigma_{k=0}^{n-1}(n-k)^2=\frac{n(n+1)(2n+1)}{6}$ ways. So $\mathcal{B}_2$ has at most $\binom{m}{2}\frac{n(n+1)(2n+1)}{6}$ lements. In the definition of the set $\mathcal{P}'$, we must have $k<n-i-j-1$. For iven k, $0\le k\le n-2$, (i,j) can be chosen in $\Sigma_{h=0}^{n-k-2}(h+1)=\binom{n-k}{2}$ ways. Hence i,j,k) can be chosen in $\Sigma_{k=0}^{n-2}\binom{n-k}{2}=\binom{n+1}{3}$ ways. So $\mathcal{P}'$ has at most $m\binom{n+1}{3}$ lements. Altogether, the augmented projection has at most $\binom{m}{2}\frac{n(n+1)(2n+1)}{6}$ $m\binom{n+1}{3}$+mn elements. For n=1, this reduces to $\binom{m}{2}+m=\binom{m+1}{2}\le m^2$. For $n\ge 2$, $\binom{m}{2}\frac{n(n+1)(2n+1)}{6}+m\binom{n+1}{3}+mn\le\frac{m^2}{2}\cdot\frac{(15/4)n^3}{6}+m\frac{n^3}{6}+\frac{1}{4}mn^3<m^2n^3$. So in all ses the augmented projection of $\mathcal{A}$ has at most m^2n^3 elements.

By the definition of a principle subresultant coefficient, each ement of $\mathcal{B}_2$ or $\mathcal{P}'$ is the determinant of a matrix with at most 2n rows d columns, whose entries are coefficients of elements of $\mathcal{A}$. Hence the de- ee of any element of the augmented projection, in any variable, is at st $2n^2$.

In order to analyze the growth of coefficient length under the gmented projection operation, we need the concept of the norm of a lynomial. If A is any integral polynomial, the <u>norm</u> of A, denoted by $|_1$, is defined to be sum of the absolute values of the integer coeffi- ents of A. This "norm" is actually just a semi-norm, having the im- rtant properties $|A+B|_1\le|A|_1+|B|_1$ and $|A\cdot B|_1\le|A|_1\cdot|B|_1$. Using these operties, it is easy to show (see [22]) that if deg(A)=m and deg(B) , then any square submatrix of the Sylvester matrix of A and B has a terminant whose norm is at most $|A|_1^n|B|_1^m$.

Let c be the maximum of the norms of the elements of $\mathcal{A}$. For any ynomials A with deg(A)=n, $|A'|_1\le n|A|_1$. Hence it is easy to see that $P\epsilon\mathcal{P}'$ then $|P|_1\le(n^jc)^{n-j-1}(n^{j+1}c)^{n-j}\le n^{n^2/2}c^{2n}$, while if $P\epsilon\ \mathcal{L}\cup\mathcal{B}_2$ n $|P|_1\le c^{2n}$.

The <u>length</u> of any non-zero integer a, L(a), is the number of bits the binary representation of a, and L(0)=1. It is easy to show that b)$\le$L(a)+L(b) and hence $L(a^n)\le nL(a)$ if n>0. Also, $L(a)\le a$ if a>0. So P is any element of the augmented projection of $\mathcal{A}$, then $L(|P|_1)\le\frac{1}{2}n^2$)+2nL(c)$\le\frac{1}{2}n^3$+2nL(c).

The following theorem summarizes the several things we have prove

Theorem 9. Let $\mathcal{A}$ be a non-empty finite set of integral polynomials in r variables, $r \geq 2$. Let $\mathcal{A}^*$ be the augmented projection of $\mathcal{A}$. Let m be the number of elements of $\mathcal{A}$, n the maximum degree of any element of $\mathcal{A}$ in any variable , $n \geq 1$. Let d be the maximum of the lengths of the norms of the elements of $\mathcal{A}$. Let m^*, n^* and d^* be the same functions of $\mathcal{A}^*$. Then

$$m^* \leq m^2 n^3, \tag{2}$$

$$n^* \leq 2n^2, \tag{3}$$

$$d^* \leq \tfrac{1}{2}n^3 + 2nd. \tag{4}$$

When $\mathcal{A}$ is a set of polynomials in r variables, algorithm DECOMP computes a sequence of r-1 projections or augmented projections. Usin Theorem 9 we can now derive bounds for all such projections.

Theorem 10. Let $\mathcal{A}$,m,n and d be defined as in Theorem 9. Let $\mathcal{A}_1 = \mathcal{A}$ and let $\mathcal{A}_{i+1}$ be the augmented projection of $\mathcal{A}_i$ for $1 \leq i < r$. Let m_k be the number of elements of $\mathcal{A}_k$, n_k the degree maximum for $\mathcal{A}_k$, d_k the norm length maximum for $\mathcal{A}_k$. Then

$$m_k \leq (2n)^{3^k} m^{2^{k-1}}, \tag{5}$$

$$n_k \leq \tfrac{1}{2}(2n)^{2^{k-1}}, \tag{6}$$

$$d_k \leq (2n)^{2^k} d. \tag{7}$$

Proof. One may first prove (6) by a simple induction on k, using (3). (5) obviously holds for k=1. Assuming (5) holds for k, by (2) we have $m_{k+1} \leq \frac{1}{8}(2n)^a m^{2^k}$ where $a = 2\cdot 3^k + 3\cdot 2^{k-1} \leq 6\cdot 3^{k-1} + 3\cdot 3^{k-1} = 3^{k+1}$, proving (5). (7) obviously holds for k=1. Assuming (7) holds for k, by (4) we have $d_{k+1} \leq \frac{1}{16}(2n)^a + (2n)^a d \leq 2(2n)^a d \leq (2n)^{a+1} d$ where $a = 3\cdot 2^{k-1}$. But $a+1 \leq 2^{k+1}$ so (7) is established.

Using Theorem 10, we can now bound the time to compute all proje tions.

Theorem 11. Let $\mathcal{A}$,m,n,d and $\mathcal{A}_1, \ldots, \mathcal{A}_r$ be defined as in Theo

10. Then there is an algorithm which computes $\mathcal{A}_2,\ldots,\mathcal{A}_r$ from $\mathcal{A}_1=\mathcal{A}$ in time dominated by $(2n)^{3^{r+1}}m^{2^r}d^2$.

Proof. Let A and B be integral polynomials in r variables, with degrees in each variable not exceeding $n\geq 2$, and with norms of lengths d or less. There is described in (5) an algorithm for computing the resultant of A and B, whose computing time is dominated by $n^{2r+2}d^2$. It is easy to see how to generalize this algorithm to compute $psc_k(A,B)$, for any k, within the same time bound. By (6) and (7), any derivative of any element of $\mathcal{A}_k$ has a norm whose length is at most $d_k+L(n_k!)\leq d_k+n_k^2 \leq \frac{5}{4}(2n)^{2^k}d=d_k'$. Since the elements of $\mathcal{A}_k$ have r-k+1 variables, each p.s.c. of $\mathcal{A}_{k+1}$ can be computed in time dominated by $n_k^{2(r-k+1)}d_k'^2$, and there are at most m_{k+1} such p.s.c.'s to be computed. Using the inequality $(r-k+1)\leq 2^{r-k+1}$, we thus find that the time to compute all p.s.c.'s of $\mathcal{A}_{k+1}$ is dominated by $(2n)^a m^{2^k} d^2$ where $a=3^{k+1}+2^r+2^{k+1}\leq 3^r+2^r+2^r\leq 9\cdot 3^{r-2}$ $8\cdot 3^{r-2}\leq 17\cdot 3^{r-2}<2\cdot 3^r$. Hence the p.s.c.'s of $\mathcal{A}_{k+1}$ can be computed in time $(2n)^{2\cdot 3^r}m^{2^r}d^2$. Multiplying by r and using $r\leq 2^{2^{r-1}}$, the p.s.c.'s of $\mathcal{A}_2,\ldots,\mathcal{A}_r$ can be computed in time $(2n)^{3^{r+1}}m^{2^r}d^2$. We have ignored the time required to compute reducta and derivatives, but this is relatively trivial. ∎

Let S be the c.a.d. of R^r computed by DECOMP and let S_k be the c.a.d. of R^k induced by S, for $1\leq k\leq r$. Thus $S=S_r$. Let c_k be the number of cells in S_k. The cells of S_1 are determined by the real roots of m_r polynomials, each of degree n_r at most. There are at most $m_r n_r$ such roots and hence $c_1\leq 2m_r n_r+1$. For each value of k, $2\leq k\leq r$, step (6) substitutes the k-1 coordinates of each sample point of S_{k-1} for the first k-1 variables of the k-variable polynomials in $\mathcal{A}_{r-k+1}$, thereby obtaining $u_{r-k+1}\leq c_{k-1}m_{r-k+1}$ univariate polynomials with real algebraic number coefficients, each of degree n_{r-k+1} at most. These polynomials have at most $c_{k-1}m_{r-k+1}n_{r-k+1}$ real roots, and hence $c_k\leq 2m_{r-k+1}n_{r-k+1}c_{k-1}+1$. For convenience, we set $u_r=m_r$. We can now prove the following theorem

Theorem 12. For $1\leq k\leq r$, both u_k and c_k are less than $(2n)^{3^{r+1}}m^{2^r}$.

Proof. We have shown above that $c_1\leq 2m_r n_r+1$; hence $c_1\leq 4m_r n_r$. Similarly, from $c_k\leq 2m_{r-k+1}n_{r-k+1}c_{k-1}+1$ it follows that $c_k\leq 4m_{r-k+1}n_{r-k+1}c_{k-1}$.

By induction on k, we then have $c_k \leq \Pi_{i=r-k+1}^{r} 4m_i n_i$. Hence $c_k \leq 2^{2r} \Pi_{i=1}^{r} m_i n_i$ for all k. In a similar manner it is easy to show that $u_k \leq 2^{2r} \Pi_{i=1}^{r} m_i n_i$ for all k. By (5) and (6) we then deduce that $2^{2r} \Pi_{i=1}^{r} m_i n_i \leq (2n)^{a+b+2r} m^b$ where $a = \Sigma_{k=1}^{r} 3^k < \frac{1}{2} \cdot 3^{r+1}$ and $b = \Sigma_{k=1}^{r} 2^{k-1} < 2^r$. Hence it suffices to show that $2^r + 2r \leq \frac{1}{2} \cdot 3^{r+1}$. But $2^r + 2r \leq 2 \cdot 2^r \leq 4 \cdot 2^{r-1} \leq 4 \cdot 3^{r-1} < \frac{1}{2} \cdot 3^{r+1}$. ∎

Our next goal is to bound the time for step (1) of DECOMP. We must first obtain bounds for the computing times of the subalgorithms BASIS and **ISOL**.

There exist (see [6]) polynomial greatest common divisor algorithms for univariate integral polynomials which, when applied to two polynomials of degree n or less and with norms of length d or less, have a maximum computing time dominated by $n^3 d^2$, Mignotte has recently shown, [23], that if A is a univariate integral polynomial with degree n and norm c, and if B is any divisor of A, then $|B|_1 \leq 2^n c$. From these two facts it easily follows that the squarefree factorization of A can be computed by the algorithm described in [14] in time dominated by $n^6 + n^4 d^2$ where d is the length of $c = |A|_1$ and $n = \deg(A)$.

Now suppose the coarsest squarefree basis algorithm outlined in Section 3 is applied to a set of m univariate integral polynomials, with degrees and norm lengths bounded by n and d respectively. In each of the m applications of Loos' algorithm, each input basis set will contain at most mn polynomials, with degrees and norm lengths bounded by n and n+d respectively. Hence the time for all applications of Loos' algorithm will be dominated by $m(mn)^2 n^3 (n+d)^2$, hence by $m^3 n^5 (n^2+d^2) \leq m^3 n^7 d^2$. The time required for the m squarefree factorizations will be dominated by $mn^6 d^2$. Hence we arrive at a maximum computing time of $m^3 n^7 d^2$ for BASIS.

Now consider the computing time of ISOL when applied to a set $\mathfrak{a}$ of m univariate integral squarefree and pairwise relatively prime polynomials, with a degree bound of n and a norm length bound of d. Collins has shown, [22], that if A is a univariate integral squarefree polynomial with deg(A)=n and $|A|_1 = c$, then the distance between any two roots of A is at least $\frac{1}{2}(e^{1/2} n^{3/2} c)^{-n}$. This theorem on root separation, together with the discussion of Heindel's algorithm in [6], implies that Heindel's algorithm will isolate the real roots of A in time dominated by $n^8 + n^7 d^3$. Hence the real roots of the m polynomials in $\mathfrak{a}$ can be separately isolated in time dominated by $mn^8+mn^7d^3$. An isolating interval for a root of $A_i\varepsilon$ can be refined to length less than 2^{-h} in time dominated by $n^2h^3+n^2d^2h$. By application of the root separation theorem to the product $A=\Pi_{i=1}^{m}A_i$ of the elements of $\mathfrak{A}$, the distance between any two roots of A is at least $\frac{1}{2}(e^{1/2}(mn)^{3/2}c^m)^{-mn}=\delta$. Hence if the isolating intervals for each A_i are refined to length 2^{-h} with $\delta/4\leq 2^{-h}$ $<\delta/2$ then all intervals for all A_i are disjoint. We then have h codominant with $mnL(mn)+m^2nd$, so the time to refine each interval is dominated by $m^3n^5L(mn)^3+m^6n^5d^3$, hence by $m^4n^6+m^6n^5d^3$. Since there are at most mn intervals to refine, the total time for ISOL is dominated by $(mn^8+mn^7d^3)+mn(m^4n^6+m^6n^5d^3)$, hence by $mn^8+m^7n^7d^3$.

Theorem 13. The computing time for step (1) of DECOMP is dominated by $(2n)^{3^{r+3}}m^{2^{r+2}}d^3$.

Proof. The time to apply BASIS in step (1) is dominated by $m_r^3n_r^7d^2$. By Theorem 10, since $d+1\leq 2d$, $m_r^3n_r^7d^2$ is dominated by $(2n)^am^bd^2$ where $b=3\cdot 2^{r-1}<2^{r+1}$ and $a\leq 3\cdot 3^r+7\cdot 2^{r-1}+2\cdot 2^r\leq 9\cdot 3^{r-1}+7\cdot 2^{r-1}+4\cdot 2^{r-1}\leq 20\cdot 3^{r-1}<3^{r+2}$. The coarsest squarefree basis $\mathcal{B}$ obtained will have at most m_rn_r elements, with degrees bounded by n_r and norm length bounded by n_r+d_r by Mignotte's theorem. Hence the time to apply ISOL will be dominated by $(m_rn_r)n_r^8$ $(m_rn_r)^7n_r^7(n_r+d_r)^3$, which is dominated by $m_r^7n_r^{17}d^3$. By Theorem 10, $m_r^7n_r^{17}d^3$ $(2n)^am^bd^3$ where $b\leq 7\cdot 2^{r-1}<2^{r+2}$ and $a\leq 7\cdot 3^r+17\cdot 2^{r-1}+3\cdot 2^r\leq 21\cdot 3^{r-1}+17\cdot 3^{r-1}$ $6\cdot 3^{r-1}=44\cdot 3^{r-1}<3^{r+3}$. ∎

Next we turn our attention to the "sizes" of the real algebraic numbers which arise in DECOMP. Two different representations are used, and hence there are two different definitions of "size". Regarded as an element of the field P of all real algebraic numbers, a real algebraic number α is represented by a primitive squarefree integral polynomial A(x) such that $A(\alpha)=0$ and an interval $I=(r,s)$ with rational endpoints r and s such that α is the unique root of A in I. We will assume moreover that r and s are <u>binary rationals</u>, that is, numbers of the form $a\cdot 2^{-k}$ where a and k are integers, $k\geq 0$, and a is odd if $k>0$. Let λ be the minimum distance between two real roots of A. By the root separation theorem, $\lambda^{-1}\leq 2(e^{1/2}n^{3/2}c)^n$ where n=deg(A) and $c=|A|_1$. Hence $\log_2 \lambda^{-1}<1+n(1+\frac{3}{2}L(n)+d)$ and $2^{-k}<\lambda$ if $k\geq 1+n(1+\frac{3}{2}L(n)+d)$, where d=L(c). Hence we assume that $r=a\cdot 2^{-h}$ and $s=b\cdot 2^{-\bar{k}}$ with $h, k\leq n(2+2L(n)+d)$. Since it follows from $A(\alpha)=0$ that $|\alpha|<c$, we may also assume that $L(a),L(b)\leq$

$2n(1+L(n)+d)$. Then the "size" of α will be characterized by $n=\deg(A)$ and $d=L(|A|_1)$.

Regarded as an element of the real algebraic number field $Q(\alpha)$, the real algebraic number β is represented by a polynomial $B(x) \varepsilon Q[x]$ with $\deg(B)<n=\deg(A)$. The rational polynomial $B(x)$ is itself represented in the form $B(x)=b^{-1}\cdot \bar{B}(x)$ where b is an integer, $\bar{B}(x)$ is an integral polynomial, and $\gcd(b,\bar{B})=1$. In this case the "size" of β is characterized by $L(b)$ and $L(|\bar{B}|_1)$.

Let P_k be the set of all points $\beta=(\beta_1,\ldots,\beta_k)$ belonging to the c.a.s. computed by DECOMP for the c.a.d. S_k. For each such point ther is computed a real algebraic number α such that $Q(\beta_1,\ldots,\beta_k)=Q(\alpha)$, an a pair (A,I) which represents α. A is a squarefree univariate integra polynomial such that $A(\alpha)=0$ and I is an isolating interval for α as a root of A. Let $\mathcal{A}_k^*$ be the set of all such polynomials A. Let n_k be th maximum degree of the elements of $\mathcal{A}_k^*$ and let d_k^* be the maximum norm length of the elements of $\mathcal{A}_k^*$.

For each coordinate β_i of a point $\beta \varepsilon P_k$, DECOMP computes a ratio nal polynomial $B_i=b_i^{-1}\bar{B}_i$ which represents β_i as an element of $Q(\alpha)$. Le $\mathcal{B}_k'$ be the set of all such rational polynomials B_i associated in this way with points β of P_k, and let d_k' be the maximum of $\max(L(b),L(|\bar{B}|_1$ taken over all $B=b^{-1}B\varepsilon\ \mathcal{B}_k'$.

Our next goal is to obtain recurrence relations for n_k^*, d_k^* and d_k'. For k=1, each algebraic number β_1 is a root of some element of $\mathcal{A}_r$, $\alpha=\beta_1$, and the polynomial A is an element of the basis for $\mathcal{A}_r$ which is computed in step (1). By Mignotte's theorem,

$$n_1^* \leq n_r, \tag{8}$$

$$d_1^* \leq n_r+d_r. \tag{9}$$

If β_1 is irrational, then $B(x)=x$ represents $\beta_1=\alpha$ as an element of Q If β_1 is rational then $B(x)=\beta_1$ represents $\beta_1=\alpha$ as an element of $Q(\alpha)$ Referring to step (2) of DECOMP, β_1 arises as an endpoint of an isol ting interval produced in step (1) by the application of ISOL to a b $\mathcal{B}$ for $\mathcal{A}_r$. Let $\bar{B}$ be the product of the elements of $\mathcal{B}$. Then $\deg(\bar{B})$ $\leq m_r n_r$ and, since $\bar{B}$ is the product of at most $m_r n_r$ polynomials, each h a norm length of at most n_r+d_r, the norm length of $\bar{B}$ is at most

$m_r n_r(n_r+d_r)$. In accordance with our previous discussion of the root separation theorem, we may therefore assume that the numerator and denominator of β_1 have lengths not exceeding $2m_r n_r\{1+L(m_r n_r)+m_r n_r(n_r+d_r)\} \leq 4m_r^2 n_r^2(n_r+d_r)$. Hence,

$$d_1' \leq 4m_r^2 n_r^2(n_r+d_r) \tag{10}$$

For each point $\beta=(\beta_1,\ldots,\beta_k)$ in P_k, and each polynomial $C(x_1,\ldots,x_{k+1})$ in $\mathcal{A}_{r-k}$, step (6) of DECOMP substitutes β_i for x_i, obtaining a polynomial $C^*(x)=C(\beta_1,\ldots,\beta_k,x)$ belonging to $Q(\alpha)[x]$, $Q(\alpha)=Q(\beta_1,\ldots,\beta_k)$. This substitution may be performed in two stages. In the first stage we substitute $B_i(y)$ for x_i, where B_i represents β_i as an element of $Q(\alpha)$, resulting in $\hat{C}(y,x)=C(B_1(y),\ldots,B_k(y),x)$, an element of $Q[y,x]$. In the second stage, $\hat{C}(y,x)$ is reduced modulo $A(y)$, where A represents α, resulting in $C^*(y,x)\varepsilon Q[y,x]$. $C^*(y,x)$ may be identified with $C^*(x)$ since the coefficients of $C^*(y,x)$ are elements of $Q[y]$ which represent the coefficients of $C^*(x)$ as elements of $Q(\alpha)$.

Instead of computing $\hat{C}(y,x)$ directly, we compute instead the integral polynomial $\bar{C}(y,x)=\{\Pi_{i=1}^{k} b_i^{\nu_i}\}\hat{C}(y,x)$, where ν_i is the degree of C in x_i. To illustrate, suppose $k=1$ and let $C(x_1,x_2)=\Sigma_{i=0}^{\nu_1} C_i(x_2)x_1^i$. Then $\bar{C}(y,x) =\Sigma_{i=0}^{\nu_1} C_i(x)\bar{B}_1(y)^i b_1^{\nu_1-i}$. Since $|C|_1=\Sigma_{i=0}^{\nu_1}|C_i|_1$, we see that $|\bar{C}|_1\leq|C|_1\cdot f^{\nu_1}$ where $f=\max(|b_1|,|B_1|_1)$. In general, recalling the definition of d_k', we see that the length of the norm of $\bar{C}$ is at most $d_{r-k}+kn_{r-k}d_k'$. Also, $\hat{C}(y,x)=c^{-1}\bar{C}(y,x)$ with $L(c)\leq kn_{r-k}d_k'$. Furthermore, the degree of $\bar{C}(y,x)$ in y is at most $kn_{r-k}n_k^*$ since the degree of each B_i is less than n_k^*.

In reducing $\hat{C}(y,x)$ modulo $A(y)$, we compute the pseudo-remainder, $C'(y,x)$, of $\bar{C}(y,x)$ with respect to $A(y)$. $C'(y,x)\varepsilon Z[y,x]$ and we have $c'\bar{C}(y,x)=A(y)\cdot Q(y,x)+C'(y,x)$ for some $c'\varepsilon Z$ and some $Q(y,x)\varepsilon Z[y,x]$, with the degree of C' in y less than $\deg(A)$. Hence $\hat{C}(y,x)=A(y)\{(cc')^{-1}Q(y,x)\}+(cc')^{-1}C'(y,x)$, and $C^*(y,x)=(cc')^{-1}C'(y,x)$. Regarding the pseudo-remainder as a subresultant, we have $|C'|_1\leq|\bar{C}|_1\cdot|A|_1^n$ where n is the degree of $\bar{C}$ in y. Since $L(|\bar{C}|_1)\leq d_{r-k}+kn_{r-k}d_k'$, $L(|A|_1)\leq d_k^*$ and $n\leq kn_{r-k}n_k^*$, $L(|C'|_1)\leq d_{r-k}+kn_{r-k}d_k'+kn_{r-k}n_k^*d_k^*$. Also, $c'=\{\mathrm{ldcf}(A)\}^h$ with $h\leq n$, so $L(cc')\leq kn_{r-k}d_k'+kn_{r-k}n_k^*d_k^*$.

The polynomial $C^*(x)$ arises from a point $\beta\varepsilon P_k$ and a polynomial

$C \in \mathcal{A}_{r-k}$. Keeping β fixed while C ranges over all elements of $\mathcal{A}_{r-k}$, we obtain a set $\mathcal{C}^*$ of univariate polynomials over $Q(\alpha)$. Step (6) of DECOMP specifies the application of ABASIS to $\mathcal{C}^*$ to produce a coarsest squarefree basis $\mathcal{B}^*$. However, at present no theorem is known which provides a reasonable bound for the "sizes" of the coefficients of the elements of $\mathcal{B}^*$. As an alternative we may therefore apply the algorithm NORMAL to α and $C^*(x)$, for each C^* in $\mathcal{C}^*$, producing an integral polynomial D(x) such that every root of C^* is a root of D. Let $\mathcal{D}$ be the set of all polynomials D so obtained as C^* ranges over $\mathcal{C}^*$.

Given α, represented by the integral polynomial A(y) and the isolating interval I, and the rational polynomial $C^*(y,x)=c^{-1}C'(y,x)$ representing $C^*(x)$, NORMAL proceeds as follows. Let $C'(y,x)=\sum_{i=0}^{m} C_i'(y)x^i$, where $C_m(\alpha)\neq 0$. The integral polynomial $C'(y,x)$ is divided by $\gcd(C_m(x),$ $(x))$, producing an integral polynomial $C''(y,x)$. Then D(x) is the resultant, with respect to y, of $C''(y,x)$ and A(y).

deg(A) and the degree in y of $C''(y,x)$ in y are both at most n_k^*. The degree of $C'(y,x)$ in x is at most n_{r-k}, the degree of $C(x_1,\ldots,x_{k+1})$ in x_{k+1}. Hence the degree of D is at most $n_k^* n_{r-k}$. Since the norm length of $C'(y,x)$ is at most $d_{r-k}+kn_{r-k}d_k'+kn_{r-k}n_k^*d_k^*$ and the norm length of A is at most d_k^*, the norm length of D is at most $n_k^*d_k^*+n_k^*d_{r-k}+kn_{r-k}n_k^*d_k'+kn_{r-k}n_k^{*2}d_k^*$.

Let $\bar{\mathcal{D}}$ be the coarsest squarefree basis of $\mathcal{D}$. Then every β_{k+1} with $(\beta_1,\ldots,\beta_k,\beta_{k+1})\in P_{k+1}$ will be represented by a polynomial $\bar{D}\in\bar{\mathcal{D}}$ and, by Mignotte's theorem, the norm length of $\bar{D}$ is at most $n_k^*n_{r-k}+n_k^*d_k^*+n_k^*d_{r-k}+kn_{r-k}n_k^*d_k'+kn_{r-k}n_k^{*2}d_k^*$.

Next algorithm SIMPLE is applied to α and β_{k+1}, producing α' such that $Q(\alpha,\beta_{k+1})=Q(\alpha')$. α and β_{k+1} are represented by the polynomials A and $\bar{D}$. α' is represented by a polynomial $A'(x)$, which is the resultant A(x-hy) and $\bar{D}(y)$ with respect to y, where h is some integer with $|h|<$ $\deg(A)\cdot\deg(\bar{D})$. Since $|x-hy|_1=|h|+1$, we have $|A(x-hy)|_1\leq|A|_1\cdot(|h|+1)^{\deg}$ Hence $L(|A(x-hy)|_1)\leq d_k^*+n_k^*(2L(n_k^*)+L(n_{r-k}))$. Since $\deg(\bar{D})\leq n_k^*n_{r-k}$ and the degree of A(x-hy) in y is $\deg(A)\leq n_k^*$, we have $L(|A'|_1)\leq n_k^*n_{r-k}\{d_k^*+2n_k^*L(n_k^*)+n_k^*L(n_{r-k})\}+n_k^*\{n_k^*n_{r-k}+n_k^*d_k^*+n_k^*d_{r-k}+kn_{r-k}n_k^*d_k'+kn_{r-k}n_k^{*2}d_k\}$. Since the degree of A(x-hy) in x is $\deg(A)\leq n_k^*$, we have $\deg(A')\leq n_k^{*2}n_{r-k}$. Thus we have proved

$$n^*_{k+1} \le n^{*2}_k n_{r-k}. \qquad (11)$$

lso, replacing $L(n^*_k)$ by n^*_k, $L(n_{r-k})$ by n_{r-k}, and making other simpli- ications in the inequality above for $L(|A'|_1)$, we have also

$$\ast_{k+1} \le (d^*_k n_{r-k}) n^*_k + (2n^2_{r-k} + d_{r-k} + d^*_k + k n_{r-k} d'_k) n^{*2}_k + (k+2) n_{r-k} d^*_k n^{*3}_k. \qquad (12)$$

It remains to obtain a relation for d'_{k+1}. Algorithm SIMPLE, when pplied to α and β_{k+1}, produces, besides α' such that $Q(\alpha,\beta_{k+1})=Q(\alpha')$, ational polynomials E and F which represent α and β_{k+1} as elements of (α'). The polynomial $A'(y)$ which represents α' is the resultant of $(x-hy)$ and $\bar{D}(y)$. The monic greatest common divisor of $A(\alpha'-hx)$ and $x)$ in $Q(\alpha')$ is the polynomial $x-\beta_{k+1}$. This implies that if $G(y,x)=$ $(y)x+G_0(y)$ is the first subresultant of $A(y-hx)$ and $\bar{D}(x)$ then β_{k+1} $G_0(\alpha')/G_1(\alpha')$. Let $H=\gcd(A',G_1)$ and $\bar{A}'=A'/H$. Since A' is squarefree, and G_1 are relatively prime integral polynomials. Applying the exten- d Euclidean algorithm, we obtain integral polynomials U and V such at $\bar{A}'U+G_1V=c$, where $c\neq 0$ is the resultant of $\bar{A}'$ and G_1. Also, $G_1(\alpha')$ so $H(\alpha')\neq 0$ and $\bar{A}'(\alpha')=0$. Hence $G_1(\alpha')V(\alpha')=c$. Let $G_2=-G_0V$. Then $^1G_2(\alpha')=-G_0(\alpha')c^{-1}V(\alpha')=-G_0(\alpha')/G_1(\alpha')=\beta_{k+1}$. Hence if $bG_2(y)=Q(y)A'(y)$ $_3(y)$ where G_3 is the pseudo-remainder of G_2 and A', then $(bc)^{-1}G_3$ re- esents β_{k+1}. Also, $\alpha'=\alpha+h\beta_{k+1}$ so if $G_4(y)=bcy-hG_3(y)$ then $(bc)^{-1}G_4(y)$ presents α in $Q(\alpha')$.

The same degree and norm length bounds, (11) and (12), which were rived for the resultant A' apply also to the subresultant coefficients and G_1. Since $\bar{A}'$ is a divisor of A', $\deg(\bar{A}')\le n^*_{k+1}$ and, by Mignotte's eorem, $L(|\bar{A}'|_1)\le n^*_{k+1}+d^*_{k+1}$. $\deg(V)\le\deg(\bar{A}')\le n^*_{k+1}$ and resultant bounds ply to c and $|V|_1$. Thus $L(c)$, $L(|V|_1)\le n^*_{k+1}(2n^*_{k+1}+d^*_{k+1})$. Hence $\deg(G_2)$ $^*_{k+1}$ and $L(|G_2|_1)\le 2n^{*2}_{k+1}+n^*_{k+1}d^*_{k+1}+d^*_{k+1}$. Therefore, $L(|G_3|_1)\le (2n^{*2}_{k+1}+n^*_{k+1}$ $_1+d^*_{k+1})+2n^*_{k+1}d^*_{k+1}=2n^{*2}_{k+1}+3n^*_{k+1}d^*_{k+1}+d^*_{k+1}$, $L(b)\le 2n^*_{k+1}d^*_{k+1}$ and $L(bc)\le$ $_{+1}+3n^*_{k+1}d^*_{k+1}$. Since $L(|h|+1)\le L(n^*_{k+1})\le n^*_{k+1}$, $L(|G_4|_1)\le 2n^{*2}_{k+1}$ $^*_{k+1}d^*_{k+1}+n^*_{k+1}+d^*_{k+1}\le 2n^{*2}_{k+1}+4n^*_{k+1}d^*_{k+1}$.

Let $B_i=b_i^{-1}\bar{B}_i$ represent β_i as an element of $Q(\alpha)$, $i\le k$. Let $G'=g^{-1}\bar{G}'$ re $g=bc$ and $\bar{G}'=G_4$. Then G' represents α as an element of $Q(\alpha')$. Hence $\alpha')=\alpha$ and $B_i(\alpha)=\beta_i$ so $B_i(G'(\alpha'))=\beta_i$. Let $B^*_i(y)=g^{\nu_i}\bar{B}(G'(y))$ where ν_i $g(\bar{B}_i)$. B^*_i is an integral polynomial with $\deg(B^*_i)\le\deg(\bar{B}_i)\cdot\deg(G')$ n^*_{k+1} and $L(|B^*_i|_1)\le L(|\bar{B}_i|_1)+\deg(\bar{B}_i)\cdot(2n^{*2}_{k+1}+4n^*_{k+1}d^*_{k+1})\le d'_k+n^*_k(2n^*_{k+1}+4n^*_{k+1}$ $_1)$. Also,

$L(b_i g^{\nu_i}) \leq d_k' + n_k^*(2n_{k+1}^{*2} + 4n_{k+1}^* d_{k+1}^*)$. Let $\bar{B}_i'$ be the pseudo-remainder of B_i^* and A', $b_i^* B_i^* = A'Q + \bar{B}_i'$, and $b_i' = b_i^* b_i g^{\nu_i}$. Then $B_i' = b_i'^{-1} \bar{B}_i'$ represents β_i as an element of $Q(\alpha')$. $L(|\bar{B}_i'|_1) \leq L(|B_i^*|_1) + n_k^* n_{k+1}^* d_{k+1}^* \leq d_k' + 2n_k^* n_{k+1}^{*2} + 5n_k^* n_{k+1}^* d_{k+1}^*$, and $L(b_i')$ satisfies the same bound.

Combining the last two paragraphs, $d_k' + 2n_k^* n_{k+1}^{*2} + 5n_k^* n_{k+1}^* d_{k+1}^*$ is a norm length bound for the polynomials which represent $\beta_1, \ldots, \beta_{k+1}$ as e ments of $Q(\alpha')$ whenever β_{k+1} is a root of one of the polynomials which is obtained by substituting $\beta_1, \ldots, \beta_k$ for $x_1, \ldots, x_k$ in a polynomial of $\mathcal{A}_{r-k}$. But we must also consider the case that β_{k+1} is a rational endpoint of some isolating interval. We have seen that, for fixed $\beta_1, \ldots, \beta_k$, the isolated roots are all roots of the polynomials in the basis $\bar{\mathcal{D}}$ of $\mathcal{D}$. Let $\hat{D}$ be the product of the elements of $\mathcal{D}$. $\mathcal{D}$ has at most m_{r-k} elements, each of degree $n_k^* n_{r-k}$ at most. Hence $\bar{\mathcal{D}}$ has at most $m_{r-k} n_k^* n_{r-k}$ elements, each of degree $n_k^* n_{r-k}$ at most. We observed previously that $n_k^* d_k^* + n_k^* d_{r-k} + kn_{r-k} n_k^* d_k' + kn_{r-k} n_k^{*2} d_k^*$ is a norm length bou for the elements of $\mathcal{D}$. Hence $\deg(\hat{D}) \leq n_k^* m_{r-k} n_{r-k}$ and $L(|\hat{D}|_1) \leq (n_k^* d_k^* + n_k^*$ $+ kn_{r-k} n_k^* d_k' + kn_{r-k} n_k^{*2} d_k^*) m_{r-k}$. If D^* is the greatest squarefree divisor $\hat{D}$ then by Mignotte's theorem $L(|D^*|_1) \leq (n_k^* n_{r-k} + n_k^* d_k^* + kn_{r-k} n_k^* d_k' + kn_{r-k} n_k^{*2}$ $m_{r-k} = L_k$, say. According to our earlier discussion, we may assume that the lengths of the numerators and denominators of the rational endpoint of isolating intervals for the roots of D^* do not exceed $2n_k^* m_{r-k} n_{r-k}$($(2n_k^* m_{r-k} n_{r-k}) + L_k) \leq 2n_k^* m_{r-k} n_{r-k} + 4n_k^{*2} m_{r-k}^2 n_{r-k}^2 + 2n_k^* m_{r-k} n_{r-k} L_k \leq 2\{kn_{r-k} d_k'$ $+ n_{r-k} d_{r-k} + (k+4) n_k^* n_{r-k}^2 d_k^*\}\, n_k^{*2} m_{r-k}^2$. Adding to this the bound $d_k' + 2n_k^* n_{k+1}^{*2}$ $+ 5n_k^* n_{k+1}^* d_{k+1}^*$, we find that

$$d_{k+1}' \leq d_k' + 2n_k^* n_{k+1}^{*2} + 5n_k^* n_{k+1}^* d_{k+1}^* + 2\{kn_{r-k} d_k' + n_{r-k} d_{r-k} + (k+4)\, n_k^* n_{r-k}^2 d_k^*\} n_k^{*2} m_{r-k}^2. \quad (13)$$

Now we use the recurrence relations (11), (12) and (13) to prove the following theorem.

<u>Theorem 14.</u> With n_k^*, d_k^* and d_k' as defined above, we have

$$n_k^* \leq (2n)^{2^{r+k-1}}, \quad (14)$$

$$d_k^* \leq (2n)^{2^{r+k+2}} (2n)^{3^{r+1}} m^{2^{r+1}} d, \quad (15)$$

$$d_k' \leq (2n)^{2^{r+k+2}} (2n)^{3^{r+1}} m^{2^{r+1}} d. \quad (16)$$

Proof. To establish (14), we will show that $n_k^* \leq (2n)^{s_k}$ where $s_k = \Sigma_{i=1}^{k} 2^{r+k-2i}$. For k=1, by (8) and (6), $n_1^* \leq n_r \leq (2n)^{s_1}$ since $s_1 = 2^{r-1}$. Assuming $n_k^* \leq (2n)^{s_k}$, by (11) and (6), $n_{k+1}^* \leq (2n)^a$ where $a \leq 2s_k + 2^{r-k-1}$. But $2s_k + 2^{r-k-1} = \Sigma_{i=1}^{k} 2^{r+k+1-2i} + 2^{r+k+1-2(k+1)} = s_{k+1}$, completing the induction. And $s_k \leq 2^{r+k-2}(1+2^{-2}+2^{-4}+\ldots) < 2^{r+k-1}$, proving (14).

Using (14), we can now simplify the recurrence relation (12). We observe first that $k+2 \leq 2^{2^k}$, from which it follows by (6) that $(k+2)n_{r-k} \leq (2n)^{2^r}$. It is then not difficult to derive from (12), using (6), (7) and (14), the inequality

$$d_{k+1}^* \leq (2n)^{2^{r+k+1}} (d+d_k^*+d_k'). \tag{17}$$

Similarly, we can simplify (13) using (5), (6), (7) and (14). We obtain

$$d_{k+1}' \leq (2n)^{2^{r+2}} (2n)^{2\cdot 3^{r-k}} m^{2^{r-k}} (d+d_k^*+d_{k+1}^*+d_k'). \tag{18}$$

Let $\bar{D}_k$ be the common right hand side of (15) and (16). Substituting from (17) for d_{k+1}^* into (18), we obtain

$$d_{k+1} \leq 2\ (2n)^{2^{r+k+1}+2^{r+2}} (2n)^{2\cdot 3^{r-k}} m^{2^{r-k}} (d+d_k^*+d_k'). \tag{19}$$

Since, by (17), (19) also holds with d or d_{k+1}^* in place of d_{k+1}', we have

$$D_{k+1} \leq 6 \left\{ (2n)^{2^{r+k+1}+2^{r+2}} (2n)^{2\cdot 3^{r-k}} m^{2^{r-k}} \right\} D_k, \tag{20}$$

where $D_k = d+d_k^*+d_k'$. It suffices then to show that $D_k \leq \bar{D}_k$ for $1 \leq k \leq r$. We will prove instead the stronger inequality

$$D_k \leq (2n)^{2^{r+k+2}} (2n)^{u_k} m^{v_k} d, \tag{21}$$

where $u_k = 2\Sigma_{i=1}^{k} 3^{r-i+1}$ and $v_k = \Sigma_{i=1}^{k} 2^{r-i+1}$. For $k \geq 2$, $6 \leq 2^3 \leq (2n)^3$ and 2^{r+k+2} $2^{r+k+1}+2^{r+2}+3 \leq 2^{r+k+3}$. Since also $u_k + 2\cdot 3^{r-k} = u_{k+1}$ and $v_k + 2^{r-k} = v_{k+1}$, (20) implies that (21) holds for k+1 if it holds for $k \geq 2$. It remains then to prove (21) for k=1 and k=2. By (9), (6) and (7),

$$d_1^* \leq (2n)^{3\cdot 2^{r-1}} d. \tag{22}$$

By (10), (5), (6) and (7),

$$d_1' \leq (2n)^{5\cdot 2^{r-1}} (2n)^{2\cdot 3^r} m^{2^r} d. \qquad (23)$$

If r=1, then (22) and (23) imply (15) and (16). Otherwise, $r \geq 2$, $3 \leq (2n)$ and $5\cdot 2^{r-1}+2 \leq 2^{r+2}$, so (22) and (23) imply

$$D_1 \leq (2n)^{3\cdot 2^r} (2n)^{u_1} m^{v_1} d, \qquad (24)$$

which proves (21) for k=1. Now (20) and (24) yield (21) for k=2 since $6 \leq (2n)^3$ and $2^{r+3}+2^{r+2}+3\cdot 2^r+3 \leq 2^{r+4}$. ∎

As an easy corollary of Theorem 14, we obtain the following theorem.

<u>Theorem 15.</u> For $1 \leq k \leq r$,

$$n_k^* \leq (2n)^{2^{2r-1}}, \qquad (25)$$

$$d_k^*, d_k' \leq (2n)^{2^{2r+3}} m^{2^{r+1}} d. \qquad (26)$$

<u>Proof.</u> This follows immediately from Theorem 14 by observing that $3^h \leq 2^{2h}$. ∎

We now have all of the information necessary to complete an analysis of the computing time of algorithm DECOMP. Theorem 12 bounds the number of cells in the decomposition as a function of m, n and r. Theorems 10 and 15 together bound the degrees and coefficient lengths of polynomials which arise in the mainstream of the calculation. From th bounds and from known computing time bounds for the various subalgori it is straightforward, but tedious, to complete the analysis. We have given above computing time bounds for some, but not all of these subalgorithms. Those which we have not given may be found by the interested reader in the various references listed at the end of this paper. The critical property of these subalgorithms is that their computing times are all dominated by fixed powers of natural parameters such as degree products and maximum coefficient lengths or, as in the case of the BASIS algorithm, the number of polynomials in a list. Theorems 11 and 13 have illustrated the analysis of the computing time of certain parts of DECOMP. Thus the completion of the analysis of DECOMP does r involve any novel techniques or subtleties. The seriously interested or skeptical reader may complete the analysis for himself. We therefore now state without additional proof the result of such analysis.

<u>Theorem 16.</u> The computing time of DECOMP is dominated by $(2n)^{2^{2r+8}} m^{2^{2r+6}} d^3$.

The exponents occurring in this theorem can likely be decreased in several ways. In the first place, the computing times used for the subalgorithms all presuppose that classical algorithms are used for integer multiplication and division. With the use of fast algorithms such as the Schönberg-Strassen algorithm, [25], for integer arithmetic, it is evident that the exponent of d can be reduced from 3 to $2+\epsilon$ for every $\epsilon > 0$. Secondly, it is probable that a tighter analysis without change of the subalgorithm would yield some improvement, for example perhaps the 2r+8 could be reduced to 2r+4. Thirdly, it is likely that improved mathematical knowledge would also improve the bound without change of the algorithms. For example, the analysis depends strongly on the root separation theorem, and it seems likely that this theorem is far from optimal. It should also be noted that the theorem bounds the maximum computing time, and the average computing time is likely much smaller.

By the remarks preceding the algorithm EVAL, if ϕ^* is a standard prenex formula with matrix ϕ, $\mathfrak{A}$ is the set of polynomials occurring in , and β is a sample point, the truth value of each atomic formula in can be determined by at most one evaluation of sign(A(β)) for each $\varepsilon\ \mathfrak{A}$. Thus the application of EVAL to ϕ^*, a c.a.s. β, and a standard efinition ψ involves mainly the evaluation of sign(A(β_i)) for each $\varepsilon\ \mathfrak{A}$ and each sample point $\beta_i \varepsilon \beta$. This is not essentially different rom the calculations performed during the last phase of the application of DECOMP, and the bound of Theorem 16 again applies. However, one ust not overlook the time required to compute the truth value of ϕ rom the truth values of its atomic formulas, for each sample point β. he time required for this is obviously dominated, for each β, by the umber, a, of occurrences of atomic formulas in ϕ. Thus the computing ime bound of DECOMP, multiplied by a, is a bound for EVAL. Finally, onsider step (1) of ELIM, which extracts from ϕ the set $\mathfrak{A}$ of distinct olynomials occuring in ϕ. This involves, at most, ma polynomial comarisons, one comparison for each atomic formula with each element of the ist of distinct polynomials already extracted. The time for each comparison is at most $(n+1)^r d \leq (2n)^r d \leq (2n)^{2^r} d$. We therefore obtain our final result:

<u>Theorem 17.</u> The computing time of ELIM is dominated by $(2n)^{2^{2r+8}} m^{2^{r+6}} d^3 a$.

As a corollary of this analysis, we can obtain a computing time bound for ELIM as a function only of the length N of the formula ϕ. Obviously we must have m,r,d and a less than or equal to N and, assuming as is usual that x^k must be expressed as the product of k x's, we also have $n \le N$. Since $r \ge 1$ and $N \ge 3$ for every formula, we have $2r+8 \le 5N$ and $r+6 \le 3N$. Hence by Theorem 17, the computing time is dominated by $(2N)^{2^{5N}} N^{2^{3N}} N^4$. But it is easy to prove by induction on h that $h^{2^k} \le 2^{2^{h+k}}$. Hence $(2N)^{2^{5N}} N^{2^{3N}} N^4 \le 2^{2^{7N}} 2^{2^{4N}} 2^{2^{2N}} \le 2^{2^{8N}}$.

<u>Theorem 18.</u> For a fomula of length N, the computing time of ELIM is dominated by $2^{2^{8N}}$.

In Theorem 17, d is the maximum norm length of the polynomials in ϕ, whereas in the Introduction the result of Theorem 17 was stated with coefficient d defined as the maximum coefficient length. But if d' is the maximum coefficient length then, since a polynomial in r variables with grees bounded by n has at most $(n+1)^r$ integer coefficients, $d \le L((n+1)^r) + d' \le rL(2$ $+d' \le 2rL(n) + d' \le 2rn + d' \le 2rnd'$, and $d^3 \le (2n)^3 r^3 d'^3 \le (2n)^{2^2} 2^{2^{2r}} d'^3 \le (2n)^{2^{2r+1}} d'^3$. Thus as a corollary of Theorem 17, the computing time of ELIM is dominated by $(2n)^{2^{2r+9}} m^{2^{r+6}} d'^3 a$. But in fact the exponent 2r+9 can be replaced by 2r+8 by converting from d to d' while carrying out the proof of Theorem 17.

<u>5. Observations</u>. For the sake of conceptual simplicity, and to facilitate the analysis, we have kept our quantifier elimination algorithm as simple as possible. But for practical application many refinements

improvements are possible, some of which will now be described.

It is unnecessary to form reducta when projecting a set of poly-
ıials in two variables. The leading coefficient of a non-zero bivari-
polynomial A is a non-zero univariate polynomial, which vanishes
only a finite number of points. If the leading coefficient of A is
ariant on a connected set $S \subseteq R$ then either S is a one-point set, on
.ch the roots of A are trivially delineable, or else $\mathrm{ldcf}(A) \neq 0$ on

We recall ([19], Chapter 4) that the discriminant of a polynomial
which we will denote by discr(A), satisfies $\mathrm{discr}(A)=\mathrm{res}(A,A')/\mathrm{ldcf}(A)$.
A is a squarefree bivariate polynomial, then discr(A) is also a non-
o univariate polynomial, which vanishes at only a finite number of
.nts. Thus it is easy to prove (confer Theorem 4) that if $A(x_1,x_2)$ is
squarefree polynomial, $\mathcal{L}=\{\mathrm{ldcf}(A):\deg(A)\geq 1\}$, $\mathcal{D}=\{\mathrm{discr}(A):\deg(A)\geq 2\}$,
.s a connected subset of R, and every element of $\mathcal{L} \cup \mathcal{D}$ (there are at
t two elements) is invariant on S, then the roots of A are delinea-
on S.

If now $\mathcal{A}$ is a set of bivariate polynomials and $\mathcal{B}$ is a squarefree
is for $\mathcal{A}$ then any two distinct elements of $\mathcal{B}$ have a non-zero resul-
.t, which again vanishes at only a finite number of points. Thus we
that in this case we can define $\mathrm{proj}(\mathcal{A})=\mathcal{P}=\mathcal{L} \cup \mathcal{D} \cup \mathcal{R}$ where $\mathcal{L}$
$\mathrm{dcf}(B):B\varepsilon\mathcal{B}\ \&\deg(B)\geq 1\}$, $\mathcal{D}=\{\mathrm{discr}(B):B\varepsilon\mathcal{B}\ \&\deg(B)\geq 2\}$ and $\mathcal{R}=\{\mathrm{res}(B_1,$
$:B_1,B_2\varepsilon\mathcal{B}\ \&B_1<B_2\&\deg(B_1)\geq 1\&\deg(B_2)\geq 1\}$, and Theorem 5 will still hold.

For the augmented projection of a set of bivariate polynomials,
must be cautious; although A is squarefree, some derivative of A may
.l to be squarefree. But if A is any polynomial, $\mathcal{B}$ is a squarefree basis
{A}, and the roots of $\mathcal{B}$ are delineable on a connected set S, then the
ts of A are delineable on S. So, with $\mathrm{proj}(\mathcal{A})$ defined as in the
ceeding paragraph, we can define the augmented projection of $\mathcal{A}$ as
.lows. Let $\mathcal{D}=\{\mathrm{der}^j(A):A\varepsilon\mathcal{A}\ \&1\leq j\leq \deg(A)-2\}=\{D_1,\ldots,D_k\}$. Let $\mathcal{B}_i$ be a
arefree basis for $\{D_i\}$ and $\mathcal{P}_i=\mathrm{proj}(\mathcal{B}_i)$. Then $\mathrm{proj}(\mathcal{A})=\bigcup\{\bigcup_{i=1}^{k}\mathcal{P}_i\}$
.l suffice for the augmented projection of $\mathcal{A}$. Actually, this still
es us a little more than necessary; the leading coefficients of the
ments of the $\mathcal{B}_i$ are superfluous. One might suppose that these basis
.culations would be time-consuming, but in most cases one will quickly
scover that D_i is squarefree so that $\mathcal{B}_i=\{D_i\}$ and for $\mathcal{P}_i$ we can then
just $\{\mathrm{discr}(D_i)\}$.

Now let $\mathfrak{A}$ be a set of polynomials in three variables. According to our earlier definition, we begin the projection by forming the set $\mathfrak{B}$ of all reducta of elements of $\mathfrak{A}$ such that the degree of the reductum is positive. In general, this set $\mathfrak{B}$ is much larger than necessary The objective is just to ensure that for each $A\epsilon\mathfrak{A}$, $\mathfrak{B}$ contains some reductum of A whose leading coefficient is invariantly non-zero on each cell S of the induced c.a.d. Indeed even this is unnecessary for one-poi cells S, because then the roots of A are trivially delineable on S. So if the first i coefficients of A are simultaneously zero at only a finite number of points of R^2, then $red^k(A)$ can be excluded from $\mathfrak{B}$ for $k\geq i$ Also, if the leading coefficient of A has no zeros in R^2, as when its degree in both x_1 and x_2 is zero, then $red^k(A)$ can be excluded from $\mathfrak{B}$ for $k\geq 1$.

For the case i=2, let $A_1=ldcf(A)$, $A_2=ldcf(red(A))$. If $A_1(\alpha_1,\alpha_2)$ $=A_2(\alpha_1,\alpha_2)=0$ then $R_1(\alpha_1)=0$ where $R_1(x_1)$ is the resultant of $A_1(x_1,x_2)$ and $A_2(x_1,x_2)$ with respect to x_2. Hence if $R_1\neq 0$ there are only a finite number of α_1's. Similarly, if R_2 is the resultant with respect to x_1 and if $R_2\neq 0$ then there are only finitely many α_2's. If $R_1\neq 0$ and $R_2\neq 0$ then there are only finitely many points (α_1,α_2).

Of course if either A_1 or A_2 has degree zero in either x_1 or x_2, then the resultants R_1 and R_2 can not both be formed, but then there ar alternatives. If A_1 is of degree zero in x_2 and A_2 is of degree zero in x_1 (or vice versa) then there are only finitely many solutions. Suppose A_1 is of degree zero in x_2 and A_2 is of positive degree in both x_1 and x_2, say $A_2(x_1,x_2)=\Sigma_{i=o}^{n}A_{2,i}(x_1)\cdot x_2^i$. Then there are only finitely many so lutions if $gcd(A_1,A_{2,n},\ldots,A_{2,1})$ is of degree zero. Also, there are onl finitely many solutions if A_1 and A_2 are both degree zero in x_2 (or x_1) and the degree of $gcd(A_1,A_2)$ in x_1 (respectively x_2) is zero.

If the cases i=1 and i=2 fail, then we may try i=3. Let $A_3=ldcf(r$ (A)). Then it suffices to show, as above, that A_1 and A_3, or A_2 and A_3 have only finitely many common solutions. Better still, we may compute $res(gcd(A_1,A_2),A_3)$.

There are obvious reasons to expect that in most cases it will be unnecessary to include in $\mathfrak{B}$ $red^k(A)$ for $k\geq 2$ when $\mathfrak{A}$ is a set of polynom in three variables. The reader can easily see for himself how to exten these methods to polynomials in $r\geq 4$ variables. For example, when r=4 w can compute $res(A_1,A_2)$, $res(A_2,A_3))$ with respect to x_1,x_2 and x_3. It w usually be unnecessary to include in $\mathfrak{B}$ $red^k(A)$ for $k\geq r-1$.

By a similar argument, for a given $B\in\mathcal{B}$, it is in general unnecessary to include in the set $\mathcal{S}_1$ $\mathrm{psc}_k(B,B')$ for all k such that $0\leq k<\deg(B')$. If we can show that the equations $\mathrm{psc}_i(B,B')=0$, for $0\leq i\leq k$, have only a finite number of solutions then $\mathrm{psc}_i(B,B')$ may be omitted from $\mathcal{S}_1$ for $i>k$.

Thus, if A is a polynomial in r variables, it will usually suffice to include in $\mathcal{S}_1$ $\mathrm{psc}_j(\mathrm{red}^i(A),\mathrm{der}(\mathrm{red}^i(A)))$ only for $0\leq i\leq r-2$ and $0\leq j\leq r-2$, a total of $(r-1)^2$ polynomials. One can even do better than this. For example, if the equations $\mathrm{ldcf}(A)=0$ and $\mathrm{psc}_0(\mathrm{red}(A),\ \mathrm{der}(\mathrm{red}(A)))=0$ have only finitely many common solutions, then we need not include $\mathrm{psc}_1(\mathrm{red}(A),\mathrm{der}(\mathrm{red}(A)))$. Thus we will usually need to include $\mathrm{psc}_j(\mathrm{red}^i(A),\mathrm{der}(\mathrm{red}^i(A)))$ only for $0\leq i+j\leq r-2$, a total of $\binom{r}{2}$ polynomials. Similar considerations apply to the set $\mathcal{S}_2$ of the projection and to the set $\mathcal{P}'$ of the augmented projection. Whereas we derived an upper bound of m^2n^3 for the number of polynomials in the augmented projection, the expected number will now be about m^2r^2 when n is larger than r.

It is important to realize that the resultants used in testing for finitely many solutions need not be computed; it is only necessary to decide whether or not they are zero. If, in fact, a resultant is nonzero then this can usually be ascertained very quickly by computing the resultant modulo a large single-precision prime and modulo linear polynomials x_i-a_i.

As an experiment, we have computed the two successive projections of a set $\mathcal{A}=\{A_1(x_1,x_2,x_3),\ A_2(x_1,x_2,x_3)\}$ where A_1 and A_2 are polynomials of total degree two with random integers from the interval $[-9,+9]$ as coefficients. Each A_i is then a polynomial with 10 terms, of degree 2 in x_3, with constant leading coefficient. $\mathcal{A}_1$, the projection of $\mathcal{A}$, is then a set consisting of four elements, $B_1=\mathrm{discr}(A_1)$, $B_2=\mathrm{discr}(A_2)$, $B_3=\mathrm{res}(A_1,A_2)$ and $B_4=\mathrm{psc}_1(A_1,A_2)$. The leading coefficient of each B_i has degree zero in x_1 so the content of B_i is an integer. Dividing B_1 by its content, we obtained the primitive part $\bar{B}_i$. We then found that each $\bar{B}_i$ was an irreducible polynomial in $Z[x_1,x_2]$ so $\mathcal{B}_1=\{\bar{B}_1,\bar{B}_2,\bar{B}_3,\bar{B}_4\}$ was a finest basis for $\mathcal{A}_1$. $\bar{B}_1$ and $\bar{B}_2$ are of degree 2 in each variable and have total degree 2. Their integer coefficients are two of three decimal digits in length. $\bar{B}_3$ is of degree 4, in each x_i separately and in total, with 4-digit coefficients. $\bar{B}_4$ has degree 1 and 2-digit coefficients.

$\mathcal{A}_2$, the projection of $\mathcal{B}_1$, has as its elements D_i=discr($\bar{B}_i$) for i=1,2,3 and $R_{i,j}$=res($\bar{B}_i$,$\bar{B}_j$) for $1\leq i<j\leq 4$. Again we set $\bar{D}_i$=pp(D_i) (the primitive part of D_i) and $\bar{R}_{i,j}$=pp($R_{i,j}$). The contents of the D_i and R_i are from 1 to 5 decimal digits in length. The largest of these primiti parts is $\bar{D}_3$, with degree 12 and coefficients about 22 to 24 decimal digits in length. Now we factor each $\bar{D}_i$ and each $\bar{R}_{i,j}$ to obtain a finest basis, $\mathcal{B}_2$, for $\mathcal{A}_2$. The results are as follows:

$$\bar{D}_1,\bar{D}_2,\bar{R}_{1,2},\bar{R}_{1,4},\bar{R}_{2,4} \text{ irreducible,}$$
$$\bar{D}_3=P_1P_2^2,$$
$$\bar{R}_{3,4}=P_2^2,$$
$$\bar{R}_{1,3}=P_4^2,$$
$$\bar{R}_{2,3}=P_5^2. \tag{27}$$

Here each P_i is irreducible. Note that P_2 is a common factor of $\bar{D}_3$ an $\bar{R}_{3,4}$.

Since random polynomials are almost always irreducible, the factorizations (27) strongly suggest some theorems. To help preclude cha events, the entire experiment was repeated using polynomials A_1 and A with different random coefficients, With the new A_1 and A_2, the structure of the factorization (27) was exactly repeated; even the degrees of the irreducible factors remained the same.

Let us consider briefly what kinds of theorems are suggested by Ignoring primitive parts, $\bar{D}_3$=discr(res(A_1,A_2)), $R_{1,3}$=res(discr(A_1), res(A_1,A_2)),$\bar{R}_{2,3}$=res(discr(A_2), res(A_1,A_2)) and $\bar{R}_{3,4}$=res(psc$_o$(A_1,A_2), psc$_1$(A_1,A_2)). Note that in each case the general form is a resultant ot two psc's with "common ancestors". On the other hand, there are nc "common ancestors" in the irreducible cases $\bar{D}_i$=discr(discr(A_i)) and $\bar{R}_1$ =res(discr(A_1),discr(A_2)). The cases $\bar{R}_{i,4}$=res(discr(A_i), psc$_1$(A_1,A_2)) appear anomalous.

A number of other experiments have been performed which tend to substantiate the rather vague conclusions suggested by the above results. For example, we find that, "in general", res(res(A_1,A_2), res(A_2,A_3)) is reducible. These observations suggest very strongly t merit of performing basis calculations preceding each projection. Ho ever, it is not entirely clear whether a finest or coarsest squarefree basis should be used. Note that in the above example the two coincide.

We have seen now how to reduce substantially the number of polynomials which arise when the projections are performed, and we have seen empirical evidence, though not yet theorems, which indicates that the growth of degrees can be controlled somewhat by basis calculations. Also, the factorizations which reduce degrees tend to reduce coefficient lengths correspondingly. Hence there is some reason for optimism regarding the potential applicability of this method. A full implementation of the method within the SAC-1 computer algebra system [6], is still in progress. Nearly all of the necessary algebraic subalgorithms are already available, and some parts of the elimination algorithm itself exist in preliminary form. The completion of the implementation and its application to several non-trivial "real" problems within the next year or two is anticipated.

Ferrante and Rackoff, [26] , have recently published a quantifier elimination method for the first order theory of the additive ordered group of the real numbers, which they show to have a computing time dominated by $2^{2^{cN}}$ for some unknown constant c. We obtain an alternative to their method as the special case of the method above in which every polynomial occurring in the formula ϕ has total degree 1. Setting n=1 in Theorem 18, we obtain their result with c=8. Their computing time bound is obtained as a function of N, the length of ϕ, only. Setting n=1 in Theorem 17, we obtain the more informative bound $2^{2^{2r+8}} m^{2^{r+6}} d^3 a$.

We can easily improve this result. It is easy to see that in the special case we are considering, we may define $\text{proj}(\mathfrak{A})=\{\text{res}(A_i,A_j):1\leq i<j\leq m\}$ where $\mathfrak{A}=\{A_1,\ldots,A_m\}$. Thus $\text{proj}(\mathfrak{A})$ has at most $\binom{m}{2}\leq m^2/2$ members, and the augmented projection is never needed. With m_k and d_k defined as before, we then easily obtain

$$m_k\leq 2(m/2)^{2^{k-1}}, \tag{28}$$

$$d_k\leq 2^{k-1}d. \tag{29}$$

Instead of isolating roots, since they are rational, we now compute them exactly. If $r_1<r_2<\ldots<r_l$ are all the roots of a set of polynomials, then for the sample points s_i between roots we use the averages

$(r_i+r_{i+1})/2$. If $r_1<0$ then we also use the sample point $s_0=2r_1<r_1$; if $r\geq 0$ then we use instead the sample point $s_0=-1$. Similarly we use $s_l=2r_l$ or +1 as a greatest sample point. The rational number $r=a/b$ is represented by the linear integral polynomial $bx-a$ with norm $|a|+|b|$; we ma call this the norm, $|r|_1$ of r. Note that $|s_i|_1\leq 2|r_i|_1\cdot|r_{i+1}|_1$, $|s_0|_1$ $\leq 2|r_1|_1$ and $|s_{l+1}|_1\leq 2|r_l|_1$.

The result of substituting $r=a/b$ for x_1 in a polynomial $C(x_1,\ldots,$ $=c_1x_1+\ldots+c_kx_k+c_0$ and then multiplying by b to obtain an integral polynomial is the same as the resultant of bx_1-a and $C(x_1,\ldots,x_k)$ with respect to x_1.

If c_k is the number of cells as before, then we have $c_1\leq 2m_r+1$ and $c_{k+1}\leq 2c_km_{r-k}+1$, from which it follows that

$$c_k\leq 2^{k+1}(m/2)^{2^r}. \qquad (30)$$

Let d'_k be the maximum norm length of the kth coordinate of any sample point. Then $d'_1\leq 2d_r+1$ amd $d'_{k+1}\leq 2(d_{r-k}+d'_1+d'_2+\ldots+d'_k)+1$. It follo that

$$d'_k\leq 2^{r+k}d. \qquad (31)$$

Using the bounds (28) to (31), it is not difficult to show that the computing time of the method is dominated by $m^{2^r}d^2a$ using classic arithmetic algorithms, $m^{2^r}d^{1+\epsilon}$ a using fast arithmetic algorithms.

Acknowledgements. I am indebted to numerous persons in various w in connection with this paper. First to Frank Beckman, who first made possible for me to pursue my interest in Tarski's method at IBM Corp. in 1955. Secondly, the late Abraham Robinson encouraged my interests this subject at various times in the 1960's, as did also C. Elgot an D.A. Quarles, Jr. I am perhaps most indebted to R. Loos who, during s veral weeks at Stanford University in early 1973, through his keen ap ciation and insightful discussions, persuaded me to persist to the f.

discovery of this method. Most recently I have become greatly indebted to H. Brakhage, who made it possible for me to spend a year at the University of Kaiserslautern in unencumbered pursuit of the further development of this method.

References

. Brown, W.S., On Euclid's Algorithm and the Computation of Polynomial Greatest Common Divisors, J. ACM, vol. 18, no.4 (Oct. 1971) pp.478-504.

. Brown, W.S., and Traub, J.F., On Euclid's Algorithm and the Theory of Subresultants, J. ACM, vol. 18, no.4 (Oct. 1971), pp. 505-514.

. Cohen, P.J., Decision Procedures for Real and p-adic Fields, Comm. Pure and Applied Math., vol. XXII, no. 2 (March 1969), pp. 131-151.

. Collins, G.E., Subresultants and Reduced Polynomial Remainder Sequences, J. ACM, vol. 14, no. 1, (Jan. 1967), pp. 128-142.

. Collins, G.E., The Calculation of Multivariate Polynomial Resultants, J. ACM, vol. 18, no. 4 (Oct. 1971), pp. 515-532.

Collins, G.E., Computer Algebra of Polynomials and Rational Functions, Am. Math. Monthly, vol. 80, no. 7 (Aug.-Sept. 1973), pp. 725-755.

Collins, G.E., Efficient Quantifier Elimination for Elementary Algebra (abstract), Symposium on Complexity of Sequential and Parallel Numerical Algorithms, Carnegie-Mellon University, May 1973.

Collins, G.E., Quantifier Elimination for Real Closed Fields by Cylindrical Algebraic Decomposition - Preliminary Report, Proceedings of EUROSAM 74, SIGSAM Bulletin, Vol.8, No.3 (August 1974), pp. 80 - 90.

9. Fischer, M.J., and Rabin, M.O., Super-Exponential Complexity of Presburger Arithmetic, M.I.T. MAC Tech. Memo. 43, Feb. 1974.

10. Goldhaber, J.K., and Ehrlich, G., Algebra, MacMillan Co., 1970.

11. Heindel, L.E., Integer Arithmetic Algorithms for Polynomial Real Zero Determination, J. ACM, vo. 18, no. 4 (Oct. 1971), pp. 533-548.

12. Loos, R.,G.K., A Constructive Approach to Algebraic Numbers, SIAM Journal on Computing, to appear.

13. Marden, M., The Geometry of the Zeros of a Polynomial in a Complex Variable, Am. Math. Soc., Providence, 1949.

14. Musser, D.R., Algorithms for Polynomial Factorization (Ph.D. Thesi Univ. of Wisconsin Computer Sciences Dept. Tech. Report No. 134, Sept. 1971.

15. Musser, D.R., Multivariate Polynomial Factorization, J.ACM., Vol. No. 2 (April 1975), pp. 291-308.

16. Rubald, C.M., Algorithms for Polynomials over a Real Algebraic Num Field (Ph.D. Thesis), Computer Sciences Dept. Tech. Report No. 206 Jan. 1974.

17. Seidenberg, A., A New Decision Method for Elementary Algebra, Anna of Math., vol. 60, no. 2 (Sept. 1954), pp. 365-374.

18. Tarski, A., A Decision Method for Elementary Algebra and Geometry second ed., rev., Univ. of California Press, Berkeley, 1951.

19. van der Waerden, B.L., Modern Algebra, vol. I, F. Ungar Co., New 1953.

20. Böge, W., private communication, June 1973

21. Holthusen, C., Vereinfachungen für Tarski's Entscheidungsverfahre der Elementaren Reelen Algebra (Diplomarbeit, University of Heide berg), January 1974.

22. Collins, G.E., and E. Horowitz, The Minimum Root Separation of a

Polynomial, Math. of Comp., Vol. 28, No. 126, (April 1974), pp. 589-597.

23. Mignotte, M., An Inequality About Factors of Polynomials, Math. of Comp., Vol. 28, No. 128 (October 1974), pp. 1153-1157.

24. Knuth, D.E., The Art of Computer Programming, Vol. 2: Seminumerical Algorithms, Addison-Wesley, Reading, 1969.

25. Schönhage, A., and V. Strassen, Schnelle Multiplikation großer Zahlen, Computing, Vol. 7, pp. 281-292.

26. Ferrante, J., and C. Rackoff, A Decision Procedure for the First Order Theory of Real Addition with Order, SIAM Journal on Computing, Vol. 4, No. 1 (March 1975), pp. 69-76.

DETERMINISTISCHE INDIZIERTE GRAMMATIKEN

Karl Weiß
Institut für Informatik I
Universität Karlsruhe
75 Karlsruhe

Eine wesentliche gemeinsame Eigenschaft von indizierten Grammatiken un kontextfreien Grammatiken ist die Invarianz ihrer Erzeugungskraft unte verschiedenartigen Ableitungsrelationen wie Links- oder Rechtsableitun oder Ersetzung an einer beliebigen Stelle. Es liegt deshalb nahe, mit Hilfe spezieller Ableitungen gewonnene Begriffe aus der Theorie kontex freier Grammatiken auf indizierte Grammatiken zu übertragen. Die in De finition 1 eingeführten ILL(k)-Grammatiken sind eng mit den kontextfre LL(k)-Grammatiken verwandt:

Definition 1:

Sei $G = (N,T,F,R,S)$ eine indizierte Grammatik, $k \in \mathbb{N}$, $r: A \to \alpha \in f$ und $r' : B \to \beta \in R$. Sei weiter

$$p_k\ (r) := \{u;\ u \in T^*,\ l(u) \leq k :\ \exists\ \delta,\gamma,\gamma' \in (N \cup F \cup T)^* :$$
$$\text{(a)}\ l(u) < k \curvearrowright \gamma' = \varepsilon$$
$$\text{(b)}\ Af\delta \Rightarrow_r \gamma \overset{*}{\Rightarrow} u\,\gamma'\}$$

$$p_k\ (r') := \{u;\ u \in T^*,\ l(u) \leq k :\ \exists\ \delta,\ \gamma,\ \gamma' \in (N \cup F \cup T)^* :$$
$$\text{(a)}\ l(u) < k \curvearrowright \gamma' = \varepsilon$$
$$\text{(b)}\ A\delta \Rightarrow_r \gamma \Rightarrow u\,\gamma'\ \}$$

Dabei soll $\Rightarrow$ die Relation "Linksableitung" bezeichnen. G heißt ILL(k Grammatik, wenn für alle $f \in F$ aus $r,\ s \in f \cup R$ mit $lhs\ (r) = lhs\ (s)$ folgt:

$$p_k\ (r) \cap p_k\ (s) = \emptyset\ .$$

Für eine ILL(k)-Grammatik ist zu jeder Satzform u und jedem bis zu k Zeichen langen "look-ahead" $w \in T^*$ diejenige Regel eindeutig bestimmt, die man als nächste auf u anwenden muß, um schließlich eine mit w be- ginnende Satzform zu erhalten. Diese Tatsache impliziert ein Top-Dow Syntaxanalyseverfahren für jede von einer ILL(k)-Grammatik erzeugte che: Man beginnt mit der Startvariablen S und wendet jeweils die dur die nächsten k Zeichen des zu analysierenden Wortes und die vorliege

Satzform bestimmte Regel an. Auf diese Weise erhält man für ε-freie ILL(k)-Grammatiken Verfahren, die mit einem zur Länge des analysierenden Wortes quadratischen Zeitaufwand arbeiten.

Für RIR-Grammatiken (indizierte Grammatiken mit Regeln $A \rightarrow a$, $A \rightarrow aB\alpha$, $a \in T \cup \{\varepsilon\}$, $\alpha \in F^*$ und ebensolchen Indexregeln) werden in Definition 1 δ durch $\bar{\delta} \in F^*$ und γ, γ' durch $\bar{\gamma}, \bar{\gamma}' \in NF^* \cup \{\varepsilon\}$ ersetzt; die so erhaltene Eigenschaft wird als RIRLL(k)-Eigenschaft bezeichnet. RIRLL(k)-Grammatiken erzeugen für beliebiges $k \in \mathbb{N}$ dieselbe Sprachklasse wie RIRLL-(1)-Grammatiken; die entsprechenden Syntaxanalyseverfahren arbeiten mit linearem Zeitaufwand.

Eigenschaften von ILL(k)-Grammatiken

Satz 1

Zu jeder ILL(k)-Grammatik G gibt es einen deterministischen nested-stack-automaton A mit

$$L\ (G) = T\ (A).$$

Der Beweis verläuft im wesentlichen wie der Beweis des nichtdeterministischen Falles in /2/; A wird dadurch deterministisch gehalten, daß man jeweils die nächsten k Eingabezeichen im Zustand kodiert.

Satz 2

Jede von einer ILL(k)-Grammatik G erzeugte Sprache L (G) ist präfixfrei.

Der Beweis beruht auf der leicht einzusehenden Tatsache, daß für eine ILL(k)-Grammatik aus $w \in p_k\ (r)$, $l(w) = n < k$ stets $\{wv;\ v \in T^*,\ l(v) \leq k - n\} \subset p_k\ (r)$ folgt. Es sei hier schon angemerkt, daß diese Aussage für RIRLL(1)-Grammatiken nicht gilt und es nicht-präfixfreie Sprachen gibt, die von RIRLL(1)-Grammatiken erzeugt werden.

Satz 3 befasst sich mit ε-freien indizierten Grammatiken. Um bei ihnen die am weitesten links stehende Variable zum Verschwinden zu bringen, muß mindestens ein Terminalzeichen erzeugt werden. Damit gibt es zu jeder solchen Grammatik G eine RIR-Grammatik G' mit isomorpher Regelmenge und $p_1\ (r) = p_1\ (r')$, wenn r' die r entsprechende Regel von G' ist. Unter Vorwegnahme des Resultats von Satz 4 gilt dann

Satz 3

Ist G eine ε-freie indizierte Grammatik, so ist es entscheidbar, ob G die ILL(1)-Eigenschaft besitzt oder nicht.

Eigenschaften von RIRLL(1)-Grammatiken

Satz 4

Ist G eine RIR-Grammatik, so ist es entscheidbar, ob G die RIRLL(1)-Eigenschaft besitzt oder nicht.

Die Schwierigkeit liegt hier in der Bestimmung der Mengen p_1 (r). Diese wird dadurch vorgenommen, daß man zu jeder Regel r : $A \rightarrow a\alpha \in f$ (oder $\in R$) mit $a \in T$ die Menge M aller Satzformen bestimmt, von denen aus man ohne Erzeugung eines Terminalzeichens zu einer mit Af (oder A beginnenden Regel gelangen kann. Die Menge aller $\beta \in NF^*$ einer festen Länge, für die es ein $\gamma \in F^*$ gibt, so daß $\beta\gamma$ in M liegt, ist effektiv konstruierbar und für alle Regeln r : $B \rightarrow \beta \in h$ (oder R), für die es eine Satzform $\beta\gamma \in M$ gibt, gilt $a \in p_1$ (r).

In /1/ wird gezeigt, daß RIR-Grammatiken und Kellerautomaten dieselbe Sprachklasse definieren (Kellerautomaten sollen immer unter Leeren des Kellers akzeptieren, im Gegensatz zu E-Kellerautomaten, die unter Übergang in einen Endzustand akzeptieren). Der Beweis beruht auf der strukturellen Äquivalenz der Satzformen bzw. Konfigurationen; einer δ-Rege

$$(q', \beta) \in \delta\ (q,a,f)$$

eines Kellerautomaten entspricht eine grammatikalische Regel

$$q \rightarrow a\ q'\beta \in f.$$

Diese Äquivalenz wird ausgenützt zum Beweis von

Satz 5

RIRLL(1)-Grammatiken erzeugen genau die deterministischen kontextfrei Sprachen (d. h. die Menge der von deterministischen E-Kellerautomaten akzeptierten Sprachen).

Durch Kodieren des nächsten zu erzeugenden (akzeptierenden) Zeichens in der Variablen (im Zustand) bleibt der Determinismus der Konzepte i beiden Beweisrichtungen erhalten.

Satz 6

RIR-Grammatiken mit der ILL(1)-Eigenschaft erzeugen genau die präfixfreien deterministischen Sprachen (d. h. die Menge der von deterministischen Kellerautomaten akzeptierten Sprachen).

Schließlich sei noch erwähnt, daß man die deterministischen "one counter languages" ebenfalls durch spezielle RIR-Grammatiken erzeugen ka Damit stellen RIR-Grammatiken ein wichtiges Hilfsmittel zur Simulatic von Automaten im kontextfreien Bereich dar.

Analysegrammatiken

Man kann die Erzeugungskraft deterministischer indizierter Grammatiken dadurch vergrößern, daß man sie in Analysegrammatiken einbaut. Eine Analysegrammatik G ist eine binäre Grammatik, deren erste Komponente G_1 - isoliert betrachtet - eine ILL(k)- oder RIRLL(1)-Grammatik bildet und deren zweite Komponente die Ableitungen bezüglich G_1 kontrolliert. Da sich diese Kontrolle darauf beschränkt, bestimmte bezüglich G_1 erlaubte Ableitungen auszuschließen, benötigt eine Analysegrammatik zur Analyse eines Wortes w höchstens denselben Zeitaufwand, den ihre erste Komponente benötigen würde, um w zu analysieren.

Definition 2:

Eine (RIRLL(1),RIR)-Analysegrammatik (RAG) ist eine binäre Grammatik (siehe /3/), deren Regeln die Gestalt

$$r:(A \to \alpha,\ B \to \beta)\ ,\ \alpha \in TNF^* \cup T \cup \{\varepsilon\},\ \beta \in NF^* \cup \{\varepsilon\}$$

besitzen und deren erste Komponente (die durch die ersten Komponenten der Regeln bestimmte Grammatik) die RIRLL(1)-Eigenschaft besitzt. Eine Ableitungsrelation => auf den Satzformen $(\gamma,\delta) \in T^* NF^* \times NF^*$ erhält man durch komponentenweise Übertragung der Ableitungsrelation für RIR-Grammatiken. Die von einer RAG G erzeugte Sprache ist dann

$$L(G) := \{w;\ (S,S) \overset{*}{\Rightarrow} (w,\varepsilon)\}.$$

Die Sprachklasse

$$L(RAG) = \{L;\ \exists\ RAG\ G:\ L = L(G)\}$$

besitzt folgende Eigenschaften:

Satz 7

(a) Die Menge aller deterministischen kontextfreien Sprachen ist eine echte Teilmenge von L(RAG).

(b) L(RAG) enthält nicht-kontextfreie Sprachen wie etwa
$$L = \{a^n c a^n b^{n-1} c a^{n-1} b^{n-2} c \ldots c a^2 b c a d;\ n \geq 2\} \cup \{ad\}.$$

(c) Ist M eine deterministische Turing-Maschine, deren mit einem Lese-Schreib-Kopf versehenes Speicherband die Eingabe enthält und ist $\bar{w}$ die Folge der δ-Regeln, die M mit der Eingabe w durchläuft, so liegt die Sprache $\{w\bar{w};w \in T(M)\}$ in L(RAG).

(d) Zu jedem $L \in$ L(RAG) gibt es ein Verfahren, das für jede Eingabe w anhält und dabei in O(l(w))-Schritten entscheidet, ob w in L(G) liegt oder nicht. Dieses Verfahren läßt sich auf einem deterministischen Automaten mit zwei Kellern als Speicherbändern realisieren.

(e) Jede Sprache $L \in$ L(RAG) ist kontextsensitiv.

Für Analyse-Grammatiken, deren erste Komponenten jeweils eine ε-freie ILL(1)-Grammatik bilden (IAGen), gilt (b) ebenfalls und die Eigenschaften (d) und (e) lassen sich ersetzen durch:

(d') ersetze in (d) RAG durch IAG und $O(l(w))$ durch $O(l(w)^2)$.

(e') Jede Sprache $L \in L(IAG)$ ist entscheidbar.

Die Punkte (a) und (c) lassen sich wegen der Präfixfreiheit der von IAGen erzeugten Sprachen nicht übertragen.

Die Beweise der einzelnen Punkte von Satz 7 lassen sich folgendermaßen skizzieren:

(a) Ist L eine deterministische kontextfreie Sprache, so gibt es nach Satz 5 eine L erzeugende RIRLL(1)-Grammatik G. Die Regelmenge

$$R = \{(A \to \alpha,\ A \to \bar{\alpha});\ A \to \alpha \text{ ist eine Regel bez. G und } \bar{\alpha} \text{ wurde aus } \alpha \text{ durch Streichen aller Terminalzeichen gewonnen.}\}$$

charakterisiert eine RAG, die L erzeugt.

(b) Gibt man zu jeder Komponente einer Regel an, ob sie in R oder einem Index f enthalten ist, so wird jede RAG schon durch ihre Regelmenge zusammen mit dem Startvariablenpaar eindeutig bestimmt (Indizes Variable oder Terminalzeichen, die in keiner Regel vorkommen, sollen nicht auftreten). Die RAG mit dem Startvariablenpaar (S_o,S_o) und den Regeln

$(S_o \to SZ \in R,\ S_o \to SZ \in R)$	$(A \to BZ \in Z,\ S \to S \in f)$
$(S \to aSf \in R,\ S \to S \in R)$	$(B \to bBf \in R, S \to S \in f)$
$(S \to cA \in R,\ S \to S \in R)$	$(B \to cA \in R,\ S \to SZ \in Z)$
$(A \to aA \in f,\ S \to Sf \in R)$	$(B \to d \in Z,\ S \to \varepsilon \in Z)$

erzeugt gerade die Sprache L.

(c) M ist deterministisch, also gibt es zu jeder Konfiguration $K = xgay$ (siehe /4/) genau eine auf K anwendbare δ-Regel. Durch Simulation der δ-Regeln von M erhält man die Regelmenge einer RAG, die die Behauptung erfüllt. Die K entsprechende Satzform besitzt die Gestalt

$$(w\alpha g x^r,\ SayZ).$$

Dabei ist α eine Vorsilbe von $\bar{w}$.

(d), (d') Das durch eine RAG bzw. IAG induzierte Syntaxanalyseverfahren bricht dann ab, wenn ein look-ahead-string auftritt, der von der vorliegenden Satzform aus nicht ableitbar ist, oder wenn die zweite Komponente die Ableitung beendet. Der Zeitbedarf berechnet sich nach ähnlichen Methoden wie der Zeitbedarf deterministischer Kellerautomaten.

(e), (e') folgt aus (d), (d').

Literatur:

/1/ AHO, A. "Indexed Grammars - An Extension of Context-Free Grammars", JACM 15,4 (1968), 647-671

/2/ AHO, A. "Nested Stack Automata", JACM 16,3 (1969), 383-406

/3/ CULIK, K. II, MOREY, C. "Formal Schemes for Language Translation", Intern. J. Comp. Math. Sciences A, Vol. 3 (1971), 17-48

/4/ MAURER, H. "Theoretische Grundlagen der Programmiersprachen", BI-Hochschultaschenbücher, Band 404/404 a*, (1969)

EINE BESCHREIBUNG CONTEXTFREIER SPRACHEN DURCH ENDLICHE MENGENSYSTEME

Manfred Opp

Inst. f. Informatik, Univ. Hamburg.

Gibt es eine Charakterisierung der contextfreien Sprachen durch endli Mengensysteme mit gewissen algebraischen Verträglichkeitseigenschafte analog zur Myhill,Nerode-Charakterisierung der erkennbaren Teilmengen (freier Monoide) durch Kongruenzen von endlichem Index ? (Eine vollständige Charakterisierung durch Sättigung mit gewissen i.a. unendlic Kongruenzen ist wegen der Komplementeigenschaft contextfreier Sprache nicht möglich, siehe u.a. Perrot[3].) Diese Fragestellung bildet den Ausgangspunkt unserer Untersuchungen, die wir im allgemeineren Rahmen der universellen Algebra durchführen werden.

Als für diesen Zweck passende Verallgemeinerungen der Kongruenz (von endlichem Index) definieren wir (stark) kongruente Familien (vor endlichem Index).

Im ersten Abschnitt dieser Arbeit zeigen wir, daß die gröbste Äquivalenz auf A, die jede Menge einer vorgegebenen stark kongruente Familie von (A,Ω) sättigt, bereits eine Kongruenz ist.

Im zweiten Abschnitt führen wir die Klasse der 'Ω-Algebren mit Längenabbildung' ein und geben durch eine Verstärkung des Begriffs d kongruenten Familie (zur reduzierenden kongruenten Familie) eine Charakterisierung der gleichungsdefinierten Mengen in dieser Algebrenkl an. Dies ermöglicht dann Beschreibungen der contextfreien Mengen in Termalgebren, freien Monoiden und freien kommutativen Monoiden durch derartige Mengensysteme. Mithilfe der oben erwähnten Konstruktion vo Kongruenzen aus stark kongruenten Familien läßt sich nun in algebrai übersichtlicher Weise die Gleichheit contextfreier und erkennbarer T mengen in Termalgebren (siehe Mezei,Wright[2]) herleiten.

Wir erzielen u.a. mit dieser Kennzeichnung gleichungsdefiniert Mengen eine Reihe beweistechnischer Vorteile, da wir oft auf eine vc ständige Induktion verzichten können. (Ω sei stets endlich.)

DER BEGRIFF DER STARK KONGRUENTEN FAMILIE

(1.0) Def.: (A,Ω) sei eine Ω-Algebra.

(a) Sei $t \in A$, $n \in \mathbb{N}$, $(f,t_1,..,t_n) \in \Omega_n \times A^n$ heißt Zerlegung t in A, falls $f(t_1,..,t_n) = t$. (Gleichheit von Zerlegunge ist also als Tupel-Gleichheit zu verstehen.)

(b) $\mathrm{Zerl}(t) := \{(f,t_1,..,t_n) \in \Omega_n \times A^n \mid n \in \mathbb{N}$ und $(f,t_1,..,t_n)$ ist Zerlegung von $t\}$.

(c) $\mathfrak{F} = \{F_i \mid i \in I\}$, $F_i \subset A$, sei ein Mengensystem auf A. Dann definieren wir für jedes Paar (t,F_i) mit $t \in F_i$, $i \in I$, die Menge $\mathrm{Zerl}_{\mathfrak{F}}(t,F_i) := \{(f,t_1,..,t_n) \in \mathrm{Zerl}(t) \mid \exists i_1,..,i_n \in I : t_j \in F_{i_j}$, für $j=1,..,n$ und $f(F_{i_1},..,F_{i_n}) \subset F_i\}$.

Wir wollen hier durchgehend darauf verzichten, die Algebra (A,Ω) als Index der eben definierten Mengen mitzuführen, da aus dem Kontext jeweils hervorgeht, welche Algebra gemeint ist.

Mithilfe der obigen Definition läßt sich nun der zentrale Begriff der kongruenten Familie leicht formulieren :

(1.1) Def.: (A,Ω) sei eine Ω-Algebra. $\mathfrak{F} = \{F_i \mid i \in I\}$, $F_i \subset A$, heißt kongruente Familie auf A, falls: $\forall\, i \in I\ \forall\, t \in F_i : (\mathrm{Zerl}(t) \neq \emptyset \Longrightarrow \mathrm{Zerl}_{\mathfrak{F}}(t,F_i) \neq \emptyset)$.

Eine (kongruente) Familie auf A heißt stark kongruent, falls sogar gilt: $\forall\, i \in I\ \forall t \in F_i : \mathrm{Zerl}(t) = \mathrm{Zerl}_{\mathfrak{F}}(t,F_i)$.

$\mathfrak{F}$ heißt von endlichem Index, falls I endlich ist.

$A' \subset A$ wird von $\mathfrak{F}$ 'gesättigt', falls $A' = \bigcup_{i \in I'} F_i$ für ein passendes $I' \subset I$.

Bemerkungen: (1) Kongruenzen auf (A,Ω) sind stark kongruente Familien.

(2) Für kongruente Familien $\mathfrak{F}$ gilt nicht notwendig, daß für $f \in \Omega_n$ die Menge $f(F_{i_1},..,F_{i_n})$ stets in einer der Mengen aus $\mathfrak{F}$ enthalten ist (das folgende Beispiel macht auch dies deutlich).

Beispiel: Sei $(X^+, \cdot)$ die von $X = \{a,b\}$ frei erzeugte Halbgruppe. $F_1 = \{a^n b^n \mid n > 0\}$, $F_2 = \{a^{n+1}b^n \mid n > 0\}$, $F_3 = \{a\}$, $F_4 = \{b\}$, $\mathfrak{F} = \{F_i \mid i=1,..,4\}$. Dann ist $\mathfrak{F}$ eine kongruente, jedoch nicht stark kongruente Familie auf $(X^+, \cdot)$: z.B. $a^7b^7 \in F_1$: $(\cdot, a^7b^6, b) \in \mathrm{Zerl}_{\mathfrak{F}}(a^7b^7, F_1)$, denn $a^7b^6 \cdot b = a^7b^7$ und $a^7b^6 \in F_2$, $b \in F_4$ und $F_2 \cdot F_4 \subset F_1$. $\mathfrak{F}$ ist nicht stark kongruent, da z.B. $\mathrm{Zerl}(a^7b^7) \ni (\cdot, a^7, b^7) \notin \mathrm{Zerl}_{\mathfrak{F}}(a^7b^7, F_1)$.

Wir werden nun eine dreistufige Konstruktion angeben, die ausgehend von stark kongruenten Familien auf Kongruenzen führt.

(1.2) Def.: $\mathcal{F} = \{F_i \ / \ i \in I\}$, $F_i \subset A$, sei ein Mengensystem auf A. Wir definieren dazu neue Mengensysteme $\overline{\mathcal{F}}, \overline{\overline{\mathcal{F}}}, \overline{\overline{\overline{\mathcal{F}}}}$ auf folgende Weise:

(a) $[t]_{\mathcal{F}} := \bigcap_{\substack{i \in I \\ t \in F_i}} F_i$, $\quad \overline{\mathcal{F}} := \{ [t]_{\mathcal{F}} \ / \ t \in \bigcup_{i \in I} F_i \}$.

(b) $\langle t \rangle_{\mathcal{F}} := [t]_{\mathcal{F}} \setminus (\bigcup_{t \notin [t']} [t'])$, $\quad \overline{\overline{\mathcal{F}}} := \{ \langle t \rangle_{\mathcal{F}} \ / \ t \in \bigcup_{i \in I} F_i \}$

(c) $\overline{\overline{\overline{\mathcal{F}}}} = \overline{\overline{\mathcal{F}}} \cup \{ \complement_A (\bigcup_{i \in I} F_i) \}$.

Ein einfaches Beispiel soll diese Konstruktion veranschaulichen:

$\mathcal{F} = \{F_1, F_2\}$

$\overline{\mathcal{F}} = \{F_1, F_2, F_1 \cap F_2\}$

$\overline{\overline{\mathcal{F}}} = \{F_1 \setminus F_2, F_2 \setminus F_1, F_1 \cap F_2\}$

$\overline{\overline{\overline{\mathcal{F}}}} = \overline{\overline{\mathcal{F}}} \cup \{\complement_A(F_1 \cup F_2)\}$

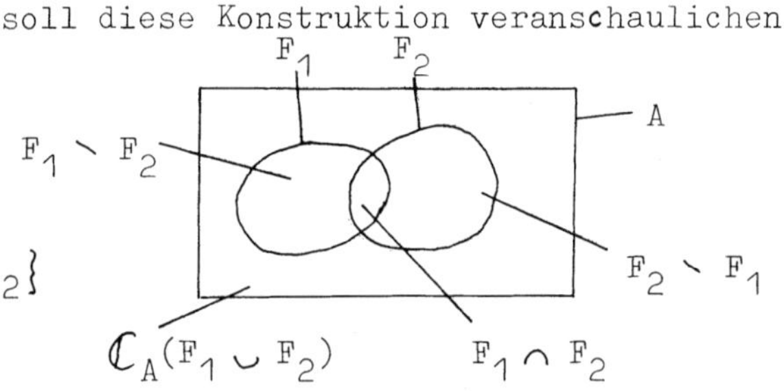

Bemerkung: (1) $\overline{\overline{\overline{\mathcal{F}}}}$ ist die gröbste Partition auf A, die jede der Mengen F_i, $i \in I$, sättigt.

(2) Mit $\mathcal{F}$ besitzt auch $\overline{\overline{\overline{\mathcal{F}}}}$ endlichen Index.

Die für das folgende wesentliche Aussage über die Invarianz star[k] kongruenter Familien gegenüber der in Definition (1.2) gegebenen Konstruktion wird nun formuliert.

(1.3) Satz: $\mathcal{F} = \{F_i \ / \ i \in I\}$ sei eine stark kongruente Familie auf (A,[Ω)]

Dann gelten folgende Aussagen:

(a) $\overline{\mathcal{F}}$ ist eine stark kongruente Familie auf A.

(b) $\overline{\overline{\mathcal{F}}}$ ist eine stark kongruente Familie auf A.

(c) $\overline{\overline{\overline{\mathcal{F}}}}$ ist eine Kongruenz auf A.

Jede Teilmenge $A' \subset A$ der Ω-Algebra (A,Ω), die von einer stark kongruenten Familie von endlichem Index gesättigt wird, kann ebenso vo[n] einer Kongruenz von endlichem Index auf (A,Ω) gesättigt werden.

Die eindeutige Zerlegbarkeit von Elementen in Termalgebren $(T_\Omega, \Omega$[)] läßt nun folgende Aussage zu:

(1.4) Lemma: (T_Ω,Ω) sei die Termalgebra über Ω. $L \subset T_\Omega$ werde von eine[r] kongruenten Familie $\mathcal{F}$ von endlichem Index gesättigt. Dann ist L eine erkennbare Teilmenge von T_Ω (d.h. wird von einer Kongruenz von endlichem Index gesättigt).

Beweis: Aus der Definition (1.1) folgt zusammen mit card(Zerl(t)) $\leq$ 1, $t \in T_\Omega$, sofort für $t \in F_i$: Zerl(t) = $Zerl_{\mathcal{F}}(t,F_i)$. Damit ergibt sich alles aus der vorigen Bemerkung.

Als eine Anwendung von Lemma (1.4) wollen wir den bekannten Satz über die Gleichheit der von deterministischen und nichtdeterministischen endlichen Automaten erkannten Wortmengen beweisen.

(1.5) Beh.: $A = (S,X,\delta,S_e,s_a)$, $S_e \subset S$, $s_a \in S$, $\delta \subset S \times X \times S$, sei ein nichtdeterministischer endlicher Automat. Die von A erkannte Wortmenge aus X^* wird ebenso von einem deterministischen endlichen Automat erkannt.

Beweis: Wir fassen X^* in bekannter Weise als monadische Termalgebra $(T_\Omega, \{f_{x_1},..,f_{x_n},\Lambda\})$ auf $(X = \{x_1,..,x_n\})$ und arbeiten von vorneherein mit dieser Identifizierung. Das Mengensystem $\mathcal{F} = \{F_s \,/\, s \in S\}$, $F_s = \{w \in T_\Omega \,/$ w wird von A im Startzustand s erkannt$\}$, ist eine kongruente Familie auf (T_Ω,Ω): Sei also $w \in F_s$ mit Zerl(w) $\neq \emptyset$, d.h. $w = f_x(w')$. Da $w \in F_s$, gibt es ein $s' \in S$ mit $(s,x,s') \in \delta$ und $(s',w',s_e) \in \delta^*$ für ein $s_e \in S_e$, d.h. $w' \in F_{s'}$. Damit ist gezeigt, daß $(f_x,w') \in Zerl_{\mathcal{F}}(w,F_s)$:

$$\begin{array}{ccc} w & = & f_x(\;w'\;) \\ \cap & & \;\;\;\;\cap \\ F_s & \supset & f_x(\;F_{s'}) \end{array}$$

$\mathcal{F}$ kann nun nach Lemma (1.4) durch eine Kongruenz von endlichem Index verfeinert werden. Dies ist interpretiert in X^* eine Rechtskongruenz, also ein endlicher deterministischer Automat.

GLEICHUNGSDEFINIERTE MENGEN IN ALGEBREN MIT LÄNGENABBILDUNG

Wir wollen nun in der Klasse der Ω-Algebren 'mit Längenabbildung' den Zusammenhang klären zwischen den durch reduzierende kongruente Familien gesättigten Teilmengen von (A,Ω) und den gleichungsdefinierten Teilmengen. Hierbei soll sofort der Gleichungstyp vom Rank = 1 herangezogen werden (dieser Typ ist bzgl. seiner Erzeugungskapazität dem allgemeinen Typ gleichwertig, siehe Mezei,Wright[2] , Lemma (3.1)).

(2.0) Def.: (Mezei,Wright[2]). Ein Ω-Gleichungssystem (vom Rank = 1) in den Variablen $X_1,..,X_m$ ist ein System der Form:

$$X_1 = \bigcup_{i \in I_1} t_{1i}, \quad .... \quad X_m = \bigcup_{i \in I_m} t_{mi} \quad \text{mit } I_1,..,I_m \text{ endlich,}$$

$t_{ji} \in \{f(X_{k_1},..,X_{k_n}) \,/\, f \in \Omega_n,\ X_{k_l} \in \{X_1,..,X_m\}\}$. t_{ji} kann also auch ein nullstelliger Operator sein.

$A' \subset A$ ((A,Ω) sei Ω-Algebra) heißt gleichungsdefiniert, falls A' als Komponente eines minimalen Lösungstupels eines Ω-Gleichung systems vorkommt.

Bemerkung: Nach allgemeinen verbandstheoretischen Sätzen erhält man die minimale Lösung $(M_1,..,M_m)$ eines Ω-Gleichungssystems in (A,Ω) durch: $M_j^o = \emptyset$, $M_j^{k+1} = \left[\bigcup_{i \in I_j} t_{ji}\right](M_1^k,..,M_m^k)$, $M_j = \bigcup_{i \geqslant 0} M_j^i$ für $j=1,..,m$

$\left[\bigcup_{i \in I_j} t_{ji}\right]$ wird in natürlicher Weise aufgefaßt als m-stellige Abbildung von $(\mathfrak{P}(A))^m$ in $\mathfrak{P}(A)$.

Zu einem Gleichungssystem GL bezeichne $\Omega_o(GL)$ die Menge aller auf den rechten Seiten von GL vorkommenden Terme aus Ω_o.

Wir benötigen nun noch folgende Definition :

<u>(2.1) Def.:</u> (A,Ω) sei eine Ω-Algebra, $A_o \subset \Omega_o$. A_o heißt 'unwesentlich für $POL(A,\Omega)$ (die Polynommenge von (A,Ω)) , oder auch kurz unwesentlich, falls gilt: $\forall n \in \mathbb{N}_o\ \forall p \in Abb(A^n,A)$: $(p \in POL(A,\Omega) \wedge p \notin A_o \Longrightarrow p \in POL(A,\Omega \setminus A_o))$.

A_o ist also unwesentlich, falls sich jedes Polynom $p \notin A_o$ in (A,Ω) auch ohne die Elemente aus A_o aufbauen läßt.

Die Bedeutung unwesentlicher nullstelliger Operationen für die Gleichungsdefiniertheit von Teilmengen ergibt sich aus der folgenden Behauptung :

<u>(2.2) Beh.:</u> (A,Ω) sei eine Ω-Algebra, $A_o \subset \Omega_o$ sei unwesentlich für $POL(A,\Omega)$. Zu jedem Ω-Gleichungssystem GL in den Variablen $X_1,..,X_m$ mit der minimalen Lösung $(M_1,..,M_m)$ gibt es dann ein Ω-Gleichungssystem $\overline{GL}$ mit $\Omega_o(\overline{GL}) \subset \Omega_o \setminus A_o$ und der minimalen Lösung $(\overline{M}_1,..,\overline{M}_m)$, wobei $\overline{M}_i = M_i \setminus A_o$ gilt.

Wir legen nun die für unsere Untersuchungen zentrale Klasse von Ω-Algebren fest.

<u>(2.3) Def.:</u> (A,Ω) sei eine Ω-Algebra. $N \in Abb(A,\mathbb{N}_o)$ heißt Längenabbildung für (A,Ω), falls folgendes gilt:

(1) $\forall n \in \mathbb{N}\ \forall f \in \Omega_n\ \forall t_1,..,t_n \in A$: $N(f(t_1,..,t_n)) \geqslant N(t_i)$ und '>' statt '$\geqslant$', falls $N(t_i) > 0$ für $i=1,..,n$.

(2) $\Omega_0 = N^{-1}(\{0,1\})$.

(3) Die Menge $N^{-1}(\{0\})$ sei unwesentlich für POL(A,Ω).

(4) $\forall t \in A \;\exists n \in \mathbb{N} \;\exists f \in \Omega_n \;\exists t_1,..,t_n \in A : \;(N(t) \geq 2 \Longrightarrow$
$t = f(t_1,..,t_n) \wedge N(t_i) < N(t),\; i=1,..,n)$.

Es sind hier folgende Standardbeispiele zu nennen :

(a) Die Termalgebra (T_Ω,Ω) über Ω mit N(t) = Tiefe des Terms $(N(\Omega_0) = \{1\})$.

(b) Das freie Monoid $(X^*,\{\cdot,\Lambda,x_1,..,x_n\})$, wobei die Erzeugenden $_1,..,x_n \in X$ als zusätzliche nullstellige Operatoren mitgeführt werden, it N(w) = Länge von w. $N^{-1}(\{0\})$ ist offensichtlich unwesentlich, da das eere Wort beim Polynomaufbau keine Rolle spielt.

(c) Das freie kommutative Monoid analog (b).

Für Ω-Algebren mit einer Längenabbildung N können wir eine Nicht-rivialitätsbedingung für kongruente Familien auf folgende Weise ein-ihren : Sei $t \in A$, unter NTZerl(t) werde die Menge aller nicht-rivialen Zerlegungen in A verstanden, d.i. NTZerl(t) := $\{(f,t_1,..,t_n) \in$ erl(t) / $0 < N(t_i)$ für $i=1,..,n\}$. Passend dazu definieren wir 'Zerl$_{\mathcal{F}}(t,F_i)$:= Zerl$_{\mathcal{F}}(t,F_i) \cap$ NTZerl(t).

.4) Def.: (A,Ω) sei eine Ω-Algebra mit Längenabbildung N. Eine kongruente Familie $\mathcal{F}$ auf (A,Ω) heißt reduzierend, falls :

$$\forall i \in I \;\forall t \in F_i : (\text{NTZerl}(t) \neq \emptyset \Longrightarrow \text{NTZerl}_{\mathcal{F}}(t,F_i) \neq \emptyset).$$

Mit dieser durch den Längenbegriff möglichen Verschärfung des griffs der kongruenten Familie können wir den Zusammenhang zu den eichungsdefinierten Teilmengen herstellen.

.5) Satz: (A,Ω) sei eine Ω-Algebra mit der Längenabbildung N. Die gleichungsdefinierten Teilmengen von A sind genau diejenigen, die durch reduzierende kongruente Familien von endlichem Index gesättigt werden.

weis: Wir geben eine kurze Beweisskizze an.

(a) Sei $(M_1,..,M_m)$ die minimale Lösung des Ω-Gleichungssystems GL den Variablen $X_1,..,X_m$. Dann gibt es ein Gleichungssystem $\overline{GL}$ (vom nk = 1) mit $\Omega_0(\overline{GL}) \cap N^{-1}(\{0\}) = \emptyset$ und der minimalen Lösung $(\overline{M}_1,..,\overline{M}_m)$, ei $\overline{M}_i = M_i \setminus N^{-1}(\{0\})$. Dann ist $\mathcal{F} = \{\overline{M}_i \;/\; i=1,..,m\} \cup \{\{a\} \;/\; a \in \Omega_0\}$

eine reduzierende kongruente Familie von endlichem Index, die jedes M_i sättigt.

(b) Sei umgekehrt $\mathcal{F} = \{F_i \mid i \in I\}$, $I = \{1,..,m\}$, eine reduzierende kongruente Familie auf (A,Ω). Dann ist die minimale Lösung des Ω-Gleichungssystems :

$$X_1 = \bigcup_{\substack{n \geq 2 \\ f \in \Omega_n \\ f(F_{i_1},..,F_{i_n}) \subset F_1}} f(X_{i_1},..,X_{i_n}) \cup (F_1 \cap \Omega_o) \quad \ldots\ldots$$

$$X_m = \bigcup_{\substack{n \geq 2 \\ f \in \Omega_n \\ f(F_{i_1},..,F_{i_n}) \subset F_m}} f(X_{i_1},..,X_{i_n}) \cup (F_m \cap \Omega_o)$$

gerade $(F_1,..,F_m)$.

Als einfache Folgerungen notieren wir die Aussagen :

(2.6) Korollar: (Mezei, Wright[2]). Gleichungsdefinierte Mengen in Termalgebren (T_Ω,Ω) sind bereits erkennbar.

Beweis: Da T_Ω eine Längenabbildung besitzt, folgt die Behauptung sofort aus Satz (2.5) und Lemma (1.4).

(2.7) Korollar: Reduzierende kongruente Familien von endlichem Index auf freien, endlich erzeugten Monoiden $(X^*,\cdot,\wedge)$ sättigen genau die contextfreien Sprachen.

Beweis: Dies folgt aus dem Zusammenhang contextfreier und gleichungsdefinierter Mengen (siehe Ginsburg, Rice[1]).

Die in der Einleitung angedeutete Möglichkeit, durch den von uns eingeführten Begriff der (reduzierenden) kongruenten Familie beweistechnische Vereinfachungen zu erzielen, soll an der abschließenden Aussage gezeigt werden.

(2.8) Beh.: (A,Ω) sei eine Ω-Algebra (mit Längenabbildung). Die Menge durch (reduzierende) kongruente Familien von endlichem Index gesättigten Teilmengen von A ist abgeschlossen gegen den Durchschnitt mit erkennbaren Teilmengen von A.

Beweis: Sei $L \subset A$ von der kongruenten Familie $\mathcal{F} = \{F_i \mid i \in I\}$ und die erkennbare Teilmenge $R \subset A$ von der Kongruenz $\mathcal{K} = \{K_j \mid j \in J\}$, I,J endlich, gesättigt. Wir zeigen, daß die $L \cap R$ sättigende Familie $\{F_i \cap K_j \mid i \in I,\ j \in J\}$ eine kongruente Familie ist:

Für alle $i \in I$, $j \in J$ und $t \in F_i \cap K_j$ mit Zerl(t) $\neq \emptyset$ ist wegen der Gültigkeit von

$$\begin{array}{c} t = f(t_1, \ldots, t_n) \\ \Cap \quad\quad \Cap \quad\quad\quad \Cap \\ F_i \supset f(F_{i_1}, \ldots, F_{i_n}) \end{array}$$

für gewisse $f \in \Omega_n$, $t_j \in A$, $F_{i_j} \in \mathfrak{F}$, und der Kongruenzeigenschaft von $\mathcal{K}$ natürlich für $t_k \in K_{j_k}$, $k=1,\ldots,n$, die Gültigkeit von

$$\begin{array}{c} t = f(t_1, \ldots, t_n) \\ \Cap \quad\quad\quad \Cap \quad\quad\quad \Cap \\ F_i \cap K_j \supset f(F_{i_1} \cap K_{j_1}, \ldots, F_{i_n} \cap K_{j_n}) \end{array}$$

gesichert.

Ebenso wird der Beweis für reduzierende kongruente Familien geführt.

LITERATUR

[1] Ginsburg, S. and H.G. Rice — Two Families of Languages Related to ALGOL. J. ACM No. 9, (1962).

[2] Mezei, J. and J.B. Wright — Algebraic Automata and Contextfree Sets. Inf. and Contr. 11, (1967).

[3] Perrot, J.F. — Monoides syntactique des langages algebriques. Inst. de Programmation, No. I.P. 74-22.

[4] Shepard, C.D. — Languages in General Algebras. Univ. of Illinois, Ph.D. 1969.

On the generative capacity of the strict global grammars

by Sorin CIOBOTARU
and Gheorghe PAUN

Universitatea Bucureşti
Secţia de studiul sistemelor
Str.Mihai Moxa 3-5 Bucureşti, s 8
Romania

In [4] Levitina introduces a new restriction in the use of the context-free (CF) rules, namely the global rules. A production rule is said to be global if in every derivation it is used to rewrite all occurrences of its left side in a sentential form. A grammar which has CF and also global rules is said a global grammar. We shall consider the grammars which have only global rules; we shall call them strict global (SG) grammars. We shall study their generative capacity by means of the parameter Rep, a parameter closely connected to the notion of index (see [1],[5]). Also, we shall analise the parameter Rep as a measure of the syntactic complexity (see [3]).

Let $G = (V_T, V_N, S, P)$ be a Chomsky CF grammar and $V = V_T \cup V_N$. For x and y in V^* (the free monoid generated by V). We put $x \underset{G}{\Longrightarrow} y$ iff $x = x_1 A x_2$, $y = x_1 Z x_2$, where $x_1, x_2 \in V^*$ and $A \longrightarrow Z$ is a rule in P. The language generated by G is the set $L(G) = \{ x \in V_T^*;\ S \underset{G}{\overset{*}{\Longrightarrow}} x \}$, where $\underset{G}{\overset{*}{\Longrightarrow}}$ is the reflexive and transitive closure of $\underset{G}{\Longrightarrow}$.

The index of a derivation $D : S = x_0 \underset{G}{\Longrightarrow} x_1 \underset{G}{\Longrightarrow} \cdots \underset{G}{\Longrightarrow} x_k$ is

$$\mathrm{Ind}(D, G) = \max_{0 \leq j \leq k} \sum_{i=0}^{n} A_i\ (x_j),$$

where $V_N = \{ S = A_0, A_1, \ldots, A_n \}$ and $A_i(x_j)$ is the number of the occurrences of the nonterminal A_i in x_j. For w in L(G) we put

$$\mathrm{Ind}(w, G) = \min_{D} \mathrm{Ind}(D, G),$$

where $D : S \underset{G}{\overset{*}{\Longrightarrow}} w$. The index of G is

$$\mathrm{Ind}(G) = \sup_{w \in L(G)} \mathrm{Ind}(w, G)$$

and the index of L is

$$\mathrm{Ind}(L) = \min \{ \mathrm{Ind}(G);\ L = L(G) \}.$$

A global rule is a rule which is used in the following way: $x \Rightarrow y$ by a rule $A \longrightarrow Z$ if and only if $x = x_1Ax_2Ax_3 \ldots x_{n-1}Ax_n$, $y = x_1Zx_2Zx_3 \ldots x_{n-1}Zx_n$, $n \geqslant 2$ and $A(x_i) = 0$ for $1 \leqslant i \leqslant n$. A grammar having only global rules is called a SG grammar.

If R is a restriction in the use of the rules of G, then we denote by G_R the grammar G with the restriction R. If Ψ is a class of grammars we put $L_\Psi = \{L$; there exists G in Ψ such that $L = L(G)\}$. We say that the restriction R modifies in the weak sense the generative capacity of the grammars of the class Ψ if there exists G in Ψ such that $L(G_R) \neq L(G)$; we write $R(\Psi)$. We say that R modifies in the strong sense the generative capacity of the grammars of Ψ if there exists G in Ψ such that $L(G_R)$ is not in L_Ψ ; we write $R[\Psi]$. Obviously, if $R[\Psi]$, then $R(\Psi)$.

Let us denote by Sg the strict global restriction.

Proposition 1. If Lin is the set of the linear grammars, then we don't have Sg(Lin).

Proposition 2. We have Sg(C) and Sg[C] where C is the class of the CF grammars.

Proof. Let us consider the grammar with the rules $S \longrightarrow Ab\,Ab\,A$, $A \longrightarrow aA$, $A \longrightarrow a$. $L(G_{Sg}) = \{a^nba^nba^n;\ n \geqslant 1\}$ is not a CF language.

Proposition 3. The class of the SG languages and the class of the matrix languages are uncomparable.

Proof. The set $L_1 = \{a^nb^nc^n;\ n \geqslant 1\}$ is a matrix language but it is not a global language (see [4]). Thus it is not a SG language. The set $L_2 = \{a^{2^n};\ n \geqslant 0\}$ is SG language (it may be generated by the SG grammar with the rules $S \longrightarrow SS$, $S \longrightarrow a$) but it is not a matrix language.

According to the notations used in the above definition of the index we define the parameter Rep in the following way:

$$\mathrm{Rep}(D, G) = \max_{\substack{o \leqslant j \leqslant k \\ o \leqslant i \leqslant k}} A_i(x_j),$$

$$\mathrm{Rep}(w, G) = \min_{D} \mathrm{Rep}(D,G),$$

$$\mathrm{Rep}(G) = \sup_{w \in L(G)} \mathrm{Rep}(w,G),$$

$$\mathrm{Rep}(L) = \min\{\mathrm{Rep}(G);\ L = L(G)\}.$$

Obviously, $\mathrm{Rep}(L) = 1$ for any linear language and $\mathrm{Rep}(L) \leqslant \mathrm{Ind}(L)$ for any CF language.

Proposition 4. For any CF language L, Rep(L) is finite if and only if Ind(L) is finite.

Proposition 5. For any CF grammar G with $\mathrm{Rep}(G) = n < \infty$ there exists a grammar G' such that L(G) = L(G') and Rep(G') = 1.

Proof. For n = 1 the assertion is true. Let us consider a grammar $G = (V_N, V_T, S, P)$ such that Rep(G) = n + 1. Let U_N be the set of the symbols of V_N which establish the value of Rep(G). If $U_N = \{A_1, A_2, \ldots, A_k\}$ let us consider $\bar{U}_N = \{\bar{A}_1, \bar{A}_2, \ldots, \bar{A}_k\}$ where A_i are not in V. Let Q be the set of the rules of P in which occurs at least a symbol of U_N. Let $\bar{Q}$ be the set of the rules obtained from the rules of Q by the substitution of at least an occurrence of each non-terminal of U_N which occurs in the rule by the corresponding symbol of $\bar{U}_N$. Let us consider the grammar $G'' = (V_N \cup \bar{U}_N, V_T, S, P \cup \bar{Q})$. Obviously L(G") = L(G). It may be proved that Rep(G") $\leqslant$ n. By the induction hypothesis there exists G' such that L(G") = L(G') and Rep(G') = 1.

Proposition 6. If $\Psi = \{G;\ \mathrm{Rep}(G) = 1\}$ then we don't have $Sg(\Psi)$.

Theorem 1. Any CF language of finite index is a SG language.

The theorem results from the propositions 4, 5 and 6.

Corollary. For any language of finite index, L, and for any $n \geqslant 1$ the language $L_n = \{w^n;\ w \in L\}$ is SG.

Theorem 2. There is a CF language of infinite index which is not a SG language.

Proof. Let us consider the language L generated by the grammar with the rules $S \longrightarrow SS$, $S \longrightarrow aSb$, $S \longrightarrow cS$, $S \longrightarrow c$. Let us consider the homomorphism defined by h(a) = a, h(b) = b, h(c) = ε . Obviously h(L) is the Dick language on the vocabulary $\{a,b\}$. Since the class of the languages of finite index is full AFL [3], it follows that Ind(L)= $= \infty$. In what follows, by the assertion "c^k is subword in w" we understand that $w = w_1 c^k w_2$ and $w_1 \neq w_1' c$, $w_2 \neq c w_2'$. We suppose that there i a grammar $G = (V_N, V_T, S, P)$ such that $L(G_{Sg}) = L$. For A in V_n we have three cases:

i) $L_A = \{w \in V_T^* \ ;\ A \overset{*}{\underset{G_{Sg}}{\Longrightarrow}} w\}$ is a finite language,

ii) $L_A = L_1 L_2 L_3$ where $L_2 \subset \{c\}^*$ and L_1, L_2 are finite languages,

iii) L_A is a finite union of languages of the form $L_1 L L_2$ where L_1, L_2 are finite languages.

Let L' be the set of w in L such that any derivation of w is of the form $S \overset{*}{\underset{G_{Sg}}{\Longrightarrow}} Z \overset{*}{\underset{G_{Sg}}{\Longrightarrow}} w$, with $A(Z) \geqslant 2$ for A with the property ii

Let be also $L'' = \{w \in L;$ if c^k and c^i are subwords in w, then $k \neq i\}$. Obviously $L' \cap L'' \neq \emptyset$. On the other hand, we have $(L' \cap L(G_{Sg})) \cap L'' = \emptyset$ Contradiction.

Open problem. Does there exist a CF language of infinite index which is a SG language ?

Following Gruska [3] a measure K of syntactic complexity is said to be nontrivial if for any $n \geqslant 1$ there exists a language L such that $K(L) > n$. K is said to be bounded if for any $n \geqslant 1$ there exists a language L such that $K(L) = n$.

Because there are languages L for which $\mathrm{Rep}(L) = \infty$, Rep is a nontrivial measure. As a consequence of the proposition 5 it results that Rep is not a bounded measure. For any language L we have either $\mathrm{Rep}(L) = \infty$, or $\mathrm{Rep}(L) = 1$. Obviously, for any $n \geqslant 1$ there exists a grammar G such that $\mathrm{Rep}(G) = n$. Moreover, we have:

Proposition 7. For any CF language L with $\mathrm{Rep}(L) = 1$, and for any $n \geqslant 1$ there exists a grammar G_n such that $\mathrm{Rep}(G_n) = n$.

Following Gruska [3], for K we put $K^{-1}(L) = \{G;\ L = L(G),\ K(G) = K(L)\}$. Then, two measures K_1 and K_2 are said to be compatible if for any CF language L we have $K_1^{-1}(L) \cap K_2^{-1}(L) \neq \emptyset$.

Proposition 8. Rep and Ind are compatible, but Rep and $K \in \{\mathrm{Var}, \mathrm{Prod}, \mathrm{Symb}\}$ (see [3]) are uncompatible.

Proof. The first assertion follows from the proposition 5 and 4. To prove the second assertion it is sufficient to find a language L such that $\mathrm{Rep}(L) = 1$ and every grammar G for L with $K(G) = K(L)$ has $\mathrm{Rep}(G) \geqslant 2$. This languages is

$$L = \{a^n\ b^n\ a^m\ b^m;\ n, m \geqslant 0\}.$$

References

1. Brainerd B. An analog of a theorem about context free languages. Information and Control 11 (1968), 561-567.
2. Ginsburg S. The mathematical theory of context free languages. Mc Graw-Hill Book Company New-York (1966).
3. Gruska J. Descriptional complexity of context free languages. Proc. of symp. and summ. school.Math. fund of computer sci. High Tatras (1973).
4. Levitina M.K. On some grammars with global productions. N.T.I. 2(1972), 32-36 (in russ.).
5. Salomaa A. On the index of a context free grammar and language. Information and Control, 14 (1968), 474-477.
6. Salomaa A. Formal languages. Academic Press New York and London (1973).

TREE-TRANSDUCERS AND SYNTAX-CONNECTED TRANSDUCTIONS

Peter Paul Schreiber
Technische Universität Berlin, Informatik PC2
Ernst-Reuter-Platz 8, Berlin 10, West Germany

Abstract

We investigate Finite Tree-Transducers operating top-down, bottom-up or both ways simultaneously. A comparative study of their transductional power is given. Syntax-Connected Transductions extending Syntax-Directed Transductions are investigated. Various types of transductions of local forests defined by Syntax-Connected Transduction Schemes can be performed by Finite Tree-Transducers.

Introduction

Operational automata like tree-transducers are extensions of classical automata. In addition to local processing like symbol-changing and state-switching, they can manipulate (permute, copy or erase) input-structures and output-structures. Finite state and push-down transducers have, so far, been very useful tools for designing and structuring the first phases of a compiler (such as the scanner and the parser). The more complicated phases consisting of semantic analysis, code generation and optimization, however, could not be supplied with such useful tools from automata theory. This is due to the fact that the objects to be dealt with in these phases are trees which have to be manipulated. As long as language translation had been understood as string processing and not as a tree-manipulating process, little effort was made to investigate machines which perform tree transductions. From the point of view of generalized automata theory, trees were used as inputs and (in a further generalization step) as outputs. Comparing these tree-transducers with syntax-directed transduction schemes performing transformations of the derivation trees of an underlying CF-Grammar, one can see that tree-transducers are more powe ful than the syntax-directed transduction schemes. Many tree-transforming phases o a compiler cannot be modelled by a syntax-directed transduction scheme, but by a tree-transducer.

1. Trees represented as terms

To represent trees labelled by elements of a set Σ we use terms over Σ. The set T_Σ of terms over Σ is the smallest subset of $(\Sigma \cup \{ (,) \})^*$ satisfying:

(0) $\Sigma \subset T_\Sigma$

(1) If $t_1, \ldots, t_k \varepsilon T_\Sigma$ and $a \varepsilon \Sigma$ then $a(t_1 \ldots t_k) \varepsilon T_\Sigma$

Let M be a set, $M \cap \Sigma = \Phi$. The set $T_\Sigma[M]$ of terms over Σ indexed by M is the smallest subset of $\Sigma \cup M \cup \{ (,) \})^*$ such that

(0) $\Sigma \cup M \subset T_\Sigma$

(1) If $t_1, \ldots, t_k \varepsilon T_\Sigma[M]$ for $k > 0$ and $a \varepsilon \Sigma$ then $a(t_1 \ldots t_k) \varepsilon T_\Sigma[M]$

A subword t' of $t \varepsilon T_\Sigma[M]$ which is a term is called subterm of t.
Notation: $t' \leq t$. Two subterms t' and t" of t are independent iff $t' \nleq t''$ and $t'' \nleq t'$.

Let $t' \leq t$ and $r \varepsilon T_\Sigma[M]$, then $t(t' \longleftarrow r)$ is the term obtained by replacing t' by r.
Let $s_1, \ldots, s_k$ be pairwise independent subterms of t and $\pi : [k] \longrightarrow [k]$ $([k] = \{1, \ldots k\})$ any permutation and $r_i \varepsilon T_\Sigma[M]$ $(1 \leq i \leq k)$, then

$$t((s_1 \leftarrow r_1) \ldots (s_k \leftarrow r_k)) = t((s_{\pi(1)} \leftarrow r_{\pi(1)}) \ldots (s_{\pi(k)} \leftarrow r_{\pi(k)}))$$

Let $X = \{x_i \mid i \varepsilon \mathbb{N}\}$ be a set of parameters and $X_k = \{x_1, \ldots, x_k\}$.

The operation of simultaneous substitutions is defined as:

$$t[t_1, \ldots, t_k] := t((x_1 \leftarrow t_1) \ldots (x_k \leftarrow t_k))$$

The frontier fr(t) of $t \varepsilon T_\Sigma[M]$ is the word obtained by concatenating the labels of the leaves from left to right.

The depth $\|t\|$ of $t \varepsilon T_\Sigma[M]$ is defined as:

$$\|t\| = \begin{cases} 1 & \text{for } t = a \varepsilon \Sigma \\ \max\limits_{i \varepsilon [k]} \|t_i\| + 1 & \text{for } t = a(t_1 \ldots t_k) \varepsilon T_\Sigma[M] \end{cases}$$

2. Finite Tree-Transducers

A Finite Tree-Transducer (FT) $P = (Q, \Sigma, \Delta, R, I)$ consists of a finite set Q of states, an inputalphabet Σ, an outputalphabet Δ, a finite set R of rules and a subset I of Q of distinguished states.

A Top-Down-rule (T-rule) is a rule of the form:

$\langle q,a\rangle(x_1 \dots x_k) \longrightarrow t$ with $\langle q,a\rangle \varepsilon Q \times \Sigma$ and $t \varepsilon T_\Delta[Q \times X_k]$

or $\langle q,a\rangle \longrightarrow t$ with $t \varepsilon T_\Delta$.

T-rules of that type with $\|t\| = n$ are called T(1,n)-rules.

A T-rule $\langle q,a\rangle(u_1 \dots u_k) \longrightarrow t$ with $a(u_1 \dots u_k) \varepsilon T_\Sigma[X]$, $\|t\| = n$ and $\|a(u_1 \dots u_k)\| = m$ is called T(m,n)-rule.

A Top-Down-Finite-Tree-Transducer (TFT) is a FT with T-rules.
A <u>move</u> of a TFT is defined as a relation $\underset{T}{\vdash}$ on $T_{\Sigma \cup \Delta \cup (Q \times \Sigma)}$.

Let $r, s \varepsilon T_{\Sigma \cup \Delta \cup (Q \times \Sigma)}$ and R a set of T(1,1)-rules then $r \underset{T}{\vdash} s$ iff

$\exists r' \varepsilon T_{\Sigma \cup (Q \times \Sigma)}$ $r' = \langle q,a\rangle(t_1 \dots t_k) \leq r$

and $\exists (\langle q,a\rangle(x_1 \dots x_k) \longrightarrow t) \varepsilon R$

such that $s := r(r' \longleftarrow t[t_1,\dots,t_k])$

$\vdash^*$ denotes the reflexive and transitive closure of $\vdash$.

$T(P) = \{\langle r,s\rangle \varepsilon T_\Sigma \times T_\Delta \mid \langle q_0,r\rangle \vdash^* s \wedge q_0 \varepsilon I\}$ is called <u>Tree-Transduction</u> from T_Σ to T_Δ performed by a TFT P.

A Bottom-Up-rule (B-rule) is a rule of the form

$a \rightarrow \langle t,p\rangle$ with $a \varepsilon \Sigma$, $t \varepsilon T_\Delta$ and $p \varepsilon Q$

or $a(\langle x_1,p_1\rangle \dots \langle x_k,p_k\rangle) \rightarrow \langle t,p\rangle$ with $a \varepsilon \Sigma$, $p, p_1, \dots, p_k \varepsilon Q$ and $t \varepsilon T_\Delta[X_k]$.

B-rules of that type with $\|t\| = n$ are called B(1,n)-rules.

A B-rule $a(u_1 \dots u_k) \rightarrow \langle t,p\rangle$ with $u_i \varepsilon T_\Sigma[X_k \times Q]$, $\|t\| = n$

and $\|a(u_1 \dots u_k)\| = m$ is called B(m,n)-rule.

A Bottom-Up-Finite-Tree-Transducer is a FT with B-rules.
A move of a BFT with B(1,1)-rules is defined as a relation $\underset{B}{\vdash}$ on $T_{\Sigma \cup \Delta \cup (\Delta \times Q)}$.

Let $r, s \varepsilon T_{\Sigma \cup \Delta \cup (\Delta \times Q)}$ then $r \underset{B}{\vdash} s$ iff

$\exists r' = a(\langle t_1,p_1\rangle \dots \langle t_k,p_k\rangle) \leq r$

and $\exists (a(\langle x_1,p_1\rangle \dots \langle x_k,p_k\rangle) \rightarrow \langle t,p\rangle) \varepsilon R$

such that $s := r(r' \leftarrow \langle t[t_1,\dots,t_k],p\rangle)$

$T(P) = \{<r,s>\varepsilon T_\Sigma x T_\Delta | r \overset{*}{\vdash} <s,p_0> \wedge p_0 \varepsilon I\}$ is the Tree-Transduction performed by a BFT P.

A rule is called rank-preserving if each parameter x_i of its left side occurs on its right side.
A rule is called linear if each parameter x_i of its left side occurs not more than once on its right side.
Rank-preserving rules can copy and do not erase subtrees while linear rules can erase and do not copy subtrees.

$$\text{A FT with } \left\{\begin{matrix}\text{rank-preserving}\\ \text{linear}\end{matrix}\right\} \text{ rules is called } \left\{\begin{matrix}\text{RFT}\\ \text{LFT}\end{matrix}\right\}$$

and LRFT if its rules are linear and rank-preserving. A FT with $|Q| = 1$ is a pure FT.

$_\Sigma FT_\Delta = \{T(P) \in T_\Sigma x T_\Delta | P \text{ is a FT}\}$ is called the class of F-Tree-Transductions and we write FT for a fixed pair (Σ,Δ).

From now on we only consider Tree-Transducers with T(1,1)-rules or B(1,1)-rules.

Generalized Finite-Tree-Transducers are composed out of a

$$\text{TFT } P_T = (Q_T,\Sigma,\Delta,R_T,I_T) \text{ and a BFT } P_B = (Q_B,\Sigma,\Delta,R_B,I_B).$$

A move of a TBFT $P = (Q_T,Q_B,\Sigma,\Delta,R_T,R_B,I_T,I_B)$ is T-move followed by a B-move and a move of a BTFT $P = (Q_B,Q_T,\Sigma,\Delta,R_B,R_T,I_B,I_T)$ is a B-move followed by a T-move.

Let P be a TBFT, then

$$T(P) = \{<r,t>\varepsilon T_\Sigma x T_\Delta | <q_0,r> \underset{T}{\vdash} s \overset{*}{\vdash} <t,p_0>,\ q_0 \varepsilon I_T \wedge p_0 \varepsilon I_B\}$$

and $$T(P) = \{<r,t>\varepsilon T_\Sigma x T_\Delta | <q_0,r> \underset{B}{\vdash} s \overset{*}{\vdash} <t,p_0>,\ q_0 \varepsilon I_T \wedge p_0 \varepsilon I_B\}$$ for a BTFT P.

Theorem 1: For the classes of Finite Tree-Transductions the following lattice exists: (including results by ENGELFRIET, ROUNDS and THATCHER)

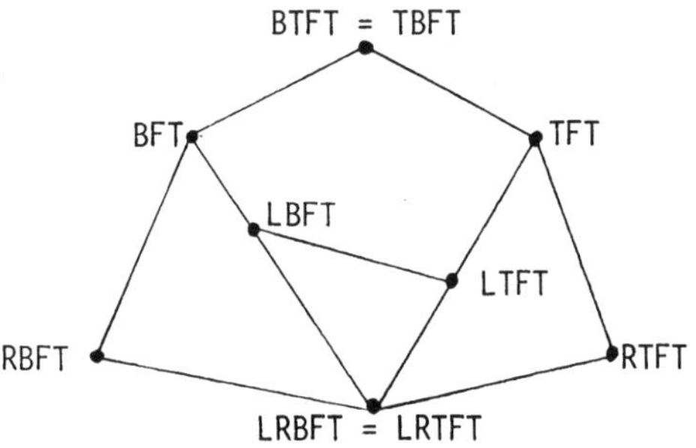

3. Syntax-Connected-Transduction-Schemes

Given a CF-Grammar $G = (\Sigma,\Sigma_0,P,S,)$ consisting of a finite alphabet Σ, subset $\Sigma_0 \subset \Sigma$ of terminal symbols, a set $P \subset (\Sigma \setminus \Sigma_0) x \Sigma^+$ productions and a start symbol $S \varepsilon \Sigma \setminus \Sigma_0$. The elements of $\Sigma \setminus \Sigma_0$ are called syntactic variables.
The set $D_S(G)$ of derivation trees of G with root S is defined as:

(0) $S \varepsilon D_S(G)$

(1) If $r \varepsilon D_S(G)$, $fr(r) = w_1 A w_2$ and $(A \rightarrow w) \varepsilon P$ with $w_1,w_2 \varepsilon \Sigma^*$, $A \varepsilon \Sigma \setminus \Sigma_0$ then $r' = r(A \leftarrow A(w))$ is in $D_S(G)$

The set $D(G) := \{t \varepsilon D_S(G) \mid fr(t) \varepsilon \Sigma_0^+\}$ is called local forest of G.

A Syntax-Connected-Transduction-Scheme (SCTS) $G = (G_E,G_A,\kappa)$ consists of a CF-inp grammar $G_E = (\Sigma,\Sigma_0,P_E,S)$, a CF-output grammar $G_A = (\Delta,\Delta_0,P_A,S)$ with $\Delta \setminus \Delta_0 \subset \Sigma \setminus \Sigma_0$ an transduction rules $A \rightarrow w,\ v[i_1,\dots,i_m]$, where $A \rightarrow w$ is an input production fro P_E, $A \rightarrow v$ is an output production from P_A such that $[i_1,\dots,i_m] \varepsilon \kappa \subset \mathbb{N}^m$ connects positions of the common syntactic variables i.e. $A \rightarrow w,\ v[i_1,\dots,i_m]$ has genera the following form:

$$A \rightarrow g_0 A_1 g_1 \dots g_{k-1} A_k g_k,\ h_0 A_{i_1} h_1 \dots h_{m-1} A_{i_m} h_m [i_1,\dots,i_m]$$

where $i_j \varepsilon [k]$ for $1 \le j \le m$, $A_i \varepsilon \Sigma \setminus \Sigma_0$, $g_i \varepsilon \Sigma_0^*$ $(0 \le i \le k)$ and $h_i \varepsilon \Delta_0^*$ $(1 \le i \le m)$.

The set $T_S(G)$ of pairs of transduction trees is defined as:

(0) $<S,S> \varepsilon T_S(G)$

(1) If $<r,s> \varepsilon T_\Sigma x T_\Delta$ such that $fr(r) = w_0 B_1 w_1 \dots w_{m-1} B_m w_m$ $fr(s) = v_0 B_{i_1} v_1 \dots v_{n-1} B_{i_n} v_n$ and $[i_1,\dots,i_n]$ with $i_j \varepsilon [m]$, $w_i \varepsilon \Sigma_0^*$ $(0 \le i \le m)$, $v_i \varepsilon \Delta_0^*$ $(0 \le i \le n)$ then $<r,s> \varepsilon T_S(G)$.

A relation $\rightarrow$ is defined on $T_S(G)$ as:

$$<r,s> \rightarrow <r',s'>$$

iff there exists a transduction rule $B_k \rightarrow w,\ v[i_1,\dots,i_1]$ such that:

1. $r' = r(B_k \leftarrow B_k(w))$
2. s' derives from s by replacing all B_{i_j} with $i_j = k$ by $B_k(v)$.

or if no i_j with $i_j = k$ exists $r' = r(B_k \leftarrow B_k(w))$ for $(B_k \rightarrow w) \varepsilon P_E$ and $s' = s$

$T(G) := \{\langle r,s\rangle \varepsilon T_S(G) \mid fr(r)\varepsilon\Sigma_0^+ \wedge fr(s)\varepsilon\Delta_0^+\}$ is called Syntax-Connected-Transduction defined by G.

A transduction rule is called rank-preserving if each $i\varepsilon[k]$ appears at least once in $[i_1,\ldots,i_m]$ and linear if all $i_j (1\leq i\leq m)$ are pairwise unequal in $[i_1,\ldots, i_m]$. If $[i_1,\ldots,i_m] = [1,\ldots,m]$ the transduction rule is called simple and regular for $[i_1] = [1]$.

$$\text{A SCTS is a} \left\{\begin{array}{c} \text{RSDTS} \\ \text{SSDTS} \\ \text{LRSCTS} \\ \text{LSCTS} \\ \text{RSCTS} \end{array}\right\} \text{if all transduction rules are} \left\{\begin{array}{l} \text{regular} \\ \text{simple} \\ \text{linear and rank-preserving} \\ \text{linear} \\ \text{rank-preserving} \end{array}\right\}$$

${}_{\Sigma}SCT_{\Delta} = \{T(G) \subset T_{\Sigma} x T_{\Delta} \mid G \text{ is a SCTS}\}$ is called the class of SC-Transductions and we write SCT for a fixed pair (Σ,Δ).

Theorem 2: For the classes of Syntax-connected Transductions the following lattice exists:

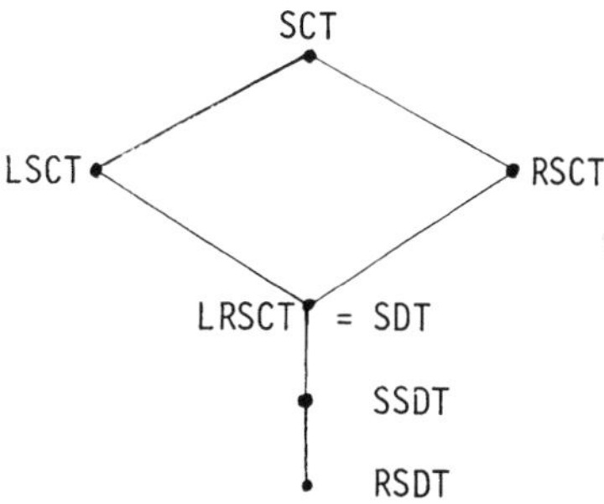

Relations between Schemes and Transducers

A SCT-Scheme defines a pair of local trees, while a tree-transducer operates on an input tree and produces an output tree.

Theorem 3: For each α-SCTS G exists a α-TFT P such that $T(G) = T(P)$. (α = L or R or LR)

This theorem implies several corollaries delivering a large variety of results dealing with special restricted cases for transducers and transduction schemes as well.

Example: Let $G = (G_E, G_A, \kappa)$ have the transduction rules:

$$A \rightarrow aBA, AAd[2,2] \qquad A \rightarrow a,c \qquad (B \rightarrow b) \varepsilon P_E$$

The following pair of trees is in T(G):

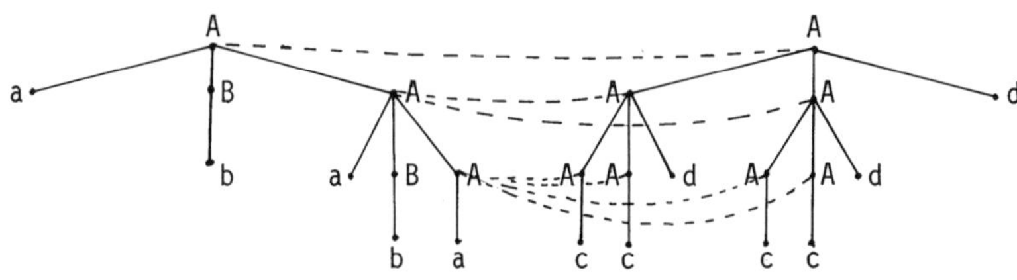

The dotted lines indicate the connections appearing in the course of generation. This Tree-Transduction can be performed by a TFT with the following rules:

$$\bar{A}(x_1 x_2 x_3) \rightarrow A(\bar{x}_3 \bar{x}_3 d) \qquad \bar{A}(x) \rightarrow A(\bar{x}) \qquad \bar{a} \rightarrow c$$

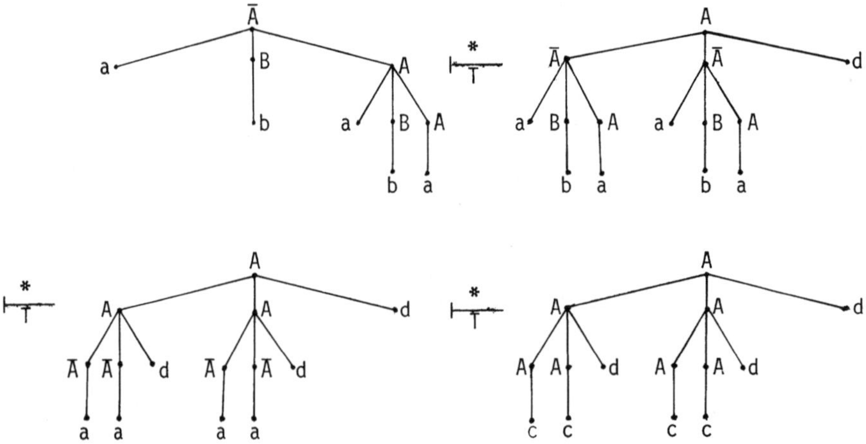

Acknowledgements:

I thank BLEICKE EGGERS for valuable discussions and GITA SARI for her excellent typi

References:

ENGELFRIET, J.: Bottom-up and Top-Down Tree Transducers - a comparison. Memorandum No. 19, 1971 Techn. Hogeschool Twente, Netherlands

ROUNDS, W.C.: Mappings and grammars on trees. MST 4, 257 - 287 (1970)

SCHREIBER, P.P.: Baum-Transduktoren (Thesis forthcoming)

SCHREIBER, P.P.: Operational Automata for Compiler Design. Bericht Nr. 75 - 13. Technische Universität Berlin, FB 20 - Kybernetik

THATCHER, J.W.: Generalized^2 Sequential Machine Maps. JCSS 4, 339 - 367 (1970)

SUR LES RELATIONS RATIONNELLES

M.P. Schutzenberger

IRIA

I. Introduction

Nous faisons référence aux chapitres IX et XI du traité de S. Eilenberg ([1]) pour les résultats de base concernant les relations rationnelles $\rho : A^* \to B^*$ entre monoïdes libres et nous appelons une telle relation *fonctionnelle* ssi l'image $a\rho$ de chaque mot a de A^* est vide (=0) ou un singleton. Nous nous proposons d'établir la propriété suivante qui peut être considérée comme une modification d'un résultat banal concernant les séries rationnelles.

Propriété : Si la relation rationnelle $\rho : A^* \to B^*$ n'est pas une somme finie de relations rationnelles fonctionnelles il existe trois mots $a,a',h \in A^*$ tels que Card $((ah^n a')\rho) \geq n+1$ pour chaque $n \in N$.

Dans ce qui suit nous supposerons d'abord la relation ρ donnée par un transducteur au sens de Nivat ([2]), c'est à dire par un morphisme μ de A^* dans le semi-anneau des QxQ matrices à entrées dans Rat(B), où Q est un ensemble d'indice fini, et la règle que pour chaque mot a, la partie $a\rho$ de B^* est certaine entrée fixe(disons, l'entrée (q_-,q_+)) de la matrice $a\mu$. En outre, on peut supposer que cette représentation est *réduite* en ce sens que pour chaque q de Q il existe des mots a,a' de A^* tels que $a\mu(q_-,q)$ et $a'\mu(q_-,q_+)$ soient non nuls. En effet s'il n'en était pas ainsi on pourrait, sans changer la valeur de ρ, remplacer par 0 les entrées des lignes et colonnes "q" dans toutes les matrices, et par conséquent, omettre q.

Sous cette hypothèse qui sera toujours faite désormais, il est clair que la propriété serait triviale si l'une des entrées de l'une des matrices génératrices $\alpha\mu$ $(a \in A)$ était une partie infinie du B^*. Nous supposerons donc aussi que toutes ces entrées sont des parties *finies* de B^*. Une autre simplification peut encore être faite : comme l'énoncé ne dépend pas du nombre d'éléments de 1ρ (où 1 est comme d'usage l'élément neutre) nous supposerons toujours que $1\rho = 0$ ou $= 1$, ces deux cas correspondant respectivement aux hypothèses que les états distingués q_- et q_+ sont distincts ou confondus.

II. Preuve de la propriété

Nous notons $\|X\|$ le nombre d'éléments d'un ensemble X quelconque et en particulier nous posons $\|Q\| = d$.

Lemme 1. La relation ρ est fonctionnelle ssi $\|a\rho\| \leq 1$ pour tous les mots a de longue $|a|$ du plus égal à $L = 1+2\,d(\,d-1\,)$.

Preuve : Soit a un mot de longueur minimum $|a| = n$ parmi ceux pour lesquels $\|a\rho\| \geq$ Si l'une des matrices $a'\mu$ ($a' \in A$) a une entrée qui n'est ni vide ni un singleton l'hypothèse que μ est un transducteur *réduit* implique que $n \leq 1+2(\,d-1\,)$, et le résultat est vérifié dans ce cas. Dans le cas contraire où chaque entrée de chacune des matrices génératrices $a'\mu$ ($a' \in A$) est au plus un singleton, soit $a = a_1a_2 \ldots a_n$ ($a_i \in A$). Il existe une suite de n-1 paires (q_j, q'_j) d'indices ($1 \leq j \leq n-1, q_j \neq q'_j$ tels que posant $q_0 = q'_0 = q_-$, $q_n = q'_n = q_+$ et $b_j = a_j\mu(\,q_{j-1}, q_j\,)$, $b'_j = a_j\mu(\,q'_{j-1}, q'_j\,)$ ($1 \leq j \leq n$) les mots $b = b_1 \ldots b_n$ et $b' = b'_1 \ldots b'_n$ soient deux éléments *distincts* de $a\rho$. Supposons que $n > L$ et montrons que l'hypothèse de minimalité sur $|a| = n$ conduit à une contradiction.

D'après $L = 1 + 2d(\,d-1\,)$ il existe trois indices $i<j<k$ pour lesquels (q_i, q'_i) = (q_j, q'_j) = (q_k, q'_k), ce qui détermine une factorisation $a = f_1f_2f_3f_4$ où $f_1 = a_1 \ldots a_i$; $f_2 = a_{i+1} \ldots a_j$; $f_3 = a_{j+1} \ldots a_k$; $f_4 = a_k \ldots a_n$ et induit de façon évidente les factorisations correspondantes $b = g_1g_2g_3g_4$ et $b' = g'_1g'_2g'_3g'_4$. Par construction on a les inclusions $g_1g_4, g'_1g'_4 \in (\,f_1f_4\,)\rho$ et $g_1g_xg_4, g'_1g'_xg'_4 \in (\,f_1f_xf_4\,)\rho$ ($x = 2$ ou 3).

En raison du caractère minimal de a, les membres de droite sont des singlet et on a donc les trois équations $g_1g_4 = g'$ et $g_1g_xg_4 = g'_1g'_xg'_4$.

Supposant, par exemple, que $|g_1| \leq |g'_1|$ il en résulte l'existence d'un mot tel que $g'_1 = g_1h$ et $g_4 = hg'_4$, d'où en reportant dans les autres équations et en s plifiant, les deux équations $hg_2 = g'_2h$ et $hg_3 = g'_3h$.

Il en résulte que

$$b = g_1g_2g_3g_4 = g_1g_2g_3hg'_4 = g_1g_2hg'_3g'_4 = g_1hg'_2g'_3g'_4 = h\,g'_1g'_2g'_3g'_4 = b'$$

en contradiction avec l'hypothèse que b et b' étaient distincts.

Par conséquent $n \leq L$.

Q.E.D.

Nous rappelons maintenant que le *support* $m\beta$ d'une QxQ matrice m est la relation binaire sur Q définie par l'ensemble de ses entrées non vides. Autrement dit, β est un morphisme du monoïde $A^*\mu$ dans un monoïde de relations binaires sur Q. On dit que μ est *irréductible* ssi l'union des relations $a\mu\beta$ ($a \in A^*$) est égale à QxQ lui-même. Nous avons donc le

Corollaire 2. Quand μ est irréductible et que ρ n'est pas fonctionnelle, il existe trois mots a,h,a' tels que $\|(ah^n a')\rho\| \geq n+1$ ($n \in N$).

Preuve : Supposons que $\|a\rho\| \geq 2$, c'est à dire que $\|a\mu(q_-,q_+)\| \geq 2$.

Puisque μ est irréductible il existe un mot a" tel que (q_+,q_-) appartienne au support de la matrice $a''\mu$. Posant h = a"a on a donc que l'entrée (q_-,q_+) de $h\mu$ contient au moins deux mots distincts. Il est trivial que la même entrée de $h^n\mu$ contient donc au moins n+1 mots distincts pour chaque $n \in N$ et l'on a par conséquent $\|(ah^n)\rho\| = \|(ah^n)\mu(q_-,q_+)\| \geq n+1$ identiquement.

Q.E.D.

Par conséquent la propriété est déjà établie dans le cas particulier où le transducteur μ est irréductible. Comme elle l'est trivialement quand le domaine de ρ est fini nous pouvons désormais procéder par induction sur $\|Q\|$ ou plus exactement, sur le nombre total des entrées non nulles des matrices génératrices $a\mu$ ($a \in A$) du monoïde $A^*\mu$.

Avant de passer au cas général nous rappelons que le produit (de concaténation) de deux relations $\rho,\sigma : A^* \to B^*$ est la relation $\pi = \rho\sigma$ telle que pour chaque mot a on ait :

$$a\pi = \Sigma \{ (a'\rho)(a''\rho) : a',a'' \in A^* ; a = a'a'' \}.$$

Supposons maintenant que μ ne soit pas irréductible. Il existe une partition $Q = Q' \cup Q''$ tel qu'aucun des supports $a\mu\beta$ ne rencontre Q" x Q'. Nous définissons un morphisme μ' par la condition que pour tout $a \in A$, $q,q' \in Q$ on ait :

$$\begin{aligned} a\mu'(q,q') &= a\mu(q,q') \text{ si } q,q' \in Q' ; \\ &= 0 \qquad\qquad \text{sinon ;} \end{aligned}$$

et un autre morphisme μ'' par la condition que $\mu = \mu' + \mu''$ et que le support des $a\mu''$ ne rencontre pas Q' x Q'. On vérifie facilement que ρ est la somme étendue à tous les $q \in Q'$ des produits $\rho'_q\rho''_q$ où $\rho'_q = \mu'(q_-,q)$ et $\rho''_q = \mu''(q,q_+)$.

Ces relations sont rationnelles et on peut leur appliquer l'hypothèse d'induction. Donc pour conclure la preuve de la propriété il nous suffit de vérifier le

Lemme 3 : Si le produit $\pi = \rho\rho'$ de deux relations rationnelles fonctionnelles n'est pas une somme finie de telles relations, il existe trois mots pour lesquels $\|(ah^n a')\pi\| \geq n+1$ ($n \in N$).

Preuve : Nous utilisons les bimachines de Eilenberg ([1], chap XI), c'est à dire que nous associons à ρ un morphisme ϕ de A^* dans un monoïde fini M et une application partielle θ : $M \times A \times M \to B^*$ telle que pour chaque mot $a = a_1 \dots a_n$ ($a_i \in A$) on ait que $a\rho$ est le produit de $i = 1$ à $i = n$ de termes (m'_i, a_i, m''_i)θ où m'_i (resp. m''_i) est l'image par ϕ du facteur gauche (resp. droit) de longueur $i-1$ (resp. $n-i$) de a. Une construction semblable avec $\phi' : A^* \to M'$ et θ' vaut pour ρ'. De fait, on peut remplacer M et M' par leur produit direct et, ceci fait, supposer simplement que $\phi = \phi'$, les deux bimachines ne diffèrant alors que par leurs fonction θ et θ'. On peut de plus exprimer ρ comme la somme sur tous les $s \in S$ des relations ρ_s qui sont définies comme la restriction de ρ à $s\phi^{-1}$. Il en est de même pour ρ' et il suffit donc d'établir le lemme sous l'hypothèse supplémentaire que le domaine de ρ est $s\phi^{-1} = D$ et que celui de ρ' est $s'\phi^{-1} = D'$.

Le domaine de $\pi = \rho\rho'$ est donc DD' et l'on a que π est fonctionnelle quand chaque mot de A^* admet au plus une factorisation comme produit d'un mot de D par un mot de D'. Dans le cas contraire, l'ensemble des mots $p \neq 1$ satisfaisant les conditions $s'.p\phi = s'$ et $p\phi.s'' = s''$ est un sous semi groupe non vide P^+ de A^* (engendré par la base P) et chaque mot a de DD' admettant plusieurs factorisations admet une factorisation maximale unique $dp_1p_2 \dots p_nd'$ où $n \geq 1$, $d \in D$, $d' \in D'$ et $p_1, \dots, p_n \in$

Nous étendons θ (et θ') à des fonctions de $M \times A^* \times M$ dans B^* par les identités :

$$(t,xy,t')\theta'' = (t,x,y\phi.t')\theta''. (t.x\phi,y,t')\theta''$$

$$(x,y \in A^*, t,t' \in S , \theta'' = \theta \text{ ou } = \theta').$$

Nous notons σ et σ' les relations rationnelles fonctionnelles de domaine P^+ envoyant respectivement chaque $p_i \in P^+$ sur $g_i = (s,p_i,s')\theta$ et $g'_i = (s,p_i,s')\theta'$

On vérifie alors que $a\rho$ est l'union pour $i = 0,1,\dots,n$ des produits $bg_1g_2\dots g_ig'_{i+1}\dots g'_nb'$ uù $b = (1,d,s')\theta$ et $b' = (s,d',1)\theta'$. Ces n+1 mots sont les mêmes ssi $g_i = g'_i$ identiquement. Si au contraire $g = p\sigma \neq g' = p\sigma$ (pour un $p \in$ on voit que les n+1 mots de (ap^na')ρ, c'est à dire les mots $d\, g^ig'^{n-i}\, d'$,($0 \leq i \leq n$ sont tous distincts. Par conséquent les deux alternatives énoncées dans la propriét correspondent respectivement aux deux cas possibles selon que $\sigma \neq \sigma'$ ou $\sigma = \sigma'$. No observons maintenant que comme σ et σ' sont fonctionnelles, on a $\sigma = \sigma'$ ssi la relation rationnelle $\sigma + \sigma'$ l'est aussi, ce que l'on peut vérifier au moyen du lemme

Q.E.D.

Remarque : Un examen plus détaillé des morphismes irréductibles permet de trouver des mots (s'il en existe) tels que Card ((ah^na')ρ) $\geq 2^n$ ($n \in \mathbb{N}$) et, de véri que, sinon, Card ($a\rho$) est au plus égal à une fonction polynomiale de la longueur d mots a. ("cas polynomial").

Quand $\|a\rho\|$ est bornée, on peut montrer que ρ est la som me d'une relation ayan un domaine fini et de d relations rationnelles fonctionnelles où d est le plus pet entier tel que $a\rho$ contienne d mots distincts de B^* pour une infinité de mots a de

Donc pour deux relations de ce type, ρ et ρ', on peut décider si l'on a ou non identiquement $a\rho \subset a\rho'$, et même si cette inclusion est vérifiée dans le complément d'une partie finie de A^*. Je présume qu'il en est de même dans le "cas polymial" mais je ne suis pas parvenu à la démontrer.

Références :

[1] S. Eilenberg. Automata languages and Machins vol. A Academic Press N.Y. 1974.

[2] M. Nivat (1968) Transductions des langages de Chomsky Annales. Inst. Fourier. XVIII. pp. 335 - 455.

PIECEWISE TESTABLE EVENTS*

Imre Simon**

Departamento de Matemática Aplicada

Universidade de São Paulo, Brasil

1. Introduction and definitions

The free monoid generated by Σ is denoted by Σ^* and has identity λ. $\Sigma^+ = \Sigma^* - \lambda$. For a word x in Σ^*, $|x|$ denotes its length. An event is a subset of Σ^*.

A word x is a *piecewise subword* of y, denoted by $x \leq y$ iff there exist $x_1,\ldots x_n, z_0, z_1,\ldots,z_n$ in Σ^* such that $x = x_1\ldots x_n$ and $y = z_o x_1 z_1\ldots x_n z_n$. For x and y in Σ^*, and a natural m, define $x \;{}_m\!\sim\; y$ iff for every s in Σ^*, $|s| \leq m$ implies that $s \leq x$ iff $s \leq y$. An event is *piecewise testable* iff there exists a natural m, such that for every x and y in Σ^*, $x \;{}_m\!\sim\; y$ implies that x [...] iff $y \in E$.

Thus, an event E is piecewise testable iff there exists a [...] m such that membership of x in E is determined by the set of piecewise subwords of length at most m, which occur in x. In its form, this definition is similar to that of locally testable events [1, 6, 7 and 11], the main difference being the substitution of leng[th] m subwords by piecewise subwords of length m. Piecewise testable ev[ents] were introduced in the author's doctoral dissertation [9], where [...] denotes the family of piecewise testable events. It has been shown [...]

---

* Part of this work has been done at the Department of Computer Scie[nce], University of Waterloo, Canada. It was supported by FAPESP (Brasi[l]) under grants 70/400 and 73/1213 and by the NRC (Canada) under gra[nt] A-1617.

** Mailing Address: Instituto de Matemática e Estatística / CP 20570 01451 São Paulo, Brasil.

that both locally and piecewise testable events constitute subfamilies of regular star-free events with dot-depth one. The dot-depth of a regular star-free event has been introduced in [3]. Indeed, combining properly these two testing concepts, one gets precisely the family of dot-depth one events [9]. Another related result is that an event whose syntactic semigroup is a monoid has dot-depth one iff it is piecewise testable [9].

As far as we know, piecewise subwords were introduced by Haines in [5] and he obtains a truly remarkable result, namely that every set of pairwise noncomparable elements (with respect to the partial order $\leq$ over Σ^*) is finite. Certain subclasses of piecewise testable events were also studied in [5] and [10].

Let a and b be elements of a monoid M. We say that $a \mathcal{J} b$ iff MaM = MbM. This is one of the well-known Green equivalence relations [2]. We say that M is *J-trivial* iff for every a and b in M, $a \mathcal{J} b$ implies a = b.

Given an event $E \subseteq \Sigma^*$, we define $x \equiv y \pmod E$, for x and y in Σ^*, iff for every u and v in Σ^*, $uxv \in E$ iff $uyv \in E$. It is easy to see that $\equiv \pmod E$ is a congruence relation over Σ^*. The quotient monoid $\Sigma^*/\equiv \pmod E$ is called the *syntactic monoid* of E. It is well-known that E is regular iff its syntatic monoid is finite; see for instance [7].

The main result of this paper is that an event E is piecewise estable iff its syntactic monoid is finite and $\mathcal{J}$-trivial. This was irst stated and proved in [9]; here we give a much improved version of hat proof. A corollary to the main result is that it is decidable hether a given regular event is piecewise testable. Indeed, it is sufficient to verify, whether its syntactic monoid is $\mathcal{J}$-trivial.

We will use the well-known left-right duality for semigroups; ee for instance [2].

. Characterization of equivalent words

In this section we study the properties of $_m\sim$ and show that $_m\sim$ y iff y can be obtained from x by a finite number of steps of a mple transformation (R_m or R_m^{-1}). Each step of this transformation consists of adding or deleting a single letter, whenever this preserves equivalence. A byproduct of the results in this section is that one can efficiently verify (in about $O((|x| + |y|)^3)$ steps), whether two given words are m-equivalent.

Lemma 1. Let x and y be in Σ^* and let m be a natural.

(a) ${}_m\sim$ is a congruence relation of finite index over Σ^*.

(b) $x \,{}_{m+1}\sim\, y$ implies $x \,{}_m\sim\, y$.

(c) If $x \leq y$ then $x \,{}_m\sim\, y$ iff for every $s \leq y$, $|s| \leq m$ implies $s \leq x$.

Proof. The proofs are left to the reader. □

Lemma 2. For every u in Σ^* and σ in Σ, there exists a natural p and a word s, such that $u \,{}_p\sim\, u\sigma$, $|s| = p$, $s \leq u$ and $s\sigma \nleq u$.

Proof. Let p be the greatest natural, such that $u \,{}_p\sim\, u\sigma$. The existence of p follows from Lemma 1(b) and the facts that $u \,{}_0\sim\, u\sigma$ and $u \,{}_{|u|+1}\not\sim\, u\sigma$. Thus, $u \,{}_{p+1}\not\sim\, u\sigma$, hence there exists a word s, such that $|s| = p$, $s \leq u$ and $s\sigma \nleq u$. □

The p and s refered to in Lemma 2 can be efficiently found by the next lemma, which will also be used in section 3. First, we have the notation: for u in Σ^*, $u\Sigma = \{\sigma \in \Sigma \mid \sigma \leq u\}$.

Lemma 3. Let u and v be in Σ^+, and let $m > 0$. Then $u \,{}_m\sim\, uv$ iff there exist $u_1, u_2, \ldots, u_m$ in Σ^+, such that $u = u_1 u_2 \ldots u_m$ and $u_1\Sigma \supseteq u_2\Sigma \supseteq \ldots \supseteq u_m\Sigma \supseteq v\Sigma$.

Proof. Let us prove the only if part by induction on m. For $m = 1$, $u \,{}_1\sim\, uv$ implies that $u\Sigma = (uv)\Sigma$, hence $u\Sigma \supseteq v\Sigma$. Suppose the assertion holds for $m \geq 1$, and let u and v in Σ^+ be such that $u \,{}_{m+1}\sim\, uv$. Let u_0 be the shortest prefix of u, such that $u_0\Sigma = (uv)\Sigma$. Such a prefix exists, since $u \,{}_{m+1}\sim\, uv$ implies $u \,{}_1\sim\, uv$, hence $u\Sigma = (uv)\Sigma$. Since u is not empty, so is u_0; and being $u_0 = u_0'\sigma$, with σ in Σ, the choice of u_0 implies that $\sigma \nleq u_0'$. Let w be such that $u = u_0 w$; we claim that $w \,{}_m\sim\, wv$. Indeed, let s in Σ^* be such that $|s| \leq m$ and $s \leq wv$, then $|\sigma s| \leq m+1$ and $\sigma s \leq u_0 wv = uv$. Since $u \,{}_{m+1}\sim\, uv$, it follows that $\sigma s \leq u = u_0'\sigma w$, and since $\sigma \nleq u_0'$, $s \leq w$. Hence, in view of Lemma 1(c), $w \,{}_m\sim\, wv$. By the induction hypothesis, there exist $u_1, \ldots, u_m$ in Σ^+, such that $u_1 \ldots u_m$

and $u_1\Sigma \supseteq \ldots \supseteq u_m\Sigma \supseteq v\Sigma$. Since $u_0\Sigma = (uv)\Sigma \supseteq u_1\Sigma$, the assertion follows.

The if part is also proved by induction on m. For $m = 1$, $u_1 = u$, and $u\Sigma \supseteq v\Sigma$ implies $u\Sigma = (uv)\Sigma$; hence $u \sim_1 uv$. Let $u_0, u_1, \ldots, u_m, v$ in Σ^+ be such that $u_0\Sigma \supseteq u_1\Sigma \supseteq \ldots \supseteq u_m\Sigma \supseteq v\Sigma$, and let $w = u_1 \ldots u_m$. Then $u_0\Sigma = (u_0 wv)\Sigma$, and by the induction hypothesis, $w \sim_m wv$. We claim that $u_0 w \sim_{m+1} u_0 wv$. Let s in Σ^* be such that $0 < |s| \leq m+1$ and $s \leq u_0 wv$. Let s' be the longest prefix of s, such that $s' \leq u_0$, and let $s = s's''$. Since $u_0\Sigma = (u_0 wv)\Sigma$, it follows that s' is not empty, hence $|s''| \leq m$. On the other hand, the choice of s' and the fact that $s's'' \leq u_0 wv$, imply that $s'' \leq wv$; hence $s'' \leq w$, since $w \sim_m wv$. Thus, $s \leq u_0 w$, which in view of Lemma 1(c) proves the claim. □

<u>Corollary 3a</u>. For every x and y in Σ^* and $m \geq 0$, $(xy)^m \sim_m (xy)^m x$.

<u>Proof</u>. It is sufficient to take $u_1 = \ldots = u_m = xy$. □

<u>Lemma 4</u>. For u and v in Σ^* and σ in Σ, $u\sigma v \sim_m uv$ iff there exist p and p', such that $p+p' \geq m$, $u \sim_p u\sigma$ and $v \sim_{p'} \sigma v$.

<u>Proof</u>. To prove the if part, let p and p' be as in the statement of the lemma. In view of Lemma 1(c), it is sufficient to show that if $s\sigma s' \leq u\sigma v$, with $s \leq u$, $s' \leq v$ and $|s\sigma s'| \leq m$, then $s\sigma s' \leq uv$. Indeed, since $p+p' \geq m$, and $|s\sigma s'| \leq m$, it follows that either $|s| < p$ or $|s'| < p'$, hence either $s\sigma \leq u$ or $\sigma s' \leq v$. In any case, $s\sigma s' \leq uv$.

Conversely, assume that $u\sigma v \sim_m uv$. By Lemma 2, there exist p and s, such that $u \sim_p u\sigma$, $|s| = p$, $s \leq u$ and $s\sigma \not\leq u$. By duality, there exist p' and s', such that $v \sim_{p'} \sigma v$, $|s'| = p'$, $s' \leq v$ and $\sigma s' \not\leq v$. It follows that $|s\sigma s'| = p+p'+1$, $s\sigma s' \leq u\sigma v$ and $s\sigma s' \not\leq uv$. Thus, if $p+p' < m$, then $u\sigma v \not\sim_m uv$, a contradiction, hence $p+p' \geq m$. □

<u>Lemma 5</u>. Let u, v and w in Σ^*, and σ and ξ in Σ, be such that $u\sigma v \sim_m u\xi w$, and $\sigma \neq \xi$. Then, either $u\sigma\xi w \sim_m u\sigma v$ or $\xi\sigma v \sim_m u\xi w$.

<u>Proof</u>. By Lemma 2 there exist p, q, s and t, such that

$$u \;{}_{p}{\sim}\; u\xi, \quad |s| = p, \quad s \leq u \quad \text{and} \quad s\xi \not\leq u, \tag{1}$$

$$\text{and} \quad u \;{}_{q}{\sim}\; u\sigma, \quad |t| = q, \quad t \leq u \quad \text{and} \quad t\sigma \not\leq u. \tag{2}$$

By duality, there exist p', q' and t', such that

$$\sigma v \;{}_{p'}{\sim}\; \xi\sigma v, \quad |s'| = p', \quad s' \leq \sigma v \quad \text{and} \quad \xi s' \not\leq \sigma v, \tag{3}$$

$$\text{and} \quad \xi w \;{}_{q'}{\sim}\; \sigma\xi w, \quad |t'| = q', \quad t' \leq \xi w \quad \text{and} \quad \sigma t' \not\leq \xi w. \tag{4}$$

If $p+p' \geq m$, then by Lemma 4, (1) and (3), $u\xi\sigma v \;{}_{m}{\sim}\; u\sigma v$, and since $u\sigma v \;{}_{m}{\sim}\; u\xi w$ by hypothesis, we have $u\xi\sigma v \;{}_{m}{\sim}\; u\xi w$. Similarly, if $q+q' \geq$ then $u\sigma\xi w \;{}_{m}{\sim}\; u\sigma v$. In either case the lemma holds.

Assume therefore that

$$p+p' < m \quad \text{and} \quad q+q' < m. \tag{5}$$

Assume further that $q' \leq p'$. Now, we claim that $t' \leq v$. Indeed, from (4), $t' \leq \xi w$. Let t_2' be the longest suffix of t' such that $t_2' \leq w$. Then $t' = t_1't_2'$ with $t_1' = \lambda$ or $t_1' = \xi$, and $|t_2'| \leq q'$. Then, from (1), $s \leq u$, hence $s\xi t_2' \leq u\xi w$. On the other hand, since $|t_2'| \leq q'$, $q' \leq p'$ by assumption, $|s| = p$ from (1), and $p+p' < m$ from (5), it follows that $|s\xi t_2'| \leq m$. This implies that $s\xi t_2' \leq u\sigma v$ since $u\sigma v \;{}_{m}{\sim}\; u\xi w$ by hipothesis. Now, from (1), $s\xi \not\leq u$, hence $\sigma \neq \xi$ implies that $\xi t_2' \leq v$. Since either $t' = t_2'$ or $t' = \xi t_2'$, follows now that $t' \leq v$. But then, $t\sigma t' \leq u\sigma v$, since $t \leq u$ by (On the other hand, from (2), (4) and (5), $|t\sigma t'| = q+1+q' \leq m$; sinc $u\sigma v \;{}_{m}{\sim}\; u\xi w$, it follows that $t\sigma t' \leq u\xi w$. This is impossible, since $t\sigma \not\leq u$ by (2), $\sigma t' \not\leq \xi w$ by (4), and $\sigma \neq \xi$ by hipothesis. Thus $q' > p'$. By a similar argument, one proves that $p' > q'$, a contradiction which shows that (5) is untenable, which in turn establishes the lemma. □

Before proceeding, we need a definition. For x and y i Σ^*, define $x\, R_m\, y$ (x m-reduces to y) iff $x \;{}_{m}{\sim}\; y$, and there exis and v in Σ^*, and σ in Σ, such that $x = u\sigma v$ and $y = uv$. Le R_m^* denote the reflexive and transitive closure of R_m, and let R_m^{-1} and R_m^{*-1} denote the inverse of R_m and R_m^*, respectively. In vie of Lemma 1(c), it is easy to see, that $z\, R_m^*\, x$ iff $x \leq z$ and $x \;{}_{m}{\sim}$

<u>Lemma 6</u>. For every x and y in Σ^*, $x \;{}_{m}{\sim}\; y$ iff there exists a in Σ^*, such that $z\, R_m^*\, x$ and $z\, R_m^*\, y$.

<u>Proof</u>. We proceed by induction on $|x| + |y| - 2|u|$, where u is longest common prefix of x and y. If $|x| + |y| - 2|u| = 0$, the $x = y = u$, and $z = u$ satisfies the proposition. Let then v' an w' be such that $x = uv'$ and $y = uw'$, with $v'w' \neq \lambda$.

If $v' = \lambda$, then $x \leq y$, and since $x \,{}_m\!\sim y$, it follows that $y\, R_m^* \,x$. Thus $z = y$ satisfies the lemma. If $w' = \lambda$, a similar argument holds. Assume therefore that $v' \neq \lambda$ and $w' \neq \lambda$; then, from the choice of u, there exist σ and ξ in Σ, such that $\sigma \neq \xi$, and $x = u\sigma v$ and $y = u\xi w$, for some v and w in Σ^*. By Lemma 5, either $u\sigma\xi w \,{}_m\!\sim u\sigma v$, or $u\xi\sigma v \,{}_m\!\sim u\xi w$. If $u\sigma\xi w \,{}_m\!\sim u\sigma v$, then, since $u\sigma v \,{}_m\!\sim u\xi w$, $u\sigma\xi w \,{}_m\!\sim u\xi w$, hence $u\sigma\xi w \,R_m\, u\xi w = y$. On the other hand, letting u' be the longest common prefix of $u\sigma\xi w$ and $u\sigma v$, we have $|u\sigma\xi w| + |u\sigma v| - 2|u'| \leq$ $\leq |\xi w| + |v| < |\xi w| + |\sigma v| = |x| + |y| - 2|u|$. Thus, by the induction hypothesis there exists a z, such that $z\, R_m^*\, u\sigma v = x$ and $z\, R_m^*\, u\sigma\xi w$. Since $u\sigma\xi w\, R_m\, u\xi w = y$, it follows that $z\, R_m^*\, y$. A similar argument holds if $u\xi\sigma v \,{}_m\!\sim u\xi w$. □

<u>Corollary 6a (Characterization of ${}_m\!\sim$)</u>. For every x and y in Σ^*, $x \,{}_m\!\sim y$ iff $x\, (R_m^{*-1} \circ R_m^*)\, y$ iff $x\, (R_m \cup R_m^{-1})^*\, y$.

<u>Proof</u>. Follows immediately from Lemma 6. □

3. The main result

In this section, we derive the main result , using the lemmas in section 2.

<u>Lemma 7</u>. Let $E \subseteq \Sigma^*$ be a piecewise testable event, and let M be its syntactic monoid. Then M is a finite $\mathcal{J}$-trivial monoid.

<u>Proof</u>. Let m be a natural, such that, for every x and y in Σ^*, $x \,{}_m\!\sim y$ implies that $x \in E$ iff $y \in E$. Since ${}_m\!\sim$ is a congruence relation (Lemma 1(a)), it follows that $x \,{}_m\!\sim y$ implies $x \equiv y \pmod E$. Thus, since ${}_m\!\sim$ is of finite index (Lemma 1(a)), so is $\equiv \pmod E$, i.e. M is a finite monoid. Let $\gamma : \Sigma^* \to M$ be the natural epimorphism defined by $\equiv \pmod E$. Assume now, that for some a and b in M, $a \,\mathcal{J}\, b$, i.e. there exist c_1, d_1, c_2 and d_2 in M, such that $a = c_1 b d_1$ and $b = c_2 a d_2$. We claim that $a = b$. Indeed, $a = (c_1 c_2)^m a (d_2 d_1)^m$. Let y_1 and y_2 in Σ^* be such that $y_i \gamma = d_i$, then by Corollary 3a, $(y_2 y_1)^m \,{}_m\!\sim (y_2 y_1)^m y_2$, and since this implies that $(y_2 y_1)^m \equiv$ $\equiv (y_2 y_1)^m y_2 \pmod E$, it follows that $(d_2 d_1)^m = (d_2 d_1)^m d_2$, i.e. $a = a d_2$. By a dual argument, $a = c_2 a$, hence $b = c_2 a d_2 = a$. Thus, M is a $\mathcal{J}$-trivial monoid. □

<u>Lemma 8</u>. Let M be a finite $\mathcal{J}$-trivial monoid, and let $\gamma : \Sigma^* \to M$ be

an epimorphism. Then for every subset X of M, $X\gamma^{-1}$ is a piecewise testable event.

Proof. It is sufficient to prove that there exists an m, such that for all x and y in Σ^*, $x \,{}_m\!\sim y$ implies $x\gamma = y\gamma$. Let k be the cardinality of M, and let $m = 2k$. First we show that if u in Σ^+ and σ in Σ are such that $u \,{}_k\!\sim u\sigma$, then $u\gamma = (u\sigma)\gamma$. Indeed, by Lemma 3, there exist $u_1, u_2, \ldots, u_k$ in Σ^+, such that $u = u_1 u_2 \ldots u_k$ and $u_1\Sigma \supseteq u_2\Sigma \supseteq \ldots \supseteq u_k\Sigma \supseteq \{\sigma\}$. Let $w_0 = \lambda$, $w_1 = u_1$, $w_2 = u_1u_2$, ... $w_k = u_1u_2\ldots u_k = u$. Since M has k elements only, there exist $i <$ j such that $w_i\gamma = w_j\gamma$. Now we claim that for all ξ in $u_{i+1}\Sigma$, $w_i\gamma = (w_i\xi)\gamma$. Indeed, if $\xi \in u_{i+1}\Sigma$, then $u_{i+1} = z_1\xi z_2$ for some z_1 and z_2 in Σ^*. Since each element in the sequence w_i, w_iz_1, $w_iz_1\xi$, w_j is a prefix of its successor, it follows that $M(w_j\gamma)M \subseteq M(w_iz_1\xi\gamma)M \subseteq M(w_iz_1\gamma)M \subseteq M(w_i\gamma)M$. Since $w_i\gamma = w_j\gamma$, it follows that all sets in the chain are equal, and since M is $\mathcal{J}$-trivial, this implies that $w_i\gamma = w_iz_1\gamma = w_iz_1\xi\gamma$. It follows that $w_i\gamma = w_i\xi\gamma$. Then, since $(u_{i+1}\ldots u_k\sigma)\Sigma = u_{i+1}\Sigma$, it follows that $u\gamma = (u\sigma)\gamma$. By a dual argument, if v in Σ^+ and σ in Σ are such that $v \,{}_k\!\sim \sigma v$, then $v\gamma = (\sigma v)\gamma$. Consider now u and v in Σ^* and σ in Σ, such that $u\sigma v \,{}_m\!\sim uv$. By Lemma 4, there exist p and p', such that $p+p' \geq m$, $u \,{}_p\!\sim u\sigma$ and $v \,{}_{p'}\!\sim \sigma v$. Since $m = 2k$, either $p \geq k$ or $p' \geq k$, hence by Lemma 1(b), either $u \,{}_k\!\sim u\sigma$ or $v \,{}_k\!\sim \sigma v$. Thus, either $u\gamma = (u\sigma)\gamma$ or $v\gamma = (\sigma v)\gamma$; in either case $(u\sigma v)\gamma = (uv)\gamma$. But this implies that for all x and y, $x \, R_m \, y$ implies $x\gamma = y\gamma$, hence by Lemma for all x and y, $x \,{}_m\!\sim y$ implies $x\gamma = y\gamma$. This completes the proof.

Thus we have:

Theorem. An event E is piecewise testable iff its syntactic monoid is finite and $\mathcal{J}$-trivial.

Proof. Immediate from Lemmas 7 and 8. □

4. Other characterizations of piecewise testable events

In this section we indicate other characterizations of piecewise testable events. Proofs and further details can be found in [9]. Our notation on automata follows [4].

First we need a few definitions. Let $\mathcal{C}$ be the smallest family of events which contains $\Sigma^*\sigma\Sigma^*$ for every σ in Σ, and is closed under concatenation. Let D be the smallest family of events which contains C and is closed under the Boolean operations.

Let $A = (Q,\Sigma,M)$ be a semiautomaton. A is a *chain-reset*, iff there exists a linear ordering $q_0,q_1,\ldots,q_m$ of Q, such that for all $q_i \in Q - \{q_m\}$, and for all $\sigma \in \Sigma$, $q_i\sigma^A$ is either q_i or q_{i+1}, and $q_m\sigma^A = q_m$ for all $\sigma \in \Sigma$. A is *partially ordered* iff for all q in Q and for all x and y in Σ^*, $q(xy)^A = q$ implies $qx^A = q$. A *component* of A is a minimal nonempty subset P of Q, such that for all $q \in Q$ and for all $\sigma \in \Sigma$, $q\sigma^A \in P$ iff $q \in P$. Let θ be a nonempty subset of Σ. The *restriction of* A *to* θ is the semiautomaton $A|\theta = (Q,\theta,N)$, where $\sigma^{A|\theta} = \sigma^A$ for all $\sigma \in \theta$. A *dead state* of A is a state $q \in Q$ such that for all $\sigma \in \Sigma$ $q\sigma^A = q$.

Now we have

__Theorem__. Let $E \subseteq \Sigma^*$ be a regular event, let E^T be the reverse of E, let $\hat{A}$ and $\hat{B}$ be the reduced automata accepting E and E^T respectively, and let M be the syntactic monoid of E. The following are equivalent:

(a) E is piecewise testable.

(b) E is in D.

(c) A can be covered by a direct product of chain-resets.

(d) A and B are both partially ordered.

(e) A is partially ordered, and for all $q \in Q$ and for all $x,y \in \Sigma^*$, $qx^A = q(xx)^A = q(xy)^A$ and $qy^A = q(yy)^A = q(yx)^A$ imply $qx^A = qy^A$.

(f) A is partially ordered and for every nonempty subset θ of Σ, each component of $A|\theta$ contains exactly one dead state of $A|\theta$.

(g) M is J-trivial.

It is relatively simple to show the equivalence of (a), (b) and c), and that of (d), (e), (f) and (g). The most difficult part in the roof of this theorem is to show that one of (d) to (g) implies one of a) to (c). In the previous section we proved that (g) implies (a). nother possibility would be to give a proof of (g) implies (b) (or ven more interesting would be (f) implies (b)) by constructing regular xpressions, of the form required to show that an event is in D, which ould denote each congruence class of $\equiv$ (mod E) (denote the event ccepted by each state of A, respectively). Such a construction has een carried out by Schützenberger in [8], constructing star-free regular expressions for events whose syntactic monoid is group-free. Unfortunately, his proof, when applied to $\mathcal{J}$-trivial monoids, does not produce expressions in D. We have been unable to carry out such a proof, unless in the very simple case of idempotent and commutative monoids.

Acknowledgment. I am indebted to Professor J.A. Brzozowski for introducing me to the fascinating world of star-free regular events.

5. References.

[1] J.A. Brzozowski and Imre Simon, Characterizations of Locally Testable Events, Discrete Mathematics 4 (1973), 243-271.

[2] A.H. Clifford and G.B. Preston, "The Algebraic Theory of Semigroups" vol. I, Mathematical Surveys nº 7, American Mathematical Society, Providence, RI, 1961.

[3] R. Cohen and J.A. Brzozowski, Dot-Depth of Star-Free Events, J. of Computer and System Sciences 5 (1971), 1-16.

[4] A. Ginzburg, "Algebraic Theory of Automata", Academic Press, New York, 1968.

[5] L.H. Haines, On Free Monoids Partially Ordered by Embedding, J. of Combinatorial Theory 6 (1969), 94-98.

[6] R. McNaughton, Algebraic Decision Procedures for Local Testabili Mathematical Systems Theory 8 (1974), 60-76.

[7] R. McNaughton and S. Papert, "Counter Free Automata", The MIT Pr Cambridge, Mass., 1971.

[8] M.P. Schützenberger, On Finite Monoids Having Only Trivial Subgr Information and Control 8 (1965), 190-194.

[9] Imre Simon, Hierarchies of Events with Dot-Depth One, Research Report CSRR 2070, Department of Applied Analysis and Computer Science, University of Waterloo, Ont., Canada, 1972.

[10] G. Thierrin, Convex Languages, in M. Nivat (ed.), "Automata, Languages and Programming", North-Holland, Amsterdam, 1973, 481-

[11] Y. Zalcstein, Locally Testable Languages, J. of Computer and Sys Sciences 6 (1972) 151-167.

São Paulo, April 28, 1975.

DIE GRÖSSE DES ZUSTANDSMINIMALEN LR(0)-ANALYSATORS

R.Kemp,Universität des Saarlandes,Saarbrücken

Die Analyse eines Wortes w,welches mittels einer LR(k)-Grammatik G (/6/) erzeugbar ist,läßt sich bekanntlich in linearer Zeit mittels eines deterministischen "push-down-transducer" DPDT(a) (LR(k)-Analysator) durchführen,dessen Schaltwerk ein endlicher Automat a (LR(k)-Automat) ist,welcher die Menge aller Anfangswörter bis zur ersten Reduktion (Handle) und die folgenden k Terminalzeichen erkennt. Dabei treten die Endzustände (Reduce-Zustände) im LR(k)-Automaten getrennt auf,d.h.es fallen keine Endzustände in Zwischenzustände (Shift-Zustände) und keine Endzustände zusammen.Im allgemeinen geht allerdings die rasche Analysezeit auf Kosten aufwendiger Analysatoren,d.h. die Zustandsmenge des LR(k)-Automaten wird sehr groß.(vergl./3/).Aus diesem Grund ist man an Verfahren interessiert,welche die Zustandsmenge vermindern,ohne auf eine korrekte Fehlererkennung bei der Analyse zu verzichten.

n der vorliegenden Arbeit werden zunächst zwei Typen von LR(k)-Autoaten definiert: Der "A-minimale LR(k)-Automat" und der "$\mathfrak{z}$-minimale R(k)-Automat".Beide definieren einen LR(k)-Analysator,welcher genau ie von der gegebenen LR(k)-Grammatik G erzeugte Sprache $\mathcal{L}(G)$ analyiert.Der A-minimale LR(k)-Analysator,welcher als Schaltwerk den A-miimalen LR(k)-Automaten besitzt,hat die Eigenschaft,daß die Entscheiung,ob das Wort in der erzeugten Sprache liegt oder nicht,in kürzester eit getroffen wird.Der $\mathfrak{z}$-minimale LR(k)-Analysator mit dem $\mathfrak{z}$-minimaen LR(k)-Automaten als Schaltwerk trifft die gleiche Entscheidung,alerdings mit stärkerer Verzögerung , besitzt dagegen aber die geringste nzahl von Zuständen unter allen Analysatoren,in deren Schaltwerk die ndzustände getrennt auftreten und die zu vorgegebenem Wort aus der prache $\mathcal{L}(G)$ den zugehörigen Ableitungsbaum bzgl.G liefern.Dabei arbeiten beide Analysatoren auf Wörtern der Sprache gleich schnell.Im esentlichen stellt sich die Konstruktion des $\mathfrak{z}$-minimalen LR(k)-Autoten aus dem A-minimalen LR(k)-Automaten als Minimierung spezieller rtieller endlicher Automaten dar.Als bemerkenswertes Ergebnis erhält n,daß i.a.auch die Mächtigkeit der Zustandsmenge des $\mathfrak{z}$-minimalen (0)-Automaten exponentiell mit der Mächtigkeit des Hilfsalphabetes r gegebenen LR(0)-Grammatik wächst.

1. NOTATIONEN - DEFINITIONEN

Definition 1

Ein 4-tupel $G=(I,T,P,\sigma)$ heißt kontextfreie Grammatik (CFG) über dem Hilfsalphabet I, dem Endalphabet T, mit dem Produktionssystem P und dem Axiom σ ($\notin I$). Jede Regel $f_i \in P, 1 \leqslant i \leqslant \#P$, ist von der Gestalt:

$$f_i : Q(f_i) \longrightarrow Z(f_i)$$

mit $Q(f_1)=\sigma, Q(f_j) \in I, Z(f_i) \in (I \cup T)^*, 1 \leqslant i \leqslant \#P, j \geqslant 2$. $Q(f)$ heißt Quelle de Regel f und $Z(f)$ heißt Ziel der Regel f.

Bemerkung 1

Wie in /1/ beschrieben, läßt sich jeder CFG eine freie X-Kategorie $\mathcal{F}(P,I\cup T)$ mit der Morphismenmenge $MOR(\mathcal{F}(P,I\cup T))$ und dem freien Erzeuge densystem P zuordnen. Jedem aus dem Axiom σ mittels der $f \in P$ ableitba ren Wort w entspricht damit ein Morphismus $g \in MOR(\mathcal{F}(P,I\cup T))$ mit $Q(g)=$ und $Z(g)=w$, wobei $Q(g)$ bzw. $Z(g)$ Quelle und Ziel von g darstellen.

Definition 2

Ist $G=(I,T,P,\sigma)$ eine CFG, dann ist

$$\mathcal{T}(G) := \left\{ w \in (I\cup T)^* \,\middle|\, (\exists g \in MOR(\mathcal{F}(P,I\cup T)))(Q(g)=\sigma \wedge Z(g)=w \right\}$$

die Menge aller aus dem Axiom σ ableitbaren Satzformen. Die Menge $\mathcal{L}(G) := \mathcal{T}(G) \cap T^*$ ist die von der CFG erzeugte kontextfreie Sprache

Definition 3

Eine CFG $G=(I,T,P,\sigma)$ heißt chomskyreduziert (CCFG), falls gilt:

(i) $(\forall A \in I)(\exists f \in P)(Q(f)=A \wedge Z(f) \in T^*)$

(ii) $(\forall A \in I)(\exists g \in MOR(\mathcal{F}(P,I\cup T)) \wedge \exists u,v \in (I\cup T)^*)(Q(g)=\sigma \wedge Z(g)=uA$

Definition 4

Ist $G=(I,T,P,\sigma)$ eine CCFG und $g \in MOR(\mathcal{F}(P,I\cup T))$, dann heißt

$$g=(1_{u_m} \times f_m \times 1_{v_m}) \circ \ldots \circ (1_{u_1} \times f_1 \times 1_{v_1})$$

mit $u_i, v_i \in (I \cup T)^*, f_i \in P, 1 \leqslant i \leqslant m$, sequentielle Darstellung von g. Bes g genau eine sequentielle Darstellung, dann ist g total unzerlegbar. sequentielle Darstellung heißt antikanonisch, wenn $l(v_i) < l(v_{i+1})+1$, $1 \leqslant i \leqslant m-1$, gilt. Dabei ist $l(w)$ die Länge des Wortes w. Wenn es zu g e antikanonische Darstellung obiger Form mit $Q(g)=\sigma$ gibt, dann heißt $(1_{u_m} \times f_m \times 1_{v_m})$ H-Faktor von g.

Definition 5

Ist $G=(I,T,P,\sigma)$ eine CCFG, dann sei mit $f \in P$ die Menge $R(f)$ wie fol definiert:

$$R(f) := \{ wZ(f) \mid (\exists v \in (I \cup T)^* \wedge \exists g \in MOR(\mathfrak{F}(P, I \cup T))(Q(g) = \sigma \wedge g \text{ total unzerlegbar} \wedge (1_w \times f \times 1_v) \text{ H-Faktor von } g) \}$$

Die Menge R(p) mit

$$R(P) := \bigcup_{f \in P} R(f)$$

heißt Menge der <u>regulären Anfangswörter</u>.

<u>Definition 6</u>

Ein <u>endlicher Automat</u> (EA) ist ein 7-tupel $a=(\mathcal{E}, \mathcal{J}, \mathcal{F}, \alpha, \mathcal{O}, \delta, \lambda)$ mit

(i) $\mathcal{E}, \mathcal{J}, \mathcal{F}, \mathcal{O}$ sind endliche Mengen (<u>Eingabezeichen</u>, <u>Zwischenzustände</u>, <u>Endzustände</u>, <u>Ausgabezeichen</u>)

(ii) $\delta : \mathfrak{D} \longrightarrow (\mathcal{J} \cup \mathcal{F}), \mathfrak{D} \subseteq (\mathcal{J} \cup \mathcal{F}) \times \mathcal{E}$ (<u>Überführungsfunktion</u>)

(iii) $\lambda : \mathcal{H} \longrightarrow \mathcal{O}, \mathcal{H} \subseteq (\mathcal{J} \cup \mathcal{F}) \times \mathcal{E}$ (<u>Ausgabefunktion</u>)

(iv) $\alpha \in \mathcal{J}$ (<u>Startzustand</u>)

Ein EA a heißt

<u>deterministisch</u> (DEA) $\Longleftrightarrow (\forall (s,x) \in \mathfrak{D})(\# \delta(s,x) \leq 1)$

<u>vollständig</u> (VEA) $\Longleftrightarrow \mathfrak{D} = \mathcal{H} = (\mathcal{J} \cup \mathcal{F}) \times \mathcal{E}$

<u>streng partiell</u> (SPEA) $\Longleftrightarrow \mathfrak{D} = \mathcal{H}$

<u>Bemerkung 2</u>

Ist a ein deterministischer VEA, dann bezeichnen wir mit $\delta(\alpha, w)$ den Zustand, in den man durch Lesen des Wortes w vom Startzustand α aus gelangt.

DER $\mathcal{G}$-MINIMALE LR(O)-ANALYSATOR

Bei der Analyse eines Wortes w, welches mittels einer LR(O)-Grammatik G erzeugbar ist, liest man das Wort von <u>l</u>inks nach <u>r</u>echts und die Entscheidung, ob an der gerade gelesenen Stelle eine Reduktion f, d.h. eine Ersetzung von Z(f) durch Q(f), vorzunehmen ist oder nicht, kann eindeutig aus dem bereits gelesenen Teilwort getroffen werden. Da in der Menge der regulären Anfangswörter (1.Def.5) alle Anfangswörter bis zur ersten Reduktion aufgelistet sind, genügt bei der Analyse eines Wortes w die Kenntnis der Menge R(P). In /1/ wurde gezeigt, daß die Menge R(P) für jede CCFG als homomorphes Bild eines Standardereignisses regulär ist und damit von einem endlichen Automaten A erkannt wird. In /2/ wurde die Berechnung der Überführungsfunktion δ dieses deterministischen VEA (DVEA) $A=(I \cup T, \mathcal{J}, \{ⓕ \mid f \in P\}, \alpha, P \cup \{1, s\}, \delta, \lambda)$ effizient gestaltet und darüberhinaus gezeigt, daß dieser VEA im automatentheoretischen Sinne reduziert und damit minimal ist. Ist $w=uxv \in (I \cup T)^*$, $uv \in (I \cup T)^*$, $x \in (I \cup T)$, dann gilt für die Überführungsfunktion δ und die Ausgabefunktion λ:

$$\delta : (\mathcal{S} \cup \mathcal{F}) \times (I \cup T) \longrightarrow \mathcal{S} \cup \mathcal{F}$$

$$\delta(Z,x) = \begin{cases} ⓕ & \text{falls } ux \in R(f), f \in P \\ Z' & \text{falls } (\exists y \in (I \cup T)^*)(uxy \in R(P)) \\ q & \text{sonst} \end{cases}$$

und

$$\lambda : (\mathcal{S} \cup \mathcal{F}) \times (I \cup T) \longrightarrow P \cup \{1,s\}$$

$$\lambda(Z,x) = \begin{cases} f & \text{falls } \delta(Z,x) = ⓕ \\ 1 & \text{falls } \delta(Z,x) \in \mathcal{S} \setminus \{q\} \\ s & \text{falls } \delta(Z,x) = q \end{cases}$$

Dabei ist q ein ausgezeichneter Zustand,in den man im Falle $w \notin \mathfrak{T}(G)$ gelangt.

Der Automat A besitzt bei vorliegender LR(0)-Grammatik die Eigenscha daß keine Endzustände zusammen- und keine Endzustände in Zwischenzustände fallen.Die Aequivalenz dieser Aussage mit dem Vorliegen einer LR(0)-Grammatik ist in /1/,/2/ gezeigt und gibt Anlaß zu folgender

Definition 7

Eine CCFG ist genau dann vom Typ LR(0),wenn für alle $f,f' \in P, f \neq f'$ gilt

(i) $R(f) \cdot T^* \cap R(f') = \emptyset$ und (ii) $R(f) \cdot T^+ \cap R(f) = \emptyset$

Es gilt der in /5a/ bewiesene

SATZ 1

Ist G eine CCFG vom Typ LR(0),dann meldet der Analysator DPDT(A) mi dem endlichen Automaten A als Schaltwerk bei dem Eingabewort w gena dann einen Analyseabbruch,wenn w ein Anfangswort w_1 besitzt,zu dem ne Verlängerung v zu einem aus $\mathfrak{S}$ ableitbaren Wort existiert.

Damit besitzt der DPDT(A) die Eigenschaft,daß er zum frühest möglic Zeitpunkt die Analyse abbricht.Wir bezeichnen ihn als A-minimalen LR(0)-Analysator der Sprache $\mathcal{L}(G)$.(Analysezeitminimal).Der Automat heißt A-minimaler LR(0)-Automat.

3. REGULÄRE LR(0)-ÜBERDECKUNGEN

Definition 8

Ist $G=(I,T,P,\mathfrak{S})$ eine CCFG vom Typ LR(0) und A der zugehörige A-min le LR(0)-Automat,welcher die reguläre Menge R(P) erkennt,dann heiß jedes Mengensystem $\hat{R}(P) := \{\hat{R}(f) \mid f \in P\}$ vermöge

(i) $(\forall f \in P)(\hat{R}(f)$ regulär) (iii) $(\forall f \in P)(R(f) \subseteq \hat{R}(f) \subseteq (I \cup T)^*$

(ii) $(\forall f \in P)(\hat{R}(f) \cdot T^+ \cap \hat{R}(f) = \emptyset)$ (iv) $(\forall f,f' \in P)(f \neq f' \Rightarrow \hat{R}(f') \cdot T^* \cap \hat{R}(f$

reguläre LR(0)-Überdeckung von R(P).

Es gilt der in /5a/ bewiesene

SATZ 2

Ist $G=(I,T,P,\sigma)$ eine CCFG vom Typ LR(0) und $\hat{R}(P)$ eine reguläre LR(0)-Überdeckung von R(P), welche von dem DEA $\hat{A}=(I\cup T,\hat{\mathcal{f}},\mathcal{F},\hat{\alpha},P\cup\{1,s\},\hat{\delta},\hat{\lambda})$ erkannt wird, dann stellt jeder DPDT($\hat{A}$) ein Analysator der Sprache $\mathcal{L}(G)$ dar.

●

Bemerkung 3

Liefert der A-minimale LR(0)-Automat A eine Reduktion f, dann ist diese auch anwendbar, d.h. der Automat gelangte durch Lesen von Z(f) in den Endzustand ⓕ. Liefert dagegen der Automat $\hat{A}$ eine Reduktion f, dann muß diese nicht notwendigerweise anwendbar sein, da $\hat{A}$ u.U. nur durch Lesen eines Endwortes von Z(f) in den Endzustand ⓕ gelangte. Aus diesem Grund müssen die zu löschenden Kellerzeichen bei einer Ausführung einer Reduktion f mittels des DPDT($\hat{A}$) mit den entsprechenden Zeichen in Z(f) auf Übereinstimmung verglichen werden.

. DER $\mathcal{J}$-MINIMALE LR(0)-ANALYSATOR

Ist A der A-minimale LR(0)-Analysator bzgl. der LR(0)-Grammatik G und $\hat{A}$ ein EA, welcher eine reguläre LR(0)-Überdeckung $\hat{R}(P)$ erkennt, dann bezeichnen wir mit A_p bzw. $\hat{A}_p$ diejenigen SPEA, welche durch Elimination des ausgezeichneten Zustandes q aus A bzw. $\hat{A}$ entstehen, d.h. z.B.

$$A_p = (I\cup T, \mathcal{f}\setminus\{q\}, \mathcal{F}, \alpha, P\cup\{1\}, \delta/(\mathcal{f}\setminus\{q\})x(I\cup T), \lambda/(\mathcal{f}\setminus\{q\})x(I\cup T))$$

Falls keine Verwechslungen auftreten, setzen wir künftig wieder:

$A_p = (I\cup T, \mathcal{f}, \mathcal{F}, \alpha, P\cup\{1\}, \delta, \lambda)$ und $\hat{A}_p = (I\cup T, \hat{\mathcal{f}}, \mathcal{F}, \hat{\alpha}, P\cup\{1\}, \hat{\delta}, \hat{\lambda})$

Es gilt der in /5a/ gezeigte

SATZ 3

Es existiert i.a. kein Automatenhomomorphismus Φ mit

(i) $\Phi(A) = \hat{A}$ bzw. (ii) $\Phi(A_p) = \hat{A}_p$

Die Menge aller regulärer LR(0)-Überdeckungen von R(P) bezeichnen wir mit $\hat{\mathcal{R}}(P)$. $\hat{\mathcal{A}}(P)$ ist die Menge aller EA $\hat{A}_p$, welche $\hat{R}(P) \in \hat{\mathcal{R}}(P)$ erkennen. Wir geben nun die

●

Definition 9

Ist $G=(I,T,P,\sigma)$ eine CCFG vom Typ LR(0), dann heißt ein Analysator DPDT($\bar{A}_p$) vermöge

$$\#\bar{\mathcal{f}} = \underset{\hat{A}_p \in \hat{\mathcal{A}}(P)}{\mathrm{MIN}} \#\hat{\mathcal{f}}$$

$\mathcal{J}$-minimaler LR(0)-Analysator. (Zustandsminimal). Der Automat $\bar{A}_p$ heißt $\mathcal{J}$-minimaler LR(0)-Automat.

Wie man leicht einsieht, erhält man jeden EA $\hat{A}_p \in \hat{\mathfrak{A}}(P)$ aus A_p durch geeig nete Identifikation von Zuständen. Es dürfen solche Zustände $z,z' \in \mathcal{S}$ nicht identifiziert werden, für die gilt:

$$(\exists v \in (I \cup T)^*)(\delta(\eta,v) = (f) \wedge \delta(\xi,v) \in (\mathcal{S} \cup \mathcal{F}) \setminus \{(f)\}), \quad \eta,\xi \in \{z,z'\}, \quad \eta \neq \xi$$

da ansonsten der Endzustand (f) in einen Zwischenzustand oder einen (f) verschiedenen Endzustand fallen würde. Zustände, welche nicht iden fizierbar sind, d.h. der angegebenen Bedingung genügen, bezeichnen wir künftig als <u>inkompatibel</u> (ansonsten: <u>kompatibel</u>). Ein Minimierungsalgo rithmus zur Konstruktion des $\mathfrak{z}$-minimalen Analysators $\bar{A}_p$ ist in /5b/ a gegeben.

5. DIE GRÖSSE DES $\mathfrak{z}$-MINIMALEN LR(0)-ANALYSATORS $\bar{A}_p$

Wir wollen nun einige Aussagen über die Mächtigkeit der Zustandsmeng $\bar{\mathcal{S}} \cup \mathcal{F}$ machen. Hierzu geben wir die

<u>Definition 10</u>

Ist $G=(I,T,P,\sigma)$ eine CCFG, dann ist

$$F(f,X) := \{ f \in P \mid Z(f) \in (I \cup T)^* X, X \in (I \cup T) \}$$

die Menge der <u>X-finalen Regeln</u> und

$$M(f,X) := \{ f \in P \mid Z(f) \in (I \cup T)^* \cdot X \cdot (I \cup T)^+ \wedge (\exists g \in P)(g \in F(f,X$$

die Menge des <u>X-medialen Regeln.</u>

Es gilt der

SATZ 4

Ist $G=(I,T,P,\sigma)$ eine CCFG vom Typ LR(0), dann gilt für die Mächtigke der Zustandsmenge $\bar{\mathcal{S}} \cup \mathcal{F}$ eines $\mathfrak{z}$-minimalen LR(0)-Automaten $\bar{A}_p$:

$$\#(\mathcal{S} \cup \mathcal{F}) \geq \#P + \underset{x \in (I \cup T)}{MAX} \left(\# F(f,X) - \delta_{0,\#M(f,X)} + 1 \right)$$

Dabei ist $\delta_{i,k}$ das "Kronecker Symbol".

<u>Beweisskizze</u>:

Betrachte im A-minimalen LR(0)-Automaten A_p alle Zustände, in die man durch Lesen eines $X \in (I \cup T)$ gelangt. Seien diese o.B.d.A. $(f_1), \dots, (f_k)$, s.., s_m mit $(f_i) \in \mathcal{F}$ und $s_j \in \mathcal{S}$, $1 \leq i \leq k$, $1 \leq j \leq m$. Es gilt:

a) Jedes $(f_i) \in \mathcal{F}$ rührt von einer X-finalen Regel

b) Jedes $s_j \in \mathcal{S}$ rührt von einer X-medialen Regel

Für jedes $(f_i) \in \mathcal{F}$ muß im Automaten $\bar{A}_p$ mindestens ein Zwischenzustand $\bar{z}_i \in \bar{\mathcal{S}}$ mit $\bar{\delta}(\bar{z}_i,X) = (f_i)$ existieren, d.h. mindestens $\# F(f,X)$ Zuständ Ungünstigenfalls sind die Zustände $s_j \in \mathcal{S}$ paarweise kompatibel und den in $\bar{A}_p$ zu einem Zustand $\bar{s} \in \bar{\mathcal{S}}$ identifiziert, was einen weiteren Zu stand s mit $\bar{\delta}(s,X) = \bar{s}$ erfordert. Damit folgt unmittelbar die Behaup

Eine unmittelbare Folgerung von SATZ 4 ist das

KOROLLAR

Ist $G=(I,T,P,\sigma)$ eine CCFG vom Typ LR(0) und endet jedes $Z(f), f \in P$, mit einem anderen Buchstaben $X \in (I \cup T)$, welcher nicht als Teilwort eines $Z(f'), f' \in P$, auftritt, dann gilt:

$$\# \mathcal{S} \cup \mathcal{F} \geq \# P + 1$$

●

Definition 11

Sei $G=(I,T,P,\sigma)$ eine CCFG und $\varphi \in \mathcal{P}(I)$ eine Hilfsalphabetkombination (HK). Wir definieren folgende Mengen:

$\{f\}_A := \{f \in P \mid Q(f)=A\}$ Bezeichnung: Regelpaket (RP)

$\{f\}_\varphi := \bigsqcup_{A \in \varphi} \{f\}_A$ Bezeichnung: Regelpaketkombination (RPK)

$V_A := \{w \in (I \cup T)^+ \mid (\exists f \in \{f\}_A)(Z(f)=wu \wedge u \in (I \cup T)^*)\}$ Bezeichnung: Zielmenge (ZM)

$V_\varphi := \bigcap_{A \in \varphi} V_A$ Bezeichnung: Zielmenge der Regelpaketkombination $\{f\}_\varphi$ (ZMRPK)

Wie in /2/,/3/ gezeigt, werden bei der Konstruktion des A-minimalen LR(0)-Automaten sukzessive HK erzeugt, deren Gesamtheit wir mit $\mathbb{T}$ bezeichnen. Jedes $\varphi \in \mathbb{T}$ erzeugt gerade $\# V_\varphi$ Zustände. Mit $i \in \mathbb{N}$ sei

$$\mathbb{T}_i := \{\varphi \in \mathbb{T} \mid \# \varphi = i\}$$

Es gilt nun der /3/,/5b/ bewiesene

SATZ 5

Ist $G=(I,T,P,\sigma)$ eine CCFG vom Typ LR(0), dann gilt für die Zustandsmenge $\mathcal{S} \cup \mathcal{F}$ des A-minimalen LR(0)-Automaten $\underset{P}{A}$:

$$\# \mathcal{S} \cup \mathcal{F} = 1 + \sum_{\varphi \in \mathbb{T}} \# V_\varphi + \sum_{A \in I \setminus \mathbb{T}_1} \Big[\# V_A - \# \bigsqcup_{\varphi \in \mathcal{H}_A} V_\varphi \Big] \leq$$

$$\leq 1 + \sum_{A \in I} \# V_A + \sum_{i=1}^{m} \# \varphi(x_i) \leq 1 + \sum_{A \in I} \# V_A + m \cdot (2^{\# I - 1} - \# I)$$

mit $\mathcal{H}_A := (\mathbb{T} \setminus \mathbb{T}_1) \cap (\mathcal{P}(I) \setminus \mathcal{P}(I \setminus \{A\}))$, $\varphi(x_i) := \{\varphi \in \mathbb{T} \setminus \mathbb{T}_1 \mid x_i \in V_\varphi\}$, $1 \leq i \leq m$

$$\bigsqcup_{\varphi \in \mathbb{T} \setminus \mathbb{T}_1} V_\varphi := \{x_i \mid 1 \leq i \leq m\}$$

●

Definition 12

Ist M eine endliche Menge und $N \subseteq \mathcal{P}(M)$ mit

(i) $(\forall \varphi, \varphi' \in N)(\varphi \nsubseteq \varphi' \wedge \varphi' \nsubseteq \varphi)$

(ii) $(\forall \varphi, \varphi' \in N)(\exists \{A,B\})(\forall \varphi'' \in N)(A \in \varphi \setminus \varphi' \wedge B \in \varphi' \setminus \varphi \wedge \{A,B\} \nsubseteq \varphi'')$

dann heißt N reduziertes Spernersystem (RSS). Ist nur (i) erfüllt, dann bezeichnen wir N in Anlehnung an /7/ als Spernersystem (SS).

Mit

$$\Theta_{RSS} := \{\Phi \subseteq \mathcal{P}(M) \mid \Phi \text{ ist RSS}\}$$

sei

$$F_{RSS}: \mathbb{N} \longrightarrow \mathbb{N}$$

$$F_{RSS}: \# M \longmapsto \underset{\Phi \in \Theta_{RSS}}{MAX} (\# \Phi)$$

Es gilt der

SATZ 6

Ist $G=(I,T,P,\sigma)$ eine CCFG vom Typ LR(0), dann gilt für die Zustandsmenge $\bar{\mathfrak{Z}} \cup \mathfrak{F}$ eines $\mathfrak{Z}$-minimalen LR(0)-Automaten $\bar{A}_P$:

$$\# \bar{\mathfrak{Z}} \cup \mathfrak{F} \leq 1 + \sum_{A \in I} \# V_A + m \cdot F_{RSS}(\# I - 1) \qquad \text{mit } m = \# \bigsqcup_{\varphi \in \Pi \setminus \Pi_1} V_\varphi$$

Beweisskizze:

Nach SATZ 5 gilt: $\# \mathfrak{Z} \cup \mathfrak{F} \leq 1 + \sum_{A \in I} \# V_A + \sum_{i=1}^{m} \# \varphi(x_i)$

Betrachte für ein $i \in [1:m]$ die HK-en $\varphi(x_i) := \{\varphi_1, \varphi_2, \ldots, \varphi_k\}$ d.h. $x_i \in V_{\varphi_j}$, $1 \leq j \leq k$

a) o.B.d.A. sei $\varphi_1 \subseteq \varphi_2 \subseteq \ldots \subseteq \varphi_r$, $r < k$

$$\Longrightarrow (\forall A \in \bigsqcup_{i=1}^{r} V_{\varphi_i})(\exists f \in P)(Q(f)=A \wedge Z(f)=x_i w)$$

Diese Regeln erzeugen im Automaten A_P r verschiedene Zustände. Da $\varphi_i \subseteq \varphi_r$, $1 \leq i \leq r-1$ und $\varphi_r \in \Pi \Longrightarrow$ Die Zustände sind kompatibel und können zu einem Zustand identifiziert werden. Dies gilt für alle Inklusionsketten in $\varphi(x_i)$, so daß $\varphi(x_i)$ höchstens soviele Zustände $\bar{A}_P$ erzeugt, wie SS über I möglich sind.

b) Nach den Identifizierungen in Teil a) ist $\varphi(x_i)$ zu $\psi(x_i)$ mit

$$(\forall \varphi, \varphi' \in \psi(x_i))(\varphi \nsubseteq \varphi' \wedge \varphi' \nsubseteq \varphi)$$

vermindert worden. Existiert in $\psi(x_i)$ eine Teilmenge η mit

$$(\exists \varphi, \varphi' \in \eta)(\forall \{A,B\})(\exists \varphi'' \in \eta)(A \in \varphi \setminus \varphi' \wedge B \in \varphi' \setminus \varphi \wedge \{A,B\} \subseteq \varphi'')$$

dann ist leicht einzusehen, daß die Zustände, welche durch φ, φ' erzeugt werden, kompatibel sind, da jedes $\{A,B\}$ mit $A \in \varphi \setminus \varphi' \wedge B \in \varphi' \setminus \varphi$ in einem $\varphi'' \in \eta$ auftritt. Sukzessive Anwendung dieses Verfahrens ergibt, daß $\varphi(x_i)$ bzgl. des $\mathfrak{Z}$-minimalen Automaten $\bar{A}_P$ höchstens soviel Zustände erzeugt, wie RSS über I möglich sind, d.h. $\psi(x_i)$ wird zu $\rho(x_i)$ mit $\# \rho(x_i) \leq F_{RSS}(\# I - 1)$ vermindert. Damit folgt die Beh. ●

Eine Untersuchung der Funktion F_{RSS} liefert den

SATZ 7

Ist M eine endliche Menge mit $\# M \geq 2$, dann gilt: $F_{RSS}(\# M) > \sqrt{2^{\# M}}$ ●

Bemerkung 4

Ist $G=(I,T,P,\sigma)$ eine CCFG und $\varphi = \{A_1, \ldots, A_s\} \in \mathcal{P}(I)$, dann sei

$$f_i : Q(f_i) \longrightarrow w\varphi = Z(f_i), \quad 1 \leq i \leq s$$

die Menge der Produktionen

$$f_i : Q(f_i) \longrightarrow wA_i \qquad 1 \leq i \leq s$$

Es gilt der

SATZ 8

Die Mächtigkeit der Zustandsmenge des $\mathfrak{Z}$-minimalen Automaten wächst i.a. exponentiell mit der Mächtigkeit des Hilfsalphabetes der zugrunde liegenden CCFG vom Typ LR(0).

Beweisskizze:

(a) Betrachte folgende Grammatikfolge $G_{2n} := (I_{2n}, T_{2n}, P_{2n}, \sigma)$ mit

$I_{2n} := \{A_i \mid 1 \leq i \leq 2n\}$ $\qquad T_{2n} := \{a\} \cup X \cup Y$ mit

$X := \{x_i \mid 1 \leq i \leq 2^n\}$

$Y := \{y_i \mid 1 \leq i \leq n\}$

$X \cap Y = \emptyset$, $a \notin X \cup Y$

$P_{2n} := \{f_i \mid 1 \leq i \leq n(2^n+5)\}$ mit

$$f_{\&n+i} : \sigma \longrightarrow x_{\&+1}\,\varphi_{\&+1} \qquad 0 \leq \& \leq 2^n-1,\ 1 \leq i \leq n$$

$$f_{n2^n+j} : \sigma \longrightarrow y_j \qquad 1 \leq j \leq n$$

$$f_{n(2^n+1)+2\beta-1} : A_\beta \longrightarrow aA_\beta \qquad 1 \leq \beta \leq 2n$$

$$f_{n(2^n+1)+2l} : A_\beta \longrightarrow y_{\left\lceil \frac{l+1}{2} \right\rceil} \qquad 1 \leq l \leq 2n$$

wobei gilt:

$$\varphi_{i+1} := M_{2^n-1+i} \qquad \text{mit} \qquad M_0 := \emptyset$$

$$M_{2^k+2\beta-1} := M_{2^{k-1}+\beta-1} \cup \{A_{2k-1}\}$$

$$M_{2^k+2\beta} := M_{2^{k-1}+\beta-1} \cup \{A_{2k}\}$$

$$0 \leq k \leq n,\ 0 \leq \beta \leq 2^{k-1}$$

Es gilt:

$$\mathcal{L}(G_{2n}) = Xa^*Y \cup Y$$

Man zeigt nun folgende Aussagen:

(b) Mit $\Phi := \varphi_1 \cup \varphi_2 \cup \ldots \cup \varphi_{2^n}$ und $y \in Y$ gilt:

$$(\forall \varphi_1, \varphi_2 \in \Phi)(\exists A_1 \in \varphi_1)(\exists A_2 \in \varphi_2)(A_1 \neq A_2 \Longrightarrow \{A_1 \rightarrow y\ , A_2 \rightarrow y\} \subseteq P_{2n})$$

(c) $\Pi = \{\sigma\} \cup \{\varphi_i \mid 1 \leq i \leq 2^n\}$

(d) Jede CCFG G_{2n} ist vom Typ LR(0).

(e) Alle Zustände im A-minimalen LR(0)-Automaten sind inkompatibel.

(f) Der A-minimale LR(0)-Automat und der $\mathfrak{Z}$-minimale LR(0)-Automat sind isomorph.

(g) Mit SATZ 5 folgt: $\#\mathfrak{F} \cup \mathfrak{F} = (n+2)2^n + 5n + 1 =$

$$= (\#I_{2n}/2 + 2) \cdot \sqrt{2^{\#I_{2n}}} + 5 \cdot \#I_{2n}/2 + 1$$

6. SCHLUSSBEMERKUNGEN

(a) Der $\mathcal{J}$-minimale LR(0)-Automat besitzt die gleiche Eigenschaft wie der A-minimale LR(0)-Automat,nämlich daß zur Reduktionsentscheidun keine Berechnung von "look-aheads" notwendig ist.Fordert man diese Eigenschaft der LR(k)-Invarianz nicht mehr,dann kann die Zustandsmenge noch weiter unter die Zustandsmenge des Automaten $\bar{A}_p$ vermindert werden.(vergl./4/,/5b/)

(b) Nach Bemerkung 3 wird die Anwendbarkeit einer Reduktion auf dem Kellerband des DPDT($\bar{A}_p$) getroffen.Der definierte Kompatibilitätsbegriff von Zuständen kann leicht dahingehend verallgemeinert werder daß gewisse Endzustände im Automaten $\bar{A}_p$ zusammenfallen,ohne die Analyse über linear anwachsen zu lassen.Es dürfen solche Endzustände nicht zusammenfallen,denen Regeln $f,f' \in P, f \neq f'$,mit $Z(f)=wZ(f')$ entsprechen,da in diesem Fall die Entscheidung zwischen f und f' auf dem Kellerband i.a. nicht mehr getroffen werden kann.

(c) Eine Minimierung des A-minimalen LR(k)-Automaten A_p zum $\mathcal{J}$-minimal LR(k)-Automaten mit $k > 1$,kann auf die gleiche Art und Weise wie f den Fall k=0 durchgeführt werden.(vergl./5b/)

7. LITERATUR

/1/ G.Hotz-V.Claus — "Automatentheorie und formale Sprachen" III.Formale Sprachen,BI.Hochschulskripten (1971), 823a

/2/ R.Kemp — "LR(k)-Analysatoren", Dissertation Saarbrücken (1973)

/3/ R.Kemp — "An Estimation of the Set of States of the minimal LR(0)-Acceptor" Automata,Languages and Programming(M.Nivat North Holland Publishing Co,Amsterdam (197 563-574

/4/ R.Kemp — "Die Größe des minimalen Analysators einer kontextfreien Grammatik" Lecture Notes in Ec.and Math.Syst.,78,(197 99-1o6

/5a/,/5b/ R.Kemp — "Minimierung von LR(k)-Analysatoren"(1,2) Berichte des Math.Inst.,Saarbrücken (A75/1

/6/ D.Knuth — "On the Translation of Languages from Left to Right" ,Inf.and Control 8,(1965),607-6

/7/ E.Sperner — "Ein Satz über Untermengen einer endlichen Menge" ,Math.Zeitsch. 27 (1928) ,544-548

FORMAL TRANSLATIONS AND THE CONTAINMENT PROBLEM FOR SZILARD LANGUAGES

H.P.Kriegel and H.A.Maurer

Institut für Angewandte Informatik und
Formale Beschreibungsverfahren
Universität Karlsruhe
D-75 Karlsruhe 1, Postfach 6380, Fed.Rep.Germany

Abstract:

One of the methods used for defining translations is the socalled syntax-directed translation scheme which can be interpreted as a pair of rather similar grammars with the productions working in parallel. Because of the similarity of the grammars each of the two grammars "fits" the other in the sense that for each derivation process in one grammar leading to a terminal word the corresponding derivation process in the other grammar also leads to a terminal word. For many practical applications it suffices to consider the case that one of the grammars fits the other, but not necessarily conversely. Investigating this idea, translations are obtained which are more powerful than the syntax-directed. It is shown that one can determine whether a given grammar fits another given grammar. As a by-product, it is established that the containment problem for Szilard languages is decidable.

I. MOTIVATION AND DEFINITIONS

The concept of transforming certain sequences of symbols into other sequences of symbols is of crucial importance in many areas of computer science. Consider e.g. a programming language such as ALGOL 60. A compiler for ALGOL 60 supposedly transforms a given ALGOL 60 program - and such a program is nothing but a sequence of symbols, after all - into another sequence of symbols, namely the corresponding machine-language or assembly-language program. Or consider a commercial environment in which certain data files are to be restructured in a specified manner: again this is a situation which can be understood as a transformation of sequences of symbols.

One possibility for defining transformations of sequences of symbols is the notion of (formal) translation.

Definition 1:

A (formal) translation T is a set of pairs (x,x') of words x and x' over some alphabets Σ and Σ'. Intuitively, if (x,x') is element of a translation T, then x is the given input word and x' the desired output word. The set of all input words of T is called the domain of T and defined by $dom(T)=\{x \mid (x,x')\in T \text{ for some } x'\}$. The range of T is the set of all output words of T and defined by $ran(T)=\{x' \mid (x,x')\in T \text{ for some } x\}$.

For a family τ of translations $dom(\tau)=\{dom(T)|T\in\tau\}$ and $ran(\tau)=\{ran(T)|T\in\tau\}$.

Notation:

A context-free grammar, called grammar, for short, is denoted by a quadrupel $G=(N,\Sigma,P$ where N is the set of nonterminals, Σ is the set of terminals, $N\cap\Sigma=\phi$, P is the set o productions and S the starting symbol.

In order to assign labels to the productions in P, we consider a set of labels Lab_P and a surjective mapping λ: $Lab_P \to P$. If $l\in Lab_P$ is one of the labels of the production $A\to\alpha$ then we write $A\overset{l}{\to}\alpha\in P$. The usual relation $\Rightarrow^*$ for derivations in G is extended in the following way:

(1) $\alpha_1 \overset{\varepsilon}{\Rightarrow^*}\alpha_2$, if $\alpha_1=\alpha_2\in(N\cup\Sigma)^*$

(2) $\alpha_1 \overset{l}{\Rightarrow^*}\alpha_2$, if $\alpha_1=\beta A\gamma, \alpha_2=\beta\alpha\gamma$ and $A\overset{l}{\to}\alpha\in P$

(3) $\alpha_1 \overset{dl}{\Rightarrow^*}\alpha_2$, if $\alpha_1 \overset{d}{\Rightarrow^*}\alpha_3 \overset{l}{\Rightarrow^*}\alpha_2$ where $d\in Lab_P^*$, $l\in Lab_P$

We often abbreviate $\alpha_1 \overset{d}{\Rightarrow^*}\alpha_2$ to just $\alpha_1 \overset{d}{\Rightarrow}\alpha_2$ and call the word d in Lab_P^* the contro word of this derivation. The controlword indicates in which sequence the production are applied, but not at which place. Thus, different derivations may have the same controlword.

A derivation $S\overset{d}{\Rightarrow}\alpha_2$ is called terminal if α_2 is in Σ^* and in this case the termina controlword d is said to generate x. A word β in $(N\cup\Sigma)^*$ is said to be a sentential form if there is a controlword d such that $S\overset{d}{\Rightarrow}\beta$. The set $L(G)=\{x\in\Sigma^*|\ S\overset{d}{\Rightarrow}x\}$ is cal the language generated by G. The Szilard language of G, denoted by Sz(G), is the s of all control words of terminal derivations in G, i.e.

$$Sz(G)=\{d\in Lab_P^* \mid S\overset{d}{\Rightarrow}x,\ x\in L(G)\}.$$

For convenience it is assumed that grammars are always reduced, i.e. for each nont minal $A\neq S$ there are controlwords d_1 and d_2 such that

$S\overset{d_1}{\Longrightarrow}xAz \overset{d_2}{\Rightarrow} xyz$ for some x,y,z in Σ^*

Notation:

Throughout this paper, let $G=(N,\Sigma,P,S)$ and $G'=(N',\Sigma',P',S')$ be two reduced grammar such that $Lab_P=Lab_{P'}$. Now the relation Co from P to P' is defined by $(p,p')\in Co$ if and p' have the same label $l\in Lab_P=Lab_{P'}$. Whenever a production p in P is applied a derivation in G, one of the productions p' such that $(p,p')\in Co$, called a corresp ding production, has to be applied in G'. For convenience, we choose $N=\{A_1,\dots,A_n$ $N'=\{A_1',\dots,A_{n'}'\}$, $S=A_1$ and $S'=A_1'$.

Definition 1:

The translation T(G,G') generated by the grammar pair (G,G') is defined by

$T(G,G')=\{(x,x')\in\Sigma^*\times\Sigma'^*|\ S\overset{d}{\Rightarrow}x$ and $S'\overset{d}{\Rightarrow}x'$ for a terminal controlword $d\in Lab_P^*$ subje condition (1) below\}

Condition (1):

If $S \overset{d_1}{\Rightarrow} \beta \overset{1}{\Rightarrow} \gamma \overset{d_2}{\Rightarrow} x \in \Sigma^*, S' \overset{d_1}{\Rightarrow} \beta' \overset{1}{\Rightarrow} \gamma' \overset{d_2}{\Rightarrow} x' \in \Sigma'^*$ and $(A \overset{1}{\rightarrow} \alpha, A' \overset{1}{\rightarrow} \alpha') \in Co$, then

(i) the leftmost A in β is replaced and

(ii) if β' contains an A' generated at the same time as the leftmost A in β, then that A' is replaced; otherwise the leftmost A' in β' is replaced.

The above condition rules out certain undesired pairs of terminal derivations. By determining the place where to a apply a given production, there is a unique derivation in G' for each terminal controlword $d \in Lab^*_P$. Larger examples for grammar pairs translating simple ALGOL 60 programs to equivalent assembly language programs are given in KANDZIA und LANGMAACK (1973) as well as in MAURER und SIX (1974).
A major problem with translations generated by grammar pairs is the fact that a terminal controlword in one grammar is not necessarily again a terminal controlword in the other grammar.
This leads to the introduction of agreeable grammar pairs and agreeable translations.

Definition 2:
A grammar pair (G,G') is called agreeable if Sz(G)=Sz(G') that is if each terminal controlword in one of the grammars G and G' is a terminal controlword in the other grammar. A translation is called agreeable if it is generated by an agreeable grammar pair.
PENTTONEN (1974) has shown that for two reduced context-free grammars G and G', Sz(G)=Sz(G') if and only if G and G' agree up to terminals, up to a one-one renaming of nonterminals and up to a permutation of nonterminals on the right hand side of corresponding productions, the correspondence given by a bijection from P onto P'.

Since the conditions in the above theorem are exactly those LEWIS and STEARNS (1968) and AHO and ULLMAN (1969 and 1972) used for defining syntax-directed translations, the family AT of agreeable translations equals the family SDT of syntax-directed translations and dom(SDT)=ran(SDT)=CF, where CF denotes the family of context-free languages.
For many applications, the translation process is only performed in one direction. This leads to the following
Definition 3:
A grammar pair (G,G') is called fitting if $Sz(G) \subseteq Sz(G')$ that is if each terminal controlword in G is a terminal controlword in G'. The translation T(G,G') is called fitting if it is generated by a fitting grammar pair (G,G').

II. PROPERTIES OF FITTING TRANSLATIONS

Let FT denote the family of fitting translations.

Theorem 1:

$\underline{SDT} \subsetneq \underline{FT}$

Proof:

By definition of agreeable translations, $\underline{SDT} \subseteq \underline{FT}$. Now consider the translation $T=\{((abc)^n, a^n b^n c^n) \mid n \geq 1\} \notin \underline{SDT}$ (ran(T) is not a context-free language). T is generated by the fitting grammar pair (G,G'), where

$G=(\{A_1,\dots,A_6\},\{a,b,c\},P,A_1)$

$G'=\{A_1',\dots,A_4'\}, \{a,b,c\},P',A_1'),$

$Lab_P = Lab_{P'} = \{1,2,\dots,7\}$ and

productions in P		corresponding productions in P'
$(A_1 \xrightarrow{1} A_2$	,	$A_1' \xrightarrow{1} A_2'A_3'A_4')$
$(A_2 \xrightarrow{2} aA_3$	,	$A_2' \xrightarrow{2} aA_2'$)
$(A_3 \xrightarrow{3} bA_4$	,	$A_3' \xrightarrow{3} bA_3'$)
$(A_4 \xrightarrow{4} cA_2$	,	$A_4' \xrightarrow{4} cA_4'$)
$(A_2 \xrightarrow{5} aA_5$	,	$A_2' \xrightarrow{5} a$)
$(A_5 \xrightarrow{6} bA_6$	,	$A_3' \xrightarrow{6} b$)
$(A_6 \xrightarrow{7} c$	,	$A_4' \xrightarrow{7} c$) ■.

By definition, dom($\underline{FT}$) = $\underline{CF}$.

It can be shown easily that for a fitting grammar pair (G,G') the language ran(T(G is a matrix language. By the following theorem this inclusion is proper.

Theorem 2:

Let T be a fitting translation. Then the Parikh-mapping of the language ran(T) is semilinear set.

For the proof, a system of linear diophantine equations associated with G is used. meaningful set of solutions of this system is considered and proved to be a semilinear set. Now a linear transformation is applied to yield the Parikh-mapping of ran(T).

Since there are matrix languages whose Parikh-mapping is not semilinear, this impl

Corrollary 3:

The family ran($\underline{FT}$) is a proper subset of the family $\mathcal{M}^\varepsilon$ of matrix languages: ran($\underline{FT}$) $\subsetneq \mathcal{M}^\varepsilon$. (The upper index ε indicates that productions $A \to \varepsilon$ are allowed).

For practically applying the concept of fitting translations, it is important to d termine whether a given grammar pair is fitting or not. In an earlier report by KRIEGEL and MAURER (1974) it has been shown that this "fitting problem" and the e valent containment problem for Szilard languages are decidable. An outline of the proof follows. It is obvious, to apply Parikh's theorem to the sentential forms the grammar G. Since we are interested neither in the terminals nor in the positi of the nonterminals, but only in the number of occurrences of the nonterminals, we characterize sentential forms in G by n-vectors whose i-th component indicates the number of occurrences of the nonterminal A_i, $1\leq i\leq n$.

Notation:

For some fixed natural number n, an n-vector is an ordered n-tupel of integers, an n_+-vector an ordered n-tupel of nonnegative integers.

0 denotes the zero-vector, e_i, $1\leq i\leq n$, the i-th unitary vector.
n-vectors are denoted by u,v,w,t,b, specially $0,e_i,1\leq i\leq n$, n'-vectors by u',v',w',t',b', specially $0',e_i'$, $1\leq i\leq n'$. Let V,V',V_+ and V_+' denote the sets of all n-vectors, n'-vectors, n_+-vectors and n_+'-vectors, respectively.

Let the grammars $G=(N,\Sigma,P,S)$ and $G'=(N',\Sigma',P',S')$ now be in vector representation,i.e. $N=\{e_1,\ldots,e_n\},\Sigma=\emptyset$, $S=e_1$ and a production in P has the form $e_i \xrightarrow{l} u$, $1\leq i\leq n$, u an n_+-vector and $l\in Lab_P$. The usual relation $\overset{d}{\Rightarrow}$, $d\in Lab_P^*$, for sentential forms is carried over to n_+-vectors. Clearly, d is a terminal controlword if $e_1 \overset{d}{\Rightarrow} 0$. An n_+-vector v is a sentential form in G if there is a controlword d such that $e_1 \overset{d}{\Rightarrow} v$. Since G is reduced, for each nonterminal e_i, $2\leq i\leq n$, there are controlwords d_1 and d_2 such that $e_1 \overset{d_1}{\Longrightarrow} e_i \overset{d_2}{\Longrightarrow} 0$.

G' is given in the analogous way. Clearly, for a fitting grammar pair (G,G') in vector representation $e_1 \overset{d}{\Rightarrow} 0$ implies $e_1' \overset{d}{\Rightarrow} 0'$. Now by Parikh's theorem it follows immediately:

Lemma 4:

The set $M=\{v\in V_+ | v \text{ is a sentential form in } G\}$ is semilinear.

Definition 4:

Let $d=l_1\ldots l_m\in Lab_P^*$, such that $e_{j_i}' \xrightarrow{l_i} u_i'\in P'$, $1\leq j_i\leq n'$ and $1\leq i\leq m$. The value of d, in symbols z(d), is defined by

$$z(d) = \sum_{i=1}^{m} (e_{j_i}' - u_i')\in V'$$

Clearly, if d is a terminal controlword in G' such that $v' \overset{d}{\Rightarrow} 0'$, then $z(d)=v'\in V_+'$.
For any sentential form $v\in V_+$ in G the set f(v) is defined by $f(v)=\{z(d)\in V' | v \overset{d}{\Rightarrow} 0,$ d cycle-free$\}$.
Additionally, define $f(0) = \{0'\}$.
A controlword d in G such that $v \overset{d}{\Rightarrow} 0$ is called cycle-free if in no branch of an associated derivation tree any nonterminal occurs more than once.
Note that the elements of f(v) may have negative components.
An n_+'-vector $w'\in f(v)$ can be considered a nonterminal balance vector which should be generated by the same controlword as v.
Let #(S) denote the number of elements of the set S. For the following definition, we suppose $\#(f(v))=1$ for each sentential form v in G, which will turn out to be reasonable in Theorem 5.

Definition 5:

Let $E\subseteq V_+$ be a linear set in the semilinear set M and $b_0,b_1,\ldots,b_k\in V_+$ be a basis of E.

E is termed <u>well-formed</u>, if for all $t \in V_+$ such that $t=b_0+b_i$, $1 \leq i \leq k$, and for $t=b_0$, $t \overset{l}{\Rightarrow} w$, $l \in Lab_P$, implies $f(t) \overset{l}{\Rightarrow} f(w)$.

The <u>grammar pair</u> (G,G') is <u>well-formed</u>, if M is the finite union of well-formed line sets.

Now we can state necessary and sufficient conditions that a grammar pair (G,G') is fitting.

<u>Theorem 5:</u>

(G,G') is a fitting grammar pair if and only if the conditions (1)-(4) hold:

(1) $\#(f(e_i))=1$ for all i, $1 \leq i \leq n$

(2) $f(e_1) = \{e_1'\}$

(3) Let $E \subseteq V_+$ be a linear set in the semilinear set M and $b_0,b_1,\ldots,b_k \in V_+$ be a basis of E. Then $f(b_i)$ is an n_+'-vector for all i, $0 \leq i \leq k$.

(4) The grammar pair (G,G') is well-formed.

Obviously, the conditions (1)-(4) in Theorem 5 are decidable. They can be easily formulated as algorithm for deciding whether or not a given grammar pair (G,G') is fitting.

Given a grammar pair (G,G'), we use the above algorithm to test whether (G,G') is fitting. If the result is "yes", we parse a given inputword $x \in L(G)$ (e.g. with Earley algorithm) yielding a controlword d such that $S \overset{d}{\Rightarrow} x$. Observing condition (1) of definition 1 this d generates an outputword x' such that $(x,x') \in T(G,G')$.

<u>References:</u>

AHO,A.V. and ULLMAN,J.D. (1972) The theory of parsing, translation and compiling, Vol. I: Parsing, Prentice-Hall, Series in automatic computation, Englewood Cliffs, N.J. (1972).

AHO,A.V. and ULLMAN,J.D. (1969), Syntax-directed translations and the pushdown assembler, Journal of Computer and System Sciences <u>3</u> (1969), 37-56.

AHO,A.V. and ULLMAN,J.D. (1969), Properties of syntax-directed translations, Journal of Computer and System Sciences <u>3</u> (1969), 319-334.

KANDZIA,P. und LANGMAACK,H. (1973), Informatik: Programmierung, Teubner Studienbücher Informatik, Bd. 18, Stuttgart (1973)

KRIEGEL,H.P. and MAURER,H.A. (1974), Formal translations and the containment problem for Szilard languages, Report No. 23 of the Institut für Angewandte Informatik und Formale Beschreibungsverfahren, Universität Karlsruhe

LEWIS,P.M. and STEARNS,R.E. (1968), Syntax-directed translations, Journal of the ACM <u>15</u> (1968), 271-281.

MAURER,H.A. und SIX,H.W. (1974), Datenstrukturen und Programmierverfahren, Teubner Studienbücher Informatik, Bd. 25, Stuttgart (1974)

PENTTONEN,M. (1974),On Derivation Languages Corresponding to Context-Free Grammars, Acta Informatica <u>3</u> (1974), 285-291.

A CHARACTERIZATION OF BOUNDED REGULAR SETS

Antonio Restivo

Laboratorio di Cibernetica del CNR
Arco Felice, Napoli.

1. INTRODUCTION

Let X be a finite alphabet and X^* the free monoid generated by X. A subset L of X^* is <u>bounded</u> iff there exists a finite number of words $w_1, w_2, \ldots, w_k$ of X^* such that $L \subset w_1^* w_2^* \ldots w_k^*$. Bounded languages were introduced in [1] by Ginsburg and Spanier as a special family of context-free languages which has "simple" structural properties and is intimately related to certain algebraic concepts. In [2] Ginsburg and Spanier considered also the particular case of bounded regular sets for which derived some characterization results.

In this paper the boundedness of a language is related with the presence in it of strings "without repetitions" of arbitrary length, and a new characterization of bounded regular sets is given (theorem 2). The problem of existence of strings "without repetitions" of arbitrary length was first considered and solved by Thue [3] giving an explicit construction of such strings. Later the same property was rediscovered by other people in different context as symbolic dynamics and the theory of semigroups. Many references on the subject can be found in [4]. To formalize these notions let us now introduce for any positive integer the following subset of X^* :

$$L_p = \{ f \in X^* \mid f \neq uv^p w \text{ for all } u, v, w \in X^* \text{ with } |v| > 0 \}.$$

In the sequel, if it is necessary, we shall use the symbol $L_p(X)$ to specify the alphabet X on which L_p is defined. We note that if

$p \leqq p'$, $L_p \subset L_{p'}$. The basic result of Thue for our pourposes can be stated as follows

<u>Theorem 1</u> (Thue). Let $|X|$ be the cardinality of the alphabet X. If $|X| = 2$, L_3 is infinite; if $|X| > 2$, L_2 is infinite.

Given an arbitrary subset L of X^*, we consider now the intersections $L \cap L_p$ for any p. We have the following

<u>Proposition 1</u> If L is bounded, $L \cap L_p$ is finite for any p.

Proof. Let $L \subset w_1^* w_2^* \dots w_k^*$. If $f \in L$, there exist k positive integers $n_1, n_2, \dots, n_k$ such that $f = w_1^{n_1} w_2^{n_2} \dots w_k^{n_k}$. The length of f is then $|f| = n_1|w_1| + n_2|w_2| + \dots + n_k|w_k|$. Let r be the maximal length of the words $w_1, w_2, \dots w_k$. For any $p > o$, if $|f| \geqq pkr$, there exists an index j such that $n_j \geqq p$. Hence, for any $f \in L$ such that $|f| \geqq pkr$, $f \notin L_p$. This completes the proof of the proposition.

Proposition 1 in the case $L = X^*$ gives immediately, by theorem 1, the following result of Ginsburg and Spanier [1] concernin the existence of unbounded sets.

<u>Corollary</u> If $|X| \geqq 2$, X^* is not bounded.

The converse of the proposition 1 is not generally true. The main result of the paper is the following

<u>Theorem 2</u>. Let L be a <u>regular</u> set. L is bounded if and only if $L \cap L_p$ is finite for any p.

The hypothesis that L is regular is essential, as shown b the following counterxample.

Let $|X| \geqq 3$, $x \in X$ and $Y = X \setminus \{x\}$. Consider the language

$$L = \{f = gx^{|g|} \mid g \in Y^*\}$$

L is context - free and is not bounded; however, for any $p > o$, $L \cap L_p$ is finite. Indeed if $f \in L$ and $|f| = 2p$, then $f = gx^p$

for some $g \in Y^p$ Hence $f \notin L_p$

The proof of theorem 2 is based on a certain number of technical lemmas which are reported in the next section without proof. In Section 3 we give in detail the kernel of the proof of the theorem.

2. SOME PRELIMINARY LEMMAS.

In this section we give, without proof, some lemmas which will be used in the proof of theorem 2 in the next section.

The first lemma concerns the problem of the invariance, under a morphism θ, of the sets L_p.

<u>Lemma 1</u>. Let X and Y be two <u>finite</u> alphabets and let θ be a <u>monomorphism</u> from Y^* to X^*. For all words $v \in Y^*$

$$v \in L_p(Y) \Rightarrow \theta(v) \in L_{|\theta|p}(X)$$

where $|\theta|$ is the maximal length of words in $\theta(Y) \subset X^*$.

Lemma 1 is not generally true if Y is not finite and θ is not one-to-one. The next lemma concerns regular sets.

<u>Lemma 2.</u> Let L be a regular set. There exist two positive integers m,k, such that for all $u,v,w \in X^*$ and for all $n \geq m$

$$uv^n w \in L \Longleftrightarrow uv^{n+k} w \in L.$$

The following notations will be now introduced. Let f and v be words of X^*. v is a <u>subword</u> of f iff there exist $u, w \in X^*$ such that $f = uvw$. If L is a subset of X^*, we denote by $S(L)$ the set of all the subwords of words in L.

<u>Lemma 3</u> Let L be a regular set.

$$S(L) \cap L_p \text{ finite for any } p \Longleftrightarrow L \cap L_p \text{ finite for any } p.$$

In order to state the next lemma let us now give some other definitions. An element $f \in X^*$ is <u>primitive</u> iff any relation $f = g^k$ implies $f = g$. Let L be a subset of X^*. An element $v \in X^*$ is an <u>iterating factor</u> of L iff there exist $u,w \in X^*$ such that $uv^*w \cap L$ i infinite. If v is an iterating factor of L and $v = g^k$ for some $g \in X^*$ and $k > o$, then also g is an iterating factor of L. We are here inter ested only to primitive iterating factors of a set L. The proof of th following lemma makes use of theorem 1.1 of Ginsburg and Spanier in [2

<u>Lemma 4</u>. Let L be a <u>regular</u> set having only a <u>finite</u> number of primiti ve iterating factors. Then L is bounded.

3. PROOF OF THEOREM 2

Suppose L be a regular set such that $L \cap L_p$ is finite for any p. To prove that L is bounded it is sufficient to prove, by lem 4, that L has a finite number of primitive iterating factors. The ar ment is by contradiction. By lemma 3, if $L \cap L_p$ is finite for any p, also $S(L) \cap L_p$ is finite for any p. Let $\gamma(p)$ be the maximal length words in $S(L) \cap L_p$, and let m,k be positive integers as in the lemma If L has not a finite number of primitive iterating factors, there exists a primitive iterating factor v such that $|v| > \gamma(m)$. The condi tions $v \in S(L)$ and $|v| > \gamma(m)$ imply that $v \notin L_m$, and then there exist $a,b,c \in X^*$, with b primitive, such that $v = ab^m c$. Since v is an ite ating factor of L, there exist $u,w \in X^*$ and $n > \frac{1}{|v|}\gamma(3(|v|+k|b|))$ such that $uv^n w \in L$. We may write

$$uv^n w = u\underbrace{a\,b^m\,c\,a\,b^m\,c\,a\,b^m\,c\,\ldots\ldots\,a\,b^m\,c}_{n\ \text{times}}w \in L$$

By lemma 2, if we substitute, as exponent of each factor b in $uv^n w$, r for m, we obtain again a word of L. Consider now the alphabet $Y = \{y_o, y_1\}$ and a map τ from Y to the integers $\{o,1\}$ defined as f lows: $\tau(y_o) = o$, $\tau(y_1) = 1$. Let s be a word of Y^* of length n s that $s \in L_3(Y)$. If $s = s_1 s_2 \ldots s_n$, $s_i \in Y$, consider now the followi word f of X^*, which, by the above remark , belongs to L:

$$f = uab^{m+\tau(s_1)k}cab^{m+\tau(s_2)k}cab^{m+\tau(s_3)k}c\ldots ab^{m+\tau(s_n)k}cw \in L.$$

The subword h of f defined by the equality $f = uhw$ plays an essential role in the rest of the proof.

We have clearly $|h| > n|v|$.

Let θ be the morphism from Y^* to X^* defined as follows

$$\begin{cases} \theta(y_o) = cab^m \\ \theta(y_1) = cab^{m+k} \end{cases}$$

We prove now that θ is a monomorphism. Let us introduce a new alphabet $Z = \{z_1, z_2\}$, and exprime θ as the composition of the morphism θ_1 from Y^* to Z^* and θ_2 from Z^* to X^* defined as follows:

$$\begin{cases} \theta_1(y_o) = z_1 z_2^m \\ \theta_1(y_1) = z_1 z_2^{m+k} \end{cases} \qquad \begin{cases} \theta_2(z_1) = ca \\ \theta_2(z_2) = b \end{cases}$$

θ_1 is clearly a monomorphism. θ_2, by a well known result in the theory of free monoids [5], is a monomorphism if and only if ca and b are not powers of the same word. Since b is primitive by hipothesis if ca and b are powers of the same word, there exists $q > o$ such that $ca = b^q$. We have then

$$\begin{cases} c = b^{q_1} b_1 \\ a = b_2\ b^{q_2} \end{cases}$$

with $b_1\ b_2 = b$ and $q_1 + q_2 = q - 1$. If follows that the word

$$v = ab^m\ c = b_2 b^{q_2}\ b^m\ b^{q_1}\ b_1 = (b_2\ b_1)^{q+m}$$

is not primitive in contradiction with the hypothesis. Then θ_2 is a monomorphism. Since the composition of two monomorphisms is a monomorphism, θ is also a monomorphism . This, with the condition $s \in L_3(Y)$, implies, by lemma 1, $\theta(s) \in L_{3|\theta|}(X)$, with $|\theta| = |v| + k\ |b|$.

Consider now the word $h \in S(L)$ previously defined. It is easy to see that h is a subword of $\theta(s)$ and then, clearly, h belongs to $L_{3|\theta|}$. We have then $h \in S(L) \cap L_{3\ |\theta|}$ and $|h| > n|v| > \gamma(3\ |\theta|)$, a

contradiction. Hence the starting hypothesis is not true and L has only a finite number of primitive iterating factors.
This completes the proof of the theorem.

REFERENCES

[1] S. Ginsburg and E.H. Spanier, Bounded ALGOL-like languages, Trans. Amer. Math. Soc. 113 (1964), 333-368.

[2] S. Ginsburg and E.H. Spanier, Bounded regular sets, Proc. Amer. Math. Soc. 17 (1966), 1043-1049.

[3] A. Thue, Uber die gegenseitige Lage gleicher Teile Gewisser Zeicheureihen, Skr. Vid. Kristiania I. Mat. Naturv. Klasse 1 (1912), 1-67.

[4] F. Dejean, Sur un Théorème de Thue, Journal of Combinatorial Theory (A) 13 (1972), 90-99.

[5] R.C. Lyndon and M.P. Schutzenberger, The equation $a^m=b^nc^p$ in a free group, Michigan Math. J. 9 (1962), 289-298.

Eine universelle Lambda-Kalkül-Programmiersprache und ihr Interpreter

E. Fehr
Universität Bonn

0. Zusammenfassung: Wir erweitern den λ-Kalkül von A.Church zu einer universellen Programmiersprache (λ_p-Kalkül) über einer beliebigen algorithmischen Basis. In Absatz 2 definieren wir in VDL den Lambda-Programm-Interpreter LPI, der alle im λ_p-Kalkül definierbaren Funktionen über dem Konstantenbereich der algorithmischen Basis berechnet. Der LPI ist ein 'fixed-program (reentrant)'-Interpreter mit einer Call-by-Name-Auswertungsstrategie. Auf Grund einer sorgfältigen Organisation des Symboltabellenzugriffs vermeidet der LPI jegliche Umbennung von Variablen. Die Korrektheit des LPI wird bewiesen durch Anwendung einer induktiven Beweistechnik auf eine Funktion TRACE, die Zustände des LPI abbildet auf teilausgewertete λ_p-Ausdrücke. Eine ausführliche Fassung dieser Arbeit liegt als Institutsbericht unter gleichem Titel vor (s. /FE/). Dort findet sich insbesondere eine Dokumentation der Implementierung des LPI in SIMULA.

1. Der Lambda-Kalkül als Programmiersprache

Sei $\underline{A}$ = (C;F,P) eine algorithmische Basis, wobei C der Konstantenbereich, F eine endliche Menge von Grundfunktionen über C und P eine endliche Menge von Prädikaten auf C ist. Die Menge $L_{\underline{A}}$ der Lambda-Programme (λ_p-Ausdrücke) definieren wir induktiv:

i) (Atome) $V \cup A \subset L_{\underline{A}}$, wobei V eine abzählbare Menge von Variablen ist und A aus Symbolen für die Elemente aus $\underline{A}$ besteht.

ii) (Kombinationen) $L_1, L_2 \in L_{\underline{A}} \Rightarrow (L_1 L_2) \in L_{\underline{A}}$

iii) (Abstraktionen) $x \in V, L \in L_{\underline{A}} \Rightarrow \lambda x L \in L_{\underline{A}}$

iv) $L_{\underline{A}}$ wird durch i)-iii) vollständig definiert.

Die Semantik des λ_p-Kalküls wird mathematisch definiert durch die Reduktionsregeln des reinen λ-Kalküls und einer Wertreduktion, welche die Anwendung von Systemfunktionen eines Rechners beschreibt. (Im folgenden ezeichnet $S^x_A M$ die Substitution von A für alle freien Vorkommen von x n M und das Symbol ω steht für undefiniert.)

) (α-Konversion, Variablenbenennung) Sei $x,y \in V, L \in L_{\underline{A}}$ und y nicht frei in L, dann gilt: $\lambda x L \longrightarrow \lambda y S^x_y L$

i) (β-Reduktion) Sei $x \in V, M, A \in L_{\underline{A}}$ und keine Variable kommt frei in A und gebunden in M vor, dann gilt:

$u(\lambda xMA)v \longrightarrow uS_A^x Mv$

iii) (Wertreduktion) Sei $h \in F \cup P$ n-stellig, $a_i \in C$ für $1 \le i \le n$ und sei $h(a_1,\ldots,a_n) = a$, dann gilt:

$$u(\ldots(ha_1)\ldots a_n)v \longrightarrow \begin{cases} uav & \text{falls } a \in C \\ u\lambda x\lambda yxv & \text{falls } a = \underline{true} \\ u\lambda x\lambda yyv & \text{falls } a = \underline{false} \\ \omega & \text{falls } a = \omega \end{cases}$$

Ein λ_p-Ausdruck L_2 ist Normalform eines λ_p-Ausdrucks L_1, wenn $L_1 \xrightarrow{*} L_2$ und keine ß-Reduktion und keine Wertreduktion auf L_2 anwendbar ist.

Definition (Semantikfunktion)

$$\sigma : L_{\underline{A}} \times C^* \longrightarrow C$$

$$\sigma(L,(c_1,\ldots,c_n)) := \begin{cases} c \text{ falls } c \in C \text{ und } c \text{ ist Normalform von } (\ldots(Lc_1)\ldots c_n) \\ \omega \text{ sonst} \end{cases}$$

Sei η die kanonische Einbettung der Programm-Daten-Kombinationen in d Menge $L_{\underline{A}}$ der λ_p-Ausdrücke, ν die Ergebnisfunktion der Call-by-Name-Berechnung (d.h. Reduktionsfolge stets von links nach rechts) und Ψ die Projektion der Menge $L_{\underline{A}}$ auf C, dann folgt unmittelbar aus dem Standardization-Theorem von Church-Rosser (s. /CF/ Seite 139 ff), daß folgendes Diagramm kommutiert:

$$\begin{array}{ccc} L_{\underline{A}} \times C^* & \xrightarrow{\eta} & L_{\underline{A}} \\ \sigma \downarrow & & \downarrow \nu \\ C & \xleftarrow{\Psi} & L_{\underline{A}} \end{array}$$

Bemerkung: Die Menge der im λ_p-Kalkül berechenbaren Funktionen wird nicht eingeschränkt, wenn man nur Programme zuläßt, in denen keine freien Variablen vorkommen (s. /FE/, Lemma II.4.1).
Sei im folgenden $Fr(L) := \{x \in V \mid x \text{ kommt frei in } L \text{ vor}\}$ und

$$L_{\underline{A}}^+ := \{L \in L_{\underline{A}} \mid Fr(L) = \emptyset\}.$$

Lemma: Sei $L_1 \in L_{\underline{A}}^+$ und $L_1, L_2, \ldots, L_n$ die Call-by-Name-Berechnung von L (d.h. Reduktionsreihenfolge stets von links nach rechts), dann gi

$$L_n \in C \Rightarrow \forall_{i \le i < n} (L_i \xrightarrow[\beta]{} L_{i+1} \text{ oder } L_i \xrightarrow[w]{} L_{i+1}).$$

Beweis: siehe /FE/.

2. Der Lambda-Programm-Interpreter LPI

Zur Definition der operationellen Semantik benutzen wir die Vienna Definition Language VDL. Eine Einführung in diese Sprache findet man i /WV/.

Der LPI erwartet als Eingabe ein strukturiertes Objekt, das dem VDL-

Prädikat is-expression genügt.

<u>Definition</u>: is-expression := is-atom $\cup$ is-combination $\cup$ is-abstraction

is-atom := $A \cup V$

is-combination := (<s-operator>:<is-expression>,
<s-operand>:<is-expression>)

is-abstraction := (<s-boundvar>:<is-var>,<s-body>:<is-expression>)

is-var := V

Wegen der Eindeutigkeit der Menge $L_{\underline{A}}$ existiert eine bijektive Abbildung $\gamma : L_{\underline{A}} \longrightarrow$ is-expression, so daß die Ergebnisse aus Absatz 1 analog für die Menge is-expression gelten.

Der LPI besteht aus vier Komponenten:

1. Ein Pointer s-work, der jeweils auf das nächste, auszuwertende Programmteil zeigt.
2. Ein Kellerspeicher s-proc (procedure-stack), in den ein Eintrag bei Prozeduraufrufen und Blockaktivierungen gemacht wird.
3. Eine Symboltabelle s-env, auf die Zugriff über einen Environmentvektor erfolgt, dessen Komponenten gemäß der'static-chain' geordnet sind.
4. Ein Hilfskellerspeicher s-aux, in dem Eintragungen aus s-proc vorübergehend abgespeichert werden.

Das VDL-Prädikat is-state charakterisiert die Zustandsmenge Σ des LPI:

is-state := (<s-work:is-expression>,<s-proc:is-proc-stack>,
<s-aux:is-proc-stack>,<s-env:is-environment>)

is-proc-stack := (<s-top:is-proc-entry>,
<s-rest:is-proc-stack>) $\cup$ is-null

is-proc-entry := (<s-control:is-control-symbol>,
<s-return:is-return-link>,<s-list:is-number-list>)

is-return-link:= is-expression $\cup$ is-null

is-null := $\{ \Omega \}$

is-control-symbol := {D,C,L,R}

is-number-list := (<s-top:is-number>,
<s-rest:is-number-list>) $\cup$ is-null

is-Number := $\mathbb{N}$

is-table-entry := (<s-var:is-var>,<s-wert:is-expression>,
<s-list:is-number-list>)

Das Prädikat is-environment wird durch die Angabe seines Domain und Range definiert.

is-environment(e) : <==> $D(e) \subset \{s\text{-}i \mid i \in \mathbb{N}\}$ und
$R(e) \subset$ is-table-entry

Zur Definition der Zustandsüberführungsfunktion Δ des LPI benötigen wir einige Abkürzungen und Hilfsfunktionen:

```
S-LISTE := s-list • s-top • s-proc  (Environmentvektor)
S-CONTROL := s-control • s-top • s-proc
S-RETURN := s-return • s-top • s-proc  (Rücksprungadresse)
```

Die formale Definition in VDL der nun folgenden Funktionen und Prädikate findet man in /FE/ Seite 42 ff, hier nur eine kurze Beschreibung: Die Funktion δ-value reduziert den am weitesten links stehenden Wert-Redex, falls ein solcher existiert.
Das Prädikat is-equ bezeichnet die Äquivalenz zweier Ausdrücke und das Prädikat i-C-expr wird von Konstantenausdrücken erfüllt.
Die Kellerfunktionen pushdown und popup sind wie üblich definiert, und die Funktion push angewendet auf zwei Keller überträgt den Inhalt des zweiten Kellers in der last-in-first-out-Reihenfolge auf den ersten Keller. Und schließlich die Funktion newnumber, die angewendet auf eine Symboltabelle, die erste, freie Adresse liefert.

<u>Definition</u>: (Die Transitionsfunktion Δ des LPI)

```
Δ : Σ ——> Σ
Δ(β) := is-C-expr (s-work(β)) ——>
           not is-equ(s-work(β),δ-value(s-work(β)) ——>
               μ(β;<s-work:δ-value(s-work(β))>)
           is-C or is-D(S-CONTROL(β)) ——>
               μ(β;<s-work:S-RETURN(β)>,
                   <S-RETURN:s-work(β)>,
                   <S-CONTROL:R>)
           is-R(S-Control(β)) ——>
               μ(β;<s-work:μ0(<s-operator:S-RETURN(β)>,
                              <s-operand:s-work(β)>)>,
                   <s-proc:popup(s-proc(β))>)
   is-abstraction(s-work(β)) ——>
      is-null(s-aux(β)) ——>
         μ(β;<s-top • s-aux:μ0(<s-control:D>,<s-list:
                 pushdown(S-LISTE(β),newnumber(β))>)>)
      is-L(S-CONTROL(β)) ——>
         μ(β;<s-work:s-body • s-work(β)>,
             <s-newnumber(β) • s-env:μ0(<s-var:s-boundvar(s-work(β))
             <s-wert:S-RETURN(β)>,<s-list:S-LISTE(β)>)>,
         <s-proc:push(popup(s-proc(β)),s-aux(β))>,<s-aux:Ω>)
      is-C or is-D(S-CONTROL(β)) ——>
         μ(β;<s-proc:popup(s-proc(β))>,<s-aux:pushdown(s-aux(β),
             <s-top • s-proc(β))>)
```

```
is-combination(s-work(β)) —>
   μ(β;<s-work:s-operator • s-work(β)>,
       <s-proc:pushdown(s-proc(β),
          μ₀(<s-control:L>,<s-return:s-operand • s-work(β)>,
             <s-list:S-LISTE(β)>))>)

is-var(s-work(β)) —>
   not is-C(S-CONTROL(β)) —>
      μ(β;<s-proc:pushdown(s-proc(β),
          μ₀(<s-control:C>,<s-list:S-LISTE(β)>))>)
   is-equ(s-work(β),var(S-LISTE(β),β)) —>
      μ(β;<s-work:wert(S-LISTE(β),β)>,
          <S-LISTE:list(S-LISTE(β),β)>)
   not is-null (S-LISTE(β)) —>
      μ(β;<S-LISTE:popup(S-LISTE(β))>)
```

Um die Korrektheit des LPI zu beweisen, definieren wir die Funktion TRACE, die die Zustandsmenge Σ des LPI abbildet auf die Menge $L_{\underline{A}}$ der λ_p-Ausdrücke. In der Definition von TRACE benutzen wir die Funktion SUBSTITUTE, die alle freien Variablen eines λ_p-Ausdrucks durch ihre Werte, gemäß dem aktuellen Environment, ersetzt.
Für einen Zustand β aus Σ wird TRACE(β) wie folgt berechnet:
Falls s-proc leer ist, ist TRACE(β) gleich dem Inhalt von s-work, sonst transformieren wir alle Information, die in s-proc enthalten ist sukzessive in einen λ_p-Ausdruck zurück, indem wir jeweils die Umkehrung von Δ ausführen und wenn nötig die Funktion SUBSTITUTE anwenden (Def. in VDL siehe /FE/).
Die Korrektheit des LPI ergibt sich nun aus der Kommutativität des folgenden Diagramms:

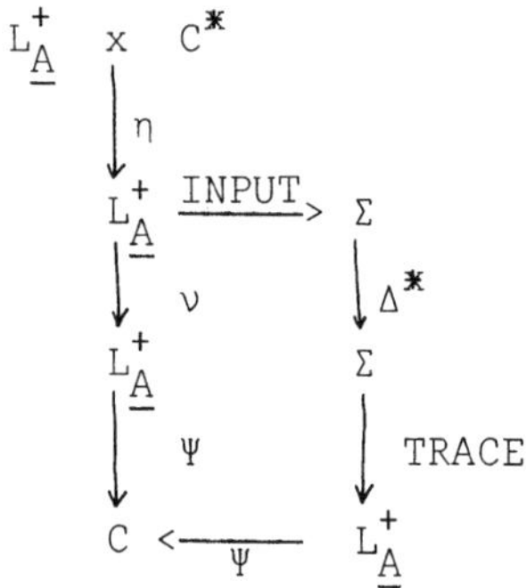

wobei $INPUT(L) := \mu_0(\langle s\text{-}work:\gamma(L)\rangle)$,
$L_{\underline{A}}^{+} := \{L / L \in L_{\underline{A}} \wedge Fr(L) = \emptyset\}$ und
η, ν, Ψ wie in Abschnitt 1

Der Beweis besteht aus drei Teilen:

Sei $(P,\bar{c}) \in L_{\underline{A}}^{+} \times C^{*}$ und $\xi^{o}_{(P,\bar{c})}, \xi^{i}_{(P,\bar{c})}, \ldots$ die entsprechende Zustands folge des LPI.

<u>Teil 1</u>: $\mathrm{trace}(\xi^{o}_{(P,\bar{c})}) = \eta(P,\bar{c})$

<u>Teil 2</u>: $\forall_{i \in N} \; \xi^{i}_{(P,\bar{c})} \neq \Omega \Longrightarrow$

$\xi^{i+1}_{(P,\bar{c})} = \Omega$ oder

$\mathrm{trace}(\xi^{i}_{(P,\bar{c})}) = \mathrm{trace}(\xi^{i+1}_{(P,\bar{c})})$ oder

$\mathrm{trace}(\xi^{i}_{(P,\bar{c})}) \xrightarrow[N]{} \mathrm{trace}(\xi^{i+1}_{(P,\bar{c})})$

<u>Teil 3</u>: $(P,\bar{c}) \neq \omega \Longrightarrow$

$\forall_{i \in \mathbb{N}} \; \xi^{i}_{(P,\bar{c})} \neq \Omega$ und $\mathrm{trace}(\xi^{i}_{(P,\bar{c})})$ nicht in

Normalform $\Longrightarrow \exists_{m \in \mathbb{N}} \; \mathrm{trace}(\xi^{i}_{(P,\bar{c})}) \xrightarrow[N]{} \mathrm{trace}(\xi^{i+m}_{(P,\bar{c})})$

Eine detaillierte Ausführung des Beweises liegt in /FE/ vor.

3. Schlußbemerkung

P.Landin hat in /LP/ die enge Beziehung zwischen dem λ-Kalkül und prozedurorientierten Programmiersprachen aufgezeigt. Nach dem Korrektheit beweis des LPI lassen sich u.a. folgende Ergebnisse auf Interpreter un Compiler höherer Programmiersprachen übertragen:

1. Auf Variablenumbenennung kann verzichtet werden.
2. Wörtliche Substitution wird vermieden durch Interpretation der gebundenen Variablen als Prozeduraufrufe unter Verwendung eines Kelle speichers (activation-record-stack).
3. Direkter Zugriff zu gültigen Eintragungen in der Symboltabelle über einen Environmentvektor, dessen Komponenten gemäß der "static-chair geordnet sind, ist korrekt.

Literaturverzeichnis:

/CA/ Church,A.; The Calculi of Lambda-Conversion, Princeton 1941

/FE/ Fehr,E.; Eine universelle Lambda-Kalkül-Programmiersprache und ihr Interpreter, Berichte der Informatik, Band 1, Universität Bonn,(erscheint)

/IK/ Indermark, K.; Semantik von Programmiersprachen, Vorlesungsmanuskript, Bonn 1973

/LP/ Landin, P.; A Correspondence between ALGOL 60 and Church's Lambda-Notation, Comm. ACM 8, 283, 1965

/ML/ McGowan,C.L.; Correctness Results for Lambda-Calculus Interpreters, Cornell-University, Ph.D., 1971

/WP/ Wegner, P.; Programming Languages, Information Structures, and Machine Organisation, McGraw Hill, 1968

/WV/ Wegner, P.; The Vienna Definition Language, Providence, Rhode Island, 02912

Potenzkategorien
und ihre
Anwendung auf den Beweis von Programmeigenschaften

Herbert A. Klaeren
Universität Bonn

Zusammenfassung

Es bietet sich an, Programmeigenschaften kategorientheoretisch zu behandeln, da Programme in Flußdiagrammform als Basen von freien Kategorien betrachtet werden können. Die freie Kategorie über diesem Programm enthält als Morphismenmenge gerade alle möglichen Kontrollflüsse durch das Programm; diese repräsentieren alle möglichen Programmläufe. Aufgr der speziellen Form der freien Kategorie (eindeutige Dekomponierbarkei lassen sich Aussagen über Programmläufe allein durch Beweise über die Instruktionen erzielen, ohne daß man noch induktive Argumente hinzuziehen muß. Floyd's inductive assertion method läßt sich auf diese Weise kategorientheoretisch beweisen.
In dieser Arbeit werden die Potenzkategorien neu definiert; in ihnen sind Schnitte und Vereinigungen von Morphismen definiert. Mit ihrer Hilfe lassen sich Berechnungsverhalten bzw. Ein/Ausgabeverhalten von Programmen eleganter formulieren und es läßt sich die Klasse der Programme vergrößern, zwischen denen sich Programmhomomorphismen (das sin im wesentlichen Programmäquivalenzen im intuitiven Sinn) herstellen lassen.
Eine vollständige Version dieser Arbeit mit allen Beweisen liegt unte gleichem Titel als Institutsbericht vor (4). Dort wird auch vorgeführ wie die Semantik von Flußdiagrammen durch Transport der Semantik der Programmiersprache in die freie Kategorie gewonnen werden kann; wir gehen hier nicht darauf ein.
Zur Erklärung der hier verwendeten Begriffe sei auf den Anhang, die Arbeiten von Burstall und Goguen und das Buch von Mac Lane verwiesen.

1. Potenzkategorien

1.1.Def.: Eine Potenzkategorie (P-Kategorie) ist eine Kategorie $\mathcal{P}$ mit den zusätzlichen Eigenschaften: (i) $(Ob_{\mathcal{P}},\cup,\cap)$ und $(Hom_{\mathcal{P}},\cup,\cap)$ sind vo ständige distributive Verbände. (ii) Die Abbildungen dom:$Hom_{\mathcal{P}} \longrightarrow Ob_{\mathcal{P}}$, cod:$Hom_{\mathcal{P}} \longrightarrow Ob_{\mathcal{P}}$ und id:$Ob_{\mathcal{P}} \longrightarrow Hom_{\mathcal{P}}$ erhalten Suprema und Infima. (Im folgenden nennen wir dies Stetigkeit.) (iii) Die Komposition von Mor

phismen ist distributiv über $\cup$ und $\cap$.
Es bezeichne $\top,\bot$ größtes und kleinstes Element von $Ob_{\mathcal{P}}$ und $\vee,\wedge$ größtes und kleinstes Element von $Hom_{\mathcal{P}}$.

1.2.Beispiel: Die Kategorie Rel(M), die als einziges Objekt eine Menge M und als Morphismen alle Relationen $r\subset M\times M$ enthält, wird mit den mengentheoretischen Operationen $\cup,\cap,\circ$ und den Definitionen $\top:=M$, $\bot:=\emptyset$, $\vee:=M\times M$, $\wedge:=\emptyset$ zur Potenzkategorie. Unterkategorien von Rel(M) werden später bei der Erklärung der Semantik eine entscheidende Rolle spielen.

1.3.Def.: Sei $B=(O,M,H)$ Basis einer Kategorie, $\hat{B}$ die davon erzeugte freie Kategorie. Definiere eine Kategorie $P(\hat{B})$ durch:
(i) $Ob_{P(\hat{B})} := \mathcal{P}(O)$ die Potenzmenge von O mit mengentheoretischer Vereinigung und Schnitt.
(ii) Es sei R die Menge aller Relationen (Aw,B) mit $A,B\in O$ und $w\in M^*$. Definiere $dom((Aw,B))=A$ und $cod((Aw,B))=B$. Auf R wird eine Komposition definiert durch $(Aw,B)\circ(Cv,A) := (Cvw,B)$ für $A,B,C\in O$ und $v,w\in M^*$. R ist dieser Komposition gegenüber abgeschlossen. Nun seien $\cup$ und $\cap$ die mengentheoretische Vereinigung und Schnitt von Relationen und $Hom_{P(\hat{B})}$ der algebraische Abschluß von R unter $\cup$ und $\cap$. Weiter sei $id:Ob_{P(\hat{B})}\longrightarrow Hom_{P(\hat{B})}$ die stetige Fortsetzung der Abbildung $A\longrightarrow(Ae,A)$ für $A\in O$, wobei e das leere Wort in M^* sei. (Also $(Ae,A)=(A,A)$.) dom und cod werden nun ebenfalls durch ihre stetigen Fortsetzungen ersetzt.

1.4.Lemma: $P(\hat{B})$ ist Potenzkategorie und der Funktor $J:\hat{B}\longrightarrow P(\hat{B})$, der durch die Basis $J(A):=\{A\}$ für $A\in O$ und $J(A\xrightarrow{f}B):=(Af,B)$ für $f\in M$ definiert ist, ist eine Einbettung.

1.5.Def.: Ein Potenzfunktor (P-Funktor) ist ein Funktor zwischen Potenzkategorien, der Suprema und Infima respektiert.

1.6.Satz: Seien B,C Basen von Kategorien, $P(\hat{B}),P(\hat{C})$ die zugehörigen freien Kategorien. Dann gilt:
(i) Zu jedem Funktor $\hat{F}:\hat{B}\longrightarrow P(\hat{C})$ gibt es einen eindeutig bestimmten Potenzfunktor $P(\hat{F}):P(\hat{B})\longrightarrow P(\hat{C})$, der das folgende Diagramm kommutativ macht

$$\begin{array}{ccc} \hat{B} & \xrightarrow{\hat{F}} & P(\hat{C}) \\ & {\scriptstyle J}\searrow \quad \nearrow{\scriptstyle P(\hat{F})} & \\ & P(\hat{B}) & \end{array}$$

(J der Inklusionsfunktor aus 1.4.)

(ii) Zu jedem Potenzfunktor $\mathfrak{F}:P(\hat{B})\longrightarrow P(\hat{C})$ gibt es einen eindeutig bestimmten Funktor $\zeta:\hat{B}\longrightarrow P(\hat{C})$, so daß $\varsigma=P(\zeta)$.

Dieser Satz gibt uns die Berechtigung, $P(\hat{B})$ die von B erzeugte freie Potenzkategorie zu nennen. Ebenso gelten die folgenden Sätze:

1.7.Korollar: Zu jedem Funktor $\hat{F}:\hat{B}\longrightarrow\hat{C}$ gibt es einen eindeutig bestimmten P-Funktor $P(\hat{F}):P(\hat{B})\longrightarrow P(\hat{C})$, so daß

$$\begin{array}{ccc} \hat{B} & \xrightarrow{\hat{F}} & \hat{C} \\ {\scriptstyle J}\downarrow & & \downarrow{\scriptstyle J} \\ P(\hat{B}) & \xrightarrow{P(\hat{F})} & P(\hat{C}) \end{array}$$

kommutiert.
$P(\hat{F})$ heißt der von $\hat{F}$ erzeugte P-Funktor.

1.8.Satz: Seien $\hat{B},\hat{C}$ freie Kategorien, $\hat{F},\hat{G}:\hat{B}\longrightarrow\hat{C}$ Funktoren, $\eta:\hat{F}\longrightarrow\hat{G}$ eine natürliche Transformation.
$P(\hat{B}),P(\hat{C})$ seien die zugehörigen P-Kategorien, $P(\hat{F}),P(\hat{G})$ die induzierte P-Funktoren.
Dann bestimmt η eindeutig eine natürliche Transformation $P(\eta):P(\hat{F})\longrightarrow P$

2. Programme, Berechnungen, Ein/Ausgabeverhalten

2.1.Def.: Ein Programm ist ein Paar (B,S), wobei B Basis einer Katego ist und S Basis eines Funktors $S:B\longrightarrow$ Rel in die Kategorie der Mengen und Relationen. Die Objekte von B heißen Marken, die Morphismen Anweisungen.

B beschreibt somit als Flußdiagramm die Kontrollstruktur des Programm S die Semantik. (Zur Definition von S mit Hilfe der Semantik einer Pr grammiersprache siehe (4)). S assoziiert mit jeder Marke eine Menge, man etwa als Menge der dort erlaubten Zustandsvektoren betrachten kan und mit jeder Anweisung eine Relation zwischen Zustandsvektoren. (Bei terministischen Programmen genügt es natürlich, sich auf partielle Fu tionen zu beschränken.) Definiert man M als die Menge der überhaupt m lichen Zustandsvektoren, so kann man sich auf die Unterkategorie Rel(von Rel beschränken; dies ist jedoch, wie gesagt, eine P-Kategorie.
S erzeugt daher einen P-Funktor $P(\hat{S})$, die die Semantik von Programmlä beschreibt. $P(\hat{S})$ heißt die von dem Programm (B,S) induzierte Berechnu Für einen Kontrollfluß $f\in Hom_{\hat{B}}$ heißt $P(\hat{S})(f)=\hat{S}(f)$ die von (B,S) längs f berechnete Relation.

2.2.Def.: Sei (B,S) ein Programm, $A,A' \in Ob_{\hat{B}}$. I und O seien ausgezeichnete Anfangs- und Endmarke von B. Zeichne in $P(\hat{B})$ die folgenden Morphismen aus:

$$C_B(A) := \bigcup \{f : \exists_{M \in Ob_{\hat{B}}} \; A \xrightarrow{f} M \in Hom_{\hat{B}}\} \quad ; \quad C_B := C_B(I)$$

$$\text{Ɔ}_B(A) := \bigcup \{f : \exists_{M \in Ob_{\hat{B}}} \; M \xrightarrow{f} A \in Hom_{\hat{B}}\} \quad ; \quad \text{Ɔ}_B := \text{Ɔ}_B(O)$$

$$Comp_B(A,A') := C_B(A) \cap \text{Ɔ}_B(A') \quad ; \quad Comp_B := C_B \cap \text{Ɔ}_B$$

Definiere außerdem $C_{(B,S)}(A) := P(\hat{S})(C_B(A))$; $\text{Ɔ}_{(B,S)}(A) := P(\hat{S})(\text{Ɔ}_B(A))$ usf.

$Comp_{(B,S)}(A,A')$ heißt die von (B,S) <u>zwischen A und A' berechnete Relation</u> und $Comp_{(B,S)}$ die von (B,S) <u>berechnete Relation.</u>

$C_B(A)$ ist also die Summe über alle Kontrollflüsse des Programms, die in A beginnen, $\text{Ɔ}_B(A)$ die Summe aller Berechnungsfolgen, die in A enden. Deshalb ist $Comp_B(A,A')$ die Summe aller Berechnungsfolgen, die von A nach A' führen. $Comp_{(B,S)}(A,A')$ ist die Semantik davon.

<u>2.3.</u>Lemma: $Comp_{(B,S)}(A,A') = \bigcup \{ \hat{S}(f) : A \xrightarrow{f} A' \in Hom_{\hat{B}} \}$

<u>2.4.</u>Lemma: Für ein Programm (B,S) mit B=(O,M,H) und $A \in O$ gilt:

$$C_B(A) = \bigcup_i \{ C_B(A_i) \circ f_i \; : \; A \xrightarrow{f_i} A_i \in M \}$$

Dieses Lemma bietet eine Möglichkeit, C_B und auch $Comp_B$ als Lösungen regulärer Gleichungssysteme darzustellen; näheres hierzu in (4). Der Semantik-P-Funktor ist mit der Lösung des Gleichungssystems verträglich; daher können auf diese Weise schon Korrektheitsbetrachtungen angestellt werden.
Auf die Behandlung von Korrektheitsproblemen mit Hilfe der kategorientheoretisch formulierten Methode von Floyd wird ebenfalls in (4) eingegangen.

2.5.Def.: Sei (B,S) Programm, I und O ausgezeichnete Anfangs- und Endmarke in B, V sei die Menge der Ein/Ausgabedaten und $e: V \to \hat{S}(I)$ und $a: \hat{S}(O) \to V$ seien Eingabe- und Ausgabeabbildung. Dann definiere das <u>Ein/Ausgabeverhalten von (B,S)</u> als $IO_{(B,S)} := a \circ Comp_{(B,S)} \circ e$.

Durch diese Definition wird es möglich, auf einfache Weise Programme miteinander zu vergleichen, die zwar auf gleichen Daten operieren, aber unterschiedlich lange oder unterschiedlich strukturierte Zustandsvektoren haben.

3. Homomorphismen und Äquivalenz von Programmen

Homomorphismen zwischen Programmen setzen die von diesen Programmen durchgeführten Berechnungen zueinander in Beziehung. Wir definieren hi zwei verschiedene Begriffe von Homomorphie: Den Goguenschen Homomorphi mus (G-Homomorphismus) und den Potenzhomomorphismus (P-Homomorphismus G-Homomorphismen sind leichter zu beweisen und reichen zur Behandlung von Korrektheits- und Terminationsproblemen nach Floyd aus; bei der Betrachtung von Äquivalenzproblemen sind jedoch die etwas kompliziert ren P-Homomorphismen allgemeiner, da sie auch die Abbildung einzelner Instruktionen auf Schleifen zulassen. G-Homomorphismen implizieren P-Homomorphismen; die umgekehrte Relation gilt nicht. Beide Homomorph men sind aufgrund der Freiheit der hier verwendeten Kategorien endlic beschreibbar.

3.1.Def.: Seien $(B,S),(B',S')$ Programme.
Ein G-Homomorphismus $h:(B,S)\longrightarrow(B',S')$ ist ein Paar $h=(\mathfrak{F},\eta)$ mit

(i) $\mathfrak{F}$ ist Funktor $\mathfrak{F}:\hat{B}\longrightarrow\hat{B}'$

(ii) η ist natürliche Transformation $\eta:\hat{S}\longrightarrow(\hat{S}'\circ\mathfrak{F})$

Ist für alle $v\in Ob_{\hat{B}}$ η_v eine Inklusion, so heißt h eine G-Simulation.

Ein P-Homomorphismus $h:(B,S)\longrightarrow(B',S')$ ist ein Paar $h=(\mathfrak{F},\eta)$ mit

(i) $\mathfrak{F}$ ist P-Funktor $\mathfrak{F}:P(\hat{B})\longrightarrow P(\hat{B}')$

(ii) η ist natürliche Transformation $\eta:P(\hat{S})\longrightarrow(P(\hat{S}')\circ\mathfrak{F})$

Definiere P-Simulation analog zu G-Simulation.

3.2.Satz: Jeder G-Homomorphismus $h:(B,S)\longrightarrow(B',S')$ induziert eindeu einen P-Homomorphismus $P(h):(B,S)\longrightarrow(B',S')$.
Beweis: 1.7. und 1.8.

3.3.Satz: $h=(\mathfrak{F},\eta):(B,S)\longrightarrow(B',S')$ ist P-Homomorphismus $\Longleftrightarrow$

$\Longleftrightarrow$ (i) $\mathfrak{F}=P(\hat{F})$, wobei $F:B\longrightarrow P(\hat{B}')$ Basis eines Funktors

(ii) $\eta=P(\mu)$, wobei μ eine Abbildung $\mu:O\longrightarrow Hom_{P(\hat{B}')}$ ist, so daß für alle $A,B\in O$ und $A\xrightarrow{f}B\in M$ das Diagramm

$$\begin{array}{ccc} SA & \xrightarrow{Sf} & SB \\ \downarrow{\scriptstyle \mu(A)} & & \downarrow{\scriptstyle \mu(B)} \\ P(\hat{S}')(FA) & \xrightarrow{P(\hat{S}')(Ff)} & P(\hat{S}')(FB) \end{array}$$

kommutiert.

Der Beweis findet sich in (4). Auf ähnliche - einfachere - Weise lassen sich G-Homomorphismen endlich beschreiben. Der folgende Satz stellt eine Beziehung zwischen den Homomorphismen und der intuitiven Äquivalenz von Programmen her. Dabei heißen zwei Programme äquivalent, wenn sie bei gleicher Eingabe die gleiche Ausgabe erzeugen. Um dies exakt zu formulieren, führen wir die Konsistenzbedingung ein.

3.4.Satz: Seien (B,S),(B',S') Programme mit Anfangs- und Endmarken A,E bzw. A',E'. Für beide Programme sei V die Menge der Ein/Ausgabedaten. e,e' und a,a' seien die Ein/Ausgabeabbildungen. Es gelte def(e)=def(e'). $h:(B,S)\longrightarrow(B',S')$ sei ein G-Homomorphismus $h=(\hat{F},\eta)$ (bzw. ein P-Homomorphismus $h=(P(\hat{F}),P(\eta))$, so daß FA=A' und FE=E'.
Falls die Konsistenzbedingung

$$\eta_A \circ e = e' \qquad \text{und} \qquad a' \circ \eta_{E'} = a$$

gilt, so ist $IO_{(B,S)} \subset IO_{(B',S')}$. Ist außerdem $\hat{F}$ (bzw. $P(\hat{F})$) voll, so gilt sogar Gleichheit.

Zum Beweis genügt es, die Kommutativität des Diagramms

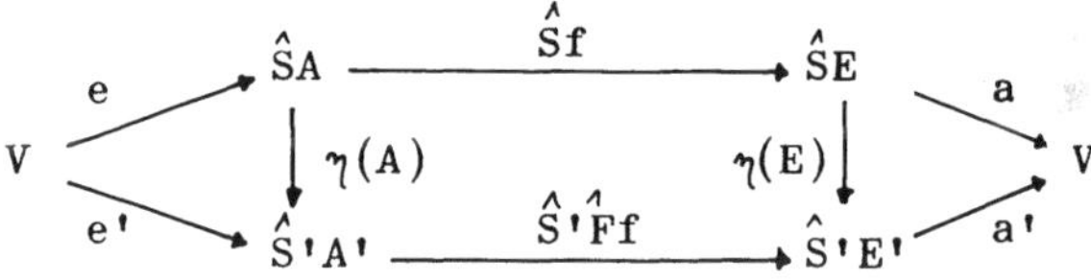

für alle $A \xrightarrow{f} E$ zu zeigen. Das mittlere Diagramm kommutiert, weil η natürliche Transformation ist, die beiden äußeren Diagramme kommutieren aufgrund der Konsistenzbedingung; daher kommutiert das ganze Diagramm. Der Rest ist nun einfach zu zeigen.

Es ist im allgemeinen nicht möglich, $Comp_{(B,S)} \subset Comp_{(B',S')}$ zu beweisen, wenn nur ein Homomorphismus vorliegt. Es läßt sich aber zeigen, daß dies bei der G-Simulation (bzw. P-Simulation) der Fall ist. Hier kann man jedoch keine Gleichheit erzielen, indem man den Funktor als voll voraussetzt.

Mit dem Satz 3.4. ergibt es sich als eine weitere Methode, die Korrektheit von Programmen zu beweisen, daß man andere Programme sucht, deren Korrektheit bereits gezeigt oder offensichtlich ist und dann versucht, Homomorphismen dazwischen zu beweisen. Hierzu bieten sich besonders die allgemeineren P-Homomorphismen an.
In (4) ist außerdem eine spezielle Klasse von Homomorphismen definiert,

welche die Termination von Programmen erhalten; hiermit lassen sich auf ähnliche Weise Terminationsbeweise erreichen.

Anhang

Eine Kategorie $\mathcal{K}$ ist ein Tripel $(Ob_{\mathcal{K}}, Hom_{\mathcal{K}}, H_{\mathcal{K}})$, wobei $Ob_{\mathcal{K}}$, $Hom_{\mathcal{K}}$ Klassen von Objekten und Morphismen und $H_{\mathcal{K}}: Hom_{\mathcal{K}} \longrightarrow Ob_{\mathcal{K}} \times Ob_{\mathcal{K}}$ eine Abbildung, so daß die üblichen Eigenschaften gelten. Wir benützen auch die Bezeichnungen $dom(f)=(pr^1 \circ H_{\mathcal{K}})(f)$ und $cod(f)=(pr^2 \circ H_{\mathcal{K}})(f)$ und $\mathcal{K}(A,B)=H_{\mathcal{K}}^{-1}(A,B)$. Die Begriffe des Funktors und der natürlichen Transformation sind wie üblich erklärt; eine Basis einer Kategorie ist ein Tripel $B=(O,M,H)$, wobei O und M Mengen und $H:M \longrightarrow O \times O$ eine Abbildung. Die von B erzeugte freie Kategorie $\hat{B}$ stellt im wesentlichen den algebraischen Abschluß von B unter einer Komposition auf M dar. In dieser Arbeit sind Basen von Kategorien stets endlich. Eine Basis einer Kategorie kann man sich als gerichteten benannten Graphen vorstellen. Ist B Basis einer Kategorie und $\mathcal{K}$ eine weitere Kategorie, so ist die Basis eines Funktors $F:B \longrightarrow \mathcal{K}$ eine Abbildung, die mit dom und cod verträglich ist. Der davon erzeugte freie Funktor ist die homomorphe Fortsetzung davon bezüglich der Komposition. Jeder Funktor von einer freien Kategorie ist selbst frei.

Literatur

1. Burstall, R.M., An Algebraic Description of Programs with Assertions Verification and Simulation, Proc. on an ACM Confr. on Provi Assertions about Programs, Las Cruces 1972, pp. 7-14
2. Goguen, J.A., On Homomorphisms, Correctness, Termination, Unfoldmen and Equivalence of Flow Diagram Programs, JCSS Vol.8 No.3,1
3. Goguen, J.A., Set-Theoretic Correctness Proofs, UCLA Comp.Sc.Dept. Reports on Semantics and Theory of Computation No.1, 1974
4. Klaeren, H.A., Potenzkategorien und ihre Anwendung auf den Beweis v Programmeigenschaften, Berichte d.Inst.f.Angew.Math. und Informatik Bonn, Band 1 (erscheint; dort weitere Literaturang
5. Mac Lane, S., Categories - for the working mathematician, Springer

WELCHER ART ERGEBNISSE ERWARTET DER COMPILERBAU VON DER THEORETISCHEN INFORMATIK?[+)]

H. LANGMAACK

Wohl in allen Naturwissenschaften und in vielen Ingenieurwissenschaften kennen wir die Aufspaltung in praktische und theoretische Forschung. Es gibt z.B. die Experimentalphysik und die theoretische Physik, es gibt die experimentelle Chemie und die theoretische Chemie, wir haben die praktische und die theoretische Elektrotechnik. Auch in der Informatik, die wir als Ingenieurwissenschaft verstehen müssen - gewiß als recht eigenartige Ingenieurwissenschaft -, haben wir die praktisch orientierte und die theoretische Informatik. Unter praktisch orientierter Informatik ist nicht angewandte Informatik zu verstehen, die Methoden der Informatik auf andere Disziplinen anwendet. Die praktisch orientierte Informatik kann durchaus in der engeren Informatik verharren. Arbeitsbereiche wie die Programmiersprachenentwicklung, der Übersetzerbau und die Betriebssystemkonstruktion zählen dazu, Bereiche, die sich also darum bemühen, die wirklichen Rechenanlagen einzusetzen und kunstvoll mit ihnen umzugehen. Die theoretische Informatik befaßt sich dagegen mit gedanklichen Modellen von Rechenanlagen und Rechenprozessen.

Seitdem die Veranstalter dieser Tagung mich gebeten haben, über das angekündigte Thema zu sprechen, habe ich mit zahlreichen Experten für

[+)] Der Autor möchte Herrn Prof. O.J.Dahl, Oslo, für die zahlreichen Gespräche danken.

Programmierung, Programmiersprachen und Compilerbau diskutiert, gewisse maßen, um Stoff zu sammeln. Um es vorweg zu sagen: Die Diskussionen sin nicht ergiebig gewesen. Zumindest hat man mir kaum konkrete Probleme nennen können, die sich zum unmittelbaren Gebrauch des Theoretikers eignen. Von einigen, sehr ernst zu nehmenden Kollegen ist sogar ganz stark bezweifelt worden, ob die Theoretiker den Praktikern in der Form von Arbeitsteilung überhaupt zur Hilfe kommen könnten. Unter Arbeitsteilung ist zu verstehen: Der praktische Übersetzerkonstrukteur formuliert seine Probleme im Rahmen präziser, mathematischer Modelle, und der theoretische Informatiker führt die Beweise.

An dieser kritischen Auffassung ist natürlich sehr vieles richtig. Wenn man als Übersetzerbaufachmann zu einer abgerundeten Problemlösung komm will, in der die Antworten ein mit präzisen Definitionen und Beweisen versehenes Gebäude bilden, dann besteht in der Tat die Hauptarbeit dar aus dem Wust von Techniken, verschwommenen Vorstellungen und ungenauer Redeweisen ein klares Modell herauszupräparieren. Jetzt noch den Theoretiker herbeizurufen, ist häufig überflüssig. Ein Praktiker, der sogar in der Lage ist, klare Modelle zu formulieren, kann auch den Rest der Arbeit erledigen.

Wenn in dem idealen Sinne der Arbeitsteilung die Hilfe des Theoretike gar nicht möglich ist, dann bleibt die Frage offen, ob der Praktiker dem Theoretiker nicht Gebiete nennen könnte, wo eine Modellbildung si und hoffnungsvoll wäre. Da ist natürlich die Frage angebracht, ob die Vorgehen den landläufigen Theoretiker nicht überforderte. Er müßte re recht in die Programmiertechniken des Praktikers voll einsteigen, um daraus das Abstrahieren zu versuchen. Dieser Theoretiker wäre gar kei Theoretiker mehr in dem Sinne, daß er es nur nötig hätte, auf vorfabr zierte Probleme zu antworten. Die Frage ist auch, ob der Theoretiker das überhaupt will; er wird sich überlegen, ob er nicht auf einfacher Weise ohne Umwege über harte praktische Probleme schneller zu Result gelangt, die der Veröffentlichung wert sind. Dem Theoretiker Arbeitsgebiete vorzuschlagen, legt dem Ratgeber außerdem eine große Verantw tung auf. Denn das Risiko des Mißerfolgs ist natürlich groß, wenn ni einmal das Modell feststeht, in dem die Antworten gesucht werden.

In dem kürzlich erschienenen und sehr informativen Band "Compiler Co struction, an Advanced Course" /1/, an dem zahlreiche international b kannte Spezialisten des Compilerbaus mitgewirkt haben, findet man ka an Theoretiker gerichtete Aufforderungen zu neuen Forschungen. Wenn aufgefordert wird, dann eher zu Experimenten, um ein Gespür zu bekommen, in welche Richtung Compilertechniken weiterentwickelt werden sollten. Solche Experimente sind natürlich in erster Linie Praktikern vorbehalten.

Trotz aller dieser Bedenken will ich jedoch versuchen, Gebiete anzuführen, auf denen eine Zusammenarbeit von Praktikern mit Theoretikern lohnend erscheint. Man möge mir verzeihen, daß die Auswahl an persönlichen Interessen orientiert sein wird. Von den Zweiflern am Unterfangen ist mir vorhergesagt worden, daß es schwer fallen dürfte, bereits allgemein akzeptierte Problemkreise zu nennen.

Um der im Titel genannten Frage näher zu rücken, sollte man sich zunächst einmal fragen: Wo hat die theoretische Informatik bisher schon Ergebnisse geliefert, die für den Compilerbau von besonderem Nutzen und Interesse gewesen sind? Hier ist als Musterbeispiel die Theorie der Analyseverfahren für kontextfreie Grammatiken zu nennen. Diese Theorie wurde durch Erscheinen des ALGOL 60-Berichts /2/ angeregt. Die Grundaufgaben wurden Anfang der sechziger Jahre durch E.T.Irons /3/ und M.Paul /4/ formuliert, die ihre Ideen aus der praktischen Konstruktion von ALGOL 60-Übersetzern empfangen haben. Weiterentwickelt worden ist die Theorie dann mit den Operatorpräzedenzgrammatiken von R.W.Floyd /5/, mit den kontextbeschränkten Grammatiken von J.Eickel /6/ und R.W.Floyd /7/, den von links nach rechts analysierbaren (LR (k)) Grammatiken von D.E.Knuth /8/, den Präzedenzgrammatiken von N.Wirth und H.Weber /9/ und den von links nach echts im top down-Verfahren analysierbaren (LL (k)) Grammatiken von .M.Foster /10/, P.M.Lewis und D.J.Stearns /11/. In dem Nachschlagewerk on A.V.Aho und J.D.Ullman /12/ ist die gesamte Theorie Anfang der siebiger Jahre in schöner Weise zusammengefaßt worden.

ür den praktischen Compilerbau werden nur wenige Grammatiktypen von edeutung bleiben. Dazu gehören die LR (0)-, die LL (1)-, die (einfachen) LR (1)-, die (look ahead-) LALR (1)- und die LR (1)- Grammatiken. Das uftreten der einfachen /13/ und der look ahead- LR (k)- Grammatiken /14/ n der Theorie ist dem Einwirken der Praxis zu verdanken. Sie sind bei em Bemühen entstanden, parser-Generatoren für LR (k)- Grammatiken zu rzeugen, wobei man einige sehr aufwendige Programmteile kurzgeschlossen at.

ch meine, daß man heute nicht mehr zu viel Arbeit in die Theorie der nalyseverfahren für kontextfreie Grammatiken investieren sollte. Wenn, dann bestenfalls für Grammatiktypen innerhalb des LR (1)- Bereichs.Ich möchte vor allem zwei Gründe näher ausführen: Einmal ist die Entwurfstechnik für Programmiersprachen weitergeschritten - man legt nicht meh bloß kontextfreie Grammatiken zugrunde -, zum anderen hat die Theorie den schwierigen Komplex der Codeerzeugung bislang nur sehr stiefmütter lich behandelt.

Bei den neueren Programmiersprachenentwürfen ist vornehmlich ALGOL 68/ zu nennen. Ihm liegt eine van Wijngaarden-Grammatik zugrunde. Solche zweistufigen Grammatiken lassen sich zwar als "pseudo"-kontextfrei mit unendlich vielen Produktionen ansehen, die bekannte Theorie der Analys verfahren läßt sich aber trotzdem nicht leicht ausdehnen. Deshalb sind bislang nur wenige Arbeiten über automatische Analyseverfahren für zwe stufige Grammatiken erschienen; ich kann hier nur C.H.A.Koster /16,17/ H.J.Bowlden /18/ und D.A.Watt /19/ erwähnen.

Ebenso existieren zur Theorie der Codeerzeugung nur wenige Arbeiten. wichtigste Publikation pflegt man gern T.R.Wilcox /20/ zu zitieren, d 1971 den Versuch gemacht hat, den Vorgang der Codeerzeugung generell und prinzipiell zu erfassen. Dabei ist das Schwierige nicht, daß sich Struktur von Rechenanlagenund Maschinenbefehlen gewandelt hat; auch T.R.Wilcox legt die klassische Struktur zugrunde. Er sieht die Codeer zeugung im Prinzip als zweistufigen Prozess, er erkennt einen Überset zungs- und einen anschließenden Codierungsprozess. Der Übersetzer geh von zwei Eingaben aus, einem in linearer Form dargestellten abstrakte Programmbaum und einer Symbolliste, beide gewonnen durch syntaktische Analyse in einem Vorlauf. Der Übersetzer erzeugt Befehle einer sog. Quellsprachenmaschine, die vom Codierer in Maschinencode verwandelt werden. Diese Sicht zeigt deutlich, daß der Strukturbaum eines Progra der ihm durch eine kontextfreie Grammatik aufgeprägt ist, hinter den abstrakten Programmbaum zurücktritt; der Strukturbaum ist zu sehr mi Künstlichem behaftet, als daß er für das Aufhängen der Semantik adäqu erscheint. Dementsprechend ist in der Übersetzerbaupraxis auch die S gewichen, die durch Sprachdefinitionen mitgegebenen Grammatiken umzu schreiben, um bequemer analysieren und um besseren Code gewinnen zu können. Die Praxis verlangt also nicht mehr um jeden Preis, mit dem Analyseproblem einer gegebenen Grammatik im strengen Sinne fertig zu werden.

Ein anderer Themenkomplex, den die Theorie mehr beachten sollte, ist der Bindung angewandter Vorkommen an definierende Vorkommen von Iden fikatoren in Programmen. Die Bindungsrelation in ALGOL 60 z.B. dürfte jedem Informatiker bekannt sein.

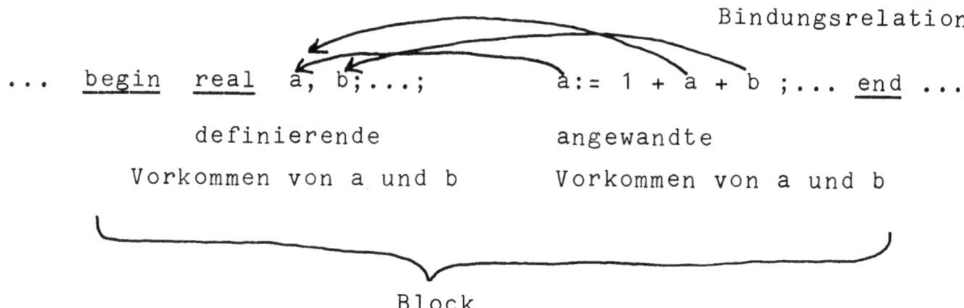

Um übersetzbares Programm zu sein, genügt nicht, daß es vermöge der kontextfreien Grammatik des ALGOL 60-Berichts auf das Axiom <program> reduziert werden kann. U.a. muß es auch folgenden Forderungen genügen: Jeder angewandt vorkommende Identifikator hat ein zugehöriges definierendes Vorkommen, und Doppeldefinitionen pro Block sind verboten.

Probleme wirft die Bindungsrelation vor allem in Zusammenhang mit Prozeduraufrufen auf. Um die Kopierregel von ALGOL 60 nicht naiv

Prozedurrumpf

.. <u>procedure</u> $f\ (x_1, \ldots, x_i, \ldots, x_m);\ \{ \ldots\ x_i\ \ldots \};$

..... $f\ (a_1, \ldots, a_i, \ldots, x_n)$ .....

$\{ \ldots\ a_i\ \ldots \}$

modifizierter Prozedurrumpf

ondern vernünftig anzuwenden, ist zuvor eine zulässige Umbenennung von dentifikatoren vorzunehmen, so daß das Ausgangsprogramm ausgezeichnet ird, d.h. daß verschiedene Vorkommen von Identifikatoren durch verschieene Identifikatoren bezeichnet sind. Die Kopierregel hat ihr Vorbild n λ -Kalkül von A.Church /21/.

ir eine Prozedur f interessiert nun häufig das Problem: Ist f aktuell kursiv? D.h. gibt es Eingabedaten, so daß f ein wiederholtes Mal akviert wird, ohne daß eine vorangegangene Aktivierung von f beendet t? Der Übersetzerkonstrukteur ist nämlich an nicht aktuell rekursiven ozeduren stark interessiert, weil diese eine wesentlich günstigere

Implementierung auf Rechenanlagen erlauben. Leider ist das Problem alg rithmisch nicht generell lösbar. Schuld daran ist die Arithmetik, die Bestandteil fast aller realistischen Programmiersprachen ist.

Die Frage ist darum: Kann man die Arithmetik in irgendeiner Weise über spielen? Etwa indem man die Programme formal oder schematisch betracht Dann eröffnet sich das neue Problem: Ist f formal rekursiv? Die Frage ist natürlich, ob dieses Abweichen vom ursprünglichen Problem sinnvol ist. Es ist deshalb sinnvoll, weil die Aussage "f ist nicht formal rekursiv" impliziert: "f ist nicht aktuell rekursiv". Wenn also die forn Rekursivität entscheidbar sein sollte und wenn durch den Entscheidungs algorithmus festgestellt wird, daß f nicht formal rekursiv ist, dann weiß man auch, daß f nicht aktuell rekursiv ist, womit man die gewüns Information in der Hand hat. Leider ist auch das neue Problem algorit misch nicht generell lösbar. Schuld daran ist jetzt die in der Kopier regel verlangte zulässige Umbenennung von Identifikatoren /22/. Die formal rekursiven Prozeduren sind zwar effektiv aufzählbar, die inter santeren nicht formal rekursiven Prozeduren sind es dagegen nicht.

Um der Entscheidbarkeit näher zu rücken, kann man daran denken, die Kopierregel naiv anzuwenden. Das führt zu dem weiteren Problem: Ist f naiv formal rekursiv? Dieses Problem ist algorithmisch generell lösba und das zugehörige Entscheidungsverfahren kann in nützlicher Weise v Compiler eingesetzt werden.

Die formale, schematische Betrachtungsweise muß natürlich gerechtfer werden. M.S. Paterson /23/ rechtfertigt seine Untersuchungen über Pr grammschemata mit der Antwort, daß für realistische Programmierspracl fast alle interessanten Eigenschaften effektiv unentscheidbar seien. Dazu zählen etwa die Korrektheit, die Äquivalenz und das Terminieren Programmen und die Erreichbarkeit und Rekursivität von Unterprogramm

Man kann die schematische Vorgehensweise aber noch viel schlagender rechtfertigen. Denn der Übersetzerkonstrukteur betrachtet zu überset de Programme auch nur schematisch. Die Übersetzung ist nämlich nicht durch die Definition der Programmiersprache eindeutig festgelegt. Vi mehr kann eine Anweisung des Quellprogramms in verschiedene Anweisun des Zielprogramms übertragen werden, die in verschiedener Weise effi sind. Weil es algorithmisch unentscheidbar ist, ob eine Anweisung hä selten oder gar nicht angesprochen wird, muß auch der praktische Übe setzerkonstrukteur den aktuellen Lauf der Rechnung vernachlässigen.

Eine Kopierregel wie für Prozeduraufrufe in ALGOL 60 gibt es auch bei Makroprozessoren, eine Umbenennung von Identifikatoren wird aber nicht verlangt. Trotzdem ist für einige Prozessoren algorithmisch unlösbar, ob die jeweilige Makroexpansion abbrechen wird. Die Umbenennungsvorschrift ist also nicht in jedem Falle schuld an der Unentscheidbarkeit. Das gilt insbesondere für den general purpose macro generator GPM von C. Strachey /24, 25/. Eine Makrodefinition für GPM hat die Gestalt

§DEF, ... , ... [....] ;

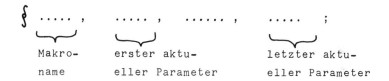

(...... = Makroname; [....] = Makrorumpf)

während ein Makroaufruf so aussieht:

§ ..... , ... , ... , ... ;

(erstes ..... = Makroname; zweites ..... = erster aktueller Parameter; letztes ..... = letzter aktueller Parameter)

i-te formale Parameter in einem Makrorumpf werden durch ~i dargestellt, und zusammengehörige eckige Klammern [ ] auf äußerstem Niveau in aktuellen Parametern sind beim Kopierprozeß fortzulassen.

hnliche Untersuchungen ließen sich auch für andere Makroprozessoren nstellen, z.B. für STAGE 2 von W.M. Waite /26/. Die Unentscheidbarkeit es Abbruchs der Makroexpansion ist gewiß unbefriedigend, und man sollte aher nach entscheidbaren Expansionsmechanismen suchen. Wählt man die echanismen zu einfach, dann vermindern sich allerdings die Steuerungsöglichleiten für Selbstaufrufe. Gleicht man den Verlust durch Makroariable, Makrowertzuweisungen und bedingte Makroanweisungen aus /27/, ann gerät man wegen der verwendeten Arithmetik unversehens wieder in ie Unentscheidbarkeitszone.

.e Überlegungen zur "most recent"-Eigenschaft von Programmen stellen n sehr schönes Beispiel theoretischer Untersuchungen dar, die aus dem mittelbaren Studium von Implementierungstechniken für übersetzte GOL 60-Programme angeregt worden sind. In einer frühen Arbeit /28/ hat

E.W.Dijkstra behauptet, alle ALGOL 60-Programme hätten die genannte Eigenschaft. Worum geht es? Wir betrachten das folgende Programm P.

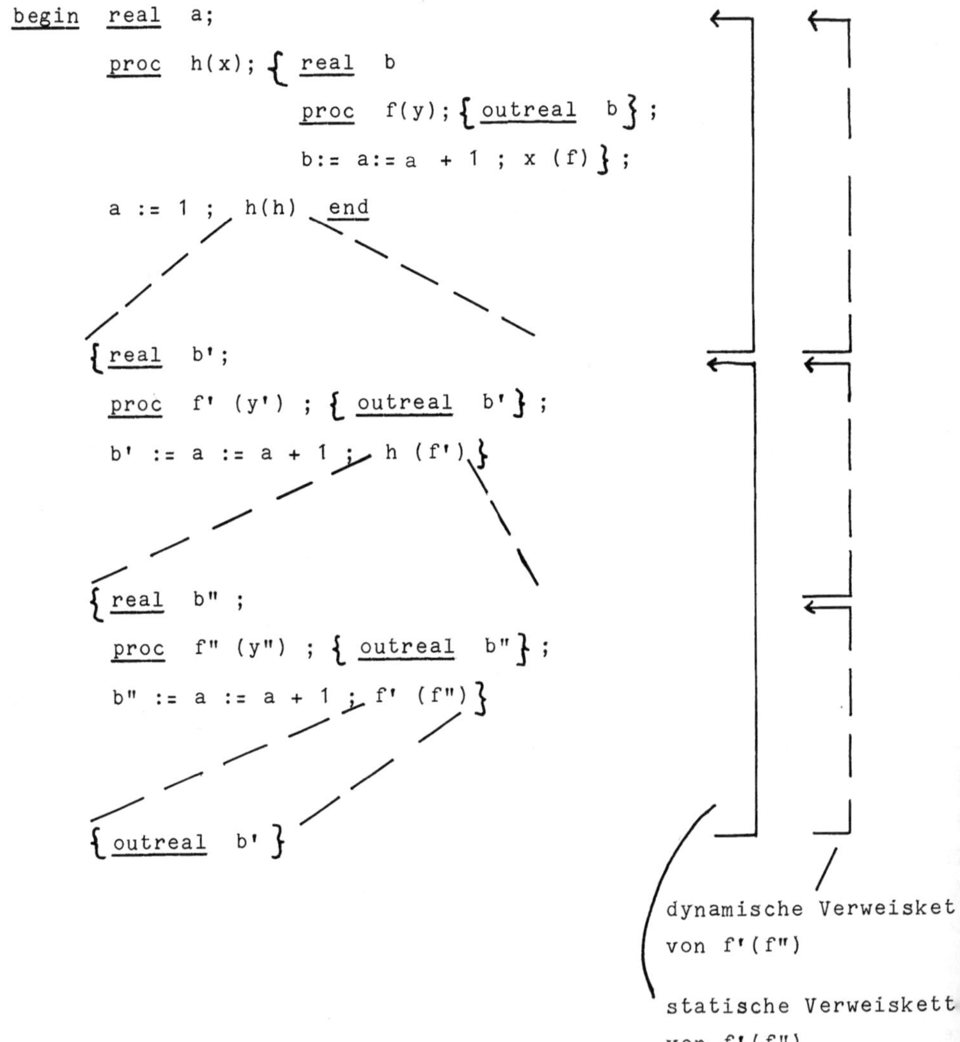

begin real a;
proc h(x); { real b
proc f(y); { outreal b };
b:= a:= a + 1 ; x (f) };
a := 1 ; h(h) end
{ real b';
proc f' (y') ; { outreal b' } ;
b' := a := a + 1 ; h (f') }
{ real b" ;
proc f" (y") ; { outreal b" } ;
b" := a := a + 1 ; f' (f") }
{ outreal b' }
dynamische Verweisket
von f'(f")
statische Verweiskett
von f'(f")

Dieses Programm besitzt nicht die "most recent"-Eigenschaft, weil di statische Verweiskette des Eintrags des Aufrufs f'(f") (activation r der Prozedur f nicht auf den jüngsten Eintrag h(f') der Prozedur h sondern auf das vorangehende h(f) zeigt. Die korrekte Ausgabe ist 2. P ist in gewissem Sinne das kleinste Programm, das die "most recent" Eigenschaft nicht erfüllt, wie man aus einer Arbeit von C.L.McGowan entnimmt. Während die aktuelle "most recent"-Eigenschaft allein sch wegen der beteiligten Arithmetik algorithmisch unentscheidbar ist, hat P.Kandzia /30/ die formale "most recent"-Eigenschaft als entscheidbar nachgewiesen, obwohl die Umbenennung von Identifikatoren beim Kopierprozeß verlangt wird.

Die Laufzeitsysteme von sehr vielen ALGOL 60-Compilern sind so konstruiert, als ob alle Programme die "most recent"-Eigenschaft hätten. Auf obiges Programm P angewendet, würden sie die inkorrekte Ausgabe 3, den Wert von b" statt von b', liefern. Die "most recent"-Eigenschaft ist nun nicht nur theoretisch interessant, sondern hat auch praktische Bedeutung. Denn die Speicherbereiche für Aufrufeintragungen einer gewissen Prozedur werden dann nur kellerartig beansprucht. Wenn bei Arbeitsspeicherüberlauf momentan nicht beanspruchte Eintragungen auf Hintergrundspeicher verdrängt werden, etwa bei virtuellem Speicherbetrieb, denn verhält sich ein Programm mit "most recent"-Eigenschaft offensichtlich günstiger als eines ohne die Eigenschaft, weil letzteres häufigeren Seitenwechsel verlangt. Wenn man ferner bedenkt, daß Benutzer nur selten gegen die in dieser Weise fehlerhaften Laufzeitsysteme protestiert haben, kann man die Idee verfolgen, die "most recent"-Eigenschaft grundsätzlich für statthaft zu erklären. Die zugehörige "most recent"- formale Rekursivität von Prozeduren und auch andere Programmeigenschaften dürften sich als entscheidbar erweisen. Man erkennt, wie eine mehr oder minder starke Manipulation an der Semantik von Programmiersprachen zu erheblichen Vorteilen für das Übersetzen und Codeerzeugen führen kann.

Übrigens gibt es verschiedene "most recent"-Eigenschaften, die alle entscheidbar sind. Es ist denkbar, daß sich in vernünftiger Weise eine ganze Hierarchie schwächer werdender "most recent"-Eigenschaften einführen läßt, womit man das allgemeine Programmverhalten approximieren könnte.

Um das Ziel besserer Übersetzungen zu erreichen, kann man auch den Weg verfolgen, Teilklassen von Programmen abzugrenzen und dann zu beweisen, daß sie wünschenswerte Eigenschaften besitzen. Eine solche Teilklasse ist z.B. die der monadischen Programme, wo für jeden Prozeduraufruf $p_o(a_1, \ldots, a_n)$ gilt: wenn a_i und a_j formale Parameter sind, dann sind sie gleich. Eine andere Teilklasse ist die der Programme mit endlichen Arten im Sinne von ALGOL 68, d.h. der Programme, die ohne den mode-Deklarator geschrieben werden können. Die formale Erreichbarkeit und Rekursivität von Prozeduren, die Makroprogrammeigenschaft und die formale Äquivalenz von Programmen sind in diesen Teilklassen vermutlich entscheidbare Eigenschaften; die bisherigen Untersuchungen /22, 25, 31/ deuten darauf hin. Die bislang betrachteten Fälle haben zu Entscheidbarkeitsfragen für reguläre Systeme /32/, stack-Systeme /33/ und Baum - grammatiken /34/ geführt. Es dürfte eine Theorie nützlich sein, die stack-Systeme auf Bäume ausdehnt, ähnlich wie die regulären Systeme au Bäume erweitert worden sind.

Für das Abgrenzen von Programmteilklassen ist wichtig, daß die Definitionstexte für Anwender einfach und verständlich sind. Wenn die Regeln effizienten Programmierens kompliziert sind, sinkt erfahrungsgemäß ihr Gebrauchswert.

Ein ganz wichtiger Problemkreis ist der der hängenden Bezüge (dangling references), wie P.Wegner /35/ ihn nennt. In ALGOL 60 tritt er gar nic auf, weil ALGOL 60 keine Bezüge, Marken oder Prozeduren als Inhalte vc Variablen und Werte von Prozeduren kennt. Als Inhalte und Werte gibt e nur die problemlosen Daten: ganze Zahlen, reelle Zahlen und Wahrheitswerte. Dementsprechend ist die Speicherverwaltung zur Laufzeit einfach Bei Block- oder Prozedurende können die reservierten Speicherbereiche ohne Vorbehalte freigegeben werden, das Laufzeitsystem arbeitet kelle artig, es darf die deletion-Strategie /36/ verfolgen.

Anders in den Programmersprachen LISP /37/, EULER, ALGOL 68, GEDANKEN /38/ und OREGANO /39/, in denen auch Bezüge, Marken und Prozeduren wi Daten behandelt werden. Dort können hängende Bezüge auftreten, wenn Bezüge, Marken oder Prozeduren an Variablen oder Prozeduren zugewiese werden, so daß erstere eine kleinere Reichweite (scope) als letzere b sitzen. J.C.Reynolds /38/ und D.M.Berry /39/ vertreten daher den Stan punkt, daß Speicherplätze erst dann wieder freizugeben seien, wenn ni mehr auf sie zugegriffen werden kann, und daß man sinnvollerweise die retention-Strategie verfolgen müsse. Abgesehen davon, daß vollständig Sprachen /38/ dafür sorgen, daß Laufzeitfehler weniger häufig gemacht werden, erhebt sich die Frage, ob die retention-Strategie mächtiger a die deletion-Strategie ist. M.J.Fischer /40/ hat bewiesen, daß beide Strategieen gleichmächtig sind, sogar in dem starken Sinne, daß es e effektives Verfahren gibt, womit jedes Programm in ein anderes verwa delt wird, welches auch mit deletion-Strategie korrekt ausgeführt wi

Dies wird nicht die einzig mögliche Aussage über den Mächtigkeitsver gleich sein. Da die Programmiersprachenentwicklung stark zu den voll ständigen Sprachen tendiert, sollte man sich überlegen, ob und in we

Sinne retention echt mächtiger als deletion ist, ähnlich wie man in den letzten Jahren die Wirksamkeit des goto theoretisch beleuchtet hat /41, 42/.

Zum Abschluß möchte ich die Aufmerksamkeit auf die bootstrapping-Technik im Compilerbau lenken. Sie ist seit langem bekannt, die Programmiersprache PASCAL /43, 44/ ist in dieser Technik auf vielen Rechenanlagen erfolgreich implementiert worden, jedoch fehlt bisher eine ansprechende Theorie. Um eine Programmiersprache S zu implementieren, konstruiert man eine aufsteigende Folge von Teilsprachen S_o, $S_1, \ldots, S_n = S$, wobei in jedem Schritt neue Sprachelemente hinzutreten. Es soll in Maschinensprachen M_o, $M_1, \ldots, M_n$ übersetzt werden, wobei der Einfachheit halber alle M_i von derselben Rechenanlage R verstanden werden mögen. M_{i+1} werde als Verbesserung von M_i angesehen, z.B. durch lokale Optimierung, die zu neuen Kombinationen von Maschinenbefehlen führt, oder durch globale Optimierung, etwa durch Vorwegziehen identischer Programmstücke oder durch rekursive Adressenberechnung. Dabei kann das Vorhandensein zusätzlicher Akkumulatoren, Adreß- und Indexregister ausgenutzt werden.

Einen Übersetzer Ü, geschrieben in der Sprache C, der Programme der Quellsprache Q in die Zielsprache Z überträgt, stellt man nach W.M.McKeeman /45/ im T-Diagramm

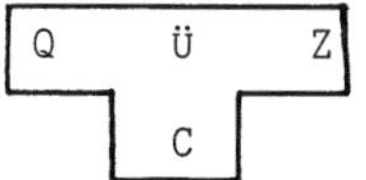

dar, und eine Gleichung (Übersetzung eines Übersetzers)

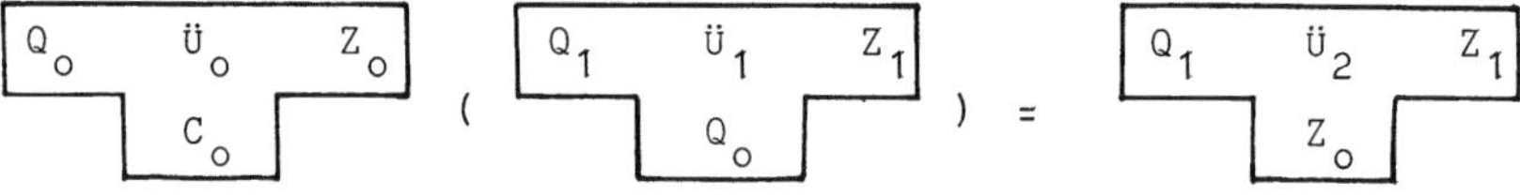

repräsentiert man so:

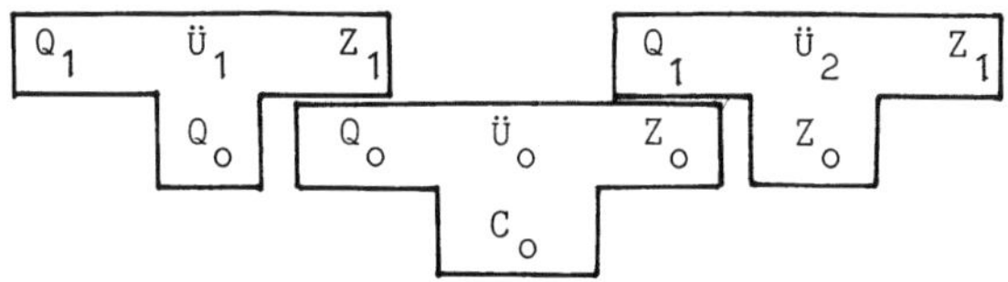

Die Generierung eines Übersetzers von S_n=S nach M_n, geschrieben in M_n, kann nach folgendem Schema geschehen:

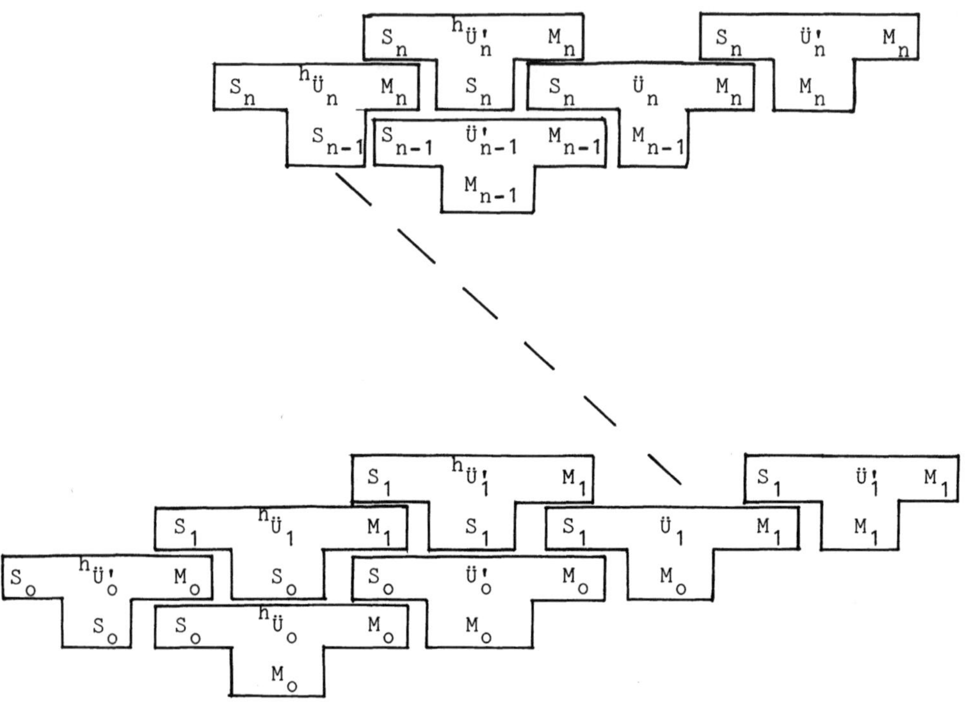

Dieses Schema geht von einer Sequenz handgeschriebener Übersetzer $^h\ddot{U}_o$, $^h\ddot{U}'_o$, $^h\ddot{U}_1$, $^h\ddot{U}'_1$,..., $^h\ddot{U}_n$, $^h\ddot{U}'_n$ aus, und es erlaubt, ein komplexes Übersetzerprojekt übersichtlich zu organisieren. In den Übersetzern $^h\ddot{U}_i$ treten jeweils neue Quellsprachelemente hinzu und verbesserter Maschine code wird erzeugt, in den $^h\ddot{U}'_i$ wirken sich diese Verbesserungen rekursi auf die Übersetzungsprozesse selbst aus. Eine mathematische Theorie übe die bootstrapping-Technik und deren Effizienzverbesserung wäre sehr interessant und wünschenswert.

Die bootstrapping-Technik bietet außerdem einen guten Ansatz, um die Korrektheit von Übersetzern zu beweisen, ein Problem, dessen Bedeutung wohl nicht erst betont zu werden braucht. Weil in jedem Schritt $^h\ddot{U}_i$, $^h\ddot{U}'_i$ geringe Modifikationen hinzutreten, dürften die Beweise auch von Hand mit vertretbarem Aufwand durchzuführen sein. Bezüglich der Method und der Strenge sollte man sich von Numerikern leiten lassen, die ja a stets Eigenschaften über ihre Algorithmen beweisen müssen und dies per Hand tun. Die Genauigkeit automatischer Beweismethoden scheint nicht i jedem Falle erforderlich zu sein.

Literatur:

/1/ F.L.Bauer, J. Eickel (Ed.): Compiler Construction, an advanced Course. Lecture Notes in Computer Science 21, Springer, Berlin-Heidelberg-New York 1974

/2/ P.Naur (Ed.): Report on the algorithmic Language ALGOL 60. Num. Math. 2, 106-136 (1960)

/3/ E.T. Irons: A syntax-directed Compiler for ALGOL 60. Comm.ACM 4, 51-55 (1961)

/4/ M.Paul: ALGOL 60 Processors and a Processor Generator. Information Processing 1962, 439-447, North Holland, Amsterdam 1963

/5/ R.W.Floyd: Syntactic Analysis and Operator Precedence. J. ACM 10, 316-333 (1963)

/6/ J.Eickel: Generation of Parsing Algorithms for Chomsky 2-Type Languages. Math. Inst. Techn. Univ. München, Bericht 6401, 1964

/7/ R.W.Floyd: Bounded Context syntactic Analysis. Comm. ACM 7, 62-67 (1964)

/8/ D.E.Knuth: On the Translation of Languages from left to right. Inform. and Control 8, 607-639 (1965)

/9/ N.Wirth, H.Weber: EULER - a Generalisation of ALGOL and its formal definition, Parts 1 and 2. Comm. ACM 9, 13-23, 89-99 (1966)

/10/ J.M.Foster: A Syntax improving Device. Computer J. 11, 31-34 (1968)

/11/ P.M.Lewis, R.E.Stearns: Syntax directed Transduction.J. ACM 15, 464-488 (1968)

/12/ A.V.Aho, J.D.Ullman: The Theory of Parsing, Translation, and Compiling. Vol.I and II, Prentice Hall, Englewood Cliffs 1972 and 1973

/13/ F.L. De Remer: Simple LR(k) Grammars. Comm.ACM 14, 453-460 (1971)

/14/ W.R. La Londe, E.S.Lee, J.J.Horning: An LALR(k) Parser Generator. Proc. IFIP Congress 71, TA-3, North Holland, Amsterdam 1971

/15/ A. van Wijngaarden (Ed.): Report on the algorithmic Language ALGOL 68. Num. Math. 14, 79-218 (1969)

/16/ C.H.A.Koster: Affix Grammars. In: J.E.L.Peck (Ed.): ALGOL 68 Implementation. North Holland, Amsterdam 95-109 (1971)

/17/ C.H.A.Koster: Using the CDL Compiler-Compiler. In /1/, 366-426 (1974)

/18/ H.J.Bowlden: Cascaded SLR(k) Parser in ALGOL 68. In: Zweite GI-Fachtagung über Programmiersprachen, Saarbrücken 1972. GMD, St. Augustin, 189-200 (1972)

/19/ D.A.Watt: Analysis-oriented two-level Grammars. Ph.D. Thesis, Glasgow 1974

/20/ T.R.Wilcox: Generating Machine Code for high-level Programming Languages. Ph.D. Thesis, Cornell Univ. 1971

/21/ A.Church: The Calculi of Lambda-Conversion. Princeton Univ. Press 1941

/22/ H.Langmaack: On correct Procedure Parameter Transmission in highe Programming Languages. Acta Informatica 2, 311-333 (1973)

/23/ M.S.Paterson: Decision Problems in computational Models. SIGPL Notices 7, 1, 74-82 (1972)

/24/ C.Strachey: A general Purpose Macrogenerator. Comp. Journal 8 225-241 (1965/66)

/25/ H.Langmaack: On Procedures as open Subroutines I, II. Acta Informatica 2, 311-333 (1973), 3, 227-241 (1974)

/26/ W.M.Waite: The mobile Programming System: STAGE 2. Comm. ACM 415-421 (1970)

/27/ G. Seegmüller: Einführung in die Systemprogrammierung. Bibl.I Zürich 1974

/28/ E.W.Dijkstra: Recursive Programming. Num. Math. 2, 312-318 (1

/29/ C.L.McGowan: The "most recent" Error: its Causes and it Corre tion. SIGPLAN Notices 7, 1, 191-202 (1972)

/30/ P.Kanzia: On the "most recent" property of ALGOL-like progran In: J.Loeckx (Ed.): Automata, Languages and Programming. 2nd Coll. Univ. Saarbrücken 1974, Lecture Notes in Comp. Science Springer, Berlin-Heidelberg-New York 97-111 (1974)

/31/ W.Lippe: Entscheidbarkeitsprobleme bei der Übersetzung von P grammen mit einparametrigen Prozeduren. In: W.Frielinghaus, B.Schlender (Ed.): Dritte GI-Fachtagung über Programmierspra Kiel 1974, Lecture Notes in Comp. Science 7, Springer, Berli Heidelberg- New York 11-24 (1974)

/32/ J.R.Büchi: Regular canonical Systems. Arch. Math. Logik u. Grundlagenforsch. 6, 91-111 (1964)

/33/ S.Ginsburg, S.A.Greibach, M.A.Harrison: Stack-Autoamta and Compiling. J. ACM 14, 172-201 (1967)

/34/ W.C.Rounds: Mappings and Grammars on Trees. Math. Systems The 4, 257-287 (1970)

/35/ P.Wegner: Data Structure Models for Programming Languages. S PLAN Notices 6, 2, 1-54 (1971)

/36/ J.B. Johnston: The Contour Model of Block structured Process SIGPLAN Notices 6, 2, 55-82 (1971)

/37/ J. McCarthy et al.: LISP 1.5 Programmer's Manual. The M.I.T. Press, Cambridge, Mass. (1962)

/38/ J.C.Reynolds: GEDANKEN, a simple typeless Language based on the Principle of Completeness and the Reference Concept. Comm. ACM 13, 5, 308-319 (1970)

/39/ D.M.Berry: Introduction to OREGANO. SIGPLAN Notices 6, 2, 171-190 (1971)

/40/ M.J.Fischer: Lambda Calculus Schemata. SIGPLAN Notices 7, 1, 104-109 (1972)

/41/ D.E.Knuth, R.W.Floyd: Notes on Avoiding "goto" statements. Inform. Proc. Letters 1, 23-31 (1971)

/42/ E.Ashcroft, Z.Manna: Inform. Proc. 71, North-Holland, Amsterdam 250-255 (1972)

/43/ N.Wirth: The Programming Language PASCAL. Acta Informatica 1, 35-63 (1971)

/44/ U.Ammann: Die Entwicklung eines PASCAL-Compilers nach der Methode des strukturierten Programmierens. Diss. ETH 5456, Zürich (1975)

/45/ W.M.McKeeman: Compiler Construction. In /1/, 1-36 (1974)

Hans Langmaack

Institut für Informatik

und Praktische Mathematik

der Universität Kiel

<u>23 K i e l 1</u>

Olshausenstr. 40-60

PRÄDIKATIVES PROGRAMMIEREN

Wolfgang Bibel
Technische Universität München

Einleitung

Alle bekannten Programmiersprachen sind im weiteren Sinne Maschinensprachen; denn zu ihrem Verständnis ist eine gewisse Kenntnis der Struktur einer Rechenmaschine unerläßlich, sei es auch nur in Form eines abstrakten Modells. Elemente wie Variable, Wertzuweisungen, Referenzstufen, Sprünge etc., die in keiner dieser Sprachen fehlen, können hier als Beispiele angeführt werden. Genau diese Elemente sind es auch, die

1. dem durchschnittlichen Benützer die Aufgabe des Programmierens so erschweren,
2. die Schwierigkeiten im Zusammenhang mit der Semantik dieser Programmiersprachen hervorrufen und
3. einer fortschreitenden Automatisierung des Programmierprozesses im Wege stehen.

Noch bevor die ältesten dieser algorithmischen Sprachen entstanden sind, war den Logikern bekannt, daß jede Berechnung auch deduktiv durchgeführt werden kann (vgl. [4, Theorem 62]); diese Tatsache bedeutet, daß die Sprache der Prädikatenlogik zusammen mit einem allgemeinen Beweisverfahren eine Programmiersprache darstellt, die völl frei ist von Elementen, wie sie oben beschrieben sind.

Erst jetzt, da man sich bewußt wird, daß die oben erwähnten Schwieri keiten bei den algorithmischen Sprachen von inhärenter Natur sind, beginnt man, diese Möglichkeit als ernstzunehmende Alternative zu de algorithmischen Sprachen zu diskutieren [11; 7; 10; 6; 8], wobei offenbar auch die zunehmende Leistungsfähigkeit der entwickelten Beweisverfahren eine entscheidende Rolle spielt.

Diese Arbeit versucht, die enormen Vorteile, die sich bei diesem Ansatz im Vergleich zu den herkömmlichen Sprachen ergeben, exemplaris herauszuarbeiten. Sie sind summarisch in den Feststellungen F1 - F8 innerhalb des Textes zusammengefaßt und bilden die Grundlage für ei zukünftiges Programmiersystem, dessen Umrisse in der Figur 3 skizzi sind.

1. Berechnung der Fakultätsfunktion

Anhand eines sehr einfachen Beispiels, nämlich der Fakultätsfunktion, soll zunächst die Möglichkeit einer deduktiven Berechnung demonstriert werden. Als zugehöriges Beweisverfahren wird ein vom Autor entwickeltes Verfahren zugrundegelegt, das auf einem Gentzen-artigen Kalkül des natürlichen Schließens basiert. Obwohl für ein tieferes Verständnis des folgenden eine gewisse Kenntnis dieses (oder eines ähnlichen) Verfahrens nötig wäre, muß - von wenigen Andeutungen abgesehen - aus Platzgründen hierzu auf die Arbeiten [3; 2; 4; 5] verwiesen werden.

Ausgangspunkt ist eine exakte Problembeschreibung in Form der üblichen Definition der Fakultätsfunktion:

1.1. Induktive Definition der Funktion fak(x):
   (1) fak(0) = 1 und
   (2) ist y der Wert von fak(x), dann ist fak(x+1) = y·(x+1).

Von hier ist es nur ein minimaler (und daher weitgehend automatisierbarer) Schritt zur Formalisierung dieser Definition in der Sprache der Prädikatenlogik:

1.2. $\mathrm{fak}(0) = 1 \wedge \forall x \forall y(\mathrm{fak}(x) = y \rightarrow \mathrm{fak}(x+1) = y\cdot(x+1)) \rightarrow \forall x \exists_1 y\ \mathrm{fak}(x) = y.$

Jun soll der Wert von fak($\bar{x}$) für einen bestimmten Eingabewert $\bar{x}$ berechnet werden, was, so behaupten wir, durch Erarbeitung eines Beweises für die Spezialisierung von 1.2 auf $\bar{x}$ möglich ist. Wählen wir $\bar{x} = 2$, so autet diese Spezialisierung:

.3. $\mathrm{fak}(0) = 1 \wedge \forall x \forall y(\mathrm{fak}(x) = y \rightarrow \mathrm{fak}(x+1) = y\cdot(x+1)) \rightarrow \exists_1 y\ \mathrm{fak}(2) = y.$

in solcher Beweis (genauer Ableitung im formalen System) ist in Figur 2 ür eine zu 1.3 äquivalente Formel F dargestellt. Dabei ist die Dartellung so gewählt, daß sie in etwa das Vorgehen des Beweisverfahrens otiviert. Tatsächlich operiert dieses in seiner weitestentwickelten orm nicht wie in Figur 2 auf einer Menge von Formeln, sondern auschließlich auf der gegebenen Formel, so daß man insbesondere aus dieser arstellung unmittelbar keine Rückschlüsse auf den erforderlichen Aufand ziehen kann. Dieses Operieren besteht grob gesprochen aus einer olge von Vergleichen von je zwei *Literalen*, womit die Grundeinheiten iner Formel nach Abzug der logischen Zeichen bis auf ¬ bezeichnet erden (so besteht F aus den Literalen L1 ≡ ¬fak(0) = 1, L2 ≡ fak(x) = y, 3 ≡ ¬fak(x+1) = y·(x+1), L4 ≡ fak(2) = y). Jedem solchen Vergleich tspricht ein Vergleich in Figur 1, weshalb wir uns nun zur Illustraon auf sie konzentrieren.

$$\underbrace{\neg fac(0) = 1 \vee \exists x \exists y \left(fac(x) = y \wedge \neg fac(x+1) = y \cdot (x+1) \right)}_{F1} \vee \underbrace{\exists_1 y\, fac(2) = y}_{F2}$$

$$\underbrace{\neg fac(0) = 1 \vee F1 \vee F2}_{F3} \vee fac(d1) = d2 \wedge \neg fac(d1+1) = d2 \cdot (d1+1) \vee \underbrace{fac(2) = d}_{F4}$$

$$\neg fac(0) = 1 \vee F1 \vee F2 \vee fac(d1) = d2 \vee F4 \quad (d1 = 0,\ d2 = 1)$$

$$F3 \vee \neg fac(d1+1) = d2 \cdot (d1+1) \vee F4$$

$$F3 \vee \underbrace{\neg fac(d1+1) = d2 \cdot (d1+1) \vee fac(2) = d}_{F5} \vee fac(d3) = d4 \vee \neg fac(d3+1) = d4 \cdot (d3+1)$$

$$F3 \vee \neg fac(d1+1) = d2 \cdot (d1+1) \vee F4 \vee fac(d3) = d4 \quad (d3 = d1+1 = 1,\ d4 = d2 \cdot (d1+1) = 1)$$

$$F3 \vee F5 \vee fac(2) = d \vee \neg fac(d3+1) = d4 \cdot (d3+1) \quad (d = d4 \cdot (d3+1) = 2)$$

Fig. 1. Berechnung von fac(2) durch Herleitung

In der zweiten Zeile dieser Figur sind die durch Existenzquantoren in gebundenen Variablen durch Platzhalter (Dummies) für Terme ersetzt, da man ja diese, deren Existenz behauptet wird, nicht von vornherein kenn Nur bei dem letzten Quantor wird auch die Eindeutigkeit gefordert; be den anderen kann (und muß) daher diese Ersetzung mit anderen Dummies wiederholt werden (Zeile 4). Jeweils nach Zeile 2 und 4 wird eine Kon junktion "aufgespalten". Bei den unterstrichenen Literalpaaren stellt man fest, daß sie nach Ersetzung der Dummies durch die in den angegeb Gleichungen stehenden Terme *komplementär* sind, d.h. sich nur durch ei unterscheiden. Formeln, die solche komplementären Literalpaare enthal sind im logischen Sinne Axiome und brauchen nicht weiter reduziert zu werden. Alle Endformeln in Figur 1 sind solche Axiome; die Figur stel also eine Ableitung von F dar und für den gesuchten Wert d ergibt sic das gewünschte Resultat 2.

Durch Auffinden einer Ableitung wurde also der gesuchte Wert bestimmt Es ist eine in der Logik seit langem bekannte Tatsache, daß sich in d ser Weise uneingeschränkt jede rekursive Funktion berechnen läßt [12; In der Informatik muß man sich aber zugleich Gedanken darüber machen, inwieweit ein solches Berechnungsverfahren hinsichtlich des Aufwandes auch praktikabel ist, was im folgenden Abschnitt geschehen soll.

2. Das Programmkonzept für die Prädikatenlogik

In Figur 2 ist das Flußdiagramm für die übliche iterative Berechnung Fakultätsfunktion angegeben. Vergleichend kann man feststellen, daß der Aktionen im Flußdiagramm bei dem Eingabewert 2 sich in einem ent

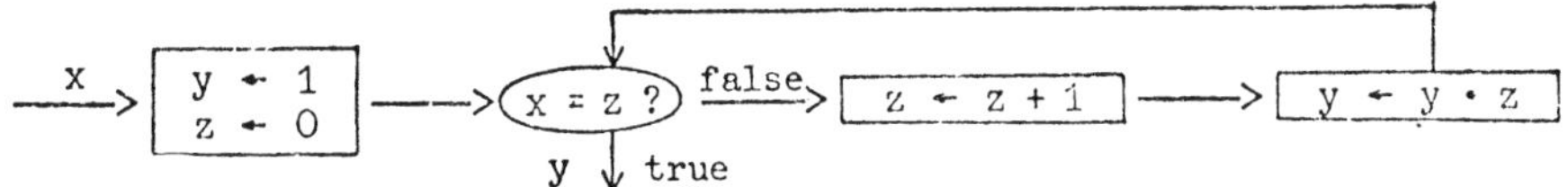

Fig. 2. Flußdiagramm zur Berechnung der Fakultätsfunktion

sprechenden Literalvergleich in der Figur 1 des ersten Abschnitts wiederfindet, was dort durch Unterstreichung bzw. -strichelung gekennzeichnet ist. So entsprechen den Initialisierungen in Figur 2 die Ersetzungen in Zeile 3 der Figur 1, dem ersten (nicht erfolgreichen) Test in Figur 2 der (nicht erfolgreiche) Literalvergleich in Zeile 2 der Figur 1, usw.. Wie man sich leicht überlegt, ist diese Aussage vom Eingabewert unabhängig.

Wie verhält es sich mit der Umkehrung dieser Aussage? Nun, das Verfahren, das ja völlig allgemein und problemunabhängig konzipiert ist, weiß natürlich ohne zusätzliche Information nicht von vornherein, welche Literalvergleiche zu einer vollständigen Ableitung führen, und wird daher eine Reihe von Literalvergleichen durchführen, die sich im nachhinein als überflüssig erweisen. Die Menge dieser überflüssigen Literalvergleiche wächst exponentiell mit dem Eingabewert, einem Mehraufwand, dem auf der Seite des Flußdiagramms nichts Vergleichbares gegenübersteht.

Dieses Mißverhältnis macht uns jedoch lediglich darauf aufmerksam, daß der Vergleich der beiden Verfahren unter inadäquaten Bedingungen ausgeführt wurde. Die Information, die in einem durch Figur 2 repräsentierten Programm steckt, umfaßt nicht nur die (implizit gegebene) exakte Problemstellung, sondern darüberhinaus eine genaue Vorschrift, in welcher Reihenfolge bestimmte Aktionen ausgeführt werden sollen. Eine solche zusätzliche Vorschrift, die wir im folgenden *Steuerung* nennen, fehlt in dem deduktiven Vorgehen noch vollständig, so daß der obige Vergleich gar nicht besser ausfallen *kann*.

Es liegt jedoch nach dem Vorangegangenen bereits auf der Hand, welche Information eine solche Steuerung dem Beweissystem zusätzlich zur Problemstellung an die Hand geben müßte: nämlich daß es im Beispiel der Figur 1 die unterstrichenen bzw. -strichelten Literalvergleiche und nur diese durchzuführen hat, womit überflüssige Vergleiche entfallen würden. Mit einer solchen zusätzlichen Steuerung ergibt sich offenbar für die beiden Berechnungsmethoden, der deduktiven und der algorithmischen, wie wir sie nennen wollen, ein vergleichbarer Berechnungsaufwand. Diese Erkenntnis wurde am Beispiel der Fakultätsfunktion gewonnen; sie läßt sich jedoch ohne Einschränkungen verallgemeinern. Doch gilt sie natürlich nur in erster Näherung, da für eine vollständige Analyse das Beweisverfahre im Detail mit einem Compiler verglichen werden müßte (was erfahrungsgemäß sicher nicht zum Nachteil des Beweisverfahrens ausfallen würde). Aufgrund dieser Überlegungen geben wir also folgende Definition.

2.1. Ein prädikatives Programm ist ein Paar (D,S), wobei der Definitionsteil D eine Formel in der Sprache der Prädikatenlogik darstellt und der Steuerungsteil S die Reihenfolge der Literalvergleiche bei einem Beweis (einer Spezialisierung) von D bestimmt.

Zur Vervollständigung dieses Ansatzes müssen wir uns noch eine Darstellung für eine solche Steuerung überlegen. Sie muß die Reihenfolge der vergleichenden Literalpaare in D angeben und dabei verschiedene Inkarnationen des gleichen Literals unterscheiden. Zur Erläuterung ziehen w nochmals das Beispiel der Figur 1 heran und wählen die Darstellung

2.2. $S_{fak(2)}=((L1^1,L4^1);(L1^1,L2^1);(L3^1,L4^1);(L2^2,L3^1);(L3^2,L4^1))$

Würde man sich die zu Figur 1 analoge Figur für den Fall des Eingabewertes 3 erarbeiten, so ergäbe sich analog

2.3. $S_{fak(3)}=((L1^1,L4^1);(L1^1,L2^1);(L3^1,L4^1);(L2^2,L3^1);(L3^2,L4^1);$
$(L2^3,L3^2);(L3^3,L4^1))$

Vergleicht man nun 1.5. und 1.6., so drängt sich die Vermutung auf, d für einen beliebigen Eingabewert die folgende Steuerung zum Ziel führ

2.4. $S_{fak}=((L1^1,L4^1);(L1^1,L2^1);[(L3^i,L4^1);(L2^{i+1},L3^i)]_{i=1;2;...})$

Bezeichnen wir jetzt die Formel 1.2 mit D_{fak}, so bildet (D_{fak},S_{fak}) e prädikatives Programm. Offenbar ist jedoch eine solche Steuerung zu g gebenem D nicht eindeutig bestimmt. Selbst zu dem einfachen D_{fak} habe wir ja bereits im ersten Abschnitt die durch das Beweisverfahren vorg gebene Grundsteuerung S^o_{fak} kennengelernt, bei der auch die überflüss Literalvergleiche mit durchgeführt werden.
Im Hinblick auf das Problem, die Erarbeitung der Steuerung zu automa sieren, halte man sich den Weg von S^o_{fak} nach S_{fak} vor Augen: Mithilf von S^o_{fak} wurde für kleine Testwerte S_{fak} berechnet und durch einen s len Vergleich zweier Zeichenlisten S_{fak} erschlossen. Auch unter Berü sichtigung des erforderlichen Aufwands ist ersteres immer automatisc möglich, während letzteres mit bekannten heuristischen Methoden in n allzu komplexen Fällen ebenfalls automatisch gelingen kann.

Zusammenfassend ergeben sich also aus der bisherigen Diskussion in (lässiger) Verallgemeinerung die folgenden Feststellungen.

F1. Das prädikative Programmkonzept ist so allgemein wie jedes ander Konzept.

F2. Unter gleichen Voraussetzungen unterscheidet es sich auch im erforderlichen Aufwand (in erster Näherung) nicht von den bekannten Programmkonzepten. - Soweit erscheint es also als völlig gleichwertig mit anderen Konzepten.

F3. Die natürliche Trennung zwischen Definitions- und Steuerungsteil schafft eine begriffliche Klarheit, die in anderen Konzepten nicht gegeben ist. Diese Klarheit schlägt sich in einer natürlichen und jedem logisch Denkenden geläufigen Semantik nieder. (Ein Blick auf den Definitionsteil verrät, worum es im Programm geht, was sich im Vergleich dazu bei einem algorithmischen Programm oft zu einer höchst komplizierten Interpretationsaufgabe ausweitet.)

F4. Diese einfachere Semantik zieht eine Vereinfachung der Programmierung eines Problems nach sich, die sich hier auf das Auffinden einer effizienten Steuerung (auf der Basis einer Grundsteuerung S^o) reduziert. Die sich dabei bietenden Möglichkeiten einer Automatisierung sind in anderen Konzepten in so einfacher Form nicht gegeben.

F5. Das Problem der Korrektheit eines Programms ist hier von untergeordneter Bedeutung (und einfach zu bewältigen), da der durch das Beweisverfahren vorgegebene Rahmen eine falsche Berechnung grundsätzlich ausschließt (da schlimmstenfalls die Berechnung ergebnislos abbricht).

3. Vertiefung des Konzepts

as Beispiel der Fakultätsfunktion erlaubte es, das grundsätzliche Vorehen beim prädikativen Programmieren in relativ einfacher Weise zu deonstrieren. Es ist jedoch nur von bedingter Überzeugungskraft, weshalb n diesem Abschnitt zwei weitere weniger triviale Probleme kurz behanelt werden sollen, an denen sich weitere Vorteile des Konzeptes zeigen erden.

as erste ist die größter-gemeinsamer-Teiler-Funktion GGT. Ihre Definiion ist praktisch durch ihren Namen gegeben und lautet in prädikatenogischer Schreibweise

.1. $\forall x\forall y\forall z(GGT(x,y)=z\leftrightarrow\exists x1(x1\cdot z=x)\wedge\exists y1(y1\cdot z=y)\wedge$
$\forall z1(\exists x1(x1\cdot z1=x)\wedge\exists y1(y1\cdot z1=y)\rightarrow z1\leq z))\rightarrow\forall x\forall y\exists_1 zGGT(x,y)=z$

ie in 1.2. enthält die Prämisse (kurz PR) die Definition (hier in einer xpliziten Form), während in der Konklusion die Funktionseigenschaft sgedrückt wird. Entsprechend dem prädikativen Konzept müßte sich etwa r Wert von GGT(12,8) durch einen Beweis der folgenden Formel bestimmen ssen:

2. $PR\rightarrow\exists_1 zGGT(12,8)=z$

Wenn man dies in einer in Figur 1 illustrierten Weise durchführt, so ergibt sich das Unterproblem, Werte für die Dummies d,d1,d2 so zu bestimmen, daß die folgende Formel gilt:

3.3. $d1 \cdot d=12 \wedge d2 \cdot d=8 \wedge (\neg x1 \cdot z1=12 \vee \neg y1 \cdot z1=8 \vee z1 \leq d)$.

Tatsächlich würde dies mit einem allgemeinen Beweissystem auch gelinge jedoch würde sein Vorgehen dem am wenigsten effizienten Algorithmus er sprechen, der etwa alle Tripel natürlicher Zahlen in einer aufsteigend Ordnung durchtestet. Hier kann die mangelhafte Effizienz offenbar nicl durch einen besseren Steuerungsteil der im 2. Abschnitt beschriebenen Art verbessert werden.

Man hat in dieser Situation auch das Gefühl, daß hier die Definition Problems allein zu dürftig ist, um auf so einfache Weise wie im zweit Abschnitt zu einem effizienten Programm zu gelangen; zur Ansteuerung eines bestimmten unter allen möglichen Algorithmen, die in der Definition stecken, muß man diese durch weitere Kenntnisse über das Problem gewissermaßen einschränken. Im Falle des GGT könnte man es z.B. mit d Eigenschaft GGT(x-y,y)=GGT(x,y) für x>y versuchen, was anstelle vom 3 die Formel

3.4. $PR \wedge \forall x \forall y \forall z (x>y \wedge GGT(x-y,y)=z \rightarrow GGT(x,y)=z) \rightarrow \exists_1 z GGT(12,8)=z$

ergibt. Mit einer naheliegenden Steuerung führt dies zum folgenden Unterproblem:

3.5. $d1 \cdot d=4 \wedge d2 \cdot d=8 \wedge (\neg x1 \cdot z1=4 \vee \neg y1 \cdot z1=8 \vee z1 \leq d)$,

also einem gegenüber 3.3 wegen des kleineren Eingabewertes merklich facheren Problem.

Fährt man in dieser Weise fort und fügt zwei weitere offensichtliche Eigenschaften des GGT hinzu, so erhält man

3.6. $PR \wedge \forall x \forall y \forall z (x>y \wedge GGT(x-y,y)=z \rightarrow GGT(x,y)=z) \wedge$
$\forall x \forall y \forall z (GGT(x,y)=z \rightarrow GGT(y,x)=z) \wedge$
$\forall x GGT(x,x)=x \rightarrow \exists_1 z GGT(12,8)=z$.

Zu dieser Formel findet man mit wenig Übung (oder automatisch) leich eine Steuerung, so daß das resultierende Berechnungsverfahren dem Eu klidischen Algorithmus entspricht.

Dieses Beispiel lehrt das folgende:

F6. Zum effizienten Programmieren ist es im allgemeinen nötig, zur I finition noch weitere Kenntnisse über das Problem hinzuzuziehen, bei man schrittweise und interaktiv vorgehen wird ("strukturier Programmieren"). Da diese Kenntnisse wiederum in ihrer natürlic Form verarbeitet werden können, läßt sich z.B. der reiche Wisse fundus der Mathematik direkt einsetzen. Die Korrektheit der Eigenschaften (d.h. ihre Verträglichkeit mit der Definition) kann auf Wunsch das Beweisverfahren automatisch nachprüfen.

Das zweite Beispiel dieses Abschnitts ist die Fibonacci-Funktion FIB. Statt der iterativen Darstellung in 1.2. sei hier eine rekursive Definition gewählt.

3.7. $FIB(0)=1 \wedge FIB(1)=1 \wedge \forall z(FIB(z+2)=FIB(z+1)+FIB(z)) \rightarrow \forall x \exists_1 y FIB(x)=y$

Wie man sich leicht überlegt, erfordert zum Eingabewert $\bar{x}$ eine prädikative Berechnung $\bar{x}$ Inkarnationen des gleichen Programms genau wie beim üblichen rekursiven Programm. Neue Inkarnationen sind aber hier wie dort kostspielig und redundant. Im prädikativen Fall lassen sie sich aber generell durch (automatische) Anwendung der folgenden Regel vermeiden:

3.8. Ersetze jedes rekursive Auftreten einer Funktion durch eine neue Variable, füge die Identifizierung mit dieser Variablen als Prämisse hinzu, und quantifiziere solche Variablen.

Wendet man diese Regel auf 3.7. an, so ergibt sich

3.9. $FIB(0)=1 \wedge FIB(1)=1 \wedge \forall z \forall u \forall v(FIB(z+1)=u \wedge FIB(z)=v \rightarrow FIB(z+2)=u+v)$
$\rightarrow \forall x \exists_1 y FIB(x)=y$

Hierzu findet man wiederum leicht die folgende Steuerung

3.10. $S_{FIB}=((L1^1,L6^1);(L2^1,L6^1);(L1^1,L3^1);(L2^1,L4^1);([(L5^i,L6^1);$
$(L4^i,L3^{i+1});(L5^i,L4^{i+1})]_{i=1;2;\ldots})$

Aus diesem Beispiel ergibt sich

F7. In der Prädikatenlogik gibt es wohlbekannte Methoden (für weitere siehe etwa [4]), deren Anwendung auf ein gegebenes (prädikatives) Programm dieses automatisch zu einem effizienten transformieren.

In einem letzten Beispiel soll die Handhabung von Datenstrukturen allgemeinerer Art angedeutet werden. Im prädikativen Ansatz wäre eine allgemeine Listenstruktur wie folgt als geordnete, endliche Menge definiert:

3.11. $\forall x \forall <(list(x,<) \leftrightarrow finset(x) \wedge ord(x) \wedge$
$\forall u \forall v(u \in x \wedge v \in x \wedge \neg u=v \rightarrow u<v \wedge \neg v<u \vee v<u \wedge \neg u<v))$

Dabei wird angenommen, daß finset,ord, bereits definierte oder primitive Prädikate darstellen. Ohne auf eine Reihe von interessanten Aspekten im Zusammenhang damit eingehen zu können, halten wir fest:

F8. Wie in algorithmischen Sprachen kann in der Prädikatenlogik auf Daten beliebigen Typs operiert werden. Ihre Definition, soweit sie nicht als primitiv angenommen sind, fügt sich zwanglos in den gegebenen Rahmen, d.h. erfolgt in der gleichen Sprache wie die Programmierung der Probleme selbst, womit eine Forderung erfüllt ist, wie sie etwa auch in [1] an ein Programmiersystem gestellt wird.

Abschließend sind die erarbeiteten Aspekte in Form einer groben Skizze eines zukünftigen prädikativen Programmiersystems in der Figur 3 zusammengefaßt.

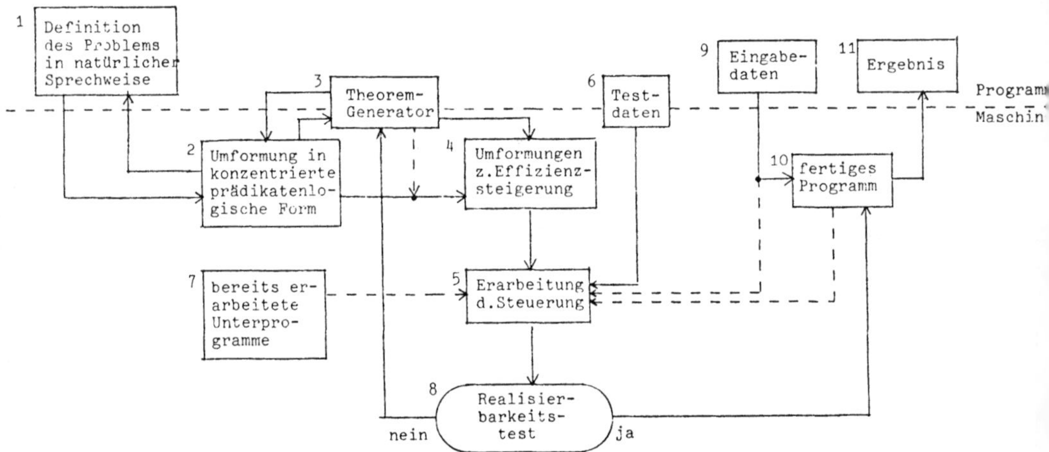

Fig. 3. Schema des Gesamtsystems

Danach wird die in 1 vom Programmierer gegebene Problemstellung interaktiv auf eine präzise maschinengerechte Form gebracht (2). Sodann werd Umformungen, wie sie am Beispiel der Fibonaccifunktion illustriert wurd zur Steigerung der Effizienz in 4 vorgenommen. Zu diesem nunmehr vorliegenden Definitionsteil versucht die Maschine nun in 5, eventuell unter Ausnutzung bekannter Steuerungen (7), aus Steuerungen für Testdaten (6) auf eine allgemeine Steuerung heuristisch zu schließen. Das entstehende Programm wird in 8 daraufhin getestet, ob es für realistische Eingabewerte praktikabel ist. Ist dies nicht der Fall, so verlangt das System weitere Kenntnisse über das Problem. Auf lange Sicht erscheint auch hi für eine teilweise Automatisierung denkbar, jedenfalls ist sie theoretisch möglich. Mit neuen Kenntnissen ausgestattet beginnt der Kreislau von neuem, bis die in 8 gestellten Kriterien an Effizienz erfüllt sind Damit ist dann die Programmierphase beendet und das resultierende Programm kann nun zu Berechnungen herangezogen werden.

Literaturverzeichnis

[1] Balzer, R.M.: *A global view of automatic programming.* Proc. Int. J. Conf. Artif. Intell. 3, Stanford, 494-499 (1973).

[2] Bibel, W.: *An approach to a systematic theorem proving procedure in first-order logic.* Computing 12, 43-55 (1974).

[3] Bibel, W. and Schreiber, J.: *Proof search in a Gentzen-like system of first-order-logic.* Bericht Nr. 7412, Techn.Universität München (1974). Erscheint in Proceedings of the International Computing Symposium (ICS 75), N.Holland P.C. (1975).

[4] Bibel, W.: *Programmieren in der Sprache der Prädikatenlogik.* Eingereicht als Habilitationsarbeit am Fachbereich Mathematik der Technischen Universität München (1975).

[5] Bibel, W.: *Predicative programming.* Unveröffentlichte Fassung in englischer Sprache (1975).

[6] Colmerauer, A., Kanoni, H., Roussel, P. and Pasero, R.: *Un système de communication homme-machine en francais.* Rapport, Université d'Aix-Marseille, Luminy (1972).

[7] Hayes, P.J.: *Computation and deduction.* Proc. Math. Foundations Comp. Science Symp., Czechoslovakian Acad. Science (1973).

[8] Hewitt, C.: *PLANNER: a language for proving theorems in robots.* Proc. Int. J. Conf. Artif. Intell. 1, Washington D.C., 219-239 (1969).

[9] Kleene, S.C.: *Introduction to Metamathematics.* North-Holland, Amsterdam (1952).

[10] Kowalski, R.: *Predicate logic as programming language.* Preprints IFIP 74, Stockholm, 569-574 (1974).

[11] Manna, Z. and Waldinger, R.J.: *Towards automatic program synthesis.* Comm. ACM 14, 151-165 (1971).

[12] Shoenfield, J.R.: *Mathematical logic.* Addison-Wesley, Reading (1967).

ANALYZING FAMILIES OF GRAMMARS

Eberhard Bertsch
Universität des Saarlandes

The problem of designing general parsing procedures for arbitrary families of languages has hardly been studied. One will usually be satisfied with general procedures for the class of LR(k)-languages, the class of precedence languages, the class of regular languages, e For the types of abstract families of languages (AFL) studied by Cremers and Ginsburg [3] , the availability of general procedures ma be of equal importance, however. To put it more precisely, if two grammars are related by belonging to the same family, it will be desirable to be able to use the same parser for both of them.
In the present paper we investigate the relationship between structurally similar grammars from the parsing point of view. Apart from providing an interesting parsing method, our approach will yie time bounds for the word problems of related grammars [2] .
Our technique is basically a three-pass mechanism which will analyz given language L(G), if the first pass analyzes a language L(G′) su that G can be mapped on G′. The second pass is based on a construct in [7] which is there used to obtain a decidability result. It take the output of the first pass as its input. The third pass produces derivation of the original word, if one exists, or else prints an error message.

Some definitions of structural relatedness

Definitions 1 and 2 are slight modifications of concepts defined in

Definition A context-free grammar form is a 6-tuple $F=(V,T,V_F,T_F,P,$
where (i) $T \subseteq V$, $T_F \subseteq T$, $(V_F \setminus T_F) \subseteq (V \setminus T)$, $T_F \subseteq T$

(ii) $G_F=(V_F,T_F,P,S)$ is a context-free grammar.

G_F is called the form grammar of the grammar form F.

<u>Definition</u> A <u>strict interpretation</u> of a grammar form $F=(V,T,V_F,T_F,P,S)$ is a 5-tuple $I=(\mu, V_I, T_I, P_I, S_I)$ where

(1) μ is a substitution on V^* such that

(a) $\mu(a)$ is a finite subset of T for each $a \in T_F$

(b) $\mu(A)$ is a finite subset of $V \setminus T$ for each $A \in V_F \setminus T_F$

(c) $\mu(A) \cap \mu(B) = \emptyset$ for $A,B \in V_F$, $A \neq B$

(2) P_I is a subset of

$$\mu(P) = \bigcup_{p \in P} \mu(p)$$

where $\mu(A \to B) := \{u \to v \mid u \in \mu(A),\ v \in \mu(B)\}$

(3) S_I is in $\mu(S)$

(4) T_I is the set of symbols in T occurring in P_I.
V_I is the set of symbols in V occurring in P_I augmented by S_I.

The context-free grammar $G_I=(V_I,T_I,P_I,S_I)$ is called the <u>grammar of I</u>.

Definition 3 is an essential concept for the categorial treatment of grammars presented in [5], [6]. By M we mean the set of derivations m of a grammar G, s(m) is the source of m, t(m) is the target of m.

<u>Definition</u> For two grammars $G_1=(V_1,T_1,P_1,S_1)$ and $G_2=(V_2,T_2,P_2,S_2)$, an <u>x-functor</u> $\varphi: G_1 \to G_2$ is a pair of mappings (φ_1, φ_2) where $\varphi_1: V_1^* \to V_2^*$, $\varphi_2: M_1 \to M_2$ such that φ_1 and φ_2 are homomorphisms, that is

$$\varphi_1(AB) = \varphi_1(A)\varphi_1(B) \qquad \text{for } A,B \in V_1^*$$

$$\left.\begin{aligned} \varphi_2(m_1 \circ m_2) &= \varphi_2(m_1) \circ \varphi_2(m_2) \\ \varphi_2(m_1 \times m_2) &= \varphi_2(m_1) \times \varphi_2(m_2) \end{aligned}\right\} \text{ for } m_1,m_2 \in M_1$$

and φ_1 is compatible with φ_2, that is

$$\left.\begin{aligned} \varphi_1(s(m)) &= s(\varphi_2(m)) \\ \varphi_1(t(m)) &= t(\varphi_2(m)) \end{aligned}\right\} \text{ for } m \in M_1$$

φ is a <u>length-preserving</u> functor if $\varphi_1(V_1 \setminus T_1) \subseteq V_2 \setminus T_2$, $\varphi_2(P_1) \subseteq P_2$, $\varphi_1(S_1) = S_2$, $\varphi_1(T_1) = T_2$.

Using a proposition in [5], it can be shown that the following theorem connects functors with interpretations of grammar forms:

<u>Theorem</u>: Let G_F be the form grammar of a c.f.grammar form F. G_I is the grammar of a strict interpretation of F, if and only if there exists a length-preserving x-functor $\varphi: G_I \to G_F$.

Our parsing mechanism

The intuitive meaning of a tree-automaton is easy to understand [7] , [8] , [2] . We will therefore skip the formal definition and explain the underlying idea in less rigorous terms.

Imprecise definition A tree-automaton $\mathfrak{A}$ relative to a grammar G possesses an alphabet T and a transition function h. Given any derivati tree m of G, whose terminal nodes are $X_1,\ldots,X_n$ in left-to-right order, h assigns a value $h_m(X_1\ldots X_n)$ to the top node of m. This value is calculated by going from bottom to top and assigning a letter of T to each node. Which letter is taken, depends on which letters have been assigned to the immediately dependent nodes.

Now we need some notation which will be used in the proof of the following theorem. Suppose that we have two grammars $G_1=(V_1,T_1,P_1,s_1)$, $G_2=(V_2,T_2,P_2,s_2)$ and a length-preserving x-functor $\varphi : G_1 \longrightarrow G_2$. We construct an automaton $\mathfrak{A} = (T,h)$ relative to G_2. T is identified wit $2^{(V_1)}$. h is given by

$$h_p(X_1\ldots X_{|t(p)|}) := \{ A\in V_1 \mid \exists \ \bar{p} = A \rightarrow A_1\ldots A_{|t(p)|} \in P_1 \text{ with } \varphi_2(\bar{p}) = p \text{ and } A_i \in X_i \ (i \leq |t(p)|) \}$$

for all $p \in P_2$.

By a lemma in [7], we know that then for all $m \in M_2$ $h_m(X_1\ldots X_{|t(m)|}) = \{ A \in V_1^* \mid \exists \ \bar{m} \in M_1$ with $s(\bar{m}) = A$, $t(\bar{m}) = A_1\ldots A_{|t(m)|}$, $\varphi_2(\bar{m}) = m$ and $A_i \in X_i$ $(i \leq |t(m)|)\}$.

The main result

This gives us our next theorem, whose proof will also contain a description of how the tree-automaton is to be employed.

Theorem: Let $\varphi : G_1 \rightarrow G_2$ be a length-preserving functor, where G_1 and are c.f.grammars and G_2 is unambiguous. Suppose there is an algorithm which will construct a parse for $w \in L(G_2)$ and reject $w \notin L(G_2)$ in less than $f(|w|)$ steps. Then there is a constant c and an algorithm which w accept $w \in L(G_1)$ and reject $w \notin L(G_1)$ in less than $cf(|w|)$ steps.

roof: Let $w \in T_1^*$. If there is an $m \in M_1$ with $t(m)=w$ and $s(m)=s_1$, then by he definition of φ there exists an $m' \in M_2$ with $\varphi_2(m)=m'$, $s(m')=s_2$, $(m')=w' \in T_2^*$. By the unambiguity of G_2, there is no $m'' \in M_2$ with $(m'')=s_2$, $t(m'')=w'$, such that $\varphi_2(m) \neq m''$. So we construct $w'=\varphi_1(w)$ n realtime and try to find a parse of w' in G_2. If there is none, we ave $w \notin L(G_1)$. If there is one, we have to check whether there is a image m of $m' \in M_2$ such that $s(m)=s_1$, $t(m)=w$. By the construction of our nite automaton, this amounts to calculating $h_{m'}(\{a_1\}\{a_2\} \dots \{a_n\})$ ere $w=a_1 \dots a_n$. m' has a coimage whose root is s_1 if and only if s_1 is element of the resulting set. Let n_m be the number of nodes in a rivation tree $m \in M_2$. Simulating tree-automata in time cn_m poses no oblem. We simply represent parse trees by words of the bracketed f.language [4] which is generated by the rules $P_b := \{\alpha \rightarrow [_p \beta]_p \mid = \alpha \rightarrow \beta \in P_2\}$. Then each transition of our tree-automaton corresponds an obvious way to a reduction step on a sentential form. As shown in] , a reduction sequence can be obtained in linear time.

far we have just specified how a yes-no decision can be reached. To e our mechanism as a parser in the strict sense of the word, some litional considerations are necessary. What we have to do, is to store race of all direct transitions and walk back from top to bottom. hin our categorial framework, this can be compactly stated as follows:

pose $h_m(X_1 \dots X_z)=X$ where $m=\bar{m} \circ \hat{m} \circ \tilde{m}$, $h_{\bar{m}}(X_1 \dots X_z)=\bar{X}_{11} \dots \bar{X}_{1k_1} \dots \bar{X}_{lk_l}$ h that $h_{\hat{m}}(\bar{X}_{11} \dots \bar{X}_{1k_1} \dots \bar{X}_{lk_l})=\hat{X}_1 \dots \hat{X}_l$ and $\hat{m}=(m_1 \times \dots \times m_l)$, $\in P_1 \cup Id_{V_2}$ with $(\bar{X}_{i_1} \dots \bar{X}_{ik_i})= \hat{X}_i$ for $i \leq l$.

pose further that $Tree(\tilde{m},\hat{X}_1 \dots \hat{X}_l)$ has been defined. If $m_i \in P_1$, take a e $p_i \in P_1$ with $s(p) \in \hat{X}_i$, $t(p) \in \bar{X}_{i1} \dots \bar{X}_{ik_i}$ $(i \leq l)$ and construct $e(\hat{m} \circ \tilde{m}, \bar{X}_{11} \dots \bar{X}_{lk_l}) := (m'_1 \times \dots \times m'_l) \circ Tree(\tilde{m},\hat{X}_1 \dots \hat{X}_l)$ where p_i if $m_i \in P_1$ and $m'_i \in Id_{V_2}$ otherwise.

start this top-to-bottom process, we have to set $Tree(p,X_1 \dots X_n)$ a rule $p_{start}=A \rightarrow A_1 \dots A_n$ in P_2 with $A \in X$, $A_i \in X_i$ for $i \leq n$ and $X_1 \dots X_n)=X$.

<u>List of references</u> (necessarily incomplete, as the subject matter touches several rapidly growing fields of study):

1) Bertsch,E.: Surjectivity of functors on grammars, appearing in Mathematical Systems Theory, vol.10, no.1
2) Bertsch,E.: An observation on relative parsing time, appearing in Journal of the ACM, vol.22, no.3
3) Cremers,A. and S.Ginsburg: Context-free grammar forms, in Lecture Notes in Computer Science, vol.14
4) Ginsburg,S. and M.Harrison: Bracketed context-free languages, Journal of Computer and System Sciences (1967)
5) Hotz,G.: Eindeutigkeit und Mehrdeutigkeit formaler Sprachen, Elektr. Inform. und Kybern. (1966)
6) Hotz,G. and V.Claus: Automatentheorie und formale Sprachen, vol.3 BI-HTB 823a, Duden-Verlag (1973)
7) Schnorr,C.: Transformational Classes of Grammars, Information and Control (1969)
8) Thatcher,J.: Characterizing derivation trees of context-free gram through a generalization of finite automata-theory, Journal of Computer and System Sciences (1967)

CONTROL STRUCTURES AND MONADIC LANGUAGES *)

Klaus Indermark **)

GMD - Universität Bonn

1. Introduction The theory of program schemes allows to investigate the impact of control mechanisms on the computation power of programs. Those properties which do not depend on the state structure and which hold for arbitrary base functions and data structures can be analysed by means of monadic schemes with one variable. Two such schemes are equivalent iff the sets of computation sequences of their standard forms coincide. This shows how control constructs can be treated syntactically, namely by comparing classes of languages |2|.
The purpose of this paper is to study the particular structure of these languages, called monadic languages (with conditions). A complete version with proofs can be found in |3|.

2. Monadic languages

Let A and B be disjoint sets with $|A| \geqslant 1$ and $|B| \geqslant 2$. $\Sigma := A \cup B$. The elements of A are called actions, those of B conditions, and those of $C(A,B) := (BA)^{*}B$ computations over (A,B).
A set L of computations over (A,B) is called a monadic language over (A,B) iff it satisfies (M):

$$(M)\quad \forall\,(w,v,v' \in \Sigma^{*},\ a \in A)\ \exists (v'' \in \Sigma^{*})\quad wav,\ wv' \in L \Rightarrow v' = av''$$

This property means that an action is uniquely determined by the preceding condition. In other words: a monadic language can be represented by a tree (finite or infinite) which branches out via B.

Example $A = \{a,\ldots\}$, $B = \{b_o, b_1, \ldots\}$

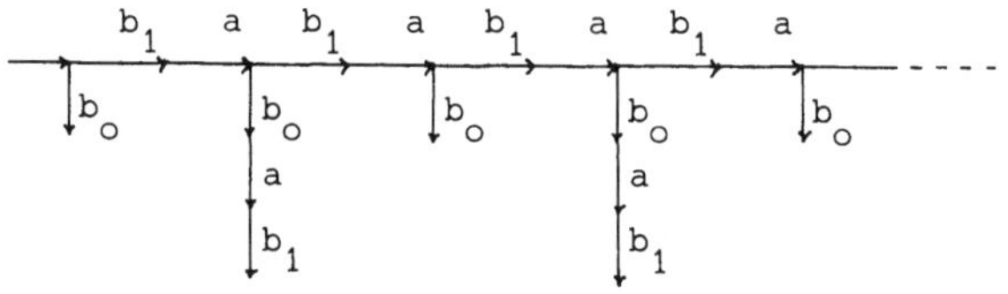

represents the same monadic language L_o as the regular expression
$(b_1\ a\ b_1\ a)^{*}\ (b_o \vee b_1\ a\ b_o\ a\ b_1)$.

---

*) This research has been supported by the Gesellschaft für Mathematik und Datenverarbeitung mbH., Bonn (GMD)
**) Address: Institut für Informatik, 53 Bonn, Wegelerstr. 6, W-Germany

By $\mathfrak{M}(A,B)$ we denote the class of monadic languages over (A,B). They coincide with Engelfriet's deterministic standard L-schemes |2|. In fact, the sets of computations of Ianov schemes and de Bakker/Scott schemes in standard form are languages of this type. Moreover, if $\underset{\sim}{D} = (D;\ \phi,\ \pi)$ is an interpretation of (A,B), i.e. (i) D is a nonvoid set, (ii) $\phi : A \to D^D$, (iii) $\pi : D \to B$, then $(L,\underset{\sim}{D})$ with $L \in \mathfrak{M}(A,B)$ represents a partial function $f_{(L,\underset{\sim}{D})} : D \to D$, and this representation is unique: $f_{(L_1,\underset{\sim}{D})} = f_{(L_2,\underset{\sim}{D})}$ for all interpretations $\underset{\sim}{D}$ of $(A,B) \Longleftrightarrow L_1 = L_2$.

3. Operations on $\mathfrak{M}(A,B)$

We shall define certain operations on $\mathfrak{M}(A,B)$ in order to characterize subclasses of languages that correspond to classes of program schemes. Therefore, we simulate syntactically operations on programs such as composition, branching and iteration. However, one cannot use the algebra of regular sets as in |5| because of the particular nature of $\mathfrak{M}(A,B)$.

Let $L, L_1, L_2 \subset C(A,B)$ and $\beta \subset B$. We call

(i) $L_1 \circ L_2 := \{w\,b\,v \mid w\,b \in L_1,\ b\,v \in L_2\}$

<u>the conditional product of L_1 and L_2</u> and

(ii) $L_1 \textcircled{\beta} L_2 := (\beta \circ L_1) \cup ((B \setminus \beta) \circ L_2)$

<u>the conditional union of L_1 and L_2 w.r.t. β</u>

(iii) With $L^{\textcircled{0}} := B$ and $L^{\textcircled{n+1}} := L \circ L^{\textcircled{n}}$ $(n \in \mathbb{N})$ we call $L^{\circledast} := \bigcup_{n=0}^{\infty} L^{\textcircled{n}}$

<u>the conditional iteration of L.</u>

<u>Lemma</u> $\mathfrak{M}(A,B)$ is closed under conditional product and conditional unions. This does not hold for conditional iteration.

Conditional product and union correspond to program composition and branching, respectively:

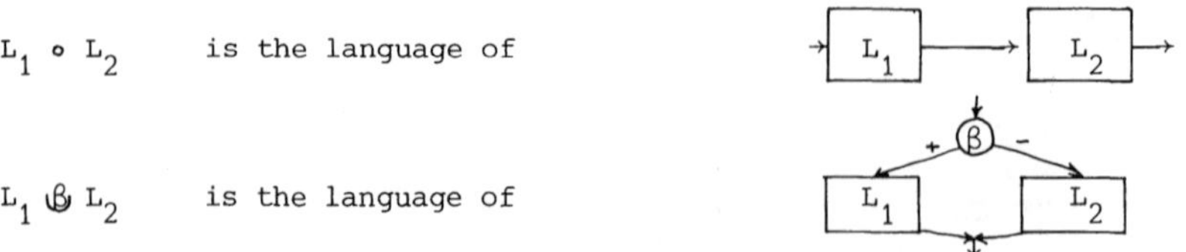

$L_1 \circ L_2$ is the language of

$L_1 \textcircled{\beta} L_2$ is the language of

Finally, the conditional iteration can be used to describe the language of the following <u>program iteration</u>

Namely, if L_i is the set of computations leading to exit i in the original program $(i = 1,2)$ then $L_1^{\circledast} \circ L_2$ describes the computations of this program iteration.

<u>Lemma</u> $\mathfrak{M}(A,B)$ is closed under program iteration, i.e.,

$$L, L_1, L_2 \in \mathfrak{M}(A,B) \quad , \quad L = L_1 \cup L_2 \Rightarrow L_1^{\circledast} \circ L_2 \in \mathfrak{M}(A,B)$$

A special case of program iteration is the so-called <u>while iteration</u>:

$(\beta \circ L)^{\circledast} \circ (B \setminus \beta)$ is the language of

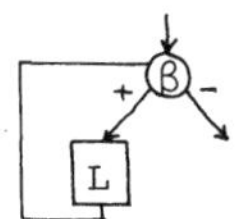

4. Goto and while languages

By means of these operations it is possible to characterize the languages of while and goto schemes. While schemes are Ianov schemes with while loops only whereas goto schemes are arbitrary Ianov schemes.

The class $\mathfrak{L}(A,B)$ of <u>base languages over (A,B)</u> is defined by $\mathfrak{L}(A,B) := \{\beta \mid \beta \subset B\} \cup \{B\,a\,B \mid a \in A\}$. Clearly, $\mathfrak{L}(A,B) \subset \mathfrak{M}(A,B)$.

The class $\mathcal{G}(A,B)$ of <u>goto languages over (A,B)</u> is defined as the smallest subclass of $\mathfrak{M}(A,B)$ that contains $\mathfrak{L}(A,B)$ and that is closed under conditional product, conditional unions and program iteration.
If we replace in the definition of $\mathcal{G}(A,B)$ program iteration by while iteration we get the class $\mathcal{W}(A,B)$ of <u>while languages over (A,B)</u> .

<u>Theorem</u> $\mathcal{G}(A,B) = \mathfrak{M}(A,B) \cap \mathrm{Reg}(A \cup B)$

This theorem shows that the goto languages are just the regular monadic languages, hence, the computation sets of Ianov schemes in standard form.

From the definition of while schemes and while languages it follows that while languages are the computation sets of while schemes. Moreover, we can prove that $\mathcal{W}(A,B) \subsetneq \mathcal{G}(A,B)$ using a generalization of Brzozowski's derivations |1|.

<u>Theorem</u> $L_o \in \mathcal{G}(A,B) \setminus \mathcal{W}(A,B)$

This proves syntactically that, in general, goto's cannot be eliminated by while statements unless one allows boolean variables, e.g.

5. Conclusion We defined an algebraic structure on $\mathfrak{M}$ (A,B) in order to give inductive descriptions of computation sets of goto and while schemes. However, the characterization of $\mathfrak{G}$ (A,B) is unsatisfactory insofar as the program iteration is a partial operation: it can be applied only to certain pairs of monadic languages. But, what are the permissible pairs?

In a forthcoming paper |4| , we remove this draw-back by means of so-called vector languages. Moreover, they can be used to characterize computation sets of repeat exit schemes.

References

|1| J.A. Brzozowski: Derivatives of Regular Expressions. Journal ACM 11 (1964), 481 - 494

|2| J.Engelfriet: Simple Program Schemes and Formal Languages. Springer Lecture Notes in Computer Science 2o (1974)

|3| K. Indermark: On a Class of Schematic Languages. GMD-ITAS-Seminarbericht 82 (1974); to appear in: Proc. International Seminar on Languages and Programming Theory, Madrid (North Holland P.C.

|4| K. Indermark: The Continuous Algebra of Monadic languages. Proc. Mathematical Foundations of Computer Science, Mariánské Lázne, Czechoslovakia (1975); to appear in: Springer Lecture Notes in Computer Science

|5| D.E. Knuth and R.W. Floyd: Notes on Avoiding goto-Statements. Information Processing Letters 1 (1971), 23 - 31

Lecture Notes in Economics and Mathematical Systems

Vol. 48: M. Constam, FORTRAN für Anfänger. VI, 148 Seiten. 1973. DM 18,–

Vol. 65: W. Everling, Exercises in Computer Systems Analysis. VIII, 184 pages. 1972. DM 20,–

Vol. 68: J. Loeckx, Computability and Decidability. An Introduction for Students of Computer Science. VI, 76 pages. 1972. DM 18,–

Vol. 75: GI-Gesellschaft für Informatik e. V. Bericht Nr. 3. 1. Fachtagung über Programmiersprachen. München, 9.–11. März 1971. Herausgegeben im Auftrag der Gesellschaft für Informatik von H. Langmaack und M. Paul. VII, 280 Seiten. 1972. DM 27,–

Vol. 78: GI-Gesellschaft für Informatik e. V. 2. Jahrestagung, Karlsruhe, 2.–4. Oktober 1972. Herausgegeben im Auftrag der Gesellschaft für Informatik von P. Deussen. XI, 576 Seiten. 1973. DM 40,–

Vol. 81: Advanced Course on Software Engineering. Edited by F. L. Bauer. XII, 545 pages. 1973. DM 35,–

Vol. 83: NTG/GI-Gesellschaft für Informatik, Nachrichtentechnische Gesellschaft. Fachtagung „Cognitive Verfahren und Systeme", Hamburg, 11.–13. April 1973. Herausgegeben im Auftrag der NTG/GI von Th. Einsele, W. Giloi und H.-H. Nagel. VIII, 373 Seiten. 1973. DM 32,–

Printed in the United States
by Baker & Taylor Publisher Services